Lecture Notes in Computer Science   8438

Commenced Publication in 1973
Founding and Former Series Editors:
Gerhard Goos, Juris Hartmanis, and Jan van Leeuwen

Rainer Böhme · Michael Brenner
Tyler Moore · Matthew Smith (Eds.)

Financial Cryptography and Data Security

FC 2014 Workshops, BITCOIN and WAHC 2014
Christ Church, Barbados, March 7, 2014
Revised Selected Papers

 Springer

Editors
Rainer Böhme
University of Münster
Münster
Germany

Michael Brenner
University of Hannover
Hannover, Niedersachsen
Germany

Tyler Moore
Southern Methodist University CS
and Engineering Department
Dallas, TX
USA

Matthew Smith
University of Bonn
Bonn
Germany

ISSN 0302-9743
ISBN 978-3-662-44773-4
DOI 10.1007/978-3-662-44774-1

ISSN 1611-3349 (electronic)
ISBN 978-3-662-44774-1 (eBook)

Library of Congress Control Number: 2014950823

LNCS Sublibrary: SL4 – Security and Cryptology

Springer Heidelberg New York Dordrecht London

Printed on acid-free paper

Springer is part of Springer Science+Business Media (www.springer.com)

Preface

This volume contains the papers and poster abstracts from the two workshops held along with the 18th International Conference on Financial Cryptography and Data Security, in Christ Church, Barbados on March 7th, 2014.

BITCOIN 2014: 1st Workshop on Bitcoin Research

When we conceived this workshop, one Bitcoin traded just below 100 US dollars. At the time of the submission deadline, one Bitcoin was worth almost 900 US dollars, close to the historical peak. The exchange rate stabilized between 500 and 600 US dollars from the time FC 2014 and the Bitcoin research workshop concluded until the time of writing this preface. This recent success of Bitcoin and other so-called cryptographic currencies has raised many new research questions. Hot topics of interest include design methods, security properties, and threat models for innovative decentralized payment systems. It is worth noting that the opportunities and risks presented by virtual currencies in general have received attention from scholars of varied communities, including computer science, economics, and law. Until 2013, a handful of research papers appeared in various disciplines, spanning a range of outlets, including security conferences, legal journals, and reports of governmental or international organizations. The objective of this workshop was to bring together interested scholars who study virtual currencies, Bitcoin in particular, and the supporting ecosystems from a technical or socio-economic perspective.

The proceedings in this volume contain the revised versions of 10 accepted papers, selected by rigorous peer-review from a total of 19 submissions, and abstracts of three poster presentations. The workshop also featured a panel on *Bitcoin's Past, Present and Future* with members of the Bitcoin Foundation and representatives of the Bitcoin startup scene.

We thank the authors of all submissions, the members of the Program Committee and the external reviewers for their efforts; the presenters, panelists and almost 100 workshop participants for attending; and the organizers of Financial Cryptography and Data Security 2014 for hosting this workshop (who, it is worth noting, accepted registration fees in Bitcoin for the first time). We are especially grateful to the Bitcoin Foundation, who acted as Bitcoin-grade sponsor – thought to be more precious than bronze, silver, and gold – of the main conference and the workshop.

April 2014

Rainer Böhme
Tyler Moore

Organization

BITCOIN 2014 Program Committee

Elli Androulaki	IBM Research, Switzerland
Rainer Böhme	University of Münster, Germany
Dominic Breuker	University of Münster, Germany
Srdjan Capkun	ETH Zurich, Switzerland
David Chen	Lightspeed Venture Partners, USA
Nicolas Christin	Carnegie Mellon University, USA
Jeremy Clark	Concordia University, Canada
Benjamin Edelman	Harvard Business School, USA
Matthew Green	Johns Hopkins University, USA
Ghassan Karame	NEC Labs, Germany
Stefan Katzenbeisser	TU Darmstadt, Germany
Joshua Kroll	Princeton University, USA
Kirill Levchenko	UC San Diego, USA
Ian Miers	Johns Hopkins University, USA
Andrew Miller	University of Maryland at College Park, USA
Tyler Moore	Southern Methodist University, USA
Fergal Reid	University College Dublin, Ireland
Meni Rosenfeld	Bitcoil, Israel

BITCOIN 2014 External Reviewers

Giuseppe Ateniese	Tatsuaki Okamoto
Pern Hui Chia	Paulina Pesch
Kay Hamacher	Raimo Radczewski
Malte Möser	Marie Vasek

BITCOIN 2014 Shepherds

Rainer Böhme	Tyler Moore
Kirill Levchenko	Fergal Reid

WAHC 2014: 2nd Workshop on Applied Homomorphic Cryptography and Encrypted Computing

Homomorphic Cryptography is one of the hottest topics in mathematics and computer science since Gentry presented the first construction of a fully homomorphic encryption scheme in 2009. Recently, a number of extensions to the original approach, as well as new paradigms have been proposed, creating a diverse basis for further theoretical research. On the other hand, we need research on practical applications of homomorphic encryption which is still less advanced. The cloud hype and different recent disclosures clearly show that there is a strong demand for secure delegation of computation. The technologies and techniques discussed in this workshop are a key to extend the range of applications that can be securely outsourced.

The goal of the workshop was to bring together researchers with practitioners and industry to present, discuss, and to share the latest progress in the field. We want to exchange ideas that address real-world problems with practical approaches and solutions. Special thanks belong to Seny Kamara from Microsoft Research for giving an excellent keynote on a proposal to *Restructuring the NSA Metadata Program*.

The workshop received 11 submissions, each of which was reviewed by at least 3 Program Committee members. While all the papers were of high quality, only 5 papers were accepted to the workshop. We want to thank the researchers of all 11 submissions, the members of the Program Committee for their effort, the workshop participants for attending and the FC organizers for having us.

April 2014
Michael Brenner
Matthew Smith

WAHC 2014 Program Committee

Jose Maria Alcaraz Calero	University of the West of Scotland, UK
Dario Fiore	Max Planck Institute for Software Systems, Germany
Seny Kamara	Microsoft Research, USA
Vladimir Kolesnikov	Bell Labs, USA
David Naccache	École Normale Supérieure, France
Maire O'Neill	Queen's University Belfast, UK
Elizabeth O'Sullivan	Queen's University Belfast, UK
Pascal Paillier	CryptoExperts, France
Henning Perl	Universität Hannover, Germany
Kurt Rohloff	BBN Technologies, USA
Christoph Sorge	Universität Paderborn, Germany
Osman Ugus	AuthentiDate International AG, Germany
Yevgeniy Vahlis	AT&T Labs, USA

Marten van Dijk   University of Connecticut, USA
Fre Vercauteren   Katholieke Universiteit Leuven, Belgium
Adrian Waller   Thales, UK
Xun Yi   Victoria University, Australia

Contents

Part I First Workshop on Bitcoin Research

Bitcoin Poster Abstracts

Part II Applied Homomorphic Cryptography and Encrypted Computing

Part I First Workshop on Bitcoin Research

Bitcoin Transactions, Policy and Legal Issues

How Did Dread Pirate Roberts Acquire and Protect his Bitcoin Wealth?

Dorit Ron[✉] and Adi Shamir

Department of Computer Science and Applied Mathematics,
The Weizmann Institute of Science, Rehovot, Israel
{dorit.ron,adi.shamir}@weizmann.ac.il

Abstract. The Bitcoin scheme is the most popular and talked about alternative payment scheme. One of the most active parts of the Bitcoin ecosystem was the Silk Road marketplace, in which highly illegal substances and services were traded. It was run by a person who called himself Dread Pirate Roberts (DPR), whose bitcoin holdings are estimated to be worth hundreds of millions of dollars at today's exchange rate. On October 1-st 2013, the FBI arrested a 29 year old person named Ross William Ulbricht, claiming that he is DPR, and seizing a small fraction of his bitcoin wealth. In this paper we use the publicly available record to trace the evolution of his holdings in order to find how he acquired and how he tried to hide them from the authorities. In particular, we trace the amounts he seemingly received and the amounts he seemingly transferred out of his accounts, and show that all his Silk Road commissions from the months of May, June and September 2013, along with numerous other amounts, were not seized by the FBI. This analysis demonstrates the power of data mining techniques in analyzing large payment systems, and especially publicly available transaction graphs of the type provided by the Bitcoin scheme.

Keywords: Bitcoin · Silk road · Dread pirate roberts · DPR

1   Introduction

Silk Road was an online marketplace which provided infrastructure for sellers and buyers to trade over the internet. In this sense it was similar to eBay, but with two major differences: most of the items offered for sale were illegal, and there was great emphasis on trying to ensure, as much as possible, the anonymity of both sellers and buyers. In particular, all the communication with the website was carried out through TOR ("The Onion Router"), in order to conceal the true IP addresses and therefore the identities of the network's users [1].

The Silk Road website was visited by hundreds of thousands of unique users from countries across the globe (about 30 % of whom indicated upon registration that they were from the United States) [2]. It grew rapidly, and in September 2013 had nearly 13,000 listings of drugs such as Cannabis, Ecstasy, etc. In addition, it offered a variety of services such as computer-hacking and items such as forged passports.

© IFCA/Springer-Verlag Berlin Heidelberg 2014
R. Böhme et al. (Eds.): FC 2014 Workshops, LNCS 8438, pp. 3–15, 2014.
DOI: 10.1007/978-3-662-44774-1_1

The only form of payment accepted on Silk Road was bitcoins. This is a decentralized form of electronic currency invented in 2008 by Satoshi Nakamoto [3]. In this scheme, all the transactions of all the users are publicly available (for instance via the so called block explorer [4]) but in an anonymous way [5,6]. Silk Road's payment system essentially consisted of an internal bitcoin "bank", where every Silk Road user had to hold at least one account in order to conduct transactions on the site. These accounts were stored on wallets maintained on servers controlled by Silk Road. Each user had to deposit bitcoins in advance into his Silk Road account, and then he was free to use them in order to buy multiple items on Silk Road. When a purchase was made, the appropriate number of bitcoins was first transferred to an escrow account maintained by Silk Road, pending completion of the transaction. When the transaction was completed, the buyers' bitcoins were transferred from the escrow account to the Silk Road bitcoin address of the vendor involved in the sale. Silk Road also used a so-called "tumbler" which, as the site explained, "sent all payments through a complex, semi-random series of dummy transactions making it nearly impossible to link your payment with any coins leaving the site" [2].

The paper is organized as follows. Section 2 describes what is known about the alleged owner and operator of the Silk Road marketplace website. In Sect. 3 we trace backwards all the accounts and amounts which are related to those which were seized by the FBI when they arrested Ulbricht and confiscated his computer, in order to better understand his financial activity and mode of operation. Finally, in Sect. 4 we discuss the power and limitations of such data mining techniques in various investigative scenarios.

2   Who Operated the Silk Road Marketplace?

The Silk Road marketplace opened in February 2011. Throughout its existence, it was operated by an unknown person who called himself Dread Pirate Roberts (DPR), who controlled every aspect of its operation: He acquired the computer infrastructure, maintained the Silk Road website, and determined vendor and customer policies (including deciding what can be sold on the site). He was paid a commission for each transaction, which varied depending on the size of the transaction: 10 % for the first $50 down to 1.5 % for purchases over $1000 [1]. On October 1-st 2013 the FBI arrested in San Francisco an American citizen named Ross William Ulbricht, claimed that he is DPR, and seized control of the Silk Road website (see Fig. 1). As expected, a different website calling itself "The New Silk Road" was opened on November 6, 2013 [7], offering a similar collection of illegal items for sale (see Fig. 2).

According to a press release from the United States attorney's office [2], Silk Road was used during its two and a half year existence by several thousand drug dealers to distribute hundreds of kilograms of illegal drugs, to supply unlawful services to more than a hundred thousand buyers, and to launder hundreds of millions of dollars derived from these transactions. The site generated sales revenue of more than 9.5 million bitcoins and collected commissions from these

The old site of the Silk Road

Seized by the FBI on October 1th 2013

Fig. 1. The Silk Road's front page [1] and the seized FBI's announcement.

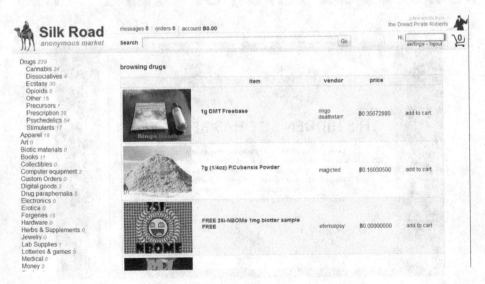

Fig. 2. A message from the administrator of the new Silk Road announcing the reopening of the new site and its new front page [8].

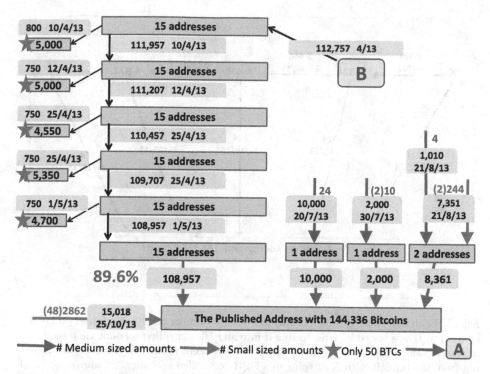

Fig. 3. The backtracking of the published address (at the bottom). 89.6 % of the entire seized amount originated from only 19 addresses shown above the published address and connected to it by four red arrows, explained in Fig. 4. (The identities of the published address and the 19 directly connected to it are given in Appendix A). The remaining 10.4 % was seized from 2,862 small accounts grouped into 48 transactions as shown in green to the left of the published address. In the (x)y notation on the arrows, x indicates the number of involved transactions and y indicates the number (not the sum!) of the transferred amounts. The sum and the associated date of the transfer are written on the arrow. If there is just one transaction with y "from" accounts, (x) is omitted. Green arrows are associated with multiple small amounts of less than 60 BTCs and blue arrows are associated with multiple medium amounts of less than 1,000 BTCs.

sales totaling more than 600,000 bitcoins. At the bitcoin exchange rate in effect when the Silk Road website was seized, these figures are roughly equivalent to $1.2 billion in sales and $80 million in commissions. At today's exchange rate, DPR's wealth is estimated to be several hundred million dollars, and only a small fraction of this amount was seized so far by the FBI.

3 Tracing Backwards the Published Account

At the time of his arrest on October 1-st 2013, Ulbricht was using a laptop computer, which was seized by the FBI. Through forensic analysis which lasted 25

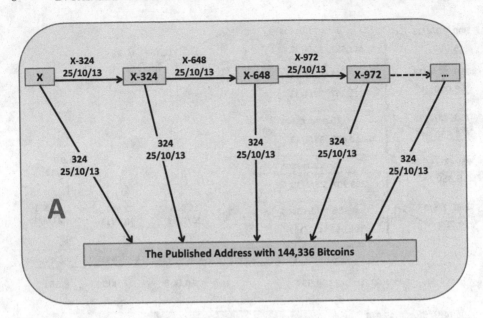

Fig. 4. Each red arrow in Fig. 3 represents a large number of bitcoins found on DPR's computer. It was seized by transferring it into an FBI-controlled account via a sequence of transactions, each moving exactly 324 bitcoins (except in the last transaction). Starting from the top-left with X bitcoins in a DPR-controlled account, 324 were seized and the remaining X-324 were moved to an intermediate address from which again 324 were seized, etc., until the entire amount was seized. All these transactions took place on 25/10/13 between 01:27:54 and 06:50:27.

days, federal law enforcement agents found on this laptop a bitcoin wallet containing approximately 144,336 bitcoins [2]. Immediately afterwards, on October 25-th between 01:27:54 to 06:50:27, the FBI transferred the full amount (then worth about $28 million) in a series of 446 transactions to a single new account that they created and controlled. Each one of the first 445 transactions transferred exactly 324 BTCs (which is the numeric equivalent of "FBI" on a phone's keypad), and the last one transferred the remaining 156 BTCs, as described in Fig. 4. On the same day, they published the identity of the new account [9] which contained all the seized bitcoins, but even if they had refrained from doing so, the public nature of the Bitcoin scheme, the highly unusual series of identical transactions and the fact that the receiving address had one of the highest balances in the Bitcoin scheme, would have revealed its identity in any case. In the block explorer this address is titled "DPR Seized Coins".

An interesting comment we would like to make is that the notion of seizing bitcoins from a suspect's laptop is much trickier than the notion of seizing cash from a suspect's safe, even if all the necessary keys are found by the FBI in both cases. In the case of cash, once the money is hauled away, it is no longer available to the suspect. However, let us assume that the Bitcoin community had noticed the unusual activity, and had refused to pick up these FBI-initiated transactions for verification as part of the official block chain. In this case, it would not help the FBI that they set up the new account and had initiated those transfers - their holdings would not be recognized as valid, and thus they would not be able to exchange or auction them off. In addition, they could still be used by either the suspect or by any one of his accomplices who happens to know the secret key! Even if the community had been late in recognizing these events and some miners would have picked up those transactions in the meantime, a 51 % majority of the computing power available to miners could have forked the block chain just before these transactions, and grown a longer side chain which would invalidate all the blocks that contain the FBI transactions. However, by now it is probably too difficult to take such measures, and the seized bitcoins are no longer usable by DPR.

Immediately after hearing about DPR's arrest, we decided to use the publicly available transaction data in the block chain in order to understand and analyze DPR's mode of operation, and in particular how he acquired and how he tried to conceal his bitcoin wealth. Our starting point was the FBI-controlled account, and we tried to trace it backwards. Out of the 446 incoming transactions into the FBI account, 48 had many sending accounts, and the remaining 398 had between one and four sending accounts. Figure 3 summarizes the structure of the accounts which were the immediate predecessors of the FBI account. The FBI address is shown at the bottom of the figure. The five arrows entering it, one green and four red, represent its entire incoming flow of bitcoins. The green arrow indicates many transactions involving relatively *small* amounts of less than 60 BTCs each, and the notation along it indicates that a total of 15,018 bitcoins were transferred on October 25-th 2013 in 48 transactions with a total number of 2,862 "from" addresses included in all of them (the same notation will be used later on for the blue arrows, which represent *medium* sized transfers of between 60 and 1,000 BTCs). When there is only a single transaction, we omit the (1) from the label of the edge. The other 398 transactions backtracked to precisely 19 addresses which contained 89.6 % of the 144,336 bitcoins which were seized from DPR's wallet. As described in Fig. 3, the four rightmost addresses received a total of 20,361 bitcoins during July and August 2013 from 244 small amounts and 38 medium ones, but most of the bitcoins which were seized by the FBI were kept by DPR in the 15 accounts shown to the left. He moved all these bitcoins simultaneously from one set of 15 accounts into another set of 15 accounts several times in April and May 2013, but then kept them in the same set of 15 accounts created on May 1-st 2013 until his arrest on October 1-st 2013. Each of these 15 addresses were used to send on the same dates exactly 50 bitcoins to certain accounts. On the left we show five such addresses marked by magenta asterisk, meaning that all its incoming transactions are exactly of 50 bitcoins. Backtracking some of these 50-bitcoin-transactions leads to several accounts which had hundreds of transactions with a huge total volume of hundreds of thousands of bitcoins.

Table 1. Bitcoins seemingly received by DPR over time

Date	Amount	# of incoming transactions	# of small amounts	# of medium amounts	How much was seized	How much was moved
10/12	12,564	2	-	540	-	5,502	7,062
11/12	42,263	6	-	1,596	-	12,463	29,800
12/12	5,275	-	1	-	50	0	5,275
1/13	63,000	5	3	2,580	71	41,350	21,650
2/13	6,000	2	-	586	-	2,650	3,350
3/13	44,642	1	3	466	66	43,442	1,200
4/13	5,000	-	-	-	6	3,550	1,450
5/13	0	-	-	-	-	0	0
6/13	0	-	-	-	-	0	0
7/13	27,018	2,862	3	8,586	34	27,018	0
8/13	8,361	2	1	244	4	8,361	0
9/13	0	-	-	-	-	0	0
	214,123					**144,336**	**69,787**

One of the largest among these accounts had more than 100,000 incoming BTCs and the last transaction in the account happened at 8AM on October 1-st 2013, just before DPR's arrest. It is not clear whether they belong to DPR, and none of these bitcoins were seized by the FBI. Further backtracking of the 15 addresses which are believed by the FBI to belong to DPR are shown in Fig. 5.

The remaining 4 addresses at the bottom of Fig. 3 behave differently. From right to left are shown: two addresses which contributed 8,361 bitcoins which had been accepted on August 21, 2013 from one transaction of 1,010 bitcoins involving four medium sized amounts and two other transactions of 7,351 bitcoins involving 244 small amounts. Next to the left, there is one address with 2,000 bitcoins and another with 10,000, both originating in July, 2013.

Figures 3 and 5 summarize all the large-amount transactions which contributed bitcoins to accounts that the FBI believes were owned by DPR. We stopped the backtracking when the amounts became too small or when the number of involved addresses became too large. We traced 30 such origins: seven already appear in Fig. 3: six on the right on top of the published address and one entering it from the left. The other 24 are shown in Fig. 5. For instance, the nine transactions in the top-left took place already in 2012 and contributed 60,102 BTCs to a single address. Interestingly, four addresses had at some point many more bitcions than the number finally seized by the FBI. These addresses are marked by a brown cloud.

In Table 1 we summarize all the incoming transactions which seemingly belonged to DPR that our analysis discovered. We arranged them according to the month (left most column) they entered the accounts. For each month,

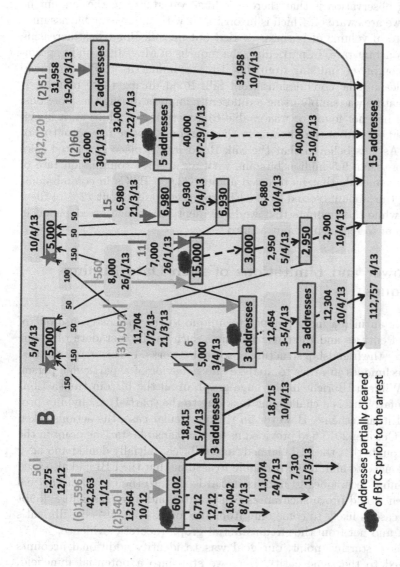

Fig. 5. Further backtracking of the largest accounts that the FBI claims to be owned by DPR reveals additional chunks of bitcoins that were there at some point, but were transferred elsewhere before October 1-st 2013 and thus were not seized. The sum of all these amounts is about 70,000 BTCs as listed in Table 1. Most of it was included in the addresses marked with a brown cloud, and their identities are listed in Appendix B.

from left to right, we describe the total number of received BTCs; the total number of transactions (how many transactions involving only small amounts and how many involving medium amounts); how many accounts participated in those transactions (small and medium amounts); how many BTCs were seized on 25/10/12 and finally how many BTCs were moved by DPR prior to his arrest. An interesting observation is that there is a huge variability in the amount he earned which we are aware of, which is inconsistent with the reasonable assumption that the total volume of business carried out on Silk Road was increasing at a roughly constant rate. In particular, the months of May, June and September 2013 are completely missing from this list. Assuming that DPR continued to receive at least some commissions from Silk Road during these months, it seems likely that he was simply using a different computer during these periods, which the FBI had not found or was unable to penetrate. In addition, it is evident that about a third of the bitcoins in these accounts, were moved out prior to his arrest. As it is believed that the Silk Road marketplace generated sales revenue of more than 9.5 million bitcoins with an average commission rate of 6.67 %, we can conclude that he received about 633,000 BTCs in commissions. Consequently, the amounts seized by the FBI represent only about 22 % of these commissions, while the amounts that we have identified, which are depicted in our figures, seem to represent about a third.

4   The Power and Limitations of such Data Mining Techniques

Data mining is an increasingly popular technique to try to make sense out of huge graphs of entities and their relationships, such as the metadata of phone conversations or the friendship structure of social networks. In this paper we tried to use such techniques in order to analyze the behavior of a particular person named Ross William Ulbricht in the huge graph of all the bitcoin transactions carried out so far. This is a challenging task due to the (partial) anonymity provided by the Bitcoin scheme. However, in this particular case, the actions taken by the FBI in October 2013 had provided us with a plausible starting point in the form of 19 accounts that the FBI claimed (and Ulbricht initially denied and later admitted) belonged to him. It is reasonable to assume that the FBI had also used some data mining techniques to find its initial leads into the case, but the real evidence which would prove such an association beyond any reasonable doubt in a criminal case is likely to come only from the forensic analysis of Ulbricht's seized laptop, and not from the circumstantial graph-theoretic evidence.

Given such a starting point, our goal was to identify additional accounts which belonged to the same entity. Here we step into a potential minefield, since unlike the FBI we do not possess any forensic evidence and thus all our identifications are conjectured rather than proven. None of the conclusions in this paper can be presented as a smoking gun in a court of law, but they are quite convincing: For example, if we see several sets of 15 accounts whose bitcoins are all moved in parallel on the same day from one set to the next, the balance of probability indicates that if the last set is known to belong to Ulbricht, then all the other sets are also likely to belong to him. However, it is still possible that someone else will come out of the blue and conclusively prove that he is the rightful owner of all the other sets.

One of the most interesting challenges in such a data mining project is to decide which pattern of behavior forms a sufficiently strong evidence to make a prima facia case that two accounts belong to the same entity (or alternatively, how careful should a privacy-conscious person be in diversifying his activities in order to avoid such identification). For example, credit card companies often use a particular pattern of ATM withdrawals (times, places, amounts, etc.) to try to fingerprint its customers, and to flag any deviation from such a pattern as a cause for suspicion (but not as a proof of guilt!). Can we claim that two bitcoin accounts which interact in very similar ways with the rest of the system necessarily belong to the same entity? Our personal opinion is that for the sake of an academic analysis, we do not need proofs beyond any reasonable doubt in order to draw such conclusions, provided that we carefully describe our methodology and explain why our conclusions are the best way to explain the currently available data. This is exactly the same level of assurance that all researchers in biology, medicine, and the social sciences are using when they discover a new correlation between two things such as eating substance A and getting disease B: This could be a complete coincidence, but it is still a noteworthy discovery which could have important consequences.

Acknowledgments. This research was supported by a research grant provided by the Citi Foundation. We would like to thank Ronen Basri, Uriel Feige, Michal Irani, Robert Krauthgamer, Boaz Nadler, Moni Naor and David Peleg from the Computer Science and Applied Mathematics Department of the Weizmann Institute of Science for many interesting and informative discussions. We would also like to thank Aharon Friedman for his help in acquiring and processing the bitcoin data base. Finally, we would like to thank all the members of the Bitcoin community that we talked to, and especially Meni Rosenfeld.

Appendix A: The Identities of Some of the Addresses in Fig. 3

We list below the identities of the addresses appearing at the bottom of Fig. 3. The first one is the one with the 144,336 DPR Seized Coins. The next 19 are the addresses from which 89.6 % of the above amount was received. In the figure, these 19 addresses are grouped (from left to right) in four subgroups of 15,1,1 and 2 addresses as listed below.

Appendix B: The Identities of Some of the Addresses in Fig. 5

We list below the identities of the addresses marked with a brown cloud in Fig. 5. There are 10 addresses which are grouped (from left to right) in four groups of

DPR Seized Coins	1FfmbHfnpaZjKFvyi1okTjJJusN455paPH
1/15	1M2TBBkAESfiyKsmqDKsLxD6oC4bvM8WQx
2/15	1JwL9bWB4RJ29Cc3ccW6M1mWA8hrfidPzm
3/15	1NfvKnqRk8wSutfWitJdMSF1cAMfG4Q9sG
4/15	1FAVjwR4ZRRUYuZKdGwbWhDrfASP5Vg5vk
5/15	1B6UsR4HK5Zn7ggN4pUZkhwJt8c65Th67G
6/15	19XmwMdRspwNN55eYLincbf1xDenNajU8R
7/15	1Fdi7uUBiYQogFEgTEsPCQZv2qC8WRLwGD
8/15	1Nt6HwcysgRMehHHwoKV9KkswmBQSLmicQ
9/15	1HGVEWBZ4MBEUw9VGf6AbQNMtoCZ8BUyj3
10/15	1KQoi5wAq6zCuQmL67adAMipWZ8apui6hP
11/15	1Pt42pTpy1i4D1XfFtvuvL7CMLMo4tVF8v
12/15	1AG6FDBg934ikpGPeeik3rabnSea8r6wGJ
13/15	1FvxZn2dkbz8AQnBkEgRq8ttH6czwADwQW
14/15	17YqeNog4t5YgbKLgh99UwSjUQAFEjuFtN
15/15	14xCmiFcddLuiTfeH6r1vgLUjro2qskCzp
1/1	19GUoeGq7hf9KyYfRVLx68SA4NJ4uDDQRF
1/1	1Az2kHto3AqCQmmnFAXtcPkGdLqNWRxnSV
1/2	1EdsvQfKkV8dWo179AgHMH52XAZ4gccoz2
2/2	1Bbwcvmtx3xd1GDLJopCX4PgftT5PkqDfa

1,3,1 and 5 addresses. In the forth group there is actually only one interesting address, the one from which 8,000 BTCs were moved prior to the FBI's action. These six relevant addresses are listed below.

1/1	1NnqM24fFeAGf7NWxmhhFkQAciPqeWo3L
1/3	1Gx49gkDDeGvPGuWNdzwvVz7pP984VX1wf
2/3	14xrNSxfQ2FwmsaQNKAYY4ENMsrDnhQW4x
3/3	1FpzHKV3yeK1jh21VG1cq5emVPuSz63wSS
1/1	1Esg7ZoXh1oytd7GwJagHoq3AijfSbAeLg
1/5	1HBxVRovvUW17wn8L9JGkxVeb5ibTU1bjs

References

1. Christin, N.: Traveling the Silk Road: a measurement analysis of a large anonymous online marketplace. In: Proceedings of the 22nd International World Wide Web Conference (WWW'13), Rio de Janeiro, Brazil, May 2013, pp. 213–224 (2013). https://www.andrew.cmu.edu/user/nicolasc/publications/Christin-WWW13.pdf
2. The United States attorney's Office: Manhattan U.S. Attorney Announces Seizure of Additional $28 Million Worth of Bitcoins Belonging to Ross William Ulbricht, Alleged Owner and Operator of Silk Road Website, 25 October 2013. http://www.justice.gov/usao/nys/pressreleases/October13/SilkRoadSeizurePR.php

3. Nakamoto, S.: Bitcoin: a peer-to-peer electronic cash system (2008)
4. The blockexplorer. http://blockexplorer.com/
5. Ron, D., Shamir, A.: Quantitative analysis of the full bitcoin transaction graph. In: Sadeghi, A.-R. (ed.) FC 2013. LNCS, vol. 7859, pp. 6–24. Springer, Heidelberg (2013)
6. Meiklejohn S., Pomarole M., Jordan G., Levchenko K., McCoy D., Voelker G.M., Savage S.: A fistful of bitcoins: characterizing payments among men with no names. In: Proceedings of the 2013 Conference on Internet Measurement Conference, pp. 127–140 (2013). http://cseweb.ucsd.edu/~smeiklejohn/files/imc13.pdf
7. Greenberg A.: 'Silk Road 2.0' Launches, Promising a Resurrected Black Market for the Dark Web, Forbes, 6 November 2013. http://www.forbes.com/sites/andygreenberg/2013/11/06/silk-road-2-0-launches-promising-a-resurrected-black-market-for-the-dark-web/
8. Cox, J.: Good News, Drug Users - Silk Road is Back!, 6 November 2013. http://www.vice.com/read/good-news-drug-users-silk-road-is-back
9. Greenberg A.: FBI Says It's Seized $28.5 Million in Bitcoins from Ross Ulbricht, Alleged Owner of Silk Road, Forbes, 25 October 2013. http://www.forbes.com/sites/andygreenberg/2013/10/25/fbi-says-its-seized-20-million-in-bitcoins-from-ross-ulbricht-alleged-owner-of-silk-road/

Towards Risk Scoring of Bitcoin Transactions

Malte Möser[(✉)], Rainer Böhme, and Dominic Breuker

Department of Information Systems, University of Münster, Münster, Germany
malte.moeser@uni-muenster.de

Abstract. If Bitcoin becomes the prevalent payment system on the Internet, crime fighters will join forces with regulators and enforce blacklisting of transaction prefixes at the parties who offer real products and services in exchange for bitcoin. Blacklisted bitcoins will be hard to spend and therefore less liquid and less valuable. This requires every recipient of Bitcoin payments not only to check all incoming transactions for possible blacklistings, but also to assess the risk of a transaction being blacklisted in the future. We elaborate this scenario, specify a risk model, devise a prediction approach using public knowledge, and present preliminary results using data from selected known thefts. We discuss the implications on markets where bitcoins are traded and critically revisit Bitcoin's ability to serve as a unit of account.

1 Introduction

Whenever a merchant receives a 100-dollar note, she is well advised to carefully check whether it is authentic. Bitcoin is a decentralized cryptographic currency with the ambition to take over the role of dollar notes at least in the domain of online transactions. As bitcoins[1] are mere references in a public ledger, the Bitcoin equivalent to checking the authenticity of conventional banknotes would be to rule out inconsistencies in the global system state which could nullify an incoming payment. The recommended and well-known defense against the so-called double spending risk is patience. The merchant has to wait until a transaction is sealed deep enough in the block chain to make revisions extremely costly, and hence unlikely [17]. But sooner or later, patience will not be enough.

The popularity of Bitcoin among criminals [13], allegedly for its anonymity and loose to absent regulation, has called for new approaches to fighting financial crime committed in or settled through Bitcoin. A promising strategy is to blacklist transaction prefixes to invalidate assets originating from criminal proceeds [25]. This strategy is effective and practical because the blacklists can be enforced at the services accepting bitcoins. Those are not decentralized and therefore cannot evade law enforcement in their jurisdiction of residence; and, by extension of mutual legal assistance, the set of internationally recognized provisions for the fight against financial crime. In fact, the ability to enforce such a blacklisting

---

[1] Convention: We capitalize Bitcoin when referring to the name of the system and use lower case for the monetary unit (like dollar, euro). BTC is shorthand for the unit.

© IFCA/Springer-Verlag Berlin Heidelberg 2014
R. Böhme et al. (Eds.): FC 2014 Workshops, LNCS 8438, pp. 16–32, 2014.
DOI: 10.1007/978-3-662-44774-1_2

policy thwarts the very idea of a decentralized currency by projecting power of the legal system into Bitcoin. This is why blacklisting practices are controversial among Bitcoin enthusiasts [6]. We leave this philosophical debate aside and concentrate on the effect of blacklisting policies on transactions in general. In practice, blacklisting is reality in Bitcoin [10] and new ventures seek to offer whitelisting services with similar effect [16].

This paper contemplates a future of Bitcoin where blacklisting of known bad transaction prefixes is common practice and the resulting blacklists are observed by all relevant parties where bitcoins can be spent. As a result, end users receiving payments in Bitcoin must screen incoming transactions as well. We can safely assume that suitable services and APIs will be offered by third parties.

However, even when payments appear benign, recipients can never be certain if a prefix of their incoming transactions will be blacklisted *in the future*. They have to accept a risk of invalidation while holding bitcoin. This specific risk is probably small compared to all other risks involved with Bitcoin for the time being, but the proportions may change as the currency gains popularity. Unlike other risks, this risk is idiosyncratic for the transaction history of the specific incoming transaction. For example, a transaction that forwards freshly mined bitcoins (so-called coinbase transactions) has less likely been involved in a crime than a transaction consisting of bitcoins that have changed ownership more often. This gives raise to the idea of *predicting the risk of blacklisting* to valuate incoming transactions and manage the spending risk.

This paper sets out to specify a risk model and outline a prediction approach using public knowledge from the Bitcoin block chain. We also present preliminary results for selected known thefts; although the low number of events and heterogeneity of data prevent us from actually calibrating and running the model. As an equally important contribution, we discuss the implications on the future of Bitcoin. The paper is organized as follows. Section 2 recalls essential features of the Bitcoin system and ecosystem with special emphasis on risks in general. Section 3 develops a model for the specific risk of transaction blacklisting. Section 4 presents our empirical findings, and Sect. 5 discusses implications. The paper concludes with an outlook on future work (Sect. 6).

2 Background

2.1 Bitcoin and the Real World

To reason about Bitcoin and its relation with the real world, it is useful to introduce some terminology. Our conceptual model in Fig. 1 distinguishes the core Bitcoin system from a surrounding ecosystem. The core system consists of a protocol, implicitly specified by the reference implementation of the client software, and data representing the global consensus system state. This state is stored in the public block chain and continuously being updated by all clients participating in the Bitcoin peer-to-peer network. The core system is decentralized and designed with the aim to withhold control by central entities.

The Bitcoin *ecosystem* is the set of market operators leveraging the Bitcoin system. It includes Bitcoin-specific financial *intermediaries*, such as exchanges, mining pools, remote wallets, or transaction anonymizers. Some intermediaries are necessary to make Bitcoin usable as a global Internet currency, but unlike the core system, Bitcoin intermediaries are *not* decentralized. To avoid single points of failure and to discipline the intermediaries, competition between intermediaries offering substitutable services is desired and required.

The outer layers in Fig. 1 reflect the conventional separation of the financial from the real sector. As some Bitcoin intermediaries, notably exchanges, interface with conventional financial intermediaries, notably payment systems, we can depict the financial sector as another layer shielding Bitcoin from the real world. The intersection of all layers at the top of the figure symbolizes the possibility to skip layers. For example, the externality of cycles burned to reach consensus via proof-of-work materializes in energy consumption and heat production in the real world without necessarily involving the layers in between [3].

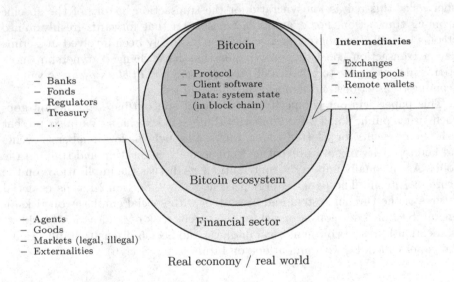

Fig. 1. Bitcoin's relation to the real world

2.2   Implications for Crime Fighters

The description in this section draws on our prior work [25]. Recall that markets in the real economy include legal and illegal activities alike. As criminals use the financial sector (and Bitcoin) to commit crimes and to launder criminal revenues, law enforcement has to take precautions. Fighting crime in the conventional financial sector lasts on the Know-Your-Customer (KYC) principle. The principle mandates financial intermediaries to verify the identity of clients before doing business with them. KYC was tightened in the US Patriot Act in order to strengthen efforts of anti-money laundering (AML) and combating the financing of terrorism (CFT). Many jurisdiction followed this US initiative. However, KYC is only one cornerstone. It must be complemented by risk assessment, monitoring, reporting and enforcement. Once identities are established via KYC, they become the identifiers enabling all downstream activities. Standard procedures include suspicious activity reports filed with financial intelligence units (FIUs), or automatic cross-checks against blacklists maintained by financial crime fighters, such as the US Office of Foreign Assets Control. In simple terms, fighting financial crime in conventional payment systems relies on known identities and does not require a full picture of all transactions.

Bitcoin, by contrast, is designed with pseudonymous identities. Account numbers are public keys of a digital signature system. Account ownership is established by knowing the corresponding private key. Everyone with a computer can create valid key pairs from large random numbers and thus open one or many Bitcoin accounts. Although the relation between Bitcoin accounts and civil identities of their owners is a priori unknown, Bitcoin transactions are not anonymous. A simple abstraction for Bitcoin is to think of it as a *public* distributed ledger that records all transactions between valid Bitcoin accounts. In short, fighting financial crime in Bitcoin means dealing with imperfect knowledge of identities, but may exploit perfect knowledge of all transactions.

2.3   Risks of Holding Bitcoin

Individuals or organizations holding bitcoins are faced with several types of risks, some of which can be managed by taking appropriate precautions. Most prominently, there is exchange rate risk. Compared to ordinary currencies, Bitcoin is still very volatile. Within just four weeks in fall 2013, Bitcoin soared as the exchange rate increased from 200 USD to 800 USD, i.e., by 400 %. On the contrary, when the Bitcoin exchange Mt. Gox was hacked in June 2011, the perpetrators caused the exchange rate to drop from 17,50 USD to just a single cent [18]. (But the exchange rate recovered minutes after the event.) The uncertainty of the exchange rate is one of many factors that might impede businesses accepting bitcoin. A mitigation strategy is to regularly convert bitcoins into local currency and keep only a small transaction budget at risk. Commercial payment providers, for instance BitPay [1], offer services to automate this process.

Closely related to exchange risk is the risk of a systemic Bitcoin failure. This means that a catastrophic event dries out the market and lets the exchange rate plummet close to zero. One reason could be a major government intervention. Although no government can stop Bitcoin from existing, a coordinated action of large countries can nevertheless force the currency into the underground. While some jurisdictions appear to tolerate Bitcoin, others, such as Thailand [20], are more reserved. Moreover, any glitch in the implementation of the Bitcoin protocol could easily cause a failure, too. Namecoin, a special-purpose Bitcoin derivate, was affected by such a failure recently. The attempt to recover it was still ongoing at the time of writing [7]. Obviously, this kind of risk can only be managed by not holding more bitcoins than one can afford to lose.

Whenever users deal with intermediaries, they are exposed to counterparty risk. There are many reported cases where Bitcoin intermediaries closed their business with their clients' deposits as loot. Whether the root causes were fraudulent motives or plain bankruptcy is of secondary interest in the absence of effective means of fund recovery. Moore and Christin [24] have empirically analyzed factors behind exchange failures and calibrated a prediction model for such events.

The risks described above affect all users (or all users within a large group) alike, but there are also risks idiosyncratic to users. First, users face the risk of making mistakes when sending transactions. As Bitcoin transactions are irreversible, typos in the transaction amount require the recipient's active collaboration to undo that error. Fool-proof client implementations are necessary to mitigate the risk of making mistakes.

Careless users may lose the private keys, which are required to spend their bitcoins, e.g., due to a failure of the storage medium of their wallet. Nobody really knows to which extent users have suffered losses so far. Ron and Shamir identify large amounts of dormant coins, i.e., bitcoins which have not been used for a long time, in their transaction graph analysis and conjecture that these might be lost coins [28]. Regular backups of private keys reduce this risk.

Users may not only lose private keys by improvidence, but may also become victims of theft. Many Bitcoin users do not keep their private keys in their own domain of trust. Instead, they entrust online service providers with managing their wallets. Such providers are hacked quite regularly, which usually means their customers lose everything. Recently, the wallet provider "inputs.io" has been compromised and the bitcoin equivalent of 1.2 million USD has been stolen [21]. Replacing online services by personal devices is not necessarily a solution. For instance, wallets managed with Android devices have been found vulnerable to a weakness of Android's random number generator [2]. Hence, paying close attention to security is critical to mitigate the risk of theft.

Another risk that received considerable attention is double-spending (for example, [3,17]). Bitcoin's nature of a decentralized peer-to-peer system relying on proof-of-work to maintain the integrity of the global state puts individual clients at the risk of believing in a transaction that will be invalidated in the future. The specific risk of double-spending declines exponentially with the number of blocks after the inclusion of the transaction [26]. Hence, while double-spendings occur regularly [8], some patience when accepting Bitcoin payments is enough to avoid falling for it.

Similar to double-spending, blacklisting is another risk of receiving apparently valid bitcoins at one point in time, which become invalid at another. Although not extensively used these days, if blacklisting becomes common practice, it is in the users' best interest to account for the risk of blacklisting whenever accepting a Bitcoin payment. What is special about this risk is that whether bitcoins are blacklisted or not depends on their transaction history, i.e., on whether those transactions preceding the current one were involved in a crime. This calls for risk scoring based on the public information contained in the block chain.

Although blacklisting has been a topic in the Bitcoin community for some time, we are not aware of any attempts to set up such a scoring model.

The collection of risks provided in this section is by no means exhaustive. More subtle risks exist as well, such as losing financial privacy if the association between a Bitcoin address and its owner becomes public. This paper focuses on the blacklisting risk specifically.

3 A Risk Arrival Model for Blacklisting Events

3.1 Blacklisting Policies: Poison and Haircut

To tackle the quantification of the risk of transaction blacklisting, it is important to specify what the consequences of blacklisting can be. Transactions are blacklisted with a certain probability if they are involved in a crime. Typical Bitcoin crimes include theft from popular online wallet providers or illegally earned proceeds from blackmailing, e.g., with ransomware such as CryptoLocker [15]. The goal of blacklists is to render the criminals' bitcoins useless, thereby lowering the incentives for this criminal activity. To achieve this end, governments could mandate all legitimate businesses not to accept transactions directly associated with blacklisted transactions.

There are several problems with this approach. First and foremost, criminals can create as many identities as they want [14]. Hence, they can send their dirty bitcoins through several fake addresses. They could repeat this procedure until it appears to a ingenuous observer that there is no connection to the criminal source. To avoid this, blacklisting has to propagate through the transaction graph to punish anyone, both fake identities of criminals and ordinary users, for accepting blacklisted bitcoins. Honest users can avoid undue punishment by obeying the blacklist preemptively.

Unfortunately, there will be a certain timespan between the point in time at which an illegal transaction takes place and the point in time at which it is added to the blacklist. Thus, honest users may accept a dirty bitcoin despite their best efforts to comply with the blacklist. These users, not knowing that they have accepted a dirty bitcoin, might combine three small amounts of bitcoins A1, A2 and A3 to create a large transaction B. With the propagation mechanism in place, B would also be affected by blacklisting if only one of its input transactions A1, A2 or A3 is dirty.

Consequently, it is important to specify how exactly B would be affected. Two basic blacklisting policies are conceivable. In the first, which we call "poison", B would be invalidated just as any other blacklisted coin. The poison policy implies that every transaction is invalidated that has at least one dirty predecessor, no matter how many generations above. Note that the propagation works on the level of transactions (not addresses) and requires the recipient to act. This prevents that saboteurs can destroy other people's bitcoin wealth by routing a blacklisted transaction to their publicly known address.

The second, less drastic policy is one we call "haircut". Instead of invalidating a transaction entirely, it is devalued proportionally to the amount of blacklisted bitcoins in its inputs, again applied recursively. In the example above, if the three transactions A1, A2 and A3 were all worth one bitcoin and one of them was blacklisted, transaction B would be treated being worth 2 BTC (although nominally, in the block chain, it would be worth 3 BTC). It is easy to see how this policy propagates through the transaction graph.

Figure 2 shows an advanced transaction graph example of how the two basic policies affect transaction values. Nodes represent transactions, whereas arrows represent the flow of value between them (i.e., an output of a former transaction is used as an input in the successive transaction). The color of a node represents the state of blacklisting, where white represents clean coins and black blacklisted coins. In the poison scenario, an initial theft of 7 BTC leads to a total loss of 20 BTC, as blacklisted coins were combined with clean coins and thereby change their state. In the case of the haircut policy, different colors of grey illustrate the amount of a transactions devaluation. As the stolen 7 BTC are repeatedly combined with clean coins, the share of blacklisted value decreases (and the color gets brighter). In contrast to the poison scenario, the total amount of blacklisted value stays the same.

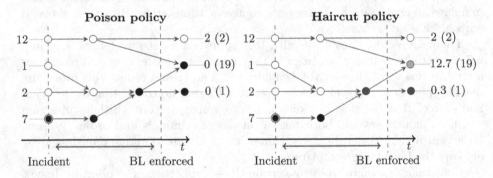

Fig. 2. Timing model of transaction blacklisting (BL) with different policies

Of course, more advanced policies that look deeper into transactions are conceivable. Imagine a "FIFO" policy, where the order of the inputs determines which outputs are affected by blacklisting. If a transaction has two inputs worth 1 BTC and only the second input originates from a blacklisted transaction, the first output(s) will be considered "clean" until they add up to a value of 1 BTC and the remaining outputs will be partially or fully invalidated. Note that as a result, such granular blacklisting policies may make the internal structure of transactions subject for negotiations between sending and receiving parties.

3.2   Risk Arrival and Impact Analysis

As discussed, blacklisting exposes all users to the risk of accepting a bitcoin which is blacklisted in the future. Rational users desire to keep this risk small. In particular, at some point in time, a user will be presented with a transaction created by another user and he will have to decide whether or not to accept it; or, more precisely, how much the bitcoins being transferred are worth to him. The user reduces the nominal value, i.e., the BTC amount specified in the transaction, by an appropriate risk premium reflecting the risk of blacklisting.

This risk is idiosyncratic for the transaction as it depends on the history of all inputs. For simplicity, we consider only one input noting that the generalization to multiple inputs is straightforward if the blacklisting policy is known. A rational user will analyze the history using suitable predictors. By observing previous thefts and the traces criminals leave behind in the block chain, he could identify characteristic patterns and search for these patterns in the given history. This information could be used to estimate the expected loss associated with accepting the transaction at face value.

For both policies, poison and haircut, users must first estimate the probability that a transaction will be affected by blacklisting as a function of time. Second, users must estimate how long they keep (parts of) this transaction in their own accounts. This is non-trivial as users may prioritize spending of risky coins or spend bitcoins faster in general, which has monetary implications not further detailed here. Third, they have to estimate their loss in case of blacklisting. This depends on the policy.

For the poison policy, the third part is straightforward. As all affected bitcoins are void, users multiply the blacklisting probability with the transaction value. Things are more complicated with a haircut policy. But the haircut policy also has advantages. Imagine the poison policy was in place and a user has accepted a transaction. When he combines this transaction with others, e.g., to consolidate his funds in cold storage, he also puts his other funds at risk. In such a policy, combining transactions would increase risk, effectively lowering the value. As a result, users would avoid doing so if not absolutely necessary. With the haircut policy, by contrast, the total value at risk does not change when transactions are combined.

Transaction histories grow substantially over time. Apart from technical challenges with analyzing such histories (e.g., finding efficient algorithms and data structures), this also causes hard-to-calculate risk. There will always be a very small but positive probability of very old incidents becoming generally known. Especially with a poison policy, this could affect very large numbers of transactions potentially causing systemic instability of the currency. Hence, some form of statutory period after which no blacklisting is done seems reasonable.

4   Prediction Approach

4.1   Model and Data

The heart of any risk scoring model is the set of predictors that separates the dangerous coins from the harmless. To test such predictors, data from real thefts is needed in order to distinguish normal from criminal behavior. While law enforcement agencies might have a comprehensive list of incidents at their hands, the only source of public information we are aware of is a list of major thefts and losses that happened from 2011 until today (November 2013). The list is maintained by users of the "Bitcoin Forum" [4]. There are a number of aspects limiting the applicability of this dataset:

– The list contains only large thefts, between 922 and 263,024 BTC.
– Only few thefts include a list of the relevant transactions.
– It is difficult to determine when a theft was "officially" announced, yet the exact point in time is needed to determine when official blacklisting could have taken place.

Out of nine thefts that contain a list of relevant transaction, we can only assign a concrete blacklisting timestamp to six incidents. We used the time of first announcement in the Bitcoin forum as the assumed time of blacklisting. Furthermore, only three of these thefts show block chain activity between the theft and the blacklisting timestamp, rendering the other three useless for our purposes (cf. Table 1). Nonetheless, we show exemplary results from our attempts to evaluate our predictors using the information from these three incidents.

Table 1. List of known incidents with transaction data

Incident	Severity	Reporting time	Coins used
Allinvain Theft	25000 BTC	2011-06-13 20:47	yes
Linode Hack	46653 BTC	2012-03-01 21:43	yes
Betcoin Theft	3172 BTC	2012-04-13 12:19	no
May 2012 Bitcoinica Hack	18548 BTC	2012-05-11 13:16	no
Bitfloor Theft	24086 BTC	2012-09-04 17:08	yes
Cdecker Theft	9222 BTC	2012-09-28 08:10	no
Mass MyBitcoin Theft	4019 BTC	unclear	–
2012 Trojan	3500 BTC	unavailable	–
Bitcoin Syndicate Theft	1852 BTC	unavailable	–

4.2   Candidate Predictors

We briefly discuss a few potential predictors for our risk model. First of all, predictors need to be powerful and efficiently measurable. As they are based on public data, criminals could try to outsmart them, hence predictors should ideally be hard to manipulate. Our list includes public information that can be gathered from the block chain only. It is conceivable to include other public information, such as references to Bitcoin addresses on the web. If the risk prediction is offered as a service, it is also possible to include private information, for instance collected by exchanges and other intermediaries; and enriched with behavioral profiles acquired from social media or search engines. It is unclear if such information is of any help to detect indications of criminal activity.

Very speculatively, a potentially powerful predictor using semi-public information would be whether transaction prefixes have been seen at exit nodes of the Tor network. If this information helps, one could even pay the operators of exit nodes for sharing such knowledge. But such ideas are clearly out of scope of our initial prediction attempts.

In the following we describe the predictors considered in this study.

Transaction Value. Ordinary users can be expected to transfer ordinary amounts of bitcoins between addresses for ordinary purposes such as changing bitcoins for local currency at a Bitcoin exchange. The number of bitcoins being transferred will be rather small. Any activity involving very large sums of Bitcoins would be suspicious, e.g., because a criminal hacked an exchange and exfiltrated all bitcoins at once. Hence, a straightforward indicator is to observe transaction volumes and to pay close attention to outliers from an expected distribution as they may stem from a major theft.

Obfuscation Patterns. If a thief is clever enough to steal a large amount of bitcoins, he is probably also clever enough to avoid leaving obvious traces of his crime behind. Instead of simply combining his entire haul to a huge lump sum to spend on a Ferrari, he may also use carefully designed obfuscation patterns, possibly involving numerous fake identities, to stop law enforcement from tracing him. Assuming that those taking on such efforts are more likely involved in criminal activities than others, risk scoring models could search for typical obfuscation strategies as indicators of blacklisting risk. Examples of such patterns have been observed in the Bitcoin transaction graph before, e.g., in the context of analyzing Bitcoin mixing services, which make extensive use of peeling chains [25]. Other studies also identified various characteristic patterns used by larger organizations in the Bitcoin ecosystem. Most importantly, these patterns involve aggregations, foldings (i.e., combining blacklisted transactions with clear transactions), splits and also peeling chains [22]. Hence, peeling chains are not necessarily associated with Bitcoin mixing but may still increase the risk.

Frequency of Usage. A thief trying to obfuscate the origin of his bitcoins may construct a complex web of transactions between multiple fake addresses to make others believe these Bitcoins were involved in ordinary business. What a thief might also want is to launder stolen coins as soon as possible. As he knows his bitcoins were involved in a crime, he is fully aware of the blacklisting risk and holding them for a long time increases his risk of loss. Hence, the thief must construct his fake transactions fast, resulting in a short time span between transactions involving these coins. This motivates measuring transaction frequency to use it is an indicator of risk. Whenever frequency increases above average values, there are reasons for suspicion.

Change Addresses and Multi-Input Transactions. The predictors presented so far make use of characteristics of the transaction graph, but do not take the addresses associated with the transactions into account. Heuristics such as the detection of change addresses [22] or the combination of addresses from multi-input transactions [27], which are likely to belong to the same user, can detect connections between apparently unrelated transactions. This allows to possibly link public keys of transaction prefixes to other blacklisted transactions. Furthermore, it can provide evidence whether obfuscation patterns or a high frequency stem from a natural origin or are constructed by a single entity.

Coinbase Transactions. Coinbase transactions are a special type of transaction of which there is one per block in the block chain. These transactions do not have inputs, i.e., they create new bitcoins without using up the bitcoins from other transactions. At the moment, their value is equal to 25 bitcoins plus the sum of all transaction fees associated with the other transactions in the block. The primary purpose of coinbase transactions is to provide an incentive for users to participate in the creation of proof of work, which is necessary to ensure manipulation resistance of the global state. Also, they solve the problem of bootstrapping the network [9]. Because coinbase transaction have no history attached to them, their risk of being involved in a theft if obviously very low – except for the case in which a thief is able to control a miner or mining pool directly and thus the coinbase transaction itself would be blacklisted. If the thief colludes with a miner to launder his coins through large transaction fees, one could apply the blacklisting policy also to transaction fees – where the haircut policy seems to be the more appropriate policy as it leaves the fixed reward of the coinbase transaction unaffected. To measure the portion of "clean" coins, we compare the value of coinbase transactions $C_i(t)$ to the value of all $V_i(t)$ transaction i steps away from the transaction of interest t, and then sum up the individual values for each i in a degressive fashion. This reduces the influence of transactions further away. One can limit i to $i = 10$, as larger values for i will influence the score only marginally:

$$X(t) = \sum_{i=1}^{10} \frac{1}{2^{(i-1)}} \cdot \frac{C_i(t)}{V_i(t)} \ .$$

Larger values of $X(t)$ imply a larger amount of value stemming from coinbase transactions and thus reduce the risk of blacklisting.

4.3 Preliminary Results

Although not adequate to calibrate our model, we calculate indicator scores for all three thefts and compare the results to a control group, where we randomly choose a transaction for each affected transaction. As n (the number of affected transactions) is low for the Allinvain and Betfloor theft, we increase n in the control group to 112. Transactions of the control groups are drawn from the same block of the blacklisted transaction to ensure comparability. (Finding the right sampling and bootstrapping approach for this purpose is deferred to specialized future work.) If there are not enough transactions available, we draw from nearby blocks. The first four predictors analyze transaction values. Due to the small number of transactions, very large values may bias the results. We therefore log-transform all transaction values. The other predictors are calibrated as follows. For peeling chains, we look if a transaction comes from a peeling chain with a minimum length of 6 transactions. To measure the portion of coinbase transactions, we use the formula stated above. However, we reduce the depth i from 10 to 8 in order to increase performance.

Table 2. Predictors for thefts and control groups

Predictor	Allinvain		Bitfloor		Linode	
	Incident	Control	Incident	Control	Incident	Control
n	7	112	8	112	82	112
Average	2.7743	1.2664	2.8249	0.3669	1.2715	0.8287
Median	3.2355	1.3573	2.8489	0.4848	1.1491	1.0553
SD	1.1687	1.1495	0.8206	1.0718	1.3929	1.0087
Variance	1.5936	1.3332	0.7695	1.1592	1.9641	1.0265
Peeling chains	0.2857	0.6639	0.6250	0.3571	0.3415	0.3482
Duration (h)	611	218	68	25	28	93
Coinbase score	0.1027	0.0575	0.0056	0.0103	0.0181	0.0948

The results (cf. Table 2) reflect our previous observation that these three thefts constitute a very special case of theft: they affect long-term user or intermediaries of the Bitcoin system, who have a large amount of bitcoins available, in parts presumably from own mining activity. The average and median transaction size in the control group is always smaller than in the incident set. There is not only heterogeneity between the particular incident and control groups, but also between the members of both incident and control groups. As a result, without better and more general data, we are currently not in a position to derive an adequate set of predictors for a risk scoring model with acceptable predictive power.

5 Market Implications

In this section we discuss how markets are affected by a regime that strictly enforces blacklists of transaction prefixes. We assume that some (imperfect) prediction models for spending risk are available, either based on public information or using proprietary information against a small fee.

5.1   1 BTC $\neq$ 1 BTC

Bitcoins are not alike. Each transaction is a descendant of a unique transaction history, which is readily available in the public block chain. Therefore, markets participants can, in principle, scrutinize the history and become selective in which transactions they accept; or, with more granularity, how much they value it. The fact that most participants do not differentiate for the time being is hard to justify with economic rationality. A necessary consequence of differentiation is that market prices reflect the information encoded in the transaction history. Dealing with bitcoins of two kinds (e.g., black and white, under the poison policy) may be manageable, essentially at the cost of lower liquidity in both market segments.[2] Pricing *every history individually* poses new challenges to the design of market mechanisms, for example at exchanges; but it also affects every small merchant who accepts bitcoins in exchange for goods or services.

As price differences reflect spending risk, we may follow the model of credit markets and introduce intermediaries who publish commonly accepted risk ratings of all unspent transactions. This comes with two issues. First, transaction rating agencies are a new kind of intermediaries that need to be paid. Second, the fact that people must rely on them conflicts with the idea of decentralization. If we try to decentralize ratings to resolve these issues (for example by trivial replication), the rating model must be confined to public information, or use non-trivial homomorphic encryption. Both options raise new questions. For example, can we generate meaningful risk ratings based on public information with public algorithms and still remain game-proof? Game-proofness is an important property that discourages whitewashing of transaction histories. If one could bounce transactions between own accounts to predictably increase their value, everybody would do it, resulting in a choked up network and block chain.

The credit rating analogy has limits. Here is one important difference: conventional credit ratings (allegedly) have an information advantage. They aggregate *private* information that is not readily available to all market participants. In the absence of better information, market participants rely on ratings as common proxy. If market participants had access to the disaggregated information—machine-readable and at no cost, like for Bitcoin transactions—some would prefer to aggregate the information using customized models. And it would be naive to assume that buyers and sellers agree on the same model, let alone on its parameters. The multitude of private valuation functions calls into question the conventional order book approach followed by popular Bitcoin exchanges. Instead, we need new efficient mechanisms that reveal and match market participants' private valuations of all transactions on a marketplace.

One thing that is conceivable under the haircut policy is risk pooling, using insurance markets and CoinJoin [5] as models: risk-averse bitcoin owners can reduce the variance of their spending risk by forming large transactions with many others, thereby distributing the impact of bad transactions equally.

---

[2] Intentionally "colored" coins have been proposed to deal with virtual goods of different value using Bitcoin as an infrastructure [29].

Of course, such schemes require coordination effort and they are vulnerable to adverse selection as parties who know that they possess dubious transactions have higher incentives to participate in the pool. This is a known issue of insurance markets.

5.2   YouMoney or Bloodcoin?

Taking the uniqueness and identifiability of Bitcoin transactions beyond the question of pricing offers interesting new insights. Precious metals or official fiat currencies are designed as homogeneous goods. This ensures fungibility: quantities are exchangeable and divisible, a precondition to fulfill the monetary function as *unit of account*. Bitcoin transactions, by contrast, are heterogeneous goods, differentiated on a quality dimension. The valuation of this quality is subject to individual preferences. This threatens the function as unit of account, as detailed above in Sect. 5.1.

On the upside, however, recipients of payments could apply ethical standards on what money they accept. This is best comparable to the Kimberly Process Certification Scheme [30], a set of international resolutions established with the aim to suspend the trade of blood diamonds, which are mined in war zones and sold to finance arms. One might wonder how well certain industries fared if the money they accept could be traced back with the ease offered by Bitcoin. Although market participants still use Bitcoin like a fungible good, being more selective in what one accepts stands to reason. At least those who have a brand or reputation to lose have every reasons to be afraid of negative publicity linking their profits to violence, with evidence publicly accessible in the block chain.

More generally, the public transaction history turns Bitcoin into *personalized money*. Because the origin of a transaction matters for spending and reputation, accepting bitcoins from one party implies a trust relationship from the payee to the payer. This trust must be established and signaled outside the Bitcoin protocol, for example by linking Bitcoin identifiers to reputation or social networking systems. Like the rating analogy above, this is another interesting feature where Bitcoin markets resemble credit markets more than foreign exchange markets: Bitcoin recipients take over the sender's spending risk in a similar vain as creditors bear their debtors' credit risk. In rough circumstances, a recipient of Bitcoin transactions may even ask for a security to cover potential losses. So at second sight, Bitcoin is not so dissimilar to systems of decentralized debt obligations, like iOwe [19].

This collection of unfinished thoughts indicates that understanding the full implications of perfectly and publicly traceable payments remains a major task for interdisciplinary research.

5.3   Alternatives

What can we do about it? In a decentralized system with a public global state, the only way to make cryptographic tokens homogeneous, and the virtual good they encode fungible, is to make transaction histories untraceable. Zerocoin [23] promises this option. Other solutions involve hierarchical structures of fast and anonymous cryptographic cash [11,12] issued by competitive intermediaries and backed with a slower and less anonymous cryptographic reserve currency, such as Bitcoin. However, all these options make it harder to fight crime by following the money. Ideally, we would like to see compromises like systems offering practically untraceable transactions for small amounts; and the computational effort needed to trace entities decreases gently as the amounts involved grow. This turns the access to transaction histories from a global binary property to a variable transaction cost, again with implications for all market participants. At the time of writing, we do not know a technical solution for this set of requirements. We conjecture that it will be hard to realize when identities are cheap.

The economics of adoption are crucial in this context [9]. All conceivable alternatives require coordinated effort to switch from Bitcoin to the new regime. This revolution is hard to achieve against vested interests. Blacklists, by contrast, are evolutionary. They can emerge without changing the core system and thus are hardly avoidable if Bitcoin remains relevant.

6 Future Work

Directions for future work include observing blacklisting practices in the Bitcoin ecosystem, collecting data for more incidents, and finding better tailored predictors to estimate and eventually validate a risk scoring model.

For simplicity, we have assumed that one blacklist is obeyed globally. In practice, synchronizing this blacklist is another problem that is prone to race conditions. Moreover, as blacklists are enforced by national law enforcement agencies, it is likely that the world will see at least one blacklist per country. So the spending risk also depends on the spending conventions. Despite people say the Internet has no borders, the would-be Internet currency becomes as messy as international trade.

Note that the authors do not approve or disapprove blacklisting of Bitcoin transactions. Our mission is to reason about the consequences of forseeable developments. A then relevant topic completely out of the scope of this work is to explore how the governance of blacklists can be put under decentralized control.

References

1. BitPay. https://bitpay.com/
2. Android Security Vulnerability (2013). http://bitcoin.org/en/alert/2013-08-11-android
3. Becker, J., Breuker, D., Heide, T., Holler, J., Rauer, H.P., Böhme, R.: Can we afford integrity by Proof-of-Work? Scenarios inspired by the bitcoin currency. In: Böhme, R. (ed.) The Economics of Information Security and Privacy, pp. 135–156. Springer, Heidelberg (2013)
4. Bitcoin Forum. List of Major Bitcoin Heists, Thefts, Hacks, Scams, and Losses. https://bitcointalk.org/index.php?topic=83794

5. Bitcoin Forum. CoinJoin: Bitcoin privacy for the real world (2013). https://bitcointalk.org/index.php?topic=279249.0
6. Bitcoin Forum. Mike Hearn, Foundation's Law & Policy Chair, is pushing blacklists right now (2013). https://bitcointalk.org/index.php?topic=333824.0
7. Bitcoin Forum. Namecoin was Stillborn, I Had to Switch Off Life-Support (2013). https://bitcointalk.org/index.php?topic=310954
8. Blockchain.info. Double Spends. https://blockchain.info/de/double-spends
9. Böhme, R.: Internet protocol adoption: learning from Bitcoin. In: IAB Workshop on Internet Technology Adoption and Transition (ITAT) (2013)
10. Buterin, V.: Mt.Gox: what the largest exchange is doing about the Linode theft and the implications (2012). http://bitcoinmagazine.com/mtgox-the-bitcoin-police-what-the-largest-exchange-is-doing-about-the-linode-theft-and-the-implications/
11. Chaum, D., Fiat, A., Naor, M.: Untraceable electronic cash. In: Goldwasser, S. (ed.) CRYPTO 1988. LNCS, vol. 403, pp. 319–327. Springer, Heidelberg (1990)
12. Chaum, D.: Security without identification: transaction systems to make big brother obsolete. Commun. ACM **28**(70), 1030–1044 (1985)
13. Christin, N.: Traveling the silk road: a measurement analysis of a large anonymous online marketplace. In: Proceedings of the 22nd International World Wide Web Conference, Rio de Janeiro, pp. 213–224 (2013)
14. Douceur, J.R.: The sybil attack. In: Druschel, P., Kaashoek, M.F., Rowstron, A. (eds.) IPTPS 2002. LNCS, vol. 2429, pp. 251–260. Springer, Heidelberg (2002)
15. Goodin, D.: You're infected-if you want to see your data again, pay us USD 300 in Bitcoins (2013). http://arstechnica.com/security/2013/10/youre-infected-if-you-want-to-see-your-data-again-pay-us-300-in-bitcoins/
16. Hill, K.: Sanitizing Bitcoin: This Company Wants To Track 'Clean' Bitcoin Accounts (2013). http://www.forbes.com/sites/kashmirhill/2013/11/13/sanitizing-bitcoin-coin-validation/
17. Karame, G.O., Androulaki, E., Capkun, S.: Two bitcoins at the price of one? Double-spending attacks on fast payments in bitcoin. In: Proceedings of the ACM Conference on Computer and Communications Security (CCS) (2012)
18. Karpeles, M.: Clarification of Mt. Gox Compromised Accounts and Major Bitcoin Sell-Off (2011). https://www.mtgox.com/press_release_20110630.html
19. Levin, D., Schulman, A., LaCurts, K., Spring, N., Bhattacharjee, B.: Making currency inexpensive with iOwe. In: Proceedings of the Workshop on the Economics of Networks, Systems, and Computation (NetEcon), San Jose (2011)
20. McLeod, A.S.: Thailand Bans The Bitcoin! National Foreign Exchange Department Rules Bitcoin Illegal, Trading Suspended (2013). http://forexmagnates.com/bitcoin-binned-thailands-foreign-exchange-department-rules-bitcoin-illegal-trading-suspended/
21. McMillan, R.: USD 1.2M Hack Shows Why You Should Never Store Bitcoins on the Internet (2013). http://www.wired.com/wiredenterprise/2013/11/inputs/
22. Meiklejohn, S., Pomarole, M., Jordan, G., Levchenko, K., McCoy, D., Voelker, G.M., Savage, S.: A fistful of bitcoins: characterizing payments among men with no names. In: Proceedings of the ACM Internet Measurement Conference (IMC), pp. 127–140. ACM, New York (2013)
23. Miers, I., Garman, C., Green, M., Rubin, A.D.: Zerocoin: anonymous distributed e-cash from bitcoin. In: IEEE Symposium on Security and Privacy, San Francisco, pp. 397–411. IEEE (2013)
24. Moore, T., Christin, N.: Beware the middleman: empirical analysis of bitcoin-exchange risk. In: Sadeghi, A.-R. (ed.) FC 2013. LNCS, vol. 7859, pp. 25–33. Springer, Heidelberg (2013)

25. Möser, M., Böhme, R., Breuker, D.: An inquiry into money laundering tools in the bitcoin ecosystem. In: Proceedings of the APWG E-Crime Researchers Summit (2013)
26. Nakamoto, S.: Bitcoin: A Peer-to-Peer Electronic Cash System (2008)
27. Reid, F., Harrigan, M.: An analysis of anonymity in the bitcoin system. In: Altshuler, Y., Elovici, Y., Cremers, A.B., Aharony, N., Pentland, A. (eds.) Security and Privacy in Social Networks, pp. 197–223. Springer, New York (2013)
28. Ron, D., Shamir, A.: Quantitative analysis of the full bitcoin transaction graph. In: Sadeghi, A.-R. (ed.) FC 2013. LNCS, vol. 7859, pp. 6–24. Springer, Heidelberg (2013)
29. Meni Rosenfeld. Overview of colored coins, December 2012. http://bitcoil.co.il/BitcoinX.pdf
30. Wikipedia. Kimberley process certification scheme (2013). http://en.wikipedia.org/wiki/Kimberley_Process_Certification_Scheme

Challenges and Opportunities Associated with a Bitcoin-Based Transaction Rating System

David Vandervort[✉]

Xerox, Webster, NY, USA
david.vandervort@xerox.com

Abstract. It has been shown that seller ratings given by previous buyers give new customers useful information when making purchasing decisions. Bitcoin, however, is designed to obfuscate the link between buyer and seller with a layer of limited anonymity, thus preventing buyers from finding or validating this information. While this level of anonymity is valued by the Bitcoin community, as Bitcoin moves toward greater adoption there will be pressure from buyers who wish to know more about who they are doing business with, and sellers who consider their reputation a strong selling point, to allow greater transparency. We consider three different models by which a reputation/rating system could be implemented in conjunction with Bitcoin transactions and consider pros and cons of each. We find that each presents challenges on both the technological and social fronts.

1 Background

Bitcoin is electronic currency. This fact has consequences for how people think about it and how they regard doing business with it. They expect to do business in a businesslike way. The promise of Bitcoin is that transactions will be quick and frictionless. Unlike businesses using more established and controlled currencies, they may also be anonymous. The Bitcoin protocol provides for monetary and other transactions to be tied to addresses, not identities. The ability to generate and use new addresses provides a degree of anonymity that non-technically inclined users are unlikely to pierce. The Bitcoin community points to this anonymity, often referred to as pseudonymity because it is not absolute, as an asset, a way of circumventing surveillance and cumbersome regulatory regimes [1]. It is also considered a defense against the user profiling/data mining practiced by large merchants such as K-Mart.

The original Bitcoin paper described the features of non-reversibility of payments and cryptographic verification as substitutes for more traditional forms of ensuring trust [2]. However, the anonymity of Bitcoin transactions removes another source of trust in transactions: Knowing who you are doing business with. It opens the possibility of counter-party risk, the danger that the other person will not live up to their obligations once the money is received. For buyers, being able to know who they are buying from can increase trust and so reduce barriers to a successful purchase. Likewise, sellers whose business grows by word of mouth or who consider good will a valuable asset may wish to share information about successful transactions with the buying public.

R. Böhme et al. (Eds.): FC 2014 Workshops, LNCS 8438, pp. 33–42, 2014.
DOI: 10.1007/978-3-662-44774-1_3

Bitcoin allows different forms of knowledge and openness from traditional forms of transaction. In the pre-cryptocurrency market, transactions are mostly anonymous and away from public view. When a buyer pays with cash, the record of the transaction contains only the amount and codes related to the items purchased. The use of a credit card creates more of a paper trail as the credit card service (i.e. Visa), the vendor and the purchaser retain records identifying both buyer and seller, as well as items and amounts. However, this information is generally not published for the world to see. Such financial records may be bought and aggregated in many ways, including scoring the credit worthiness of the buyer. They may be mined by the seller to learn much about their customers but, since virtually all companies consider financial information to be confidential, the results are not shared with customers or with other companies.

Studies have shown that buyer behavior can be influenced by knowledge of seller reputation, product quality, and experiences and sentiment of previous customers. Specifically, simulations have shown that reputation systems can improve the overall quality of an online market [3]. The Bitcoin protocol includes as a central feature, the blockchain, a public ledger of all transactions. Amounts paid, change received, and both input and output addresses are stored and cryptographically verified. The information contained therein, however, is sparse. An address is no more than a temporary identity. By intent it contains no direct links to more stable and human understandable identities. Likewise, the exact nature of the goods or services purchased is absent.

As Bitcoin and associated altcoins become more mainstream and their communities attempt the leap to general acceptance, the sparsity of information may become an issue. There is some likelihood that some buyers and sellers will seek ways to leverage and augment the information on the blockchain to learn more about each other. The ability to mine the blockchain for data is part of the promise of Bitcoin. This paper explores three ways in which such augmented information could be developed, looking specifically at the case where buyers seek information about sellers and sellers voluntarily cooperate. The three cases considered are site based systems, wallet based systems and coin based systems.

2 Characteristics of Rating Systems

For purposes of this discussion we define a rating system as a means for customers to provide feedback on a purchase that future potential customers may access and include in their decision making process. Other purposes, such as for sellers to track customer satisfaction or for regulatory bodies to monitor performance, while potentially possible are not considered here. Ratings may take different forms, such as a number of stars, a thumbs up/thumbs down, or a numerical rating. Some systems may aggregate multiple ratings. For example, a transaction may be given a separate rating in each of several categories such as price, speed of delivery and product quality. Free form product reviews are also common. Whatever method is used, the goal is to encode some concept of quality associated with the transaction, product or provider in a form that can be easily understood by future customers. This requirement does not rule out machine mediation of information, such as developing an average of ratings or converting numbers into words (1 $\sim$ 'Excellent') that are considered more readable by humans.

The potential for the computer to repackage information is relevant to the case of Bitcoin transactions. In raw form, a Bitcoin transaction contains very little data that a human finds meaningful, particularly if that human is an average, non-technical user. A Bitcoin transaction is essentially little more than a hash code that is used to identify a collection of other hash codes, with numbers representing transaction amounts, attached. Software can easily break this down into a set of inputs and outputs, showing addresses Bitcoins are drawn from and sent to. There is little meta-data that would identify the purpose of the transaction or the entities involved (that is, the owners of the associated addresses) is not present. This is an efficient system for transmitting the required information. Any system for rating Bitcoin transactions must contend with this efficiency, preferably without compromising it.

Online rating systems are subject to several weaknesses that can be exploited by malicious parties. One such weakness is falsified ratings. That is, friends or enemies of a seller may post fake ratings (possibly using multiple false identities) intended to boost or suppress a seller's reputation regardless of whether they had ever engaged in business with the seller, or of the outcome if they had done business. It may also be possible for malicious intruders in a system to tamper with authentic ratings, making them invalid [4]. It is essential for any rating system, including one involving Bitcoin transactions, to address these weaknesses.

It should be noted that rating systems are often referred to in the literature as reputation systems. This terminology is not used here largely because the question of whether ratings can be reliably related to sellers is still an open one. Therefore in this paper we use the more limited terminology of rating systems.

3 Considerations for a Bitcoin-Based Rating System

The heart of the Bitcoin protocol is the blockchain, the ledger of all transactions that is maintained by the entire Bitcoin network. Cryptographic proof-of-work makes it extremely difficult to forge transactions and ensures a high degree of integrity to the blockchain. Because the blockchain "remembers" all Bitcoin transactions, it is large and continuously growing. In the context of transaction ratings this means that adding rating meta-data directly into the blockchain may cause enough increase in the storage and transmission size of transactions to be impractical.

A more salient point than data size is the speed at which transactions become "fixed" in the blockchain. One of the attractions of Bitcoin is that transactions are very quick, with confirmations coming from around the network within minutes. Confirmation means that some number of nodes around the network have verified the cryptographic proof-of-work associated with the transaction. It also means that, once confirmed, the transaction cannot be changed. Customers who provide feedback on a transaction may wait until a product is delivered, or until it is installed, or until it breaks. The amount of time between transaction and rating varies but in virtually all cases will be greater than the brief period between creation of a transaction and confirmation. The consequence of this is straight forward. Ratings of a transaction cannot be included in the data for that transaction.

It may be possible to create a new kind of transaction that references an older one and adds meta-data to it. However, there is no such proposal at this time and any scheme that depends on such a proposal being implemented should be considered unlikely. No such proposal will be considered here.

The anonymity-by-intent nature of the Bitcoin protocol is a major consideration. The official Bitcoin client software can generate a large number of random addresses that can be used to send or receive Bitcoin payments. Nothing about any given address links it to the entity using it, although there are techniques by which addresses may sometimes be de-anonymized. For example, if several addresses are inputs to the same transaction they are all known to be owned by the same entity. Re-use of any of the addresses therefore reveals information about all of them [5]. It does not necessarily reveal the identity of the owner, however.

The poor linkage between payment addresses and identities has the effect on a rating system of making aggregation of ratings difficult or impossible. This is potentially a greater hurdle to a strong rating system than the immutable nature of the blockchain. Any attempt at a rating system must de-obfuscate the relationship between addresses and the parties in a transaction. A rating must attach to a seller and come from a buyer, not merely an address.

The above considerations are largely technical. There are also social considerations. The Bitcoin protocol does not merely allow anonymous transactions, it is intentionally built on them. The community up to now has seen this as a virtue. However, for a rating system to be meaningful, ratings must attach to some identity. Therefore it is a given that participating sellers must give up some privacy. In deference to the values of the community, then, any rating system must be opt in, meaning that sellers who do not wish to be rated are not required to accept it and buyers are never required to provide ratings. However, those sellers who do opt in, should be prevented or discouraged from being rated selectively, cherry picking only the good transactions, or otherwise subverting the quality of ratings.

Likewise, buyers who wish to anonymously submit ratings should be permitted to do so, within the constraints of the need to verify the authenticity of the rating. This means that any effective system must still be able to weed out bogus ratings. Linking all ratings to an origin address corresponding to previous transactions may fulfill this requirement. However, the anonymity of ratings to sellers, who may have records of the buyer's identity (for example, in a shipping address) likely cannot be protected. Whether ratings might also be linked back to the buyer's identity by third parties who have access both to the ratings themselves and to the blockchain is a significant question that should be carefully explored before implementing any rating system.

4   Rating System Models

The constraints and capabilities of the Bitcoin protocol result in three major ways for a rating system to be built. These are at the website level, the wallet level and the coin level. The three methods are not mutually exclusive. The following sections will describe what each of these means and their strengths and weaknesses.

4.1 Site Based Systems

Site based rating systems are already common on the Internet, with the prototypical example being the seller ratings on eBay. These systems evolved to allow a measure of trust between non-local persons doing business with strangers [6]. The basic mechanism is therefore known. The question becomes, is it possible for such systems to extend to payments via Bitcoin? In one sense, Bitcoin is identical to any other currency. Marketplace websites ordinarily force payments to be funneled through the site interface. The alternative would be for checks to be mailed or funds to be transferred outside the system. This introduces the possibility that the seller will fail to deliver goods after payment is received or even to notify site and buyer of receipt. Keeping payments inside the site's control removes this friction.

Facilitating Bitcoin payments within a market requires that buyer and seller each establish a Bitcoin wallet (aka an account) in the site and stock it with funds, just as they would if paying with dollars. Several sites do exactly this, including localBitcoins. com, a Bitcoin trading platform and bidinBitcoins.com, a merchandise auction site. The downside of this solution is that it is not portable, meaning that a seller could easily engage in bad behavior on one site, receive bad ratings, and migrate to a different site where the ratings will not be available. This problem is independent of Bitcoin and is a result of the general anonymity of the Internet.

Web site ratings systems are usually not anonymous. They are instead tied to buyer identity on the site, which is also typically tied to an email address. Bitcoinary.com, a web site where users buy and sell Bitcoins, is an example of a site based rating system that goes to extra lengths to verify that users have some real identity beyond the site itself by linking accounts to social media profiles such as Twitter, Facebook and LinkedIn. In order to preserve anonymity, however, the site does not reveal the details of those profiles to other users. It merely indicates that they exist (Note: At the most recent check, bitcoinary.com appears to be offline).

Identity verification protects the site and its users from fake ratings but creates the potential for exposure due to careless programming or malicious attack on the database. The site is a target for such attacks simply by virtue of the presence of currency. Exposure of user information does not directly compromise their complete Bitcoin portfolio, if they maintain a separate wallet outside the market site. The Bitcoin addresses used within the site remain separate from those generated elsewhere. It is possible, though, to develop a site requiring user's to input addresses generated by an external wallet for use in transactions. If the addresses so used were ever used from the wallet, links would be created from the user's identity on the site to the rest of their wallet. Further, any such compromise of identity would link that user's ratings of others to transactions outside the site. This partial identity compromise should be considered when designing market sites or when deciding whether to open an account on one.

4.2 Wallet Based Systems

A Bitcoin wallet is software that stores Bitcoins, generates addresses and sends and receives Bitcoin transactions. Wallets can reside on a computer hard drive, on specialized hardware or on a mobile device such as a smartphone. Users can manage their own or can sign up for online wallet services (such as https://coinbase.com) that manage the details for them. The software that comprises the wallet could be written in a way that maintains meta-data about addresses and transactions as well as those items themselves. This development is already taking place. The official Bitcoin wallet allows users to tag Bitcoin addresses in its address book and to refer to the tags when creating a transaction. The Electrum wallet (https://electrum.org) has a slightly more sophisticated graphical user interface that resembles a check register, with a field for the user to enter the payee and a description line. This allows linking of sellers to their addresses, even when the address changes with every transaction. Adding a field for a transaction rating to this type of interface is trivial. What is done with the ratings afterwards is of more interest.

This wallet level rating suffers from an even worse form of the siloing problem than site based systems in that ratings are not shared with other users at all. This does not necessarily make them useless, as they can still be an aid to a buyer's memory. Their usefulness is still limited in that they provide no information about sellers previously unknown to the current user. Likewise, if the wallet software instituted a peer-to-peer exchange of such information, it would end up being shared only with other users of the same client, making them little different from self-contained web systems. As the payee and description lines are (currently) hand-entered, spelling and typos become an issue that makes aggregation of scores more difficult unless commonalities of seller Bitcoin addresses can be used to resolve them.

One development that may work to ease the problem of aggregating seller information even across clients is in the proposals related to the Bitcoin payment protocol. Specifically, Bitcoin Improvement Proposal number 72 (https://github.com/bitcoin/bips/blob/master/bip-0072.mediawiki) would create a new link type that would be embedded on a web page or in the signature of an email. When clicked, one of these links would initiate a Bitcoin payment. The web address of the seller would be included in the meta-data on the link. This proposal is currently in draft state and has not been enabled in the Bitcoin protocol. Developments like this reduce seller anonymity while increasing ease of use and also provide data that could be used by payment systems.

4.3 Coin Based Systems

Bitcoin is a protocol as well as a currency. Many other currencies have been created using variations of the protocol. Not all of these variants (called altcoins) are intended for use as currency. Namecoin, for example, uses a blockchain to store arbitrary name data, used to create an alternative domain name system for finding sites on the Internet. A system has been proposed for extending Namecoin in a way that would incorporate identity certificates, with the value of the currency as a proxy for trust [7]. "Colored coins" is a proposal to add a meta-data layer to Bitcoins that would convert them into some other type of asset, such as a stock or bond [8]. Inserting ratings directly into a Namecoin or as coloration to a Bitcoin, with the hash code of the transaction referred to included in the data, could provide several benefits over wallet and site based systems. The first is that, like the Bitcoin blockchain itself, it would be public record, accessible to anyone with an Internet connection and the right software. Another benefit is that, again like Bitcoin transactions, ratings so recorded would be immutable. Once confirmed, a transaction is a part of the blockchain forever (barring a blockchain fork, which is a rare occurrence so far).

A type of cryptocoin dedicated entirely to storing transaction ratings on its own blockchain could be designed and integrated into existing wallets (including site-based wallets). This would remove the need to update the Bitcoin protocol to accommodate the new data but would add the problem of keeping the rating blockchain in sync with the Bitcoin blockchain. This is both an opportunity and a technical hurdle. The public nature of the Bitcoin blockchain means it can be used not only to verify that a transaction has taken place but that the buyer address and seller address referred to in a transaction rating were actually also involved in the transaction. This can greatly curb fake ratings. Unfortunately, it means that sellers and buyers who use multiple addresses can frustrate the system. Some method of tying addresses to identities could mitigate this problem but would run directly counter to the Bitcoin design philosophy.

The coin based rating system suffers from technical problems in coin generation and distribution. Bitcoins themselves are created by software that solves cryptographic problems and is rewarded with currency. There is a strict upper limit to the amount of Bitcoins that can be created, meaning there will come a time when there can be no more. Would rating coins have any economic value? How would someone who wishes to rate someone acquire the coins? If they have value, then acquiring them will either require mining them as Bitcoins are mined, buying them, or being paid in them. These activities burden the blockchain with multiple types of transactions requiring multiple types of processing as well as begging the question, how much money is a rating worth? Add these questions to the need for 2-step verifications of ratings and the entire system may become unwieldy.

A coin based system also contains no defense against sellers who use multiple addresses for transactions. By associating a rating with a transaction, only the addresses used in that transaction are marked. Sellers wishing to aggregate their ratings to show their good reputation would need some mechanism to register all the addresses they use as associated with a single identity. Meanwhile, those sellers who wished to hide from their ratings would have a ready method for doing so, by simply switching addresses frequently and not relating them to their own identity, or any other.

5 Comparison

A summary of the characteristics of the different approaches is displayed in Table 1. In the table, verifiability refers to the ability to ensure that ratings are allowed only for real transactions. The public blockchain makes this easily enforceable. A flaw in this view is that Bitcoin is highly divisible into units of only 0.00000001 Bitcoin, an amount so small as to be virtually without value at current exchange rates. Nothing is to stop an attacker from sending very tiny payments to an address known to be associated with a seller in order to gain the ability to provide ratings.

The information sharing entries in the table refer to how public ratings are once created and how easily they can be aggregated. This is a difficult property to achieve in a system where a new payment address can be created for every transaction.

This second issue is why coin based systems are listed as having only limited information sharing. While transactions are completely public, aggregation can be made much more difficult by the use of multiple addresses.

The write-once entry in the table refers to whether rating entries are immutable once created. This can be seen as a measure of data integrity. A database entry is entirely mutable if compromised by malicious or dishonest entities, therefore site and wallet based systems are seen as lacking this property. A blockchain entry, as in a coin based system, once confirmed, is immutable because of the cryptographic proof involved.

The entries for buyer and seller verifiability are references to the ability to verify that buyer and seller are real entities, rather than bogus identities created solely for the purpose of corrupting the system with fake ratings or even fake transactions. This is one of the most difficult properties to verify because of the difficulty distinguishing casual or infrequent users from those whose intent is not to participate at all.

Table 1. Comparison of rating system types

Characteristic	Site based	Wallet based	Coin based
Verifiability	Yes	Yes	Yes
Information sharing	Limited	Limited	Limited
Write-once data	No	No	Yes
Buyer verifiability	Yes	N/A	No
Seller verifiability	Yes	No	No
Distributed control	No	Possibly	Yes

The final row in the table considers distributed control of ratings. Systems in which one entity or a small group of entities stores or aggregates ratings for the whole network have centralized, rather than distributed, control. A distributed system, where all entities on the network are equally vested in the rating system would be most in keeping with the values of the Bitcoin community, however it may also be the most difficult to implement. Site and wallet based systems, in general, are seen as examples of single entity control, though it is possible for them to cooperate in a distributed fashion. No such cooperation can be assumed, however.

All of the given characteristics of a rating system are desirable if the system is to be of highest value. It can be seen that none of the considered architectures possesses all of these characteristics, thus none is a total solution. Social measures may address some of the weaknesses. For example, a standard could be created by which sellers agree to publish all of their addresses. This would aid in aggregation of results to provide something like a true reputation system. Software to manage transactions could verify transaction addresses against the published addresses as well. Creating a common method of publishing that is discoverable by all buyers would need to be very carefully crafted, however.

Business solutions may also be possible. Sellers might engage third parties to audit their practices and validate that they are adhering to policies of identity transparency. Public posting of audit results could give buyers some confidence that sellers are not gaming a rating system. This sort of heavy handed method would be expensive, however, and is clearly contrary to the values of the Bitcoin community. There is room for doubt that it would be widely accepted.

No system to police sellers can provide control of buyers. Protecting a rating system from abuse of sellers with fake ratings is an equally important issue. A coin based system, where ratings actually carry some small cost, in conjunction with minimum costs for the transactions that can be rated, may at least provide a disincentive for abuse. Such a pay-to-play system would require a balancing act between discouraging bad actors and encouraging good ones.

6 Conclusion and Future Research

Each of the systems described has strengths and weaknesses. None is a complete solution to the need for information about sellers. The structure of the Bitcoin protocol intentionally makes this difficult. The ease with which addresses are created and discarded makes it relatively simple for buyers and sellers, both, to maintain several identities for transactions, or to simply disappear into the blockchain, their Bitcoin balances known but never their habits. Therefore in each of the three systems the question of seller identification was touched on. The fact remains that honest sellers do have an incentive to allow themselves to be rated. Particularly within the context of an anonymous system like Bitcoin, the simple fact of submitting to ratings demonstrates a degree of good faith.

As described above, web-based rating systems for Bitcoin transactions already exist. Web sites, however, maintain their own infrastructure for doing so, without using the strengths of the Bitcoin blockchain in verification of transactions and in anchoring ratings to specific transactions. The strengths of the blockchain are in its public nature and in the strong cryptographic proof that its contents are valid. These strengths should also make a strong rating system. A coin-based system is most directly designed to capitalize on these strengths. One potential area of future research would be in solving the problems of multi-blockchain synchronization. Another is in designing transactions that coordinate the potential monetary value of colored coins, Namecoins and others, with entirely different uses such as transaction ratings.

The question of anonymity is one that none of the technologies considered is well able to handle. A web-based system is in the best position of any of the three to impose standards on sellers but may find enforcement extremely difficult. Transactions taking place outside the system, even if still with Bitcoin, will be unknown to the system and difficult or impossible to trace back to the specific seller.

A hybrid system, that combines two or all of the systems described in this paper is worthy of further investigation. Could a site based rating system interact with external wallets? Could a coin-based system be designed that would interact with both? At a higher level, what is the minimum level of adoption by sellers or buyers for a rating system to make it truly useful? Is this level higher, lower, or the same with wallet based systems or coin based systems than for web based systems? This question is especially interesting with a coin based system because of the peer-to-per nature of the Bitcoin protocol. Bitcoin is dependent on pure computing power to guaranty the integrity of its blockchain. Bad actors that may attempt to spend coins they do not possess or otherwise corrupt transactions are frustrated by the enormous computational capacity of the more honest part of the network. Altcoins, including a hypothetical transaction rating coin, will almost certainly have smaller networks behind them and so may be less stable. The problem might be somewhat mitigated, however, by the act of reading against the Bitcoin blockchain. A better understanding of these factors would be helpful in building new features and services for the Bitcoin ecosystem.

It has been shown in this discussion that grafting features requiring some degree of identity validation onto the Bitcoin protocol is a difficult task. It seems also to show that technology alone cannot drive a complete solution. The cooperation of sellers and buyers is also key. Changes to the way the system works, whether at the local or the global level, will require careful consideration of the incentives for all parties concerned as well as the tools they use.

References

1. de la Porte, L.A.: The Bitcoin transaction system, Utrecht, Netherlands (2012)
2. Nakamoto, S.: Bitcoin: a peer-to-peer electronic cash system (2008)
3. Jøsang, A., Hird, S., Faccer, E.: Simulating the effect of reputation systems on e-markets. In: Nixon, P., Terzis, S. (eds.) iTrust 2003. LNCS, vol. 2692, pp. 179–194. Springer, Heidelberg (2003)
4. Yao, Y., Ruohomaa, S., Xu, F.: Addressing common vulnerabilities of reputation systems for electronic commerce. J. Theor. Appl. Electron. Commer. Res. 7(1), 1–20 (2012)
5. Reid, F., Harrigan, M.: An analysis of anonymity in the Bitcoin system. In: Altshuler, Y., Elovici, Y., Cremers, A.B., Aharony, N., Pentland, A. (eds.) Security and Privacy in Social Networks, pp. 197–223. Springer, New York (2013)
6. Resnick, P., Zeckhauser, R.: Trust among strangers in Internet transactions: Empirical analysis of eBay's reputation system. Adv. Appl. Microecon. 11, 127–157 (2002)
7. Vyshegorodtsev, M., Miyamoto, D., Wakahara, Y.: Reputation scoring system using an economic trust model: a distributed approach to evaluate trusted third parties on the internet. In: 27th International Conference on Advanced Information Networking and Applications Workshops (WAINA), pp. 730–737 (2013)
8. Rosenfeld, M.: An overview of colored coins (2012). https://bitcoil.co.il/BitcoinX.pdf

Bitcoin: A First Legal Analysis
With Reference to German and US-American Law

Franziska Boehm and Paulina Pesch[(✉)]

Institute for Information, Telecommunication, and Media Law,
University of Münster, Münster, Germany
{franziska.boehm, paulina.pesch}@uni-muenster.de

Abstract. The use of Bitcoins is increasing rapidly. Bitcoins are utilized in e-commerce to purchase both legal and illegal goods, they are transferred and traded and companies have invested their capital in the new digital currency. While the technical aspects of the system are well established, the legal framework remains unclear. Legislators all over the world are just starting to discover this new virtual phenomenon. This article illustrates selected legal challenges arising in different fields of law (public, criminal and civil law). Particular attention is paid to the German situation while the US-American context is also considered.

1 Introduction

Since laws are always one step behind technological developments, governments are just starting to react to the challenges that new digital currencies pose. At the same time, the use of Bitcoin, one of the most popular virtual currencies, is growing rapidly. Important features of the Bitcoin-system are the decentralized structure that is free of any governmental influence and the possibility to pseudonymously use the currency. Bitcoin transactions are relatively easy to verify when using the publicly available blockchain and, in contrast to other online payment services, transactions costs are almost zero. These characteristics are exploited in different ways. On the one hand, online shops, companies and private users profit from the fast and transparent way to sell and purchase goods; on the other hand, criminals make use of the pseudonymous and decentralized features. As a consequence, Bitcoins serve as a quasi-anonymous sub-stitute for money in illegal activities. This development raises various legal questions. Germany is one of the few states in Europe starting to regulate the Bitcoin-system. In the sphere of public law (Sect. 2), regulatory and tax law related issues play an important role. Offences such as money laundering, blackmail, theft or offences related to data are of great significance in criminal law (Sect. 3). If Bitcoins are used in e-commerce, questions relating to the liability and enforcement in the context of civil law (Sect. 4) are essential. In addition, since neither the criminal law, nor the civil law order is accus-tomed to dealing with virtual objects, fundamental questions relating to the enforcement of long-established legal rules arise. Therefore, this work aims to give an overview of the different legal issues concerning Bitcoins under German (and to a lesser extent US-American) law, thereby illustrating the immense need for legal research. The article also shows first approaches regarding the regulation of Bitcoins in Germany.

© IFCA/Springer-Verlag Berlin Heidelberg 2014
R. Böhme et al. (Eds.): FC 2014 Workshops, LNCS 8438, pp. 43–54, 2014.
DOI: 10.1007/978-3-662-44774-1_4

2 Public Law

Public law typically establishes rules for the relationship between the government and its citizens. Since Bitcoins serve as an alternative currency and individual usage of Bitcoins has increased, administrations have begun, after a period of uncertainty, to see the need to regulate and supervise the Bitcoin-system. As every Bitcoin user is a potential taxpayer and trading platforms earn money with Bitcoin-transactions, Bitcoins raise important issues for public law, especially in the fields of regulatory and tax law.

2.1 Licensing Requirement

The initial question that must be posed in Bitcoin regulation is whether Bitcoin trading platform operators must be licensed by financial supervisory agencies. The state of New York, for instance, plans to introduce so a called BitLicence for companies trading with Bitcoins [1, 2]. The license should protect consumers from online-fraud and improve control over money-laundering activities related to Bitcoins.

In Germany, virtual currency regulation already exists and follows from § 32 Sect. 1 of the German Banking Act (Kreditwesengesetz). According to this rule any person who conducts *banking business or financial services* for commercial purposes in Germany needs a written authorization by the German Federal Financial Supervisory Agency (GFFSA). The German Banking Act defines what falls under the category of financial services (§ 1 Sects. 1a and 2). The Act specifically lists issuing and accepting of financial instruments as a financial service. Financial instruments include so called "units of account" (Rechnungseinheiten). In consequence, the GFFSA has classified "digital currencies", in particular Bitcoins, as units of account in the sense of the German Banking Act. In addition, the agency [3] and some regional courts [4] have expressed the opinion that companies need not to have their place of business in Germany, but that serving German customers would make the licensing requirement applicable. Hence commercial Bitcoin platform operators – at least those established in Germany and/or those serving German customers – need a license from the GFFSA under German law. Conducting financial services without the required license is punishable with imprisonment or a fine (§ 54 Sect. 1 Nr. 2 of the German Banking Act). In conclusion, in Germany the need for a license is directly derived from already existing laws. That is due to the fact that the German Banking Act's definitions are very broad and abstract leaving room for the inclusion of new developments such as virtual currencies. Thus the establishment of new rules for the licensing of Bitcoin businesses is not necessary under German regulatory law.

In the US – after a heated discussion [5] about the lawfulness of Bitcoins [6, 7] – Bitcoin services have been deemed subject to regulation. While, as mentioned above, the New York State Department of Financial Services is intensively considering the introduction of a special BitLicense for all businesses operating (primarily) with decentralized virtual currencies, [8, 9] there are already some legal rules in place that establish a licensing requirement for money transmitters. These rules can be used to control Bitcoin services.

Money transmitters are regulated under federal law as well as under state law in the US. Federal law includes a registration requirement for money transmitting services due to 31 U.S. Code § 5530. Thus Bitcoin services have to register with the Financial Crimes Enforcement Network (FinCEN) if they fall under the category of money transmitters in the sense of the provision. FinCEN does not differentiate between transmitters of official currencies on the one hand and Bitcoin transmitters on the other, hence affirming a registration requirement [10, 11].

Whereas US federal law does not go beyond the need for a registration, additional licensing requirements stem from US state laws [12], causing two big problems. The first problem relates to unclear definitions of the term money transmitter in state law. Therefore it is quite difficult to identify which licensing requirements actually apply to a single Bitcoin business [12]. The bigger issue is that a money transmitter probably needs a license in every state in which it offers its services [12]. The latter issue arises on the international level too, because companies offering services on the internet have to comply with diverse legal orders. The German authority for instance, takes the view that conducting financial services in Germany means offering financial products to German citizens, no matter where the company is actually located. However, discussion surrounding this question has been controversial, particularly in view of the extraterritorial effect that such an opinion involves [13].

Given the above, Bitcoin services fall under licensing provisions of both legal orders. In the US, as well as in Germany, governments are keen to license Bitcoin transactions, mainly to control (and survey) the transfer of money.

2.2   Tax Law Related Questions

The rapid rise of the Bitcoin exchange rate guarantees increasing attention from tax authorities. The following two situations are of particular concern:

First, financial authorities may have an interest in the taxation of earnings denominated in Bitcoin, though tax policy and laws are not necessarily designed to take account of virtual profits. As Bitcoins are not recognized as traditional money, tax authorities are forced to develop new definitions to categorize Bitcoin revenue as taxable. Due to this "definition gap", German tax authorities classify Bitcoins as an "economic asset" (Wirtschaftsgut) that is then subject to the income tax according to §§ 22, 23 of the German Income Tax Act (Einkommenssteuergesetz). In the US the Internal Revenue Code (IRC) includes the basic rules for taxation. According to Sect. 61 of the IRC "gross income means all income from whatever source derived". Thus, the term "income" comprises various activities leading to an increase in wealth. In light of this, Bitcoins might be subject to the rules of the IRC [14]. Similar to the German understanding, income includes any economic value received, irrespective of the form (virtual or physical existent) of that income.

Second, sales taxes on profits of Bitcoin-transactions are also discussed in academia. In Germany, the distinction between private and commercial transactions plays a crucial role. Only transactions and online trading on a commercial basis are usually subject to sales tax, according to § 1 of the German Sales Tax Act (Umsatzsteuergesetz). Non-commercial users, when using Bitcoins as a method of payment or even in context with transactions of large Bitcoin exchange platforms such as Mt. Gox, are not obliged to pay sales tax.

In the US, the question of sales tax on Bitcoin-transactions is currently subject to discussion. However, a final decision has not been reached yet.

Bitcoins can be classified as "income" under US law [15]. General taxation of Bitcoin revenue depends on whether Bitcoins are seen as property or as currency [15]. Quite recently the Internal Revenue Service (IRS) decided to treat Bitcoin as property [16].

In both legal systems regulation and taxation requirements increase. Beyond these legal questions, authorities face difficulties in detecting taxable Bitcoin transactions and identifying the taxable persons, but this problem is of a practical rather than legal nature.

3   Criminal Law

In the context of criminal law, Bitcoins are often used as a method of payment to disguise the origin of illegally obtained money. Bitcoin wallets also offer the possibility to receive payments more anonymously than transfers between normal bank accounts. Additionally, since Bitcoins, like any other virtual currency, can be used to purchase goods (in e-commerce or offline), they can be the target of criminal activities. However, as Bitcoins only exist in the virtual sphere, it is difficult to apply traditional criminal law provisions in this special context.

3.1   Bitcoins as a Substitute for Money

The pseudonymity of Bitcoin transactions makes it an attractive tool criminals can use for illegal activity. In comparison with regular money, the advantages of Bitcoins are two-fold: there is neither a need to be personally present when receiving money, nor is it necessary to use bank accounts that are controlled and enable identification. The transfer of Bitcoins, sometimes after having used Bitcoin-mixers, is much harder for law enforcement to verify and control than the use of a normal bank account, even if an intermediary is used. Due to these characteristics, the use of Bitcoins – especially as a method of payment in the online environment or when buying illegal goods via anonymous networks – is becoming more and more popular.[1] In addition, criminals use Bitcoins increasingly often as a method of payment when blackmailing individual computer users, companies or even public authorities [17, 18]. For instance, criminals install malware on computers via email attachments. The virus then hinders the affected persons' access to their data unless a ransom (of Bitcoins) is paid. The requested sum is usually not a very high one, thus many users decide to pay instead of waiting for the police to solve the problem. Another way could be a DDoS-attack of a website, in particular one that generates profits like an online shop. Recently, due to the rapid growth of the Bitcoin exchange rate, criminals even decided to reduce the sum to be paid [19].

---

[1] The best-known example is Silkroad, where drugs and other illegal commodities where sold until the shut-down in October 2013. Successor platforms already exist.

Usually, when Bitcoins are used as a substitute for money, criminal law provisions are applicable without any difficulties. Under German law the relevant crimes like fraud (§ 263 German Criminal Code) and blackmail (§ 253 German Criminal Code) specify any pecuniary loss [20] (Vermögensschaden/-nachteil) on the part of the victim whether it is a loss of official money or any other values such as Bitcoins. The US federal legal situation is quite similar. Blackmail for instance requires that the offender "demands or receives any money or other valuable thing" (18 U.S. Code § 873). Bitcoins can be easily classified as "other valuable thing".

3.2 Money Laundering

Bitcoins are suspected of being utilized in money laundering [21]. It is possible to exchange money coming from illegal activities for Bitcoins and then disguise the origin of this money again, for instance with the help of Bitcoin-mixers.[2] Different features of the Bitcoin-system play a role in this context: The traceability of Bitcoin-transfers is complicated and therefore it is very challenging for law enforcement to verify the origins of Bitcoins. Users can create a new password for each Bitcoin-transaction and are able to use a new synonym and randomly generate various new keys for transactions. In addition, due to its decentralized structure there are no general reporting duties that apply to the Bitcoin-system. While banks have to report to supervisory authorities and their financial operations are closely supervised,[3] Bitcoin transactions remain far less controlled.

Some specific events have aroused the suspicion that Bitcoins have been used to launder illegal money from tax offences. The most famous example is the very fast rise of the Bitcoin-exchange rate shortly before the compulsory bank levy on Cypriot capital in March 2013 [22, 23]. At that moment, the Bitcoin exchange rate doubled within a few days and has not fallen beneath that value since. One explanation for that rapid rise could be the attempt of bank account holders to exchange their money into a seemingly anonymous currency to disguise the origin of that money and protect it from financial authorities. While this incident shows that Bitcoins can be potentially used for money laundering purposes, the liability for such an offence according to national law provisions is far from clear.

Under German law, one of the meanings of money laundering is – concealing the origin of an economic asset obtained through unlawful action(s) (§ 261 German Criminal Code). The term economic asset is traditionally understood as tangible thing or as right which has a value [24]. Traditional money or jewelry etc. fall under this term without any difficulties. If bank notes are obtained of an unlawful action in the meaning of the provision, for example they are stolen, concealing their origin is punishable as money laundering. However, buying Bitcoins with stolen money to conceal its origin can only be money laundering if Bitcoins can be classified as economic assets in the sense of the provision. Bitcoins do not fall under the traditional understanding of this

---

[2] Bitcoin mixers are tools that allow one to disguise the original source of Bitcoins.

[3] Compare the US-supervision of bank transfers via the control of the SWIFT system: EU/US SWIFT Agreement of 1 August 2010.

term, but one could argue that this term has to be interpreted in a broader sense [24, 25], since it corresponds with the spirit and the purpose of law to cover anything which has a value. In addition, when comparing Bitcoins to other money-laundering tools, it is possible to draw parallels to book money (Buchgeld) that similar to Bitcoins exists only in a virtual sphere and is subject to the German money laundering provision. However, an official authority has not yet recognized this interpretation.

In the US, there is currently a discussion whether Bitcoin developers, e-wallet holders or Bitcoin users have to comply with the Bank Secrecy Act (BSA) and the regulations passed by the Financial Crimes Enforcement Network (FinCEN) [5]. The US American Federal Money Laundering Provision (18 U.S. Code § 1956) includes a term that leads to similar problems as those from the German provision. Object of money laundering is "property derived from an unlawful act" which leads to the question if Bitcoins are property. Unlike in Germany,[4] the US-American understanding of property covers also intangible goods that could apply to Bitcoin. This question is related to the discussion of virtual property and virtual items in online games like World of Warcraft [26, 27], but has not been clarified yet. Though, as in Germany, the spirit and purpose of the US money laundering provision is an argument for a broad interpretation of the term property including virtual items such as Bitcoins.

3.3　Offences Related to Data (Cyber Crime)

The creation of new Bitcoins requires an increasingly large amount of computing power. As a consequence, high electricity use and costly hardware has made mining new coins quite expensive. However, the situation is drastically altered if others bear the mining costs. One possibility is using botnets to support the generation of new Bitcoins through the secret use of infiltrated computers to aid in the mining process [28]. Another possibility to illegally use Bitcoins is to exchange Bitcoins against botnets conducting a dDos-attack.[5] Of course, the construction of botnets is subject to criminal law provisions, but most provisions relate to computer fraud or other data related crimes [29]. Both legal systems, the German and the American, punish such computer crimes irrespective of the exact purpose (obtaining official money or Bitcoins or something else) behind them.[6] However, the enforcement of such provisions is time-consuming and difficult due to the quasi-anonymous features of the Bitcoin-System as described above.

3.4　"Theft" of Bitcoins?

If Bitcoins or Bitcoin users are the target of criminal activity, such as theft, the application of traditional criminal law provisions is not straightforward and legal

---

[4] Property ('Eigentum') in the meaning of § 903 German Civil Code (BGB) only relates to physical/ tangible objects ('Sachen', § 90 German Civil Code).

[5] For example: http://www.hackforums.net/.

[6] Compare §§ 202a ff. §§ 303a ff. German Criminal Code and 18 U.S. Code § 1030.

recourse is unclear. Bitcoins are computer-generated and not physically existent. Such kind of immaterial object is not automatically part of national provisions protecting against theft. In Germany, for instance, only physical objects can be the object of theft [30]. Other provisions protect against the manipulation of data or computer fraud (§§ 202a et seq. and 303a et seq. German Criminal Code), but such provisions were not necessarily designed to cover theft of virtual goods. § 303a of the German Criminal Code, which protects the integrity of data, is occasionally used as alternative to prosecute such offences. Due to this uncertainty, there are very few cases available that demonstrate how the theft of virtual objects would be prosecuted [31]. Apart from such practical difficulties in enforcement, the features of Bitcoins lead to problems relating to the application of basic criminal law rules. However, the theft of virtual goods is growing and this development is profoundly challenging traditional criminal law.

In the US, state law defines theft. For instance, Article 155 New York Penal Law, punishes the stealing of property. As already seen in the context of money laundering the status of virtual goods as property has been discussed but not answered yet. This problem exists under various legal systems. In the Netherlands, usually very progressive in the field of internet law, the Supreme Court classified virtual goods as property and sentenced a teenager for stealing virtual money and virtual goods in the online fantasy role playing game Runescape [32]. Some single US courts have the tendency to appreciate virtual property as well [33, 34], nonetheless the protection against theft of Bitcoins is still unclear.

To give an interim result, criminal law provisions in the US and Germany can only apply to Bitcoins, if their scope is extended. One main problem in this regard seems to be the virtual nature of Bitcoins. If provisions, such as the German theft provision, do not allow for such extensions, other provisions have to be designed to cover these cases.

4 Civil Law

Similar to criminal law, classifying Bitcoins under German civil law is also difficult due to their virtual nature. The German civil law system distinguishes special categories of objects, which can be covered by rights, namely physical objects, claims and a strictly limited [35] number of other immaterial goods (IP rights). However, Bitcoins are neither physical objects nor are they claims because there is no issuer and a Bitcoin's value is not covered by any guarantees.

The only possible approach to classify Bitcoins under the currently existing list of IP rights is the German Copyright Act. This act protects works which represent a personal intellectual creation (§ 2 of the German Copyright Act (Urheberrechtsgesetz)), and contains special rules for the protection of software (§ 69c of the German Copyright Act). But Bitcoins are neither a personal intellectual creation (but the result of a software process) nor software (just the Bitcoin protocol is software). German civil law does not include any rules for the property of virtual goods comparable to the rules about exclusive property rights over physical objects. Given the analysis above, there does not seem to be a proper place for Bitcoins in the German legal system.

Nevertheless the Bitcoin system plays a vital and growing role in online trading. The number of Bitcoin users who mine, buy, hold and sell Bitcoins is increasing and more and more e-commerce shops accept Bitcoin payments. But all participants are confronted with considerable legal uncertainty, as described below.

4.1   E-Commerce

Since Bitcoins are used in e-commerce the following questions arise: Which types of contracts exist between the parties of a Bitcoin transaction and which legal norms are applicable? Is there a repayment claim in the case of dispute? And what impact does the use of intermediaries have on the legal classification? The answers to these questions are difficult to find, in particular since German civil law is quite complex.

First of all it has to be clarified that contracts which include Bitcoin transactions generally are legally effective in accordance with the fundamental principle of contractual freedom. But to answer the questions raised here it is necessary to identify the legal nature of Bitcoin contracts.

If somebody buys a product in exchange for money, this is classified as a contract of sale. It seems obvious this would cover a typical purchase paid for with Bitcoin. But a closer look at the legal norm that defines contracts of sale under German law (§ 433 of the German Cilvil Code (Bürgerliches Gesetzbuch)) yields a different conclusion. It defines a contract of sale as a contract that includes the duty tó transfer the ownership of a movable thing[7] in exchange for *monetary* payment [36]. Therefore this designation does not apply because Bitcoins cannot be classified as money that is meant to be an official currency. It is characteristic of money that it is linked with a general duty of acceptance.[8] But nobody is required to accept Bitcoins as payment instead of traditional money.

The situation in which somebody buys Bitcoins in exchange for money cannot be classified as a conventional contract of sale either because Bitcoins are not movable (physical) things; however, German law equates the sale of rights to the sale of movable things (§ 453 of the German Civil Code). So the rules about contracts of sale would be applicable to the discussed constellation if Bitcoins were rights. Right in this case is defined as an individual's power to require an action or an omission from somebody else. Examples are pecuniary claims or copyrights. However, Bitcoins cannot be classified as rights. A Bitcoin is not a claim and in particular there is no one who is required to take Bitcoins in exchange for money or who grants Bitcoins a certain value. One cannot have a copyright in Bitcoins either. And one cannot own them in the sense of having an exclusive right.

One only could classify the sale of Bitcoins as a sale of other miscellaneous assets. In this case the rules about contracts of sale would also be applicable (§ 453 of the German Civil Code). But it is questionable to which extent these rules – which are tailored for movable things – could be applied to Bitcoin contracts in a reasonable way.

---

[7] The US federal Uniform Commercial Code (U.C.C. Article 2 § 2-106) and the United Nations Convention on the Sale of Goods (Article 1 Sect. 1) are only applicable to the sale of movable things, too.

[8] In Germany § 14 Sect. 1 of the German Federal Bank Act classifies the Euro as legal tender. US American Law classifies United States coins and currency as legal tender in 31 USC § 5103.

Another solution seems to be the classification as a contract of barter [37]. German law equates such contracts to contracts of sale (§ 480 of the German Civil Code). Contracts of barter can include the exchange of movable things and rights [38, 39] and other miscellaneous assets of value that can be legally transferred. [40] However, in situations in which Bitcoins are exchanged against money, barter contracts are not applicable, since only exchanges not involving money can be classified as barter contracts. The legal situation in the USA is similar. Barter contracts, which are covered under the American Uniform Contract Code (UCC), are contracts of exchange without the use of money as well [41].

It could be argued, that the transfer of Bitcoins should be handled as an "atypical work and service contract" [42]. This contract, correctly worded, would require the successful transfer of Bitcoins and not merely the attempt to transfer them. This stipulation however, does not help with the issue of contracts that deal with the purchase of physical goods using Bitcoins.

4.2 Liability

One fundamental question concerns ensuring that the contractual risks are properly balanced between merchant and customer. What happens in the case of data loss or data misuse? To answer these questions it is necessary to classify the legal nature of Bitcoins and the contracts that include them. As mentioned above, there is currently no viable solution to this problem. Since one could nonetheless make a binding contract involving Bitcoins, even without classifying the type of contract, one could ask why the classification of contracts is important anyway. Under German law the identification of the contractual type is essential for the identification of the relevant liability rules, since there are special rules (about liability, consumer protection etc.) for certain types of contracts. And if any of these special rules are applicable, general rules are not. For this reason liability issues will remain unclear as long as the contractual type is not classified.

Moreover Bitcoin users face a couple of practical problems respective to the enforcement of any claims. One example is the irreversibility of transactions. Bitcoin shares this feature with some other payment methods, indeed, but in contrast to these other (central) payment methods there is no central instance who can execute a reverse transaction in cases of mistakes. Thus, the payer carries the risk of transferring Bitcoins to an unknown payee or a wrong public key.

4.3 Enforcement/Foreclosure

Finally the legal situation of Bitcoins in the field of enforcement is unclear. It has to be clarified whether and, if so, how a creditor can seize a debtor's Bitcoins (provided that he attains knowledge of it). The German Code of Civil Procedure includes a – conclusive – list of possible seizable assets.

First there exists the ability to seize (and transfer) monetary claims (§§ 829, 835 of the German Code of Civil Procedure). But, as mentioned above, Bitcoins are not claims so this legal rule is not applicable. German law also recognizes the ability to seize physical objects, but Bitcoins are not physical objects. Hence the right to seize the data storage medium on which the debtor's wallet is stored does not entitle the creditor to access and confiscate the Bitcoins connected to the wallet.

§ 857 of the German Code of Civil Procedure, which allows the seizure of "other pecuniary rights", suggests another possible type of seizure. This should serve as a catch-all provision but, as mentioned above, Bitcoins are not rights. So the legal status of Bitcoins in the area of enforcement remains uncertain as well. In US law, the nature of Bitcoins and the question of legal categorization in civil law related contexts seems to be just as challenging as in German law. It is, for instance, unclear whether Bitcoins are securities, commodities or a currency [5]. If they are a security, other regulations, "including general antifraud rules", would then be applicable [5]. Narrow definitions in both, German and US law, plus the technical features of Bitcoins currently lead to the mentioned enforcement difficulties.

4.4 Common Law

At first glance there seem to be similar problems in the field of Bitcoin contracts and e-Commerce under the US American system. But in contrast to Germany with its civil law system that is based on and bound to codified laws, the US legal system follows the common law approach that is based on case law therefore characterized by a higher level of flexibility. Thus, under US law, it is somehow easier to find solutions for the classification of Bitcoins and related issues without changing the existing law but through case-law. However, until such decisions are made Bitcoin suffers from the legal uncertainty under US law as well as under German law.

5 Conclusion

It seems that current legal rules are not designed to handle a decentralized virtual currency like Bitcoins. Traditional laws lack the flexibility to adapt quickly to new technological contexts. The article illustrates that the virtual aspect of Bitcoins plays a crucial role. One could add that Bitcoins are just one example that shows the fundamental difficulties of the legal treatment of virtual objects. Data that only exist in a digital form is another prominent example. In Germany especially the criminal and civil law systems are by no means prepared for the challenges arising outside the traditional understanding of physically existent objects. In the US, the legal situation is also still unclear in large parts, but the flexible nature of case law reshapes the issues. So far, it appears that governments have been able to adapt to the characteristics of the Bitcoin-system and hence effectively regulate only in the context of regulatory and tax law. From the users' point of view, this development raises some concerns. There is a danger of imbalance if only public law rules increase and civil as well as criminal law remain unable to adapt. Therefore, if the regulation of the Bitcoin-system increases, attention has to be paid to a balance between the different interests at stake. Some of the other critical fields of legal regulation have been addressed in this article.

References

1. Popper, N.: Virtual Money Draws Notice of Regulators (2013). http://dealbook.nytimes. com/2013/11/14/new-york-regulator-to-explore-Bitcoin-license/?_r=0
2. Foley, S.: New Yorks Finance Regulator Voices Backing for Bitcoins. Financial Times (2014). http://www.ft.com/intl/cms/s/0/2b25c21c-88a9-11e3-9f48-00144feab7de.html# axzz2ry3Inxz3
3. BaFin: Hinweise zur Erlaubnispflicht nach § 32 Abs. 1 KWG, p. 1 (2005)
4. Examples are: VG Frankfurt of 7.5.2004 – Az. 9 G 6496/03, and of 11.10.2004 – Az. 9 E 993/04 (V), and VGH Kassel of 21.1.2005 – Az. 6 TG 1568/04, and VG Frankfurt of 5.7.2007 – Az. 1 E 4355/06 (V)
5. Grinberg, R.: Bitcoin: an innovative alternative digital currency. Hastings Sci. Technol. Law J. **4:1**, 182 et seq (2012)
6. Popper, N.: Regulators See Value in Bitcoin and Investors Hasten to Agree (2013). http://dealbook.nytimes.com/2013/11/18/regulators-see-value-in-Bitcoin-and-investors-hasten-to-agree/?_r=0
7. Raskin, M.: U.S. Agencies to Say Bitcoins Offer Legitimate Benefits (2013). http://www. bloomberg.com/news/2013-11-18/u-s-agencies-to-say-Bitcoins-offer-legitimate-benefits.html
8. Fuller, C.: New York Bitcoin License? State Department of Financial Services Seeks Possible Regulation (2014). http://www.ibtimes.com/new-york-bitcoin-license-state-department-financial-services-seeks-possible-regulation-1551234
9. Jeffries, A.: New York Considers Creating a 'BitLicense' for Bitcoin Businesses (2014). http://www.theverge.com/2014/1/28/5353806/new-york-is-considering-bitlicense-bitcoin
10. Guidance FIN-2013-G001 About the Application of FinCEN's Regulations to Persons Administering, Exchanging, or Using Virtual Currencies (2013). http://fincen.gov/statutes_ regs/guidance/html/FIN-2013-G001.html
11. Santori, M.: Bitcoin Law: What US Businesses Need to Know (2013). http://www.coindesk. com/bitcoin-law-what-us-businesses-need-to-know/
12. Santori, M.: Bitcoin Law: Money Transmission on the State Level in the US (2013). http:// www.coindesk.com/bitcoin-law-money-transmission-state-level-us/
13. Fischer, R.: In: Boos, K.-H., Fischer, R., Schulte-Mattler, H. (eds.) Kreditwesengesetz (§ 32, para 17), 4th edn (2012)
14. Bal, A.: Stateless virtual money in the tax system. Eur. Tax. **53**(7), 351–356 (in particular 355) (2013)
15. Isom, J.: As Certain as Death and Taxes: Consumer Considerations of Bitcoin Transactions for When the IRS Comes Knocking, p. 9 et seq (2013). SSRN: http://ssrn.com/abstract= 2365493 or http://dx.doi.org/10.2139/ssrn.2365493
16. Rubin, R., Dougherty, C.: Bitcoin Is Property, Not Currency, in Tax System: IRS (2014). http://www.bloomberg.com/news/2014-03-25/bitcoin-is-property-not-currency-in-tax-system-irs-says.html
17. Thompson, I.: Cryptolocker Infects Cop PC: Massachusetts Plod Fork Out Bitcoin Ransom (2013). http://www.theregister.co.uk/2013/11/21/police_pay_cryptolocker_crooks_to_get_ their_computers_back/
18. Meusers, R.: Erpressersoftware: US-Polizisten zahlen Online-Kriminellen Bitcoin als Lösegeld (2013). http://www.spiegel.de/netzwelt/web/cryptolocker-angriff-us-polizei-zahlt-bitcoin-an-ransomware-a-934815.html
19. Kremp, M.: Rasanter Kursanstieg: Erpresser senken Bitcoin-Lösegeldforderung (2013). http://www.spiegel.de/netzwelt/web/cryptolocker-software-erpresser-senken-bitcoin-loesegeldforderung-a-935044.html

20. Kindhäuser, U.: In: Kindhäuser, U., Neumann, U., Paeffgen, H.-U. (eds.) Strafgesetzbuch (§ 263, para 250), 4th edn (2013)
21. FBI, Bitcoin Virtual Currency: Unique Features Present Distinct Challenges for Deterring Illicit Activity, 24 April 2012
22. Garland, E.: Cyprus Bailout Sends Bitcoin to More Heights (2013). http://www. transitionistas.com/2013/03/21/cyprus-bailout-sends-bitcoin-to-new-heights/
23. BBC News Magazine: A Point of View: Bitcoin's Freedom Promise (2013). http://www. bbc.co.uk/news/magazine-22292708
24. Ruhmannseder, F.: In: Beck'scher Online-Kommentar, B. StGB (para 8), 23rd edn (2013)
25. Kühl, K.: In: Lackner, K., Kühl, K. (eds.) StGB (§ 261, para 3), 27th edn (2011)
26. Mesiano-Crookston, J.: The Legal Status of Virtual Goods (2013). http://www. lawyersweekly.ca/index.php?section=article&articleid=1912
27. Shen, L.: Who Owns the Virtual Items? (2010). http://scholarship.law.duke.edu/dltr/vol9/ iss1/10/
28. Lemos, R. Cyber-Criminals Putting Botnets to Work on Bitcoin Mining. http://www.eweek. com/security/cyber-criminal-putting-botnets-to-work-on-Bitcoin-mining/
29. Roos, P., Schumacher, P.: Rechtliche Betrachtung von Desinfektionsmaßnahmen zur Botnetzbekämpfung durch Internet-Service-Provider. In: Informationssicherheit stärken – Vertrauen in die Zukunft schaffen, Tagungsband zum 13. Deutschen IT-Sicherheitskongress, pp. 37–53. SecuMedia (2013)
30. Fischer, T.: In: Beck'scher Kurzkommentar, Strafgesetzbuch und Nebengesetze (§ 242, para 3), 57th edn (2010)
31. One of the few cases in this context: AG Augsburg of 30 November 2010, Az. 33 Ds 603 Js 120422/09 jug
32. Feldmann, E.: Netherlands Teen Sentenced for Stealing Virtual Goods (2008). http://www. pcworld.com/article/152673/virtual_theft.html
33. Tucows.Com Co. v Lojas Renner S.A. [2011] O.J. No. 3576 for domain names
34. Guly, C.: Domain Names are 'Property': Ont. CA (2011). http://www.lawyersweekly.ca/ index.php?section=article&articleid=1495
35. Wiebe, A.: In: Wiebe, A. (ed.) Wettbewerbs- und Immaterialgüterrecht, p. 18 (2010)
36. Magnus, U.: In: von Staudinger, J. (ed.) BGB (Art. 1, para 42). CISG (2013)
37. Eckert, K.-P.: Steuerliche Betrachtung elektronischer Zahlungsmittel am Beispiel sog. Bitcoin-Geschäfte. In: Der Betrieb (DB) 2013, 2108 et seq. in the context of income tax
38. Gehrlein, M.: In: Bamberger, H.G., Roth, H. (eds.) Beck'scher Online-Kommentar zum BGB (§ 480, para 1) (2012)
39. Mader, P.: In: von Staudinger, J. (ed.) BGB, Buch 2 (§ 480, para 7), 15th edn (2014)
40. Westermann, H.P.: In: Münchener Kommentar zum BGB (§ 480, para 1) (2012)
41. Kaplanov, N.M.: Nerdy Money: Bitcoin, The Private Digital Currency, and the Case Against Its Regulation, 140, 25 Loy. Consumer L. Rev. 111 (2012)
42. Schneider, J.: Interview Legal Tribune Online. http://www.lto.de/recht/hintergruende/h/ Bitcoins-waehrung-rechnungseinheit-umsatzsteuer

Bitcoin Security

Empirical Analysis of Denial-of-Service Attacks in the Bitcoin Ecosystem

Marie Vasek, Micah Thornton, and Tyler Moore(✉)

Computer Science and Engineering Department,
Southern Methodist University, Dallas, TX, USA
{mvasek,mathornton,tylerm}@smu.edu

Abstract. We present an empirical investigation into the prevalence and impact of distributed denial-of-service (DDoS) attacks on operators in the Bitcoin economy. To that end, we gather and analyze posts mentioning "DDoS" on the popular Bitcoin forum bitcointalk.org. Starting from around 3 000 different posts made between May 2011 and October 2013, we document 142 unique DDoS attacks on 40 Bitcoin services. We find that 7 % of all known operators have been attacked, but that currency exchanges, mining pools, gambling operators, eWallets, and financial services are much more likely to be attacked than other services. Not coincidentally, we find currency exchanges and mining pools are much more likely to have DDoS protection such as CloudFlare, Incapsula, or Amazon Cloud. We show that those services that have been attacked are more than three times as likely to buy anti-DDoS services than operators who have not been attacked. We find that big mining pools (those with historical hashrate shares of at least 5 %) are much more likely to be DDoSed than small pools. We investigate Mt. Gox as a case study for DDoS attacks on currency exchanges and find a disproportionate amount of DDoS reports made during the large spike in trading volume and exchange rates in spring 2013. We conclude by outlining future opportunities for researching DDoS attacks on Bitcoin.

1 Introduction

Bitcoin [1] is the first cryptocurrency that has been widely adopted. Whereas previously digital currencies sought to be as perfect a substitute for cash as possible (e.g., DigiCash emulated the anonymity of cash with the convenience of electronic payments [2]), Bitcoin has tried to improve on the perceived shortcomings of traditional currencies. For example, Bitcoin offers a money supply with limited growth enforced by its design and without relying on a central bank. This has appealed to inflation hawks and libertarians alike.

Another key reason behind Bitcoin's meteoric rise is how its design creates opportunities for participants to strike it rich. For instance, new cash is introduced into the system by so-called miners, who are paid to solve puzzles that aid in the verification of past transactions. Additionally, the relatively fixed money supply is susceptible to deflation, which helps drive up the exchange rate against

© IFCA/Springer-Verlag Berlin Heidelberg 2014
R. Böhme et al. (Eds.): FC 2014 Workshops, LNCS 8438, pp. 57–71, 2014
DOI: 10.1007/978-3-662-44774-1_5

hard currencies and attract the attention of speculators. These opportunities for wealth have also created problems, as those competing for riches sometimes cheat in order to gain an advantage.

Indeed, the Bitcoin ecosystem remains a "Wild West" of sorts. In an environment with scores of unregulated financial products, scammers have set up Ponzi schemes to defraud those holding Bitcoins [3,4]. Because Bitcoin transactions are non-revocable, hackers have frequently stolen Bitcoins of individuals and companies, leaving the victims without any recourse [5]. Currency exchanges are frequently hit with security breaches to steal coins, prompting the weaker ones to close [6]. Other times exchanges simply shut down without explanation, often with customers losing their "deposits".

Perhaps the most common scourge to afflict Bitcoin participants, however, has been denial-of-service attacks. These are inexpensive to carry out and quite disruptive. Competing services launch them in order to improve market share, traders target exchanges to buy or sell at favorable prices [7], and miners outgunned in the rush to increase computational power could try to cripple larger pools in order to increase their odds of solving the hash puzzle first [8].

Despite their apparent frequency, very little is known about the true prevalence of service-denial attacks on Bitcoin. To that end, we carry out an empirical analysis of reports of such attacks made on the popular bitcointalk.org discussion forum. We begin in Sect. 2 by outlining how we gather reports of DDoS attacks from public sources. We employ a simple rule-based classifier that distinguishes between the discussion of those experiencing attacks from other messages mentioning DDoS attacks.

We present our analysis in Sect. 3. We identify 142 distinct DDoS attacks taking place between May 2011 and October 2013. We first explain how these attacks vary over time and by category of service affected (e.g., currency exchanges, mining pools, gambling websites). We present evidence that those services that have suffered DDoS attacks are much more likely to now take steps to prevent future DDoS-es. We examine the relationship between a mining pool's size and its susceptibility to attacks, and we look at how attacks relate to the trading volumes and exchange rate at Mt. Gox, the largest currency exchange. We review related work in Sect. 4, and we discuss opportunities for further research on DDoS attacks with the gathered dataset in Sect. 5.

2   Methodology

We first set out our approach to data collection in Sect. 2.1. Then we describe and evaluate our method for identifying posts that report DDoS attacks in Sect. 2.2. The collected data and analysis scripts are publicly available for replication purposes at doi:10.7910/DVN/25541.

2.1   Data Collection

Identifying when a denial-of-service attack has taken place can be difficult. If we knew in advance the websites to monitor, we could run a regular script that attempts to visit the websites. However, simply because we can connect to a website does not mean that others are being blocked. Furthermore, some services (e.g., mining pools) are not run as websites, so non-standardized means of connecting would be required. Finally, it would be desirable to peer back further into the past to check for historical reports of DDoS attacks.

To that end, we decided to inspect reports of DDoS attacks posted to the popular bitcointalk.org forum. Using the Google Custom Search API, we identified all posts including the term "ddos" on the website appearing between February 2011 and October 2013. Because the Google API limits the results to the top 100 results, we issued queries restricted to week-long intervals. In only 3 weeks (during April and May 2013) did the API return the maximum 100 results. In those cases we shortened the time interval further to ensure that we obtained all results including "ddos".

In total, we identified 2 940 distinct pages on bitcointalk.org that mentioned "ddos". However, many duplicates existed in these pages, such as when a single thread spans multiple pages. Consequently, we identified 1 355 distinct pages comprised of the first page of the thread. For each page, we then fetched a local copy of the page and automatically extracted the thread title, plus the first post's text, URLs, poster handle and date. We also extracted the forum title. Not all posts actually described DDoS attacks, however. In Sect. 2.2 we explain how to distinguish between discussion of perceived DDoS attacks and other DDoS-related threads.

We collected additional information to complement the information gathered on DDoS reports. For instance, we fetched a directory of 1 240 online services supporting Bitcoin [9] and 32 mining pools [10]. We extracted category and subcategory information for these services from parsing the directory. We threw out any services that did not resolve after an automatic and manual check.

Subsequently, we identified the use of anti-DDoS providers by resolving the websites of all known Bitcoin services and comparing against known IP ranges for CloudFlare [11], Incapsula [12], and Amazon Web Services [13]. CloudFlare and Incapsula are content distribution networks (CDNs), whereas Amazon hosts material. All three are identifiable by IP range. For services not resolving to these networks, we looked up their AS number using the IP address. We did not find any other content distribution networks serving more than two Bitcoin services. Therefore, we are confident we found all significant network-based anti-DDoS protections. Other forms of protection, such as DDoS detection built in to security appliances, could not be identified and are beyond this paper's scope.

Finally, we identified historical market share of mining pools from 22 Internet Archive snapshots of http://blockchain.info/pools dating to October 2011.

2.2   Classification of Posts Describing Attacks

As noted above, many of the posts mentioning "ddos" do not actually describe experiences with denial-of-service attacks. Instead, users discussed ways to defeat DDoS attacks, posted advertisements for services with built-in protections against attacks, and speculated on the motivations behind prior attacks.

We built a simple word-based classifier to identify just those threads describing DDoS attacks currently in progress. Of course, we cannot confirm that what the posters describe is actually a DDoS attack rather than a server overloaded with demand. Nonetheless, user reports do provide a useful indication of when such attacks most likely occur. We flagged all posts with the following words and phrases in the title as DDoS attacks: "unreachable", "offline", "online", "down", "flooding", "attack", "ddos", "unavailable", "blocking", and "connect". Any posts including the words "anti-ddos" or "vote" in the title were marked as not describing attacks.

Table 1. Confusion matrix plus precision, recall and accuracy measures for the word-based classifier.

	Actual	
	DDoS	Not DDoS
Predicted DDoS	42	36
Predicted Not DDoS	15	114
Precision 54 %, Recall 74 %, Accuracy 75 %		

To evaluate the classifier's accuracy, we compared it against a manually labeled set of 207 posts. The results are given in Table 1. Overall accuracy is 75 %. The false negative rate is modest (26 %), but false positives are problematic. Thus the classifier does a pretty good job at finding DDoS reports, whereas many posts flagged as DDoS in fact are not.

Consequently, we manually inspected the 362 posts identified by the classifier as describing attacks from the full dataset. We found that 200 posts actually described attacks. We use these posts in the analysis that follows below. Based on the observed recall rates, we expect that there are around 70 more posts describing attacks not included in our analysis. However, we defer improving the classifier further and identifying those posts to future work.

There is one final subtlety in the data collection that bears mentioning. Sometimes multiple posts discuss the same DDoS event. To account for that, we define distinct DDoS attacks as any post mentioning a service on a given day. For instance, if three posts describe an attack on Mt. Gox on April 26, 2013, we count that as a single attack. If however, a single post mentions a DDoS on three different services, we count that as three attacks. Using this approach, the 200 posts correspond to 142 distinct DDoS attacks.

3   Empirical Analysis

We first discuss how DDoS attack targets have changed over time in Sect. 3.1, along with an examination of which service categories are targeted more and less often. We then study attacks on mining pools in Sect. 3.3, followed by attacks on currency exchanges in Sect. 3.3.

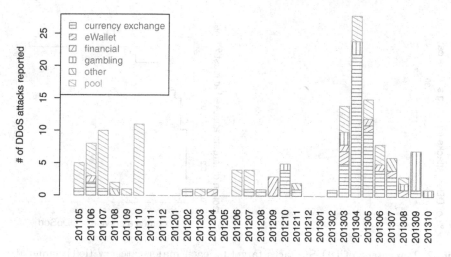

Fig. 1. Reported DDoS attacks over time, split up by category of targeted service.

3.1   DDoS Attacks Over Time and by Target

We begin by examining how reports of DDoS attacks on Bitcoin services have evolved over time. Figure 1 plots the number of reported DDoS attacks per month since May 2011. We can see that the number and target of reported attacks varies greatly over time. Initially, in the second half of 2011, most DDoS reports concerned mining pools. Then there were very few reported attacks of any kind during the first half of 2012. During the second half of 2012, DDoS attacks picked up again, initially targeting pools, but more frequently targeting currency exchanges and other websites. During 2013, attacks on pools continued, but they were joined by DDoS on gambling websites, eWallets, and currency exchanges. Attacks on currency exchanges dominated the totals from March–June 2013, coinciding with rising exchange rates and unprecedented interest in Bitcoin. While we expect that some of these reported DDoSes were in fact triggered by customer demand, it is nonetheless interesting to see the rise in reported abuses. Finally, DDoS on exchanges fell sharply in August. However, Bitcoin-based gambling websites experienced a surge of DDoS activity in its place.

Figure 2 (left) shows how DDoS attacks stack up by category over all time. The most targeted service category is currency exchanges (41 %), followed closely by mining pools (38 %). These were trailed by gambling (9 %), finance (5 %), and eWallets (4 %). DDoS attacks on other services accounted for 3 % of the total.

While some services are targeted only once by DDoS attacks, others are repeatedly hit by them. Figure 2 (right) plots a CDF of the number of times a service is DDoSed. Out of the services targeted by a DDoS attack, 44 % are only attacked once, while 15 % are attacked on at least five occasions. One service, the Mt. Gox currency exchange, suffered 29 DDoS attacks on different days. We study the timing of attacks on Mt. Gox in greater detail in Sect. 3.3 below.

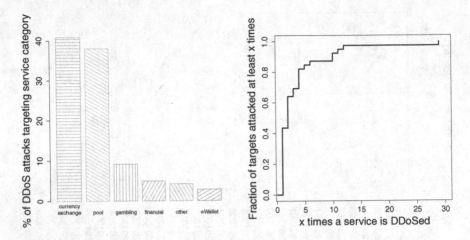

Fig. 2. Percentage of DDoS attacks targeting each major category (left); cumulative distribution function of the number of attacks targeting each service (right).

Table 2 shows another way to look at the breakdown of DDoS attacks by category. The first column lists the number of services for each category that are still operational (i.e., their listed websites resolve), followed by the percentage of services in each category that have suffered DDoS attacks. Overall, 7.3 % of services actually experienced a DDoS attack. The variation across categories is substantial: 27 % of pools have experienced DDoS attacks compared to just 0.7 % of shops selling physical products. Currency exchanges, mining pools, financial services and eWallets are targeted more frequently than other categories. These differences compared to the average are statistically significant with 95 % confidence according to a χ^2 test. One surprise is that Bitcoin payment systems are not targeted by DDoS attacks any more than average.

Given the very real threat of DDoS attacks on Bitcoin services, it is not surprising that many services take steps to defend against these attacks. Moving over to the next column grouping, we report for each category the percentage of services that use anti-DDoS services (either Amazon, Incapsula, or CloudFlare). Overall, around 20 % of online Bitcoin services have anti-DDoS protection.

Anti-DDoS protection is more popular in some categories than others. Around one third of exchanges and pools have anti-DDoS protection. This difference in proportion (compared to the 20 % average) is statistically significant according to a χ^2 test. Shops selling material and physical products and accepting Bitcoin were substantially less likely to be protected from DDoS attacks – only 10.5 % rely on these services. Financial firms and eWallets also frequently employ anti-DDoS protection, but the differences are not statistically significant.

Finally, the last grouping in Table 2 shows for each category how many services have anti-DDoS protection and have been attacked, how many have anti-DDoS and have not been attacked, and how many have been DDoSed but do not have anti-DDoS protection from Amazon, Incapsula, or CloudFlare. It is

Table 2. Prevalence of DoS attacks and anti-DDoS uptake by service category.

Category	#	Suffer DDoS %	Sig.?	Anti-DDoS (AD) %	Sig.?	AD + DDoS	AD Only	DDoS Only
Material/physical products	295	**0.7**	–	**10.5**	–	2	29	0
Internet & mobile services	225	1.8		16.9		0	38	4
Online products	185	3.8		14.6		3	24	4
Professional services	137	0		10.2		0	14	0
Currency exchanges	119	**10.9**	+	**36.1**	+	10	33	3
Travel/tourism/leisure	78	0		10.3		0	8	0
Commerce & community	71	1.4		12.7		1	8	0
Getting started	31	0		12.9		0	4	0
Financial	26	**15.4**	+	26.9		1	6	3
Pool	41	**26.8**	+	**34.1**	+	5	9	6
Bitcoin eWallets	17	**17.6**	+	35.3		2	4	1
Bitcoin payment systems	11	9.1		18.2		1	1	0
Average		*7.3*		*19.9*				

noteworthy that across categories it is far more common to have anti-DDoS protection than it is to have actually experienced a DDoS attack. Even in categories where no service has experienced a DDoS attack (e.g., travel and professional services), there is substantial uptake of anti-DDoS protection.

We can also answer a related question: Are services that have experienced DDoS in the past more likely to get anti-DDoS protection afterwards? Table 3 helps to answer the question for all services.

Table 3. Contingency table comparing the uptake of anti-DDoS protection based on whether or not the service has experienced DDoS attacks.

	Use Anti-DDoS #	Use Anti-DDoS %	No Anti-DDoS #	No Anti-DDoS %
Suffered DDoS	25	54 %	21	46 %
No DDoS	178	15 %	1012	85 %

Of the 46 distinct services that have experienced DDoS attacks, more than half now have anti-DDoS protection. It is impossible to tell whether or not they had such service at the time of attack. Among services that have not yet experienced a DDoS attack, only 15 % have anti-DDoS protection. The difference in proportion (15 % vs. 54 %) is statistically significant, according to a χ^2 test ($p \ll 0.0001$ with χ^2 value of 47.232). We conclude that providers are much more likely to obtain anti-DDoS protection if they are targeted by DDoS attacks.

3.2   DDoS Attacks on Mining Pools

Given that mining pools are frequently targeted by DDoS attacks, we now study them in greater detail. We first investigate whether the size of a mining pool affects its chances for being DDoSed. Mining pool size constantly changes, sometimes in response to DDoS attacks. Hence, we needed a historical record of mining pool market shares. Using the Internet Archive, we accessed 22 historical copies of blockchain.info/pools that breaks down hashrate by pool. We deem a pool to be "big" if it is observed to have at least a 5 % share of the hashrate during two or more observations. All other pools are deemed "small".

Table 4 shows how the incidence of DDoS attacks vary by pool size. 5 out of 8 big pools (63 %) have suffered DDoS attacks, compared to just 7 out of 41 small pools (17 %). These percentage differences are statistically significant, according to a χ^2-test with a p-value of 0.022. Why would large pools be targeted for DDoS attacks more than small pools? Attackers gain more by targeting large pools, since taking one out can substantially increase the odds of winning the round.

Table 4. Contingency table comparing the size of a mining pool to whether or not the pool has experienced DDoS attacks.

	Small pools		Big pools	
	#	%	#	%
Suffered DDoS	7	17.1 %	5	62.5 %
No DDoS	34	82.9 %	3	37.5 %

Figure 3 examines the historical hashrate-based market share for six of the larger pools. DDoS reports are indicated by the vertical dashed lines. Some pools seem unfazed by DDoS attacks (e.g., Slush's Pool, Eclipse MC, and Eligius). BTC Guild actually increased its market share following a DDoS attack in mid-2012. However, substantial declines followed a later attack in mid-2013. Furthermore, one can see that sometimes DDoS attacks target multiple pools simultaneously. For example, DeepBit was targeted by attacks at the same time as BTC Guild and Eclipse MC. DeepBit's share of the hashrate tumbled, while it appears that Eclipse MC and BTC Guild benefited as a result. Later attacks in 2013 on BTC Guild and Eclipse MC reduced their own shares, with Eligius benefiting this time even though it too had been hit by DDoS attacks.

Based on this analysis, we reject the notion that DDoS attacks always trigger a decline in market share for affected mining pools. Instead, we see that DDoS attacks often precede shakeups in pool market share. However, at this point we cannot reliably predict who the winners and losers will be as a result.

3.3   DDoS Attacks on Currency Exchanges

Currency exchanges are the most frequent target of DDoS attacks. We defer to future work a more detailed analysis of how DDoS attacks affect exchange

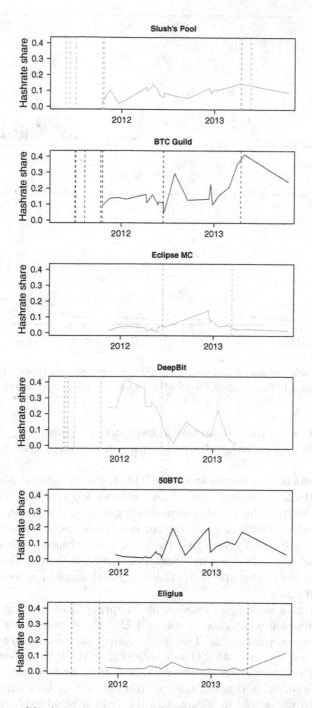

Fig. 3. Mining pool hashrate market share (solid line) over time, compared to timing of DDoS attacks (dashed lines).

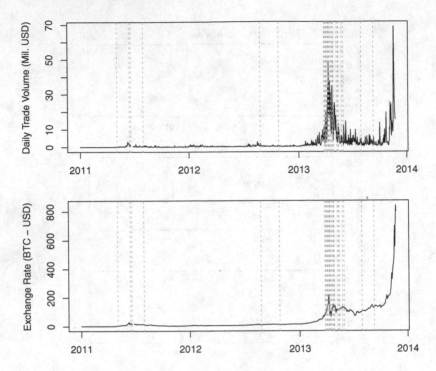

Fig. 4. Daily trade volumes (top) and USD-BTC exchange rate (bottom) at Mt. Gox. Dashed green lines indicate when DDoS attacks on Mt. Gox were reported.

operations in general. Instead, we take a closer look at attacks targeting Mt. Gox, the largest currency exchange during the time of our study and most frequent attack target.

Figure 4 plots trade volumes and USD-BTC exchange rates at Mt. Gox, along with DDoS attacks as dashed green lines. We can see that Gox suffered some DDoS attacks in 2011 shortly after experiencing unprecedented peaks in trading volume. (It can be difficult to see on the current graph since trading has exploded so much since early 2013.) Note that these early attacks, plus one in late 2012, came shortly after a fall from a new peak in the exchange rate. This behavior is consistent with the modus operandi of blocking exchanges in order to slow down a panicked sell-off.

When Bitcoin's exchange rate shot up in spring 2013, trading volume also soared to unprecedented heights. Dozens of DDoS claims were made in April and May 2013, eventually subsiding. Two more reports were made later in 2013, but these were one-off reports rather than a chorus as in the spring. Doubtless, some reports were caused by surging demand rather than by a botnet. The blogger *organofcorti* observed a drop in trading volume at Mt. Gox after Mt. Gox's Dwolla account was seized in spring 2013 [14], which could explain some of the reported attacks in times of lower trading volume.

In the (slight) majority of cases, we observe a decrease in transaction volume in the week following a DDoS attack compared to the week prior, as seen in Table 5. We also notice that the median size of the transaction volume change is greater when the transaction volume increases. Figure 5 show this trend over time. We observe that the increases and decreases tend to be clustered together in time. This suggests that certain DDoS attack campaigns can be recovered from quickly while others cannot.

Table 5. Changes in transaction volume on Mt. Gox after a DDoS attack.

Δ Transaction Vol.	# of Attacks	% Attacks	% Change (median)
Increase	12	41.4 %	53.3 %
Decrease	17	58.6 %	34.2 %

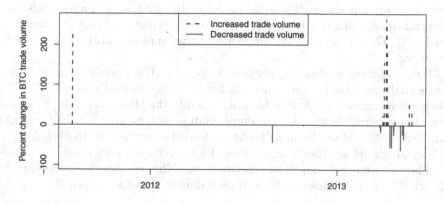

Fig. 5. Changes in transaction volume on Mt. Gox after a DDoS attack over time.

4 Related Work

As interest in Bitcoin has exploded, researchers have undertaken a number of measurement studies to improve our understanding of how Bitcoin is used and abused in practice. Ron and Shamir reconstruct a transaction graph from the Bitcoin block chain in order to find out how money changes hands and identify suspicious transactions (e.g., attempts to launder identity) [15]. Meiklejohn et al. also leverage the block chain in order to measure the traceability of transactions initiated at many Bitcoin service providers [16]. Möser et al. also investigate the traceability of Bitcoin transactions by evaluating the protection offered by three popular transaction-anonymizing services [17]. Christin crawled advertisements on the now-defunct Silk Road, which shed light on how that marketplace was employing Bitcoin-based transactions to facilitate the sale of illegal goods, notably drugs [18]. Moore and Christin gathered public records of transactions taking place at 40 Bitcoin-currency exchanges in order to find out how often the exchanges shut down [6]. They constructed statistical models to help explain why exchanges close, finding that while more popular exchanges are more likely to be hacked, they are less likely to close.

The present work continues in the vein of these measurement studies, in that it collects publicly-available data to explain better the prevalence of DDoS attacks affecting Bitcoin. We are not aware of any prior work measuring the occurrence of DDoS attacks on Bitcoin. There has been one large-scale study that measures how prevalent DDoS attacks are in the context of websites and blogs [19]. But there are several reasons why we believe Bitcoin DDoS attacks are worth studying on their own. First, there are unique incentives at play that reward DDoS attacks, such as traders who benefit by blocking others' transactions. Second, Bitcoin's unregulated environment has facilitated criminality in pursuit of profits, with DDoS an attractive tool for unscrupulous operators. Indeed, the most closely related work to our own is that of Johnson et al., who present a game-theoretic model of the trade-offs mining pools face between investing in upgrades to computing infrastructure and engaging in DDoS attacks [8]. Their model nicely complements the empirical work undertaken in this paper.

Of course, there are many other attacks besides DDoS involving miners that have been discussed in the literature. Barber et al. describe a Doomsday, "51%", attack where a miners enter false transactions into the block chain [20]. Eyal and Sirer further refine the attack assuming colluding miners, lowering the threshold from 50% to 33% of total mining hashrate needed to control the blockchain [21]. Kroll et al. model whether a miner should join a mining pool using game theory. They expand their model to describe a "Goldfinger" attack on the Bitcoin network [22]. Finally, Rosenfeld describes a double-spending attack [23].

5   Concluding Remarks

We have presented an empirical study of DDoS attacks targeting a wide range of operators in the Bitcoin ecosystem. Using posts to the popular bitcointalk.org forum, we identify and analyze 142 distinct DDoS attacks. We find that 7.4% of Bitcoin-related services have experienced DDoS attacks. Currency exchanges are targeted most often, followed by mining pools, gambling operators, financial service providers, and eWallet operators. Attack frequency is highly variable: pools were targeted most often back in 2011, followed by a wave of attacks targeting currency-exchanges in Spring 2013. DDoS on gambling operators, nonexistent until December 2012, have picked up considerably in the latter part of 2013.

We also carried out preliminary analysis into the effects of DDoS attacks on mining pools and currency exchanges. One striking finding is that over 60% of large mining pools have been DDoSed, compared to just 17% of small ones. This suggests that the large pools are big targets for unscrupulous miners hoping to increase their odds of winning freshly minted Bitcoins.

Our results indicate that Bitcoin DDoS attacks merit further investigation. Nonetheless, the findings often raise more questions than they answer. To get those answers, a richer and more robust dataset is needed. Our dataset is based on circumstantial evidence of DDoS attacks reported on a single, albeit popular, web forum. Such reports do not constitute definitive evidence that a DDoS has taken place. Future investigations could corroborate reports with supplementary evidence, such as directly measuring inaccessibility from probes and incorporating reports from additional sources besides bitcointalk.org.

Therefore, much work remains to be done. In future work, we would like investigate the following:

- Check for any consistent variation between trade volumes and exchange rate before and after a DDoS attack on a currency exchange.
- Explore the relationship between DDoS attacks on other digital currencies such as Litecoin. Mt. Gox was subject to a DDoS attack which delayed their acceptance to trade Litecoin. Furthermore, some speculate that Bitcoin enthusiasts are attacking other currencies to ensure Bitcoin's market dominance in the market of digital currencies.
- We investigated three leading forms of anti-DDoS protection, but there are others. Furthermore, protection such as CloudFlare doesn't protect against certain types of DDoS attacks.
- Study how other factors such as type of mining pool influence the prevalence and success of DDoS attacks. For instance, the supposedly DDoS-resistant P2P mining pool `altcoin.pw` was shut down. Are P2P pools inherently more "DDoS-able", or is this a function of something else?
- Moore and Christin found that transaction volume mattered more than attack susceptibility when predicting the future viability of a Bitcoin exchange [6]. Does this model carry over to Bitcoin mining pools? The case study of DeepBit which has lost its market dominance due to repeated DDoS attacks would suggest not.

In addition to these avenues for analytical investigation, we would also like to refine the classification mechanism for automatically identifying posts that describe DDoS attacks. Given that DDoS is an ongoing and sporadically-occurring problem for Bitcoin, it would be useful to develop a tool that can automatically generate reliable attack indicators that do not require manual removal of false positives.

Acknowledgments. We thank the anonymous reviewers and paper shepherd Fergal Reid for their helpful feedback. This work was partially funded by the Department of Homeland Security (DHS) Science and Technology Directorate, Cyber Security Division (DHS S&T/CSD) Broad Agency Announcement 11.02, the Government of Australia and SPAWAR Systems Center Pacific via contract number N66001-13-C-0131. This paper represents the position of the authors and not that of the aforementioned agencies.

References

1. Nakamoto, S.: Bitcoin: a peer-to-peer electronic cash system (2009). http://www.bitcoin.org/bitcoin.pdf
2. Chaum, D.: Achieving electronic privacy. Sci. Am. **267**, 96–101 (1992)
3. Gallu, J.: Bitcoin Ponzi scheme alleged by SEC in lawsuit against Texas man. Bloomberg, July 2013. http://www.bloomberg.com/news/2013-07-23/bitcoin-ponzi-scheme-alleged-by-sec-in-lawsuit-against-texas-man.html
4. Jeffries, A.: Suspected multi-million dollar Bitcoin pyramid scheme shuts down, investors revolt. The Verge, August 2012. http://www.theverge.com/2012/8/27/3271637/bitcoin-savings-trust-pyramid-scheme-shuts-down
5. Leyden, J.: Linode hackers escape with $70k in daring Bitcoin heist. The Register, March 2012. http://www.theregister.co.uk/2012/03/02/linode_bitcoin_heist/
6. Moore, T., Christin, N.: Beware the middleman: empirical analysis of bitcoin-exchange risk. In: Sadeghi, A.-R. (ed.) FC 2013. LNCS, vol. 7859, pp. 25–33. Springer, Heidelberg (2013)
7. Leyden, J.: How mystery DDoSers tried to take down Bitcoin exchange with 100Gbps crapflood. The Register, October 2013. http://www.theregister.co.uk/2013/10/17/bitcoin_exchange_ddos_flood/
8. Johnson, B., Laszka, A., Grossklags, J., Vasek, M., Moore, T.: Game-theoretic analysis of DDoS attacks against Bitcoin mining pools. In: Böhme, R., Brenner, M., Moore, T., Smith, M. (eds.) FC 2014 Workshops. LNCS, vol. 8438, pp. 72–86. Springer, Heidelberg (2014)
9. Bitcoin Wiki: Trade. https://en.bitcoin.it/wiki/Trade. Accessed 21 Nov 2013
10. Bitcoin Wiki: Category: Pool operators. https://en.bitcoin.it/wiki/Category:Pool_Operators. Accessed 21 Nov 2013
11. CloudFlare: Cloudflare IP ranges. http://www.cloudflare.com/ips. Accessed 21 Nov 2013
12. Harel, U.: Restricting direct access to your website (Incapsula's IP addresses). http://support.incapsula.com/hc/en-us/articles/200627570-Restricting-direct-access-to-your-website-Incapsula-s-IP-addresses-. Accessed 15 Jan 2014
13. Amazon Web Services: Announcement: Amazon EC2 public IP ranges. https://forums.aws.amazon.com/ann.jspa?annID=1701. Accessed 21 Nov 2013
14. organofcorti: MTGOX volume post Dwolla: a single statistical test, Neighbourhood Pool Watch, July 2013. http://organofcorti.blogspot.com/2013/07/114-mtgox-volume-post-dwolla-single.html
15. Ron, D., Shamir, A.: Quantitative analysis of the full Bitcoin transaction graph. In: Sadeghi, A.-R. (ed.) FC 2013. LNCS, vol. 7859, pp. 6–24. Springer, Heidelberg (2013)
16. Meiklejohn, S., Pomarole, M., Jordan, G., Levchenko, K., McCoy, D., Voelker, G.M., Savage, S.: A fistful of Bitcoins: characterizing payments among men with no names. In: Proceedings of the 2013 Conference on Internet Measurement Conference, ser. IMC 2013, pp. 127–140. ACM, New York (2013)
17. Möser, M., Böhme, R., Breuker, D.: An inquiry into money laundering tools in the Bitcoin ecosystem. In: 8th APWG eCrime Researchers Summit. IEEE (2013)
18. Christin, N.: Traveling the silk road: a measurement analysis of a large anonymous online marketplace. In: Proceedings of the 22nd International Conference on the World Wide Web, International World Wide Web Conferences Steering Committee, pp. 213–224 (2013)

19. Zuckerman, E., Roberts, H., McGrady, R., York, J., Palfrey, J.G.: 2010 report on distributed denial of service (DDoS) attacks. Technical report 2010-16, Berkman Center Research Publication (2010). http://ssrn.com/abstract=1872065
20. Barber, S., Boyen, X., Shi, E., Uzun, E.: Bitter to better — how to make Bitcoin a better currency. In: Keromytis, A.D. (ed.) FC 2012. LNCS, vol. 7397, pp. 399–414. Springer, Heidelberg (2012)
21. Eyal, I., Sirer, E.G.: Majority is not enough: Bitcoin mining is vulnerable. In: Proceedings of the 18th International Conference on Financial Cryptography and Data Security, ser. Lecture Notes in Computer Science, vol. (to appear). Springer (2014)
22. Kroll, J., Davey, I., Felten, E.: The economics of Bitcoin mining, or Bitcoin in the presence of adversaries. In: Proceedings of the Twelfth Annual Workshop on the Economics of Information Security (WEIS 2013), Washington, DC, June 2013
23. Rosenfeld, M.: Analysis of hashrate-based double-spending (2012). https://bitcoil.co.il/Doublespend.pdf

Game-Theoretic Analysis of DDoS Attacks Against Bitcoin Mining Pools

Benjamin Johnson[1], Aron Laszka[2], Jens Grossklags[3](✉),
Marie Vasek[4], and Tyler Moore[4]

[1] University of California, Berkeley, CA, USA
johnsonb@ischool.berkeley.edu
[2] Budapest University of Technology and Economics, Budapest, Hungary
laszka@crysys.hu
[3] The Pennsylvania State University, State College, PA, USA
jensg@ist.psu.edu
[4] Southern Methodist University, Dallas, TX, USA
{mvasek,tylerm}@smu.edu

Abstract. One of the unique features of the digital currency Bitcoin is that new cash is introduced by so-called *miners* carrying out resource-intensive proof-of-work operations. To increase their chances of obtaining freshly minted bitcoins, miners typically join *pools* to collaborate on the computations. However, intense competition among mining pools has recently manifested in two ways. Miners may invest in additional computing resources to increase the likelihood of winning the next mining race. But, at times, a more sinister tactic is also employed: a mining pool may trigger a costly distributed denial-of-service (DDoS) attack to lower the expected success outlook of a competing mining pool. We explore the trade-off between these strategies with a series of game-theoretical models of competition between two pools of varying sizes. We consider differences in costs of investment and attack, as well as uncertainty over whether a DDoS attack will succeed. By characterizing the game's equilibria, we can draw a number of conclusions. In particular, we find that pools have a greater incentive to attack large pools than small ones. We also observe that larger mining pools have a greater incentive to attack than smaller ones.

Keywords: Game theory · Bitcoin · Internet · Security · DDoS

1 Introduction

Bitcoin is a decentralized digital currency that first became operational in 2009 [1]. While cryptographically protected digital currencies have been around for decades [2], none has received the attention or experienced the same rise in adoption as Bitcoin [3].

There are many factors that contribute to the success of a currency. Most currencies are tightly associated with a particular country, and are influenced

© IFCA/Springer-Verlag Berlin Heidelberg 2014
R. Böhme et al. (Eds.): FC 2014 Workshops, LNCS 8438, pp. 72–86, 2014.
DOI: 10.1007/978-3-662-44774-1_6

by decisions regarding economic factors and political leadership. At the same time, internal stakeholders and external trade partners benefit from the adoption and maintenance of a stable currency. Wider adoption enables positive network effects, e.g., by enabling exchange of goods beyond the scope of a traditional barter community. However, currencies remain in competition with each other, and new currencies might gain a foothold if they offer comparative advantages to a certain set of stakeholders [4].[1]

One reason why Bitcoin has attracted enthusiastic backers is that its design creates opportunities for participants to shape its future and to profit from its success. The artificially constrained money supply helps drive up the exchange rate over time, rewarding those who have invested in bitcoins. Most importantly, new bitcoins are given as rewards to the miner who finds the solution to a complex mathematical problem. However, this also means that new entrants in the market for Bitcoin mining impose negative externalities on other contributors. Each new miner who contributes to Bitcoin automatically lowers the value of the relative contributions of all other miners.

Miners respond in two primary ways to increase their output during the quest to earn another bundle of bitcoins. First, they form associations with other contributors in *mining pools*. Second, they may invest in additional computing resources. For example, the increasing value of Bitcoin has also created a market for specialized hardware. At the same time, botnets have been used to increase the output of mining pools that control these illegally acquired resources. In the end, the most powerful mining pool is the most likely to win the next race.

There is one caveat to this relatively straightforward process. More recently, attacks hampering the effectiveness of mining pools have been observed. Distributed Denial of Service Attacks (DDoS) frequently target mining pools in order to disrupt their operations (e.g., the distribution and submission of delegated tasks). There are two primary objectives that attackers are following when facilitating DDoS attacks on mining pools. First, the operations at competing mining pools are slowed down which might give a decisive (but unfair) advantage in the race for the next bundle of bitcoins. Second, individual miners might become discouraged and decide to leave "unreliable" mining pools as the result of these attacks.[2]

---

[1] Rules for currency competition may differ by country. For example, in the United States the following rules are of importance. United States money, as identified by the U.S. Code, when tendered to a creditor always legally satisfies a *debt* to the extent of the amount tendered. However, no federal law mandates that a person or an organization must accept United States money as payment for *goods or services not yet provided*. That is, a business might specify a particular currency and therefore increase competition between currencies.

[2] Other attack motivations might include the facilitation of other cybercriminal activities, e.g., using DDoS as a means to extract payments from a mining pool as part of an extortion ploy [5]. Attacks might also be indicative of non-financial objectives, e.g., the earning of reputation in the attacker community or general disagreement with the goals and objectives of the Bitcoin community.

Mining pools have been sporadically targeted by DDoS attacks since 2011. According to an empirical analysis of Bitcoin-related DDoS attacks [6], mining pools are the second-most frequently targeted Bitcoin service after currency exchanges. Of 49 mining pools, 12 experienced DDoS attacks, often repeatedly. At least one mining pool, Altcoin.pw, appears to have shut down due to repeated DDoS attacks.

Our study addresses the trade-off between two different investment dimensions in the context of Bitcoin creation: construction and destruction. Under the construction paradigm, a mining pool may invest in additional computing resources to increase the likelihood of winning the next race. Under the destruction focus, a mining pool may trigger a costly DDoS attack to lower the expected success outlook of a competing mining pool.

We approach the study of this trade-off by developing a series of game-theoretical models. We begin our analysis with a simple model that presents a binary choice between investment and DDoS attack. Subsequently, we expand this baseline model to account for costs and the possibility of attack failure. Our goal is to give the reader initially an intuitive understanding about the impact of the different investment choices. With increasing model complexity, we aim for a heightened degree of realism regarding actual investment decisions.

Our work is important because it contributes to a greater understanding of the inherent risks of the Bitcoin economy. Due to its decentralized nature, international focus and lack of regulation, the existing competing and misaligned interests prevalent in the Bitcoin community can frequently lead to undesirable outcomes. For example, many Bitcoin currency exchanges have a short survival time, often leaving their customers in the lurch [7]. The scenario we study becomes an increasingly central concern to Bitcoin mining pools. With accelerating upfront investment costs to compete in the Bitcoin mining race, the associated risks are ballooning as well, e.g., interference with the mining operations becomes more costly. Responding to such threats requires a good understanding of the economic impact of attacks and potential countermeasures.

Our presentation proceeds as follows. In Sect. 2, we briefly discuss related work with a focus on theoretical research. In Sect. 3, we develop and analyze a series of game-theoretical models. We discuss the practical implications of these analyses and conclude in Sect. 4.

2   Related Work

2.1   Economics of Security Decision-Making

Our model is concerned with DDoS attacks as a strategic choice impacting the Bitcoin mining race. As such, we focus in our review on research in which adversarial interests are the subject of economic models. However, relatively little work has addressed the strategic choices of attackers and cybercriminals. Fultz and Grossklags model strategic attackers and the competition between those attackers [8]. In their model, attackers and defenders have to be cognizant of inherent interdependencies that shape the impact of offensive and defensive actions [9–11].

Similarly, Clark and Konrad present a game-theoretic model with one defender and one attacker. The defending player has to successfully protect multiple nodes while the attacker must merely compromise a single point [12]. Cavusoglu et al. [13] analyze the decision-making problem of a firm when attack probabilities are externally given compared to a scenario when the attacker is explicitly modeled as a strategic player in a game-theoretic framework.

Cremonini and Nizovtsev compare attacker decisions under different scenarios of information availability regarding defensive strength [14]. Schechter and Smith [15] draw upon the economics of crime literature to construct a model of attackers in the computer security context [16]. They derive the penalties and probabilities of enforcement that will deter an attacker who acts as an utility optimizer evaluating the risks and rewards of committing an offense.

Several surveys have summarized the achievements in this area [17–19].

2.2   Economics of DDoS

Research on the economics of DDoS attacks has focused on the organization of an effective defense [20–22]. For example, Liu et al. develop a game-theoretic model of DDoS attacker-defender interactions, and conduct a network simulation study which utilizes their model to infer DDoS attack strategies [20].

More closely related to our work is a paper by Li et al. [23]. They model the incentives of a botnet herder to maintain a zombie network for the primary purpose of renting a sufficiently large subset to a DDoS attacker. They investigate whether this business relationship can remain profitable if defenders can pollute the botnet with decoy machines (which lowers the effectiveness of a DDoS attack). Complementary to this work, Christin et al. investigate the incentives of a group of defenders when they face the threat of being absorbed into a botnet, e.g., for the purpose of a DDoS attack [24]. Their model shows how the bounded rationality of defenders can contribute to lower defensive investments and a higher risk of security compromise.

We are unaware of any economic research that investigates the potential impact of DDoS attacks on the Bitcoin economy.

2.3   Incentive Modeling of the Bitcoin Economy

In this subsection, we briefly report on research studies that investigate the stability of Bitcoin to economically-driven attacks. We do not review research on the robustness of the cryptographic underpinnings of Bitcoin.

Kroll et al. study the stability of Bitcoin mining if an outsider has motivation to destroy the currency [25]. More specifically, their "Goldfinger" attack compares on a high level the collective benefit of Bitcoin mining with some externally given incentive to destroy the economy altogether. They also study the likelihood of deviations from the consensus process of Bitcoin mining.

Similarly, Barber et al. perform an in-depth investigation of the success of Bitcoin, and study the characteristics of a "doomsday" attack in which the complete transaction history would be invalidated by an adversary with vastly superior computing power [3]. They also investigate a number of other potential weaknesses, and propose improvements to the Bitcoin protocol.

Babaioff et al. show that, as the Bitcoin protocol is currently defined, it does not provide incentives for nodes to broadcast transactions; in fact, it provides strong disincentives [26]. However, the Bitcoin economy seems to be – at least in this respect – working well in practice. The authors propose a solution for this potential problem, which is based on augmenting the Bitcoin protocol with a scheme for rewarding information propagation.

3   Game-Theoretic Model and Analysis

Our modeling approach focuses on the incentives of Bitcoin mining pool operators to initiate distributed denial of service attacks against other mining pools. Toward this end, we begin our analysis with a very simple model that presents a binary choice between investment and attack. Subsequently, we expand the baseline model to account for the possibility of attack failure, and then to consider linear investment and attack costs.

In each model, we focus on exactly two players – a big player B and a small player S. By the size comparison, we simply mean that B has more computational power to mine bitcoins than S. A third entity R represents the rest of the Bitcoin mining market. R behaves heuristically and thus is not a player in a game-theoretical sense. In equations, we overload the notation B, S, and R to represent the value of the respective player's computing power.

Each player's decision space involves a binary choice of investment – either to invest in additional computing power, or to initiate a DDoS attack against the other strategic player. The outcome of each player's decision is realized over a time scale that is long enough so that payoffs to pools in bitcoins are realized according to the mining probabilities, but short enough so that reaching an approximate equilibrium in the relative computational power of mining pools is a reasonable assumption.

3.1   Baseline Model

We assume that the Bitcoin mining market increases computational power over the game's time scale at a fixed rate ε; and that the market is at an equilibrium with respect to each player's relative computing power. Each player's base strategy is to maintain the market equilibrium by investing in computation to keep up with the market. Each player's alternative strategy is to use those resources that would have been used for increased computation to initiate a DDoS attack against the other strategic player.

In the baseline model, we assume that DDoS attacks are 100 % effective, so that a player who is subject to the attack cannot mine any Bitcoins for the duration of the game's time scale. Secondly, in the baseline model, we assume that the costs to invest or initiate an attack are negligible relative to the overall Bitcoin revenue, so that they do not factor into the players' strategic decisions.

The payoff for each player is determined by the expected value of the fraction of Bitcoins that they mine. If both players use the base strategy to keep up with the market, then the payoff of player S is

$$\frac{S(1+\varepsilon)}{(B+S+R)(1+\varepsilon)} = \frac{S}{B+S+R};$$

similarly, the payoff for player B is

$$\frac{B}{B+S+R}.$$

If both players initiate DDoS attacks against each other, then they each receive nothing. If player S initiates a DDoS attack against player B, while B keeps up with the market, then B receives nothing, and S receives

$$\frac{S}{S+R(1+\varepsilon)}.$$

These consequences are symmetric with respect to S and B.

The full payoff matrix for each player is summarized in Table 1. From this, we derive each players' best responses to each of the other player's strategies. Then we use best response conditions to classify the game's Nash equilibria. Finally, we provide numerical illustrations for the game's equilibria and analyze the corresponding implications.

Table 1. Payoff matrix for B, S

		Player B	
		Computation	DDoS
Player S	Computation	$\frac{B}{B+S+R}, \frac{S}{B+S+R}$	$\frac{B}{B+R(1+\varepsilon)}, 0$
	DDoS	$0, \frac{S}{S+R(1+\varepsilon)}$	$0, 0$

Best-Response Strategies. If player S invests in DDoS, then investing in DDoS and investing in computing are both best responses for player B, since they both yield a payoff of 0. On the other hand, if player S invests in computing, then investing in DDoS is a unique best response for player B if

$$\frac{B}{B+R(1+\varepsilon)} > \frac{B}{(B+S+R)};$$

which reduces to

$$R\varepsilon < S. \tag{1}$$

Both DDoS and computing are best responses if

$$R\varepsilon = S; \tag{2}$$

and computing is a unique best response otherwise. The best responses of player S analogous, with the constants B and S swapped.

Equilibria

- First, both players investing in DDoS is always a Nash equilibrium. However, this is only a weak equilibrium, as both players are indifferent to their strategy choices.
- Second, both players investing in computing is an equilibrium if

$$S \le R\varepsilon \tag{3}$$

and

$$B \le R\varepsilon. \tag{4}$$

Furthermore, the equilibrium is strict if both inequalities are strict.
- Finally, if only one of the above inequalities holds, then there is an equilibrium in which the player whose inequality does not hold invests in DDoS, while the other player invests in computing. This is again a weak equilibrium, since the latter player is indifferent to her strategy.

Numerical Illustrations. Figure 1 shows features of the Nash equilibria for various values of B and S. Figure 1a divides the parameter space based on the set of equilibrium profiles. Figure 1b shows the payoff of player B as a function of the relative sizes of B and S, where the average payoff is taken for regions having multiple equilibria. The average payoffs of players B and S (for a fixed S) are shown as a function of B by Fig. 1c.

   From Fig. 1a, we see immediately that it is always a weak equilibrium for each player to DDoS the other. This happens because, with perfect effectiveness of DDoS, the player being attacked loses all incentives related to their strategic choice, and thus can choose an arbitrary strategy. We extend the model in the next section to incorporate imperfect DDoS, which alleviates this phenomenon. From the same figure, we also see that if either player becomes much larger than the market growth rate, there is no incentive to mutually cooperate. In these regions, one of the players always has a greater incentive to DDoS if her opponent invests in computation. The slant of the dividing lines also shows that the tendency to avoid cooperation is slightly affected by a player's own size. Figure 1b shows that in this model, the large player fares extremely poorly against a small player if her size becomes too large relative to the market growth rate.

3.2 Baseline Model with Imperfect DDoS

In the first extension of our baseline model, we assume that DDoS attacks are successful only with fixed probability $1-\sigma$. For numerical illustrations, we take σ

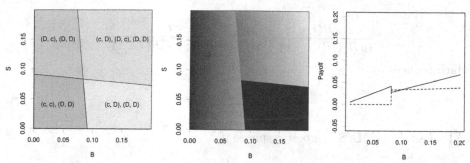

(a) Equilibrium strategy profiles for players (B, S) as a function of the players' sizes. The letters c and D abbreviate computation and DDoS, respectively.

(b) Equilibrium payoff of player B (lighter shades represent higher payoffs). Where there are multiple equilibria, the figure shows the average payoff.

(c) Average equilibrium payoffs of players B (solid) and S (dotted) as a function of B, with $S = 0.1$.

Fig. 1. Equilibria for various values of B and S. The increase in computational power is $\varepsilon = 0.1$.

Table 2. Payoff matrix for B, S with imperfect DDoS

		B	
		Computation	DDoS
S	Computation	$\frac{B}{B+S+R}, \frac{S}{B+S+R}$	$\frac{B}{B+(\sigma S+R)(1+\varepsilon)}, \frac{\sigma S(1+\varepsilon)}{B+(\sigma S+R)(1+\varepsilon)}$
	DDoS	$\frac{\sigma B(1+\varepsilon)}{(\sigma B+R)(1+\varepsilon)+S}, \frac{S}{(\sigma B+R)(1+\varepsilon)+S}$	$\frac{\sigma B}{\sigma(B+S)+R(1+\varepsilon)}, \frac{\sigma S}{\sigma(B+S)+R(1+\varepsilon)}$

to be 0.2. The new payoffs (with arbitrary σ) for players B and S are summarized in Table 2.

Best-Response Strategies. If player S invests in computation, then investing in computation is a best response for player B if

$$\frac{B}{B+S+R} \geq \frac{B}{B+(\sigma S+R)(1+\varepsilon)},$$

which reduces to

$$S \leq \frac{\varepsilon R}{1-\sigma(1+\varepsilon)}; \tag{5}$$

and investing in DDoS is a best response if

$$S \geq \frac{\varepsilon R}{1-\sigma(1+\varepsilon)}. \tag{6}$$

If player S initiates a DDoS attack, then investing in computation is a best response for player B if

$$\frac{\sigma B(1+\varepsilon)}{(\sigma B + R)(1+\varepsilon) + S} \geq \frac{\sigma B}{\sigma(B+S) + R(1+\varepsilon)},$$

which reduces to

$$S \leq \frac{\varepsilon R}{1 - \sigma - \frac{\varepsilon}{1+\varepsilon}}; \tag{7}$$

and investing in DDoS is a best response if

$$S \geq \frac{\varepsilon R}{1 - \sigma - \frac{\varepsilon}{1+\varepsilon}}. \tag{8}$$

Equilibria. The game's equilibria depend on the sizes of B and S compared to the quantities $\frac{\varepsilon R}{1-\sigma(1+\varepsilon)}$ and $\frac{\varepsilon R}{1-\sigma-\frac{\varepsilon}{1+\varepsilon}}$. Note that we would expect the first quantity to be smaller, because we typically have $\sigma < \frac{1}{1+\varepsilon}$. Concretely, for example, this desired relation holds when the growth rate ε is less than 100 % and the DDoS failure rate σ is at most 50 %.

– First, both players investing in DDoS is a Nash equilibrium whenever

$$B, S \geq \frac{\varepsilon R}{1 - \sigma - \frac{\varepsilon}{1+\varepsilon}} \tag{9}$$

and the equilibrium is strict whenever the inequality is strict.
– Second, both players investing in computing is an equilibrium if

$$B, S \leq \frac{\varepsilon R}{1 - \sigma(1+\varepsilon)} \tag{10}$$

and again the equilibrium is strict if the inequality is strict.
– Third, there exists an equilibrium in which S initiates a DDoS attack and B invests in computation whenever

$$B \geq \frac{\varepsilon R}{1 - \sigma(1+\varepsilon)} \tag{11}$$

and

$$S \leq \frac{\varepsilon R}{1 - \sigma - \frac{\varepsilon}{1+\varepsilon}}. \tag{12}$$

– Finally, there is a sub-case of the previous condition in which B can initiate a DDoS attack while S invests in computation, if

$$\frac{\varepsilon R}{1 - \sigma(1+\varepsilon)} \leq B, S \leq \frac{\varepsilon R}{1 - \sigma - \frac{\varepsilon}{1+\varepsilon}}. \tag{13}$$

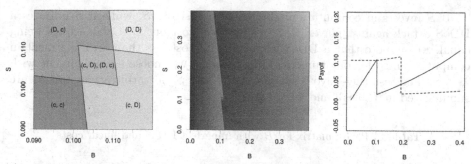

(a) Equilibrium strategy profiles for players (B, S) as a function of the players' sizes. The letters c and D abbreviate computation and DDoS, respectively.

(b) Equilibrium payoff of player B (lighter shades represent higher payoffs). Where there are multiple equilibria, the figure shows the average payoff.

(c) Equilibrium payoff of players B (solid) and S (dotted) as a function of B for $S = 0.1$.

Fig. 2. Equilibria for various values of B and S. The increase in computational power is $\varepsilon = 0.1$, and the success probability of DDoS is $1 - \sigma = 0.8$.

Numerical Illustration. Figure 2, illustrates features of the equilibria for the baseline model with imperfect DDoS. Figure 2a divides the parameter space based on the set of equilibrium profiles. Figure 2b shows the payoff of player B as a function of the relative sizes of B and S; and Fig. 2c shows the payoff of players B and S (for a fixed S) as a function of B.

From Fig. 2a, we see that, (compared to the baseline model) there is no longer a weak equilibrium in which each player initiates a DDoS attack against the other; and in most parameter configurations, there is now a unique equilibrium. For each player, this unique equilibrium strategy is primarily determined by her opponent's computational power. Once the opponent reaches a given threshold, it is in the player's best interest to DDoS that opponent. The slanted nature of the equilibrium-dividing lines shows that a player's equilibrium strategy is also determined to a weaker degree by her own computational power, with larger players having slightly more incentive to attack. Finally, there is a region for players of medium and comparable sizes, in which the game has two competing equilibria. The strategic dynamic in this region is similar to the classical game of *battle of the sexes*.

3.3 Baseline Model with Imperfect DDoS and Linear Costs

The third extension of our baseline model combines the features of imperfect DDoS attacks and linear costs for player investment choices. Here we assume that the cost of an investment to keep up with the mining market is proportional to the size of the investing player, and that the cost to initiate a DDoS attack is proportional to the size of the player who is being attacked.

If S invests in computation, she incurs a cost of γS; while if S initiates a DDoS attack against player B, it results in a cost of λB. Other things being equal, we suppose that a DDoS attack should cost less than an investment in computation, so for our numerical illustrations, we choose an assignment with $\lambda < \gamma$. The resulting payoffs for players B and S (for arbitrary γ and λ) are summarized in Tables 3 and 4.

Table 3. Payoff matrix for B with imperfect DDoS and linear costs

		B	
		Computation	DDoS
S	Computation	$\frac{B}{B+S+R} - \gamma B$	$\frac{B}{B+(\sigma S+R)(1+\varepsilon)} - \lambda S,$
	DDoS	$\frac{\sigma B(1+\varepsilon)}{(\sigma B+R)(1+\varepsilon)+S} - \gamma B$	$\frac{\sigma B}{\sigma(B+S)+R(1+\varepsilon)} - \lambda S$

Table 4. Payoff matrix for S with imperfect DDoS and linear costs

		B	
		Computation	DDoS
S	Computation	$\frac{S}{B+S+R} - \gamma S$	$\frac{\sigma S(1+\varepsilon)}{B+(\sigma S+R)(1+\varepsilon)} - \gamma S$
	DDoS	$\frac{S}{(\sigma B+R)(1+\varepsilon)+S} - \lambda B$	$\frac{\sigma S}{\sigma(B+S)+R(1+\varepsilon)} - \lambda B$

Best-Response Strategies. If player S invests in computation, then investing in computation is a best response for player B if

$$\frac{B}{B+S+R} - \gamma B \geq \frac{B}{B+(\sigma S+R)(1+\varepsilon)} - \lambda S; \tag{14}$$

and investing in DDoS is a best response if

$$\frac{B}{B+S+R} - \gamma B \leq \frac{B}{B+(\sigma S+R)(1+\varepsilon)} - \lambda S. \tag{15}$$

If player S initiates a DDoS attack, then investing in computation is a best response for player B if

$$\frac{\sigma B(1+\varepsilon)}{(\sigma B+R)(1+\varepsilon)+S} - \gamma B \geq \frac{\sigma B}{\sigma(B+S)+R(1+\varepsilon)} - \lambda S; \tag{16}$$

and investing in DDoS is a best response if

$$\frac{\sigma B(1+\varepsilon)}{(\sigma B+R)(1+\varepsilon)+S} - \gamma B \leq \frac{\sigma B}{\sigma(B+S)+R(1+\varepsilon)} - \lambda S. \tag{17}$$

Equilibria

– First, both players initiating DDoS attacks is a Nash equilibrium whenever

$$\frac{B}{B+S+R} - \gamma B \geq \frac{B}{B+(\sigma S+R)(1+\varepsilon)} - \lambda S \qquad (18)$$

and

$$\frac{S}{B+S+R} - \gamma S \geq \frac{S}{(\sigma B+R)(1+\varepsilon)+S} - \lambda B. \qquad (19)$$

– Second, both players investing in computing is an equilibrium if

$$\frac{\sigma B(1+\varepsilon)}{(\sigma B+R)(1+\varepsilon)+S} - \gamma B \leq \frac{\sigma B}{\sigma(B+S)+R(1+\varepsilon)} - \lambda S \qquad (20)$$

and

$$\frac{\sigma S(1+\varepsilon)}{B+(\sigma S+R)(1+\varepsilon)} - \gamma S \leq \frac{\sigma S}{\sigma(B+S)+R(1+\varepsilon)} - \lambda B. \qquad (21)$$

– Third, an equilibrium in which S conducts a DDoS attack against B while B invests in computation may occur when

$$\frac{\sigma B(1+\varepsilon)}{(\sigma B+R)(1+\varepsilon)+S} - \gamma B \leq \frac{\sigma B}{\sigma(B+S)+R(1+\varepsilon)} - \lambda S \qquad (22)$$

and

$$\frac{S}{B+S+R} - \gamma S \leq \frac{S}{(\sigma B+R)(1+\varepsilon)+S} - \lambda B. \qquad (23)$$

– Finally, there can be an equilibrium in which B conducts a DDoS attack against S while S invests in computation whenever the roles of B and S are interchanged in the two inequalities from the previous case.

Numerical Illustration. Figure 3 shows features of the Nash equilibria for various values of B and S. Figure 3a divides the parameter space based on the set of equilibrium profiles. Figure 3b shows the payoff of player B as a function of the relative sizes of B and S; and Fig. 3c shows the payoff of players B and S (for a fixed S) as a function of B.

The addition of costs to the model keeps the smallest players from participating in DDoS attacks, as they are best served by investing in their own computational prowess. Aside from this, the dynamics of the equilibrium strategies are largely similar to the model without costs. Namely, players are still incentivized to attack large players, and slightly more so if they are larger themselves. There still remains a small region for midsize players in which either player can attack the other; and with the possible exception of an extremely large player, the payoffs are generally higher for a player whose size lies just below the threshold for being attacked.

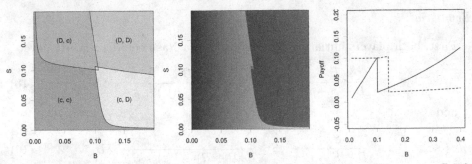

(a) Equilibrium strategy profiles for players (B, S) as a function of the players' sizes. The letters c and D abbreviate computation and DDoS, respectively.

(b) Equilibrium payoff of player B (lighter shades represent higher payoffs). Where there are multiple equilibria, the figure shows the average payoff.

(c) Equilibrium payoff of players B (solid) and S (dotted) as a function of B for $S = 0.1$.

Fig. 3. Equilibria for various values of B and S. The increase in computational power is $\varepsilon = 0.1$, the success probability of DDoS is $1 - \sigma = 0.8$, and the linear cost factors for investing into computation and DDoS are $\gamma = 0.002$ and $\lambda = 0.001$.

4   Conclusions and Future Work

We set out in this work to understand the motivation behind recent DDoS attacks against Bitcoin mining pools. To do this, we analyzed a series of game-theoretical models involving two mining pools with different sizes. Several fundamental dynamics of this game were common to all models and seem well-motivated in the context of Bitcoin. First, we saw that there is a greater incentive to attack a larger mining pool than a smaller one. This finding is intuitive because each pool battles for the reward; and eliminating the largest mining pool has the greatest impact on the chances of the remaining mining pools to win. It is also consistent with what has been observed empirically: 63 % of large mining pools have experienced DDoS attacks, compared to just 17 % of small ones [6]. Second, we observed that the larger mining pool has a slightly greater incentive to attack than the smaller mining pool. This dynamic arises because a larger mining pool has a smaller relative competitor base, and eliminating a competitor from a small base yields more benefit than eliminating one from a larger base. Finally, there is a size threshold such that mining pools larger than this threshold are subject to economically-motivated attacks; and pools smaller than the threshold are not. Furthermore, players whose sizes are just below this threshold tend to receive the highest payoffs.

From our modeling extensions we found additional insights. First, if attacks can be mitigated, then the size threshold for a mining pool to be safe from DDoS increases. That is, the market will tolerate (without attempting an attack) progressively larger pools as attacks become less effective. Second, the prevalence of costs can keep smaller players out of the DDoS market, but these do not change the core dynamics for mid-size and large mining pools.

There are many extensions to pursue in future work. A more direct economic approach to the cost dimension would have each player optimize their own investment costs relative to their current size. A player's choice of whether to initiate a DDoS attack would depend on the solution to two investment optimization problems. This extension would improve realism and reduce the game's exogenous parameters at the expense of additional model complexity. Another way to extend the model would be to give DDoS attacks a variable cost constraining their effectiveness. Finally, our work considers the incentives of mining pools as a whole, but in reality most pools consist of heterogeneous individuals who have a choice to change pools. By expanding our game to an iterated version in which individual players could switch mining pools between rounds, we might gain further insights into the strategies we see in today's Bitcoin mining market.

Acknowledgements. This research was partly supported by the Penn State Institute for CyberScience, CyLab at Carnegie Mellon under grant DAAD19-02-1-0389 from the Army Research Office, and the National Science Foundation under ITR award CCF-0424422 (TRUST). We also thank the reviewers for their comments on an earlier draft of the paper.

References

1. Nakamoto, S.: Bitcoin: a peer-to-peer electronic cash system. http://bitcoin.org/bitcoin.pdf (2008)
2. Chaum, D., Fiat, A., Naor, M.: Untraceable electronic cash. In: Goldwasser, S. (ed.) CRYPTO 1988. LNCS, vol. 403, pp. 319–327. Springer, Heidelberg (1990)
3. Barber, S., Boyen, X., Shi, E., Uzun, E.: Bitter to better — how to make Bitcoin a better currency. In: Keromytis, A.D. (ed.) FC 2012. LNCS, vol. 7397, pp. 399–414. Springer, Heidelberg (2012)
4. Dowd, K., Greenaway, D.: Currency competition, network externalities and switching costs: towards an alternative view of optimum currency areas. Econ. J. **103**(420), 1180–1189 (1993)
5. Plohmann, D., Gerhards-Padilla, E.: Case study of the miner botnet. In: Proceedings of the 4th International Conference on Cyber Conflict (CYCON), pp. 345–360 (2012)
6. Vasek, M., Thornton, M., Moore, T.: Empirical analysis of Denial-of-Service attacks in the Bitcoin ecosystem. In: Böhme, R., Brenner, M., Moore, T., Smith, M. (eds.) FC 2014 Workshops. LNCS, vol. 8438, pp. 57–71. Springer, Heidelberg (2014)
7. Moore, T., Christin, N.: Beware the middleman: empirical analysis of Bitcoin-exchange risk. In: Sadeghi, A.-R. (ed.) FC 2013. LNCS, vol. 7859, pp. 25–33. Springer, Heidelberg (2013)
8. Fultz, N., Grossklags, J.: Blue versus red: towards a model of distributed security attacks. In: Dingledine, R., Golle, P. (eds.) FC 2009. LNCS, vol. 5628, pp. 167–183. Springer, Heidelberg (2009)
9. Grossklags, J., Christin, N., Chuang, J.: Secure or insure? a game-theoretic analysis of information security games. In: Proceedings of the 2008 World Wide Web Conference (WWW'08), Beijing, China, April 2008, pp. 209–218 (2008)

10. Grossklags, J., Johnson, B., Christin, N.: When information improves information security. In: Sion, R. (ed.) FC 2010. LNCS, vol. 6052, pp. 416–423. Springer, Heidelberg (2010)
11. Varian, H.: System reliability and free riding. In: Camp, L., Lewis, S. (eds.) Economics of Information Security. Advances in Information Security, vol. 12, pp. 1–15. Kluwer, Dordrecht (2004)
12. Clark, D., Konrad, K.: Asymmetric conflict: weakest link against best shot. J. Conflict Resolut. 51(3), 457–469 (2007)
13. Cavusoglu, H., Raghunathan, S., Yue, W.: Decision-theoretic and game-theoretic approaches to IT security investment. J. Manag. Inf. Syst. 25(2), 281–304 (2008)
14. Cremonini, M., Nizovtsev, D.: Understanding and influencing attackers' decisions: Implications for security investment strategies. In: Proceedings of the Fifth Annual Workshop on Economics and Information Security (WEIS), Cambridge, UK, June 2006
15. Schechter, S.E., Smith, M.D.: How much security is enough to stop a thief? In: Wright, R.N. (ed.) FC 2003. LNCS, vol. 2742, pp. 122–137. Springer, Heidelberg (2003)
16. Becker, G.: Crime and punishment: an economic approach. J. Polit. Econ. 76(2), 169–217 (1968)
17. Anderson, R., Moore, T.: The economics of information security. Science 314(5799), 610–613 (2006)
18. Laszka, A., Felegyhazi, M., Buttyán, L.: A survey of interdependent security games. Technical report CRYSYS-TR-2012-11-15, CrySyS Lab, Budapest University of Technology and Economics (2012)
19. Manshaei, M., Zhu, Q., Alpcan, T., Bacşar, T., Hubaux, J.P.: Game theory meets network security and privacy. ACM Comput. Surv. 45(3), 25:1–25:39 (2013)
20. Liu, P., Zang, W., Yu, M.: Incentive-based modeling and inference of attacker intent, objectives, and strategies. ACM Trans. Inf. Syst. Secur. 8(1), 78–118 (2005)
21. Spyridopoulos, T., Karanikas, G., Tryfonas, T., Oikonomou, G.: A game theoretic defence framework against DoS/DDoS cyber attacks. Comput. Secur. 38, 39–50 (2013)
22. Wu, Q., Shiva, S., Roy, S., Ellis, C., Datla, V.: On modeling and simulation of game theory-based defense mechanisms against DOS and DDOS attacks. In: Proceedings of the 2010 Spring Simulation Multiconference, pp. 159:1–159:8 (2010)
23. Li, Z., Liao, Q., Striegel, A.: Botnet economics: uncertainty matters. In: Johnson, M. (ed.) Managing Information Risk and the Economics of Security, pp. 245–267. Springer, Heidelberg (2009)
24. Christin, N., Grossklags, J., Chuang, J.: Near rationality and competitive equilibria in networked systems. In: Proceedings of the ACM SIGCOMM Workshop on Practice and Theory of Incentives in Networked Systems, pp. 213–219 (2004)
25. Kroll, J., Davey, I., Felten, E.: The economics of Bitcoin mining, or Bitcoin in the presence of adversaries. In: Proceedings of the Twelfth Annual Workshop on Economics and Information Security (WEIS), Washington, DC, June 2013
26. Babaioff, M., Dobzinski, S., Oren, S., Zohar, A.: On Bitcoin and red balloons. In: Proceedings of the 13th ACM Conference on Electronic Commerce (EC), pp. 56–73 (2012)

The Bitcoin P2P Network

Joan Antoni Donet Donet, Cristina Pérez-Solà[✉],
and Jordi Herrera-Joancomartí[1]

Departament d'Enginyeria de la Informació i les Comunicacions,
Universitat Autònoma de Barcelona, 08193 Bellaterra, Catalonia, Spain
{jdonet,cperez,jherrera}@deic.uab.cat

Abstract. The Bitcoin virtual currency is built on the top of a decentralized peer-to-peer (P2P) network used to propagate system information such as transactions or blockchain updates. In this paper, we have performed a data collection process identifying more than 872000 different Bitcoin nodes. This data allows us to present information on the size of the Bitcoin P2P network, the node geographic distribution, the network stability in terms of interrupted availability of nodes, as well as some data regarding the propagation time of the transmitted information. Furthermore, although not every Bitcoin user can be identified as a P2P network node, measurements of the P2P network can be considered as a lower bound for Bitcoin usage, and they provide interesting results on the adoption of such virtual currency.

1 Introduction

Bitcoin is an online virtual currency based on public key cryptography. It was proposed in 2008 in a paper authored by someone behind the Satoshi Nakamoto pseudonym. Bitcoin became fully functional on January 2009 and its broad adoption, together with its high exchange rates with traditional currencies (EUR or USD), has made it the most successful virtual currency ever. Security issues have been solved using elliptic curve public key cryptography together with the help of hash functions. The fact that hash functions are one-way functions provides a way to define an easily verifiable and fine-grained adjustable proof-of-work. Furthermore, double-spending, probably the core problem of digital currencies, is prevented by maintaining a public non-modifiable register, the blockchain, which includes all the transactions performed on the system.

Besides its security robustness, two main properties have probably been its key to success: anonymity and decentralization. Anonymity in the Bitcoin network is based on the fact that users can create any number of anonymous Bitcoin addresses that will be used in their Bitcoin transactions. This basic approach is a good starting point, but the underlying non-anonymous Internet infrastructure, together with the availability of all Bitcoin transactions, has proven to be an anonymity threat as different authors have pointed out [1,9,11–13]. The other key point of the system is its decentralized nature. No central authority is supposed to control the Bitcoin payment system and a distributed approach based on a peer-to-peer (P2P) network has been adopted.

© IFCA/Springer-Verlag Berlin Heidelberg 2014
R. Böhme et al. (Eds.): FC 2014 Workshops, LNCS 8438, pp. 87–102, 2014.
DOI: 10.1007/978-3-662-44774-1_7

To our best knowledge, at the present time no detailed information has been published about the P2P Bitcoin Network. Therefore, this paper represents the first attempt to collect and map such data in a comprehensive way. Collected data provides information on the size of the Bitcoin P2P network, the node geographic distribution, the network stability in terms of interrupted availability of nodes, as well as some data regarding the propagation time of the transmitted information. On the other hand, the data provided in this paper sheds some light about the real adoption and usage of the Bitcoin currency. This is a difficult measurement due to the distributed architecture of the system. Some previous attempts to estimate Bitcoin adoption rates were based on the number of existing Bitcoin addresses. However, these results provided an upper bound on the number of users since multiple addresses may be generated by a single user and an average rate of such value is not straight forward to obtain. The number of P2P Bitcoin nodes is, therefore, a better estimation, and can be taken as a lower bound for the number of Bitcoin users.

The rest of the paper is organized as follows. Section 2 gives some basic ideas about the decentralized nature of the Bitcoin system and reviews some prior works. Section 3 describes the data collection process. Then, Sect. 4 presents the data analysis: we provide information about the network size, the geographic node distribution, the node stability, and measurements about information propagation. Finally, Sect. 5 concludes the paper and provides some ideas for further research.

2   Bitcoin Basics

As we have already mentioned in Sect. 1, one of the interesting properties of Bitcoin is its decentralized nature. The Bitcoin architecture does not rely on a centralized server. Instead, a distributed approach has been adopted to support the system. The distributed approach is used in many of the system facets, the most important of which are: data storage, data confirmation, and data transmission. The core information of the Bitcoin system is stored in the so called blockchain. The blockchain is stored in every full-client node of the Bitcoin system, allowing them to validate new blocks and transactions. On the other hand, new transactions are confirmed by adding them to the blockchain through the mining process, a process that is also distributed and that can be performed by any user of the network using specific-purpose software (and hardware). Mining Bitcoins helps to confirm transactions and it has been designed to be a hard task. Mining uses the concept of proof-of-work in order to provide a significant level of security.

Finally, the Bitcoin system needs to disseminate different kinds of information, essentially, the payment transactions performed by users and the blockchain (or its actualization). Since both data are generated in a distributed way, the system transmits such information over the Internet through a distributed peer-to-peer (P2P) network. This distributed network is created by Bitcoin users in a dynamic way. Nodes of the Bitcoin P2P network are machines running Bitcoin node software. This software is included by default in Bitcoin's full-client wallets, but it is not usually incorporated in light wallet versions (such as those running in mobile devices). It is important to stress this distinction, because when discovering nodes of the P2P network we do not identify all Bitcoin users, but only those running a full-client. Furthermore, the online Bitcoin accounts provided by major Bitcoin Internet sites are also not detected as independent Bitcoin nodes.

2.1 Related Work

In contrast to other virtual payments systems that have appeared so far, the seminal paper [10] describing the Bitcoin system was not published in the scientific arena but as an Internet post. Furthermore, the practical development of the ideas proposed in such paper took place on January 2009, when the first block of the blockchain appeared together with a fully functional Bitcoin wallet. For this reason, the deployment of Bitcoin has taken off without so much attention from the research community and, until now, not so many research papers have been published analyzing its particularities and properties.

Besides its legal and economic aspects, the majority of Bitcoin research papers are focused on analyzing the anonymity of Bitcoins [1,9,11–13]. They do so by exploiting the opportunity that represents the availability of all system transactions in the publicly accessible blockchain. Other few papers deal with security issues [4,8] or improvements on the payments processing time [3].

Regarding the characteristics of the P2P Bitcoin network, there are two papers related to this topic. In [2] the authors analyze the well known Sybil attack, where users of the P2P network are able to create various identities to perform different attacks and reduce, for instance, the P2P network performance. However, their approach is a theoretical one, and no real information is provided on the P2P Bitcoin network. Decker and Wattenhofer perform in [6] an interesting study on how information is disseminated in the Bitcoin network and how a network synchronization problem may affect the payment system in terms of blockchain uniqueness. In that paper, some measurements on propagation delays are provided but the results are based on a set of approximately 16000 nodes, in contrast with our 872648 node dataset.

3 Data Collection

In this Section we review the data collected to perform our analysis. We explain the procedure used to gather the information together with some numbers describing the amount of data collected. Finally, we review the limitations of both the collected data and the analysis done on its basis.

3.1 Data Collection Procedure

In order to collect data from the Bitcoin P2P network we developed an application, BTCdoNET[1], which serves, on one hand, as a frontend to interact with several utilities and, on the other hand, to store the collected data.

---

[1] The name of the application is a pun with the first author's name, who was the developer of the application.

With respect to the interaction with other applications, BTCdoNET is used as an interface to a modified Bitcoin P2P Network Sniffer [5] instance. Bitcoin Sniffer is a Python script that is able to connect to a Bitcoin node and listen to network events such as block and transaction broadcasts. We have modified the original Bitcoin Sniffer program in order to be able to listen to many nodes of the network at the same time, and to store all the collected data in a MySQL database. BTCdoNET also makes use of pynode, which is a dependency of the Bitcoin P2P Network Sniffer; and a classic LAMP installation, with a MySQL database storing all the collected data.

With respect to the data collection functionalities, BTCdoNET gathers essentially two different kinds of data:

1. **Network topology information**
   By issuing a `getaddr()` command to a set of seeds, we obtain a list of nodes that are connected to every seed. Then, by recursively applying the same procedure to the nodes connected to the seeds, that is, by sending `getaddr()` commands to the seeds' neighbors, we discover the neighbors of the neighbors, and so on. We maintain a list of already pooled nodes, so that one node is not queried twice. The process ends when there are no new nodes pending to be queried. Following the stated procedure, we perform a Breadth First Search of the Bitcoin P2P network. With this procedure we obtain, on one hand, a view over the Bitcoin P2P network structure itself and, on the other hand, a list of IPs addresses knowing to be running a Bitcoin node.
2. **Propagation of information in the network**
   The application is also able to connect to a set of already discovered nodes and to start monitoring their activity, that is, to listen to the transactions and blocks that the node is propagating to its neighbors. Apart from storing the transaction or block identifiers, BTCdoNET records the exact moment when the transaction or the block was broadcast by each of the nodes. This allows us to analyze how the information (transactions and blocks) is propagated through the network.

3.2   Collected Data

With respect to topology information, we performed 1 scan every day at 9 PM CET from November 30th, 2013 to January 5th, 2014. We will use the term *network snapshot* to refer to each of the 37 scans. Each snapshot took around 2 h to complete. The network discovery procedure used a fixed set of 600 nodes as seeds. After these 37 days of network discovering, we have detected 872648 different IP addresses corresponding to machines running Bitcoin nodes. Note, however, that only with the information of the first snapshot we already discovered 111475 nodes. This points out that there is a lot of node overlap between different snapshots and can be used as an indicator of the stability of the network. Section 4.2 analyzes node stability in a deeper way.

Concerning the propagation of information in the network, we configured the sniffer to try to simultaneously connect to 2000 different Bitcoin clients.

We selected those clients from the set of more stable nodes obtained with the network topology discover procedure. From these 2000 nodes, only 1377 accepted the connection request. We then listened to all 1377 nodes during 26 h, storing information about the exact moment when each of the nodes sent us transactions and blocks. After this period of time, we stop listening to information about transactions, but keep monitoring the block propagation information for an additional 92 h. The rationale behind this decision was to obtain a significant amount of block information without being flooded by the transaction propagation information. Over those periods of time, we received 13910769 transactions from the different nodes, representing a total of 70254 unique transactions. Regarding block information, we received 492793 block copies, getting information from 11663 different unique blocks.

3.3   Limitations

Although the amount of data collected is huge, both the dynamic nature of the P2P network and the data collection methodology introduce some limitations.

- Limitations of network topology information:
  - The number of nodes discovered is huge, but it does not represent the entire network. On one hand, some nodes do not respond to getaddr messages, so no information about their neighborhood can be extracted from them. On the other hand, the standard implementation of the Bitcoin client does not return all the node's neighbors in response to a getaddr call, but just the minimum between 23 % of the active nodes and a constant, which is set to 2500. These also limits the amount of information obtained when exploring the network through getaddr messages.
  - The paper is focused on analyzing the Bitcoin P2P network and thus we are dealing with Bitcoin nodes. Note that working with Bitcoin nodes is very different from working with Bitcoin users. It is important to stress such distinction, because the usage of light-clients as well as online Bitcoin accounts is very extended, and thus an important part of Bitcoin users can not be identified as Bitcoin nodes.
  - We identify Bitcoin nodes by their IP addresses. Although servers usually have static IP addresses, some of the Bitcoin nodes may be running on machines with dynamic IP addresses. Therefore, nodes may appear to be more unstable than they really are.
  - Each of the scans took about 2 h to complete. Therefore, some parts of the network may have changed while we were exploring other parts. However, we consider all the information in each of the snapshots as belonging to the very same instant of time.
  - We rely on geopositioning services to locate the IP addresses, which may introduce small errors when drawing their location over a map or classifying them by countries.
- Limitations about propagation information:

- When studying data propagation through the network, we simultaneously listened to around 1300 nodes. This number of nodes is far away from the total number of nodes of the network, and thus our computations can only be seen as an approximation of the values the whole network would exhibit.

4   Data Analysis

In this section we present the analysis of the collected data. We provide general information on the size of the peer-to-peer network, its geographical distribution, and the stability of the nodes. Finally, we study how transaction and block data propagate through the P2P network.

4.1   Network Size and Geographic Distribution

The Bitcoin network is global and, as such, we can find Bitcoin nodes operating all over the world. Table 1 shows the number of Bitcoin nodes discovered by country. The Table lists the 25 countries showing the highest number of Bitcoin nodes on the first day snapshot of the network, together with the 8 countries showing the least number of nodes. The country of a node is estimated from its IP address, using an IP geolocating service [7]. The Table presents the number of nodes by country analyzing all the collected data (2nd column) and for the data collected on the first day, which corresponds to the first full snapshot of the network (3rd column). Due to node overlap between different snapshots, the rankings may vary depending on the specific criteria used. Section 4.2 analyzes this fact in more depth.

We can observe that nodes placed in Unites States and China sum up to 37 % of the discovered nodes. Germany, United Kingdom, and Russia concentrate also a big amount of nodes of the network, with 9 %, 4 %, and 7 %, respectively, of the overall detected nodes. At the bottom of the table we can see that there are 8 countries with just one node detected on at least one of the snapshots. Grouped into the *others* category, there are as much as 136619 nodes (15483 on the first snapshot) coming from other 180 countries.

It is also interesting to study the Bitcoin adoption rate in each of the different countries. We have tried to evaluate this rate by comparing the number of Bitcoin nodes found in each country with the number of Internet users on that very same country.[2] Countries like Japan, Brazil, Mexico, and China present really low adoption rates, with the number of Bitcoin nodes being less than 3 per every 100000 Internet Users. On the contrary the Netherlands, Norway, Finland, and the Czech Republic have the highest adoption rates, more than 10 times higher than those showed by Brazil.

---

[2] However, as we explain in Sect. 3.3, the number of Bitcoin nodes does not map directly with the number of Bitcoin users, so the adoption rates have to be interpreted accordingly.

Table 1. Discovered nodes by country of origin

Country	# of Bitcoin nodes (37 days)	# of Bitcoin nodes (1st day)	# of Internet users [15]	Bitcoin node rate (per 100.000)
United States	145.495	24.621	254.295.536	9.68
China	172.662	16.700	568.192.066	2.94
Germany	80.067	7.695	68.296.919	11.27
United Kingdom	43.369	6.849	54.861.245	12.48
Russian Federation	66.705	6.848	75.926.004	9.02
Canada	23.308	4.664	29.760.764	15.67
Netherlands	16.490	4.070	15.559.488	26.16
France	17.249	2.752	54.473.474	5.05
Australia	15.239	2.364	18.129.727	13.04
Poland	19.242	2.265	24.969.935	9.07
Spain	14.303	1.726	33.870.948	5.10
Ukraine	13.606	1.688	15.115.820	11.17
Italy	17.098	1.572	35.531.527	4.42
Brazil	16.452	1.476	99.357.737	1.49
Czech Republic	6.019	1.403	76.32.975	18.38
Taiwan	16.335	1.375	17.656.414	7.79
Sweden	7.958	1.366	8.557.561	15.96
Norway	4.036	1.016	4.471.907	22.72
Switzerland	5.463	933	6.752.540	13.82
Finland	4.692	901	4.789.266	18.81
Japan	6.631	843	100.684.474	0.84
Austria	7.012	828	6.657.992	12.44
Belgium	5.810	726	8.559.449	8.48
Argentina	5.863	663	23.543.412	2.82
Hong Kong	4.917	648	5.207.762	12.44
...	...	...	...	...
Anguilla	1	0	9.133	0.00
Burundi	1	0	128.799	0.00
Cape Verde	1	0	181.905	0.00
Dominica	1	0	40.349	0.00
Equatorial Guinea	1	0	162.202	0.00
Samoa	1	0	25.111	0.00
Sao Tome & Principe	1	0	39.515	0.00
Timor-Leste	1	0	10.461	0.00
Others (180 countries)	136619	15483	-	-
Total	872648	111475	-	-

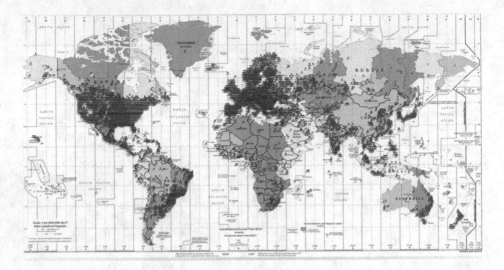

Fig. 1. Geolocation of discovered nodes

We have also used the IP geolocation service to plot the origin of the discovered nodes over a map. Figure 1 shows a map with the estimated location of all discovered nodes. Interesting information can be extracted from the map: there are Bitcoin nodes all over the world, with very low populated areas and underdeveloped countries being almost the only exceptions; western Europe and US distribution of nodes is quite uniform, with some peaks located over the most populated areas. Moreover, the map also demonstrates that the sample we have collected is broad, that is, it is not limited to a specific part of the Bitcoin network.

4.2 Node Stability

The map offered information about the location of nodes and, in a rough sense, their amount. We have also started to study the behavior of the Bitcoin nodes in terms of stability, that is, given a node, we analyze if such P2P node is available during all the 37 days of network observation. Figure 2 provides such information, showing the number of nodes still available after successive days of data collection. Notice that most of them are not connected more than the first five consecutive days and, at the end of the period, only 5769 nodes remain (which represents only a 0.66 % of the discovered ones). These 5769 nodes were permanently connected during all 37 days.

4.3 Information Propagation Analysis

In this section, we present the results of the information propagation analysis. Using the modified Bitcoin P2P Network Sniffer, we listened to various nodes of

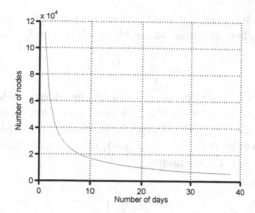

Fig. 2. Number of nodes in the intersection of the snapshots (for the 37 days)

the Bitcoin network, storing the transactions and blocks being broadcast through the network together with a timestamp signaling the exact moment when each of the nodes sent the information.

Block Propagation. Block propagation data consists on 492793 block copies representing 11663 different unique blocks. This data was captured listening to 1377 nodes during a period of 118 h (around 5 days). The data as captured is, however, very noisy. Note that if we take into account that the theoretical block production rate is 6 blocks per hour, the total number of blocks produced during this period of time should be around 708, a number significantly different from the mentioned 11663 blocks. The reason is that we receive copies of some very old blocks. For instance, even when the propagation information was captured on January 2014, we received a block whose timestamp dated from May 31th, 2013. In order to filter all this noise, we focus the block propagation analysis on the blocks created during the sniffer listening time. When adding this restriction, we obtain 737 different blocks to work on, a number much closer to the theoretical 708.

Bitcoin blocks contain a specific field in their headers with the current timestamp. This field is filled by the miner who finish the proof-of-work by solving the cryptographical challenge needed to find the block. Since the network accepts a block as valid even if the timestamp does not exactly match the network time (block timestamp is considered valid if it is not set more than two hours in the future) [14], the miner has some degree of freedom when setting the block's timestamp.

Once a miner has found a block, the miner announces it to the network by sending inv messages with the block to all of their peers, who do the very same thing if they consider the block valid, and thus propagate the block through the network.

Let us denote by $t_{\text{stamp}}(B_i)$ the timestamp contained in the header of the block B_i. Given a passive node (*i.e.*, a sniffer) with n peers, we define the registration time $t_j^{\mathrm{reg}}(B_i)$ as the moment when the sniffer receives the block B_i from peer j, with $j = 1, \cdots, n$. Then, the first time a block B_i is seen by the passive node is $t_{\min}^{\mathrm{reg}}(B_i)$:

$$t_{\min}^{\mathrm{reg}}(B_i) = \min_{\forall j}\{t_j^{\mathrm{reg}}(B_i)\}$$

Since the miners can set the timestamp of the block header, $t_{\mathrm{stamp}}(B_i)$, we analyzed the differences between the aforementioned timestamp and the first time we receive a block, $t_{\min}(B_i)$. We were specially interested in detecting, on one hand, if the network is synchronized and, on the other hand, if miners were blatantly adjusting block timestamps.

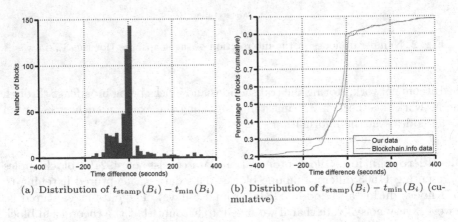

(a) Distribution of $t_{\mathrm{stamp}}(B_i) - t_{\min}(B_i)$

(b) Distribution of $t_{\mathrm{stamp}}(B_i) - t_{\min}(B_i)$ (cumulative)

Fig. 3. Distribution of $t_{\mathrm{stamp}}(B_i) - t_{\min}(B_i)$

Figure 3 shows the distribution of $t_{\mathrm{stamp}}(B_i) - t_{\min}^{\mathrm{reg}}(B_i)$ for the collected blocks, with the blue line representing the data we collected. Most of the times the difference is around 0. This is what is expected for a synchronized network with low propagation delays and where all peers well-behave. Note that more than 80 % of samples are negative, meaning that we receive the block after it is allegedly created. Positive samples illustrate that we receive a block before its header's timestamp, which indicates an altered block timestamp, either because the network time of the miner is notably different from ours, or either because the miner is intentionally modifying the block timestamp. There are around 10 % of blocks showing a positive difference less than 50 s, and another 10 % of blocks showing higher positive differences.

For the sake of comparing the data we collected with other external data, we also used the blockchain info API[3] to query for their reception time of each of the blocks. The results are presented in green in Fig. 3, where it can be seen that they are quite similar to ours. When the time difference is higher than -80 s, we

---

[3] Blockchain.info is a web page that offers information about Bitcoin blocks and transactions. They have a public API that allows to query for specific information. We used the API to obtain their *received_time* for each of the blocks.

receive the blocks a little faster than blockchain.info. However, when the time difference is lower than $-80\,\mathrm{s}$, their time difference is much lower. This may be a consequence of our shorter listening time, that make us receive copies of old blocks. Regarding the highest positive time difference, it is 7212 for our data and 7202 for blockchain.info data.

In a similar way than with the minimum registration time, we can define the last time the sniffer receives a block, $t_{\max}^{\mathrm{reg}}(B_i)$, as:

$$t_{\max}^{\mathrm{reg}}(B_i) = \max_{\forall j}\{t_j^{\mathrm{reg}}(B_i)\}$$

We can then define the observable propagation delay for block B_i as:

$$\Delta(B_i) = t_{\max}^{\mathrm{reg}}(B_i) - t_{\min}^{\mathrm{reg}}(B_i)$$

Figure 4 shows the observable propagation delay for blocks. One can appreciate that 50 % of the blocks are propagated in less than 17 min, but the rest of the nodes take a huge amount of time to get to all listened nodes. However, note that we are using the last time we receive a block to do these computations, so if only one node sends us a copy of a block with high delay, it is enough to set that block's $\Delta(B_i)$ to a huge number. The best propagation time was as low as $52\,\mathrm{s}$.

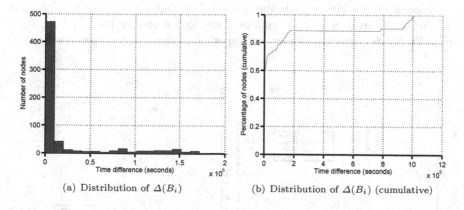

(a) Distribution of $\Delta(B_i)$ (b) Distribution of $\Delta(B_i)$ (cumulative)

Fig. 4. Distribution of $\Delta(B_i)$ for blocks

In order to try to better understand how the information is propagated through the network, we define the vector $T^{\mathrm{reg}}(B_i)$ as the vector containing all the registration times for a block, $t_j^{\mathrm{reg}}(B_i)$, in an increasing order (from the earliest to the latest):

$$T^{\mathrm{reg}}(B_i) = [T_1^{\mathrm{reg}}(B_i), \cdots, T_n^{\mathrm{reg}}(B_i)]$$

with

$$T_k^{\mathrm{reg}}(B_i) = t_j^{\mathrm{reg}}(B_i), \; \forall k \in [1, n]$$

for some peer j such that

$$T_{k-1}^{\mathrm{reg}}(B_i) \leq T_k^{\mathrm{reg}}(B_i) \leq T_{k+1}^{\mathrm{reg}}(B_i)$$

Then, we can study how information is propagated through the network by analyzing how much time is needed to get to 25 %, 50 %, 75 %, and 90 % of the nodes we were listening. Each of the percentages corresponds to a different position of the above described vector, specifically:

$$\Delta^{25\,\%}(B_i) = T_{278}^{\mathrm{reg}}(B_i) - t_{\mathrm{min}}^{\mathrm{reg}}(B_i) = T_{278}^{\mathrm{reg}}(B_i) - T_1^{\mathrm{reg}}(B_i)$$

$$\Delta^{50\,\%}(B_i) = T_{557}^{\mathrm{reg}}(B_i) - t_{\mathrm{min}}^{\mathrm{reg}}(B_i) = T_{557}^{\mathrm{reg}}(B_i) - T_1^{\mathrm{reg}}(B_i)$$

$$\Delta^{75\,\%}(B_i) = T_{836}^{\mathrm{reg}}(B_i) - t_{\mathrm{min}}^{\mathrm{reg}}(B_i) = T_{836}^{\mathrm{reg}}(B_i) - T_1^{\mathrm{reg}}(B_i)$$

$$\Delta^{90\,\%}(B_i) = T_{1003}^{\mathrm{reg}}(B_i) - t_{\mathrm{min}}^{\mathrm{reg}}(B_i) = T_{1003}^{\mathrm{reg}}(B_i) - T_1^{\mathrm{reg}}(B_i)$$

Figure 5(a) shows the time needed for the blocks to propagate to a specific percentage of the listened nodes (25 %, 50 %, 75 %, and 90 %). We can appreciate that for 70 % of the blocks it takes less than 84 s to reach 25 % of the nodes. However, just 38 % of the blocks get to 50 % of the nodes in that very same time, 6 % of the blocks get to 75 % of the nodes, and less than 1 % of the blocks get to 90 % of the nodes. Note that, for some blocks, we do not receive their copies from every node that we are connected to. This may happen because the node disconnects during our listening period. We consider the registration time of a block B_i from peer j to be infinite if we do not receive the block B_i from peer j. Therefore, the graph shows an upper bound over the propagation times.

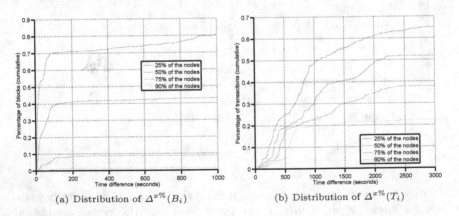

(a) Distribution of $\Delta^{x\,\%}(B_i)$ (b) Distribution of $\Delta^{x\,\%}(T_i)$

Fig. 5. Distribution of $\Delta^{25\,\%}$, $\Delta^{50\,\%}$, $\Delta^{75\,\%}$, and $\Delta^{90\,\%}$ for blocks and transactions

Finally, we studied if there is any correlation between the size of the block and the time needed to propagate the block through the network. In order to do so, we compute different correlation metrics between the size of the block, in bytes, and the time needed to propagate the block to the 25 % of the nodes of

Table 2. Number of transaction and blocks first received by each node

Node id	# of blocks	% of blocks	Node id	# of transactions	% of transactions
1	80	10.85 %	125	20695	29.46 %
2	63	8.55 %	126	7990	11.37 %
3	47	6.38 %	7	5815	8.28 %
4	42	5.70 %	10	3075	4.38 %
5	36	4.88 %	3	2285	3.25 %
6	35	4.75 %	11	1688	2.40 %
7	34	4.61 %	23	1521	2.17 %
8	28	3.80 %	12	1443	2.05 %
9	21	2.85 %	9	1138	1.62 %
10	21	2.85 %	19	964	1.37 %
11	18	2.44 %	35	818	1.16 %
12	15	2.04 %	127	655	0.93 %
13	15	2.04 %	128	602	0.86 %
14	14	1.90 %	129	564	0.80 %
15	11	1.49 %	103	560	0.80 %
16	10	1.36 %	130	530	0.75 %
17	9	1.22 %	131	475	0.68 %
18	8	1.09 %	132	436	0.62 %
19	7	0.95 %	83	431	0.61 %
20	7	0.95 %	133	413	0.59 %
Total (sum of the 20 best ranked IPs)	521	70.69 %		52098	74.16 %
Total (overall collected data)	737	100 %	-	70254	100 %

the network. The obtained Pearson correlation coefficient is 0.0172, which is a positive but low value, thus indicating that there is no strong linear correlation between the two variables. However, rank correlation coefficients, that capture the degree of similarity between the rankings of the two variables, present much higher values. The Kendall's tau correlation coefficient for these same variables is 0.3617, and the Spearman's rho coefficient is 0.4409. This indicates that there exists a correlation between the two variables, size and propagation, but that this correlation is not linear.

Transaction Propagation. In a similar way than with blocks and using the same notation, we also analyzed the propagation time of transactions over the P2P network. Transactions are broadcast through the network in a similar way than blocks, although there exists some differences on the client behavior for the two structures.

Figure 5(b) shows the time needed for the transactions to propagate to a specific percentage of the listened nodes (25 %, 50 %, 75 %, and 90 %). Transaction relaying seems to be slower than block propagation. While 50 % of blocks were broadcast to 25 % of the nodes in less than 22 s, 17 min are needed to relay 50 % of the transactions to the 25 % of the nodes. Apart from this scaling factor, blocks and transactions are propagated in a similar way, with most of them being quite fast to get to 25 % of the nodes, but really slow to get to all of the nodes. Note that if a transaction is sent to the network and it is not included in any block for a period of time, the client may try to send it again, producing latter retransmissions of the same transaction and thus an increase on $\Delta(T_i)$.

Transaction vs Block Propagation. We also studied if the first nodes that relay transactions and blocks are always the same, that is, we analyzed which nodes were sending us transactions and blocks that we do not have seen previously. Table 2 shows the nodes that are more often relaying transactions and blocks for the first time. The first thing to notice is that although we are listening to more than 1300 different nodes, the best 20 nodes (in terms of transaction and block propagation speed) are responsible for first relaying more than 70 % of both blocks and transactions. It is also interesting to note that there is some overlap between the nodes first relaying blocks and the nodes first relaying transactions: 7 of the best nodes in terms of first relaying blocks are also between the best 20 nodes in terms of first relaying transactions. However, the nodes that are first relaying most of the transactions (nodes 125 and 126) have not relayed any block for the first time.

5   Conclusion and Further Work

Bitcoin is a virtual currency that has been rapidly adopted due to its security robustness, but also for its anonymity and decentralized properties. In this paper we have presented an analysis of the collected data of the decentralized P2P network that supports its information transmission. Data shows that the Bitcoin P2P network is homogeneously spread all over the world, with some exceptions on very low populated areas and underdeveloped countries. Information about node stability shows that there exist a core of around 6000 nodes that are connected during the whole listening period, that is, 37 days. Propagation data shows that the general latency of the P2P Bitcoin network is acceptable for normal nodes but, in some cases, it could be too high for miners, causing them to be working on already mined blocks due to the network delay.

The collection process performed so far, the variety of data collected, and this first brief (due to space constraints) analysis of the information presented in this paper allows us to draw some guidelines for further research. For instance, a network topology analysis could be performed in order to plot the main topological structure of the P2P Network. On the other hand, a more in depth information propagation analysis can be performed by increasing the amount of data collected and the number of connections made to listen to the network.

Acknowledgments. This work was partially supported by a student grant of the Master in Security of Information and Communication Technologies (MISTIC), at the Universitat Autónoma de Barcelona (UAB), and by the Spanish Government projects, TIN2011-27076-C03-02 CO-PRIVACY, TIN2010-15764 N-KHRONOUS, CONSOLIDER INGENIO 2010 CSD2007-0004 ARES, and grant FPU-AP2010-0078.

References

1. Androulaki, E., Karame, G.O., Roeschlin, M., Scherer, T., Capkun, S.: Evaluating user privacy in bitcoin. In: Sadeghi, A.-R. (ed.) FC 2013. LNCS, vol. 7859, pp. 34–51. Springer, Heidelberg (2013). http://dx.doi.org/10.1007/978-3-642-39884-1_4
2. Babaioff, M., Dobzinski, S., Oren, S., Zohar, A.: On bitcoin and red balloons. In: Proceedings of the 13th Association for Computing Machinery (ACM) Conference on Electronic Commerce, EC 2012, pp. 56–73. ACM, New York (2012). http://doi.acm.org/10.1145/2229012.2229022
3. Bamert, T., Decker, C., Elsen, L., Wattenhofer, R., Welten, S.: Have a snack, pay with bitcoins. In: Proceedings of the IEEE International Conference on Peer-to-Peer Computing (P2P) 2013, Trento, Italy (2013)
4. Barber, S., Boyen, X., Shi, E., Uzun, E.: Bitter to better–how to make bitcoin a better currency. In: Keromytis, A.D. (ed.) FC 2012. LNCS, vol. 7397, pp. 399–414. Springer, Heidelberg (2012). http://dx.doi.org/10.1007/978-3-642-32946-3_29
5. Castro, S.: Bitcoin P2P network sniffer. https://github.com/sebicas/bitcoin-sniffer
6. Decker, C., Wattenhofer, R.: Information propagation in the bitcoin network. In: Proceedings of the IEEE International Conference on Peer-to-Peer Computing (P2P) 2013, Trento, Italy, (2013)
7. Geoplugin development team: Geoplugin. http://www.geoplugin.com/
8. Karame, G.O., Androulaki, E., Capkun, S.: Double-spending fast payments in bitcoin. In: Proceedings of the 2012 Association for Computing Machinery (ACM) Conference on Computer and Communications Security, CCS 2012, pp. 906–917. ACM, New York (2012). http://doi.acm.org/10.1145/2382196.2382292
9. Meiklejohn, S., Pomarole, M., Jordan, G., Levchenko, K., McCoy, D., Voelker, G.M., Savage, S.: A fistful of bitcoins: Characterizing payments among men with no names. In: Proceedings of the 2013 Conference on Internet Measurement Conference, IMC 2013, pp. 127–140. ACM, New York (2013). http://doi.acm.org/10.1145/2504730.2504747
10. Nakamoto, S., Andresen, G.e.a.: Bitcoin standard client. https://github.com/bitcoin/bitcoin/
11. Ober, M., Katzenbeisser, S., Hamacher, K.: Structure and anonymity of the bitcoin transaction graph. Future Internet 5(2), 237–250 (2013). http://www.mdpi.com/1999-5903/5/2/237
12. Reid, F., Harrigan, M.: An analysis of anonymity in the bitcoin system. In: Altshuler, Y., Elovici, Y., Cremers, A.B., Aharony, N., Pentland, A. (eds.) Security and Privacy in Social Networks, pp. 197–223. Springer, New York (2013). http://dx.doi.org/10.1007/978-1-4614-4139-7_10

13. Ron, D., Shamir, A.: Quantitative analysis of the full bitcoin transaction graph.
    In: Sadeghi, A.-R. (ed.) FC 2013. LNCS, vol. 7859, pp. 6–24. Springer, Heidelberg
    (2013). http://dx.doi.org/10.1007/978-3-642-39884-1_2
14. The Bitcoin Wiki: Bitcoin protocol rules. https://en.bitcoin.it/wiki/Protocol_rules
15. International Telecommunications Union: Percentage of individuals using the inter-
    net 2000–2012, June 2013. http://www.itu.int/en/ITU-D/Statistics/Documents/
    statistics/2013/Individuals_Internet_2000-2012.xls

Improving Digital Currencies

Fair Two-Party Computations via Bitcoin Deposits

Marcin Andrychowicz[1], Stefan Dziembowski[1,2], Daniel Malinowski[1], and Łukasz Mazurek[1]($\boxtimes$)

[1] University of Warsaw, Warszawa, Poland
{marcin.andrychowicz,stefan.dziembowski,daniel.malinowski,
lukasz.mazurek}@crypto.edu.pl
[2] University of Rome La Sapienza, Roma, Italy

Abstract. We show how the Bitcoin currency system (with a small modification) can be used to obtain fairness in any two-party secure computation protocol in the following sense: if one party aborts the protocol after learning the output then the other party gets a financial compensation (in bitcoins). One possible application of such protocols is the fair contract signing: each party is forced to complete the protocol, or to pay to the other one a fine.

We also show how to link the output of this protocol to the Bitcoin currency. More precisely: we show a method to design secure two-party protocols for functionalities that result in a "forced" financial transfer from one party to the other.

Our protocols build upon the ideas of our recent paper "Secure Multiparty Computations on Bitcoin" (Cryptology ePrint Archive, Report 2013/784). Compared to that paper, our results are more general, since our protocols allow to compute any function, while in the previous paper we concentrated only on some specific tasks (commitment schemes and lotteries). On the other hand, as opposed to "Secure Multiparty Computations on Bitcoin", to obtain security we need to modify the Bitcoin specification so that the transactions are "non-malleable" (we discuss this concept in more detail in the paper).

1 Introduction

In our recent paper [2] we put forward a new concept dubbed "secure multiparty computations (MPCs) on Bitcoin". On a high level the idea of this concept is as follows. Recall that the MPCs [20,29] are protocols that allow a group of mutually distrusting parties to "emulate" a trusted third party functionality in a secure way. Examples of such functionalities include lotteries, auctions, voting schemes and many more. It is known since 1980s that for any

This work was supported by the WELCOME/2010-4/2 grant founded within the framework of the EU Innovative Economy (National Cohesion Strategy) Operational Programme.

© IFCA/Springer-Verlag Berlin Heidelberg 2014
R. Böhme et al. (Eds.): FC 2014 Workshops, LNCS 8438, pp. 105 121, 2014.
DOI: 10.1007/978-3-662-44774-1_8

efficiently-computable functionality there exists an efficient protocol that emulates it, assuming that the majority of the participants is honest and that certain computational problems are intractable. If there is no honest majority (in particular: if there are just two parties and one of them is cheating), then such protocols also exist, but in general they do not provide *fairness*, i.e. a dishonest party can prevent the other parties from learning their outputs, after she learned it herself [10,17].

Despite of their great importance both to the theory and applications, the MPC protocols suffer from some inherent limitations. The first one is the above-mentioned lack on fairness when the majority of the participants is dishonest. The second is that the standard security definition of MPCs does not ensure that the parties provide the inputs to the computations in an honest way, and that they respect the outcome. For example, in most of the settings it is clearly impossible to guarantee in a cryptographic way that a bidder in an auction has enough money to pay his bid, or that the losing party will accept the outcome of the voting procedure. Bitcoin, due to its fully distributed nature, and the fact that the list of transactions is publicly known, gives an attractive opportunity to go beyond this barrier. In [2] we discuss this idea, and provide some examples of how it can be used. The main technical contribution of that paper is a protocol for a multiparty lottery with a very strong security property: each honest party can be sure that, once the game starts, it will be fair, and she will be paid the money in case she wins. This happens even if the other parties actively cheat, and in particular even if some (or all) of them abort the protocol prematurely. In order to achieve it we use a mechanism that financially penalizes a party that does not follow the protocol.

Our main tool is a special type of a "Bitcoin-based timed commitment scheme", that has the following non-standard property: a committer has to pay a "deposit" during the commitment phase, that he gets it back only if he opens his commitment within some specific time. Although the main application of this commitment scheme is the lottery protocol, it can actually also be used to obtain fairness in protocols where the inputs and outputs do not concern Bitcoin. One of the questions left open in [2] is to construct protocols for more general functionalities than the commitment scheme or the lottery.

Our Contribution. In this paper we show that a small modification of the Bitcoin specification would make it possible to construct protocols for a very general class of functionalities in a two-party settings. Roughly speaking (for more details see Sect. 3), for our protocols to work we need to assume that the transactions are "non-malleable" in the following sense: we assume that each transaction is identified by the hash of its simplified version (also called the "body" of a transaction), instead of the hash on the *complete* transaction (i.e. the body and the input scripts) as it is done currently in Bitcoin. Assuming this modification, we show how to achieve fairness in any two-party protocol in the following sense. Before learning the output of the computation, each party has to pay some deposit. She is guaranteed to get this money back as long as she behaves honestly until the very end of the protocol, i.e. until the other party learns the output. If she misbehaves then her money is given to the other party.

In practice it will make sense to use this protocol if the potential gain from a premature termination is lower than the deposit that the party pays. As the potential applications of our protocols let us mention the *contract signing* problem, which has been extensively studied in cryptography since 1980s [6,12,14,18]. Informally, the challenge in this line of work is to design the protocols where two parties simultaneously sign a document M in a fair way, i.e. it should be impossible for one party, say Alice, to obtain Bob's signature on M without Bob obtaining Alice's signature on M (and vice-versa). It was shown by Even and Yacobi [18] that this task is in general impossible to achieve, and since then there has been a substantial effort to overcome this impossibility result in various ways (e.g. by assuming an existence of a trusted third party). Since obviously a signing procedure can be modeled as a two-party functionality, hence one can use our protocol to achieve fairness. If the value of the contract is lower than the deposit paid by each party, then clearly the parties will have no incentive to cheat. Moreover, if one party, say Alice, cheats then Bob will earn Alice's deposit (plus he will get his own deposit back), which will compensate his loses resulting from the fact that Alice cheated during the contract signing protocol. Of course, our protocols can be used in several other applications that rely on a fair exchange of secrets, such as certified e-mail systems [1,4,31] or non-repudiation protocols [30].

We also show how to link the outputs of our protocols to the Bitcoin money in the following sense (for more information see Sect. 6). The output of the emulated functionality can contain instructions of a form "Alice sends d ฿ to Bob" or "Bob sends d ฿ to Alice" (where "฿" is the Bitcoin currency symbol). Our protocol will enforce that these transfers are indeed performed. Of course, this holds only if the parties conduct the protocol until the very end, but again, if one party decides to abort prematurely then her deposit will be paid to the other party. Hence, if this deposit is larger than d then it clearly makes no economic sense to abort. Of course, one example of a such a functionality is the lottery protocol. We would like to stress, however, that our result does not imply the result of [2], since the protocols of [2] work on the current version of Bitcoin protocol (without any modification).

One can, of course, imagine several other applications of our protocols. For example, one can construct protocols for buying digital goods that can be specified by any poly-time computable functions $\pi : \{0,1\}^* \to \{true, false\}$. More precisely: imagine that Alice promises Bob that she will pay him 1 ฿ if he sends her a file $m \in \{0,1\}^*$ such that $\pi(m) = true$, however she does not want to reveal this function neither to Bob nor to the public. Then, we can construct such protocol that emulates the following functionality: the input of Alice is π and the input of Bob is m. If $\pi(m) = true$ then the output is m and a "forced transfer of 1 ฿ from Alice to Bob", otherwise the output is $\perp$. Such π can be, e.g., a function that checks if m is a secret that concerns a certain person.[1]

On a technical level, our protocols are based on a new variant of a Bitcoin-based timed commitment scheme that we call the "simultaneous commitment" and denote SCS. It can be viewed as an extension of the Bitcoin-based commitment scheme from [2] described above. The main difference is that it forces both users to *simultaneously* commit to their secrets. In other words, the commitment of each party is valid (and she is forced to open it by some time t) only if the other party made her corresponding commitment at the same time.

Related Work. As described above our paper builds upon the ideas from our previous paper [2], and hence most of the work relevant to that paper is also relevant to this one. Usage of Bitcoin to create a secure and fair two-player lottery has been independently proposed by Back and Bentov in [5]. Similarly to [2], their protocol makes use of the time-locked transactions, but the purpose they are used for is slightly different. Their protocol uses time-locks to get the deposit back if the protocol is interrupted, while this paper and [2] use time-locks to make a financial compensation to an honest party, whenever the other party misbehaves.

Usage of timed-commitments to achieve fairness in MPC has been already proposed in a number of papers, e.g. [8,19,25], but this line of research uses a completely different approach from ours. It is based on a gradual release of information and if the protocol is interrupted prematurely than both parties can reconstruct the result with a huge computational effort. The fairness of two-party computation has been also studied by Gordon et al. [17], who showed that complete fairness can be achieved for some functions being computed, e.g. Boolean and/or, but not xor. In contrast, our construction works for an arbitrary function.

Improvements to Bitcoin have been suggested in an important work of Barber et al. [16] who study various security aspects of Bitcoin and Miers et al. [15] who propose a Bitcoin system with provable anonymity. The idea to use some concepts from the MPC literature appeared already in Sect. 7.1 of [16] where the authors construct a secure "mixer", that allows two parties to securely "mix" their coins in order to obtain unlinkability of the transactions. They also construct commitment schemes with time-locks, however some important details are different, in particular, in the normal execution of the scheme the money is at the end transferred to the receiver. Also, the main motivation of this work is different: the goal of [16] is to fix an existing problem in Bitcoin ("linkability"), while our goal is to use Bitcoin to perform tasks that are hard (or impossible) to perform by other methods.

Commitment schemes and zero-knowledge proofs in the context of the Bitcoin were already considered in [9], however, the construction and its applications are

---

[1] A real-life example of such situation is the recent case when the German tax authorities paid 4 million euro to an anonymous informant for a CD containing information about the German tax evaders with bank accounts in Switzerland [13].

different—the main idea of [9] is to use the Bitcoin system as a replacement of a trusted third party in time-stamping. The notion of "deposits" has already been used in Bitcoin (see [26], Example 1), but the application described there is different: the "deposit" is a method for a party with no reputation to prove that she is not a spambot by temporarily sacrificing some of her money.

The Bitcoin wiki "Contracts page" [26] contains several interesting multiparty protocols, and in some sense our work can be viewed as an effort to extend the set of possible types of contracts. We note that the main features that distinguishes our work from most of them is (1) we do not want to rely on any trusted third parties (like the "mediators") and (2) the focus of our protocols is to protect the input privacy.

The problem of the malleability of the transactions has been noticed before and described in [28]. Malleability is a problem for most of the protocols using time-locks (e.g. [5,27]) and Examples 1, 5, and 7 in [26], but is usually not even mentioned, probably because it is believed that it will be eliminated in the future versions of the Bitcoin protocol. In contrast, our lottery protocol from [2] is not susceptible to the malleability problem. We also note that in our subsequent work [3] we managed to solve the problem of constructing the simultaneous commitment schemes in the standard Bitcoin (without any modifications), at a cost of making the protocol more complicated. Nevertheless, we think that our modification proposal from this paper still makes sense, as it allows to construct simpler simultaneous commitment protocols, and may be useful also in other contexts.

2   A Description of Bitcoin

We assume reader's familiarity with the basic principles of the Bitcoin. Let us only briefly recall that the Bitcoin currency system consists of *addresses* and *transactions* between them. An address is simply a public key pk (technically an address is a *hash* of pk). We will frequently denote key pairs using the capital letters (e.g. A). We will also use the following convention: if $A = (sk, pk)$ then $\mathsf{sig}_A(m)$ denotes a signature on a message m computed with sk and $\mathsf{ver}_A(m, \sigma)$ denotes the result (true or false) of the verification of a signature σ on message m with respect to the public key pk.

Each Bitcoin transaction can have multiple inputs and outputs. Inputs of a transaction T_x are listed as triples $(y_1, a_1, \sigma_1), \ldots, (y_n, a_n, \sigma_n)$, where each y_i is a hash of some previous transaction T_{y_i} (our proposal, described in Sect. 3, is to change it, but for a moment let us stick to the current version of the system), a_i is an index of the output of T_{y_i} (we say that T_x *redeems the* a_i-*th output of* T_{y_i}) and σ_i is called an *input-script* The outputs of a transaction are presented as a list of pairs $(v_1, \pi_1), \ldots, (v_m, \pi_m)$, where each v_i specifies some amount of coins (called the *value of the i-th output of* T_x) and π_i is an *output-script*. A transaction can also have a time-lock t, meaning that it is valid only if time t is reached. Hence, altogether transaction's most general form is:

$T_x = ((y_1, a_1, \sigma_1), \ldots, (y_n, a_n, \sigma_n), (v_1, \pi_1), \ldots, (v_m, \pi_m), t)$. The *body of T_x^2* is equal to T_x without the input-scripts, i.e.: $((y_1, a_1), \ldots, (y_n, a_n), (v_1, \pi_1), \ldots, (v_m, \pi_m), t)$, and denoted by $[T_x]$. One of the most useful properties of Bitcoin is that the users have flexibility in defining the condition on how the transaction T_x can be redeemed. This is achieved by the input- and the output-scripts. One can think of an output-script as a description of a function whose output is Boolean. A transaction T_x defined above is valid if for *every $i = 1, \ldots, n$* we have that $\pi_i'([T_x], \sigma_i)^3$ evaluates to true, where π_i' is the output-script corresponding to the a_i-th output of T_{y_i}. Another conditions that need to be satisfied are that the time t has already passed and $v_1 + \cdots + v_m \leq v_1' + \cdots + v_n'$ where each v_i' is the value of the a_i-th output of T_{y_i}. The scripts are written in the Bitcoin scripting language.

We will present the transactions as boxes. The redeeming of transactions will be indicated with arrows (cf. e.g. Fig. 1). The transactions where the input script is a signature, and the output script is a verification algorithm are the most common type of transactions and are called *standard transactions*. The address against which the verification is done will be called a *receiver* of this transaction. Currently some miners accept only such transactions. However, there exist other ones that do accept the non-standard (also called *strange*) transactions, one example being a big mining pool called *Eligius*.

We use the security model defined in [2]. For the lack of space we only sketch it here. We assume that the parties are connected by an insecure channel and have access to the Bitcoin chain, which is the only "trusted component" in the system. We assume that each party can access the current contents of the block chain, and post messages on it. Let $\mathsf{max_{BB}}$ be the is maximal possible delay between broadcasting the transaction and including it in the block chain. We do not assume that this communication is private. For simplicity we also assume that the transaction fees are zero, but our model and security statements can be easily modified to take into account the non-zero fees.

3   Bitcoin Improvement Proposal

One of the problems with constructing multi-party protocols using Bitcoin is the "malleability" of transactions. This problem has been noticed before by the Bitcoin community [28] as it concerns several Bitcoin protocols that use the advanced features of the scripting language. Essentially, the problem is that, given a valid transaction T, it is possible for everyone to construct a different valid transaction T', which is functionally equivalent to T, but has a different hash. The malleability of transactions comes from the fact, that a hash of a transaction is computed over the whole transaction including its input scripts. On the other hand, signatures are computed only over the body of the

---

[2] In the original Bitcoin documentation this is called "simplified T_x".

[3] Technically in Bitcoin $[T_x]$ is not directly passed as an argument to π_i'. We adopt this convention to make the exposition clearer.

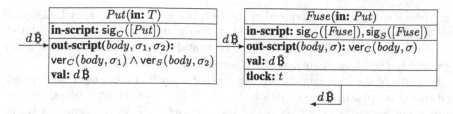

Fig. 1. The graph of transactions for a situation when a user locks d ฿. This is an exemplary situation when the problem of malleability arises. C and S denote the pairs of keys hold respectively by the client and the server. t is a moment of time, when the user can take his deposit back. T denotes an unredeemed transaction with value d ฿, which can be redeemed with key C.

transaction, which means that they do not cover the input scripts[4]. Therefore, one can tweak an input script in a way that does not change its functionality (e.g. by adding *push* and *pop* operations[5]) and create a transaction, which is also correct (the signatures are still valid as the input scripts are not signed), and functionally equivalent to the original transaction, yet its hash is different.

To understand why malleability of transactions may be a problem consider a situation, when a client wants to prove to a server that he is not a spambot by locking (making unspendable for a particular amount of time) some amount of bitcoins[6]. To achieve this, the client should create a transaction such that he can not redeem it on his own. But he has to be sure, that he will eventually get his money back after some time. This could be resolved by using a transaction with a time-lock (see Fig. 1 for a graph of transactions)—the client first creates a transaction *Put* spending his money, which can be redeemed only by a transaction signed by him and the server (so they can agree to return the deposit to the client at any time). Then he sends the hash of this transaction to the server and the server returns a transaction *Fuse* with a signature of the server on it[7]—this transaction sends back the deposit to the client after some time. So now the client may broadcast the first transaction, and after some time he may use the *Fuse* transaction to get back his deposit. This is exactly where the problem of malleability arises: if an adversary sees the transaction *Put* after it is broadcast, but before it is included in the block chain (as the transactions are broadcast in a peer-to-peer network), he can create and broadcast a transaction

---

[4] The reason is that it is impossible to construct a signature, in such a way, that it is a part of the message being signed.

[5] In this paper we usually treat input scripts as arguments for the corresponding output scripts. In reality, however, they are scripts in Bitcoin scripting language, which are supposed to push arguments for an output script on the stack.

[6] To read more about such deposits see [26].

[7] The server signs a transactions *Fuse* without seeing the transaction *Put* and a malicious client could try to send a hash of an existing transaction instead of *Put*. Therefore, the server should use a fresh key every time to prevent itself from being tricked into signing a transaction spending some other transaction of its to the client.

Put', which is functionally equivalent to *Put*, but has a different hash. Then, if *Put'* is included in the block chain first, the original *Put* becomes invalidated. As a result the *Fuse* will not be correct (it contains a hash of *Put*, which never appeared in the block chain), so the client may lose his money.

A source of the malleability problem is that a hash of a transaction depends on its input scripts. In some situation this dependence is itself a problem, because we may not know the input scripts of the transaction T while signing a transaction redeeming T. In next section we present a possible solution for these problems. It requires a small modification of the Bitcoin specification. We believe that this modification could be implemented in the future in Bitcoin. We discuss why it does not decrease the security of Bitcoin.

Our Modification. In the current version of Bitcoin protocol, each transaction contains a hash of the transaction it spends. That hash is computed over the *whole* transaction. We propose to compute those hashes over the transaction without its input scripts (i.e. over the *body* of the transaction), so they would be computed in the same way the hashes for transactions' signatures are currently being computed. That means that the transaction would have the same hash value regardless of its input scripts.

Obviously with this modification, the malleability is not a problem. An adversary can still tweak the input script of an arbitrary transaction in the network and broadcast its modified version, but the hashes of both transactions—original and modified one—are identical, so it does not make any difference, which of them will be included in the block chain.

Additionally, with this modification it is possible to sign a chain of transactions even if we do not know the input scripts of some of them. The only thing, which is necessary to compute signatures are outputs (output scripts and values) and the hashes of the transactions redeemed by the first transaction in the chain. This may be useful in constructing more complex protocols.

Now consider, what in fact is changed with this modification. The input scripts are used only to show that the transaction is authorized to redeem the other transactions. So two correct transactions which differ only in the input scripts are equivalent—they prove in two different ways that the Bitcoin transfer is authorized. It is not possible that the block chain contains two such transactions. That is why the hash still uniquely identifies the redeemed transaction.[8]

4   Simultaneous Bitcoin-Based Timed Commitment Scheme

In this section we present a modification of the Bitcoin-based timed commitment scheme introduced in [2]. To make the paper self-contained we first recall the

---

[8] The only exception are the so-called *generation* transactions, which create new bitcoins and can have arbitrary input scripts (the script is called "coinbase" in this case). However, it is not difficult to ensure that each such transaction has a different hash, by using a new pair of keys for each generation.

original timed-commitment scheme $CS(C, d, t, s)$ of [2], and then we describe our modified scheme.

Timed-Commitments of [2]. Recall that a (standard) commitment scheme is a protocol between two parties: a committer C and a receiver R. The protocol contains of two phases. In the first one, called the *commitment phase*, C *commits* to some secret string s by interacting with R. What is important is that after this interaction s should remain secret (this is called the *hiding* property of the scheme). Then comes the *opening phase* in which C *opens* the commitment by interacting again with R, which results in R learning s. What we require is that a cheating C cannot "change his mind", in other words, once the commitment phase is over, there exists at most one value s that R will accept. This property is called *binding*. A simple commitment scheme can be constructed as follows. Let H be a hash function. To commit to a string s (of some fixed length) the committer selects a random string ρ, computes $s' = (s||\rho)$ and sends $H(s')$ to the receiver. If H is modeled as a random oracle, and ρ is sufficiently large (say: linear in the security parameter), then obviously $H(s')$ does not reveal any significant information about s (hence the commitment is hiding). To open the commitment, C sends s' to R. The binding property of this commitment scheme follows from the collision-resistance of H.

Several other commitment schemes have been constructed over the last 2 decades. One inherent problem with all of them is related to the fairness issue in the two-party computation protocols (see Sect. 1). Namely, there is no way to force C to open the commitment. This problem has negative consequences for several applications. Consider, e.g., a simple protocol in which two parties (call them again C and R) want to "flip a coin", i.e., to select a bit $b \leftarrow \{0, 1\}$ uniformly at random. A simple protocol of Blum [7] for this problem works as follows: (1) C commits to some random bit $c \leftarrow \{0, 1\}$, (2) R selects a random bit $r \leftarrow \{0, 1\}$ and sends it to C, (3) C opens his commitment, and the output of the protocol is computed as $b = c \oplus r$. This protocol is obviously secure, informally because the hiding property of the commitment scheme guarantees that R does not know c when he chooses r, and the binding property prevents C from changing c after he learned r. Unfortunately, there is no way to force R to complete Step (3) and to open the commitment. Hence, C he can make the protocol "crash" without producing the output, depending on what the output is.

As a remedy to this problem [2] propose to use Bitcoin in the following way. During the commitment phase the committer has to put aside a "deposit". Assume its value is $d \, \tilde{\textrm{B}}$, and it comes from an unredeemed standard transaction T, whose receiver is C. The committer gets his money back once he opens the commitment. If he does not open the commitment within some time t then the money can be claimed by the receiver. This is implemented using the Bitcoin scripts and time-locks on top of the hash-based commitment scheme described above. Let C and R be the respective key-pairs of C and R. The transactions used in this implementation are as follows (the scripts' arguments, which are omitted are denoted by $\perp$):

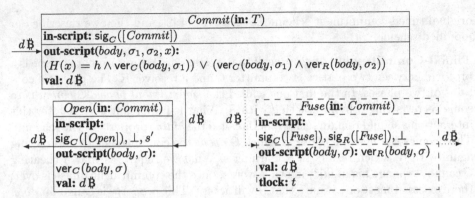

To commit to a secret s the committer first computes $s' = (s||\rho)$ (where ρ is a random string of some fixed length), and sets $h := H(s')$. He then creates the *Commit* transaction and posts it on the block chain. The role of this step is to publish h and to deposit the money. The committer also creates the body of the *Fuse* transaction with time lock set to some time t in the future, and sends it to R together with his signature on it. Hence, the only thing that is missing to obtain the complete *Fuse* transaction is the receiver's signature on the body. This, however, R can compute himself. Hence at the end of the commitment phase R holds a *Fuse* transaction. The purpose of *Fuse* is to allow the receiver to claim the money, if R did not open the commitment within time t.

In the opening phase the committer posts *Open* on the block chain. This has two consequences. Firstly, this reveals s' (and hence s), which is part of the input script. Secondly, it allows the committer to get his money back. Thanks to the way in which the scripts are created, this is actually the only way for him to get his money. If he does not do it by the time t, then R posts *Fuse* on the block chain and gets the committer's deposit.

It is easy to see how this timed-commitment scheme solves the problem of fairness in the coin-flipping protocol described above: if C did not open the commitment scheme on time then he is "punished" financially for this, and R gets a compensation. Unfortunately, this commitment scheme does not solve the fairness problem in general. This is because for the general two-party computation protocols we need something stronger. More precisely, the problem is that this commitment scheme forces the committer to reveal his secret (or to pay a fine), no matter how the other party behaves. To see why it is a problem, imagine two parties, called Alice and Bob holding secrets denoted respectively s_A and s_B. Suppose that the protocol instructs both of them to commit to their secrets and then to reveal them (in fact this is exactly the situation that we have in our two-party scheme in Sect. 5). If they just run two instantiations of the CS scheme, then one party, say Alice, can interrupt the protocol where she is the committer, after Bob has already made a commitment. In that case Bob will be forced to reveal his secret share or lose his deposit. Hence, it is important that both commitment schemes are executed *simultaneously*, i.e. it is not possible that as a result of the protocol one of the parties is committed to her secret and the other one is not. A construction of such a commitment scheme is one of our two main contributions and is presented below.

Simultaneous Bitcoin-Based Timed Commitment Scheme. The protocol is denoted by $\mathsf{SCS}(\mathsf{A}, \mathsf{B}, d, t)$, where A and B are the parties executing the protocol, d is the value of the deposits in $\mathsf{\ss}$, t is the timestamp—the parties should open the commitments before that time, and s_A, s_B are the secrets. We assume that A and B are the respective key pairs of A and B and the block chain contains unredeemed transactions T^A and T^B, both of a value d, whose receivers are A and B respectively. The protocol is depicted on Fig. 2. The commitment phase is denoted by $\mathsf{SCS.Commit}(\mathsf{A}, \mathsf{B}, d, t)$ and the opening phase is denoted by $\mathsf{SCS.Open}(\mathsf{A}, \mathsf{B}, d, t)$. Let α be the security parameter.

The security definition of the SCS protocol is very similar to the security definition of the CS protocol described above. We model the hash function H used in the protocol as a random oracle. We require that the commitment is hiding and binding. We allow a negligible (in α) error probabilities in both hiding and biding. The protocol can be interrupted during the commitment phase—in this case the parties do not lose any bitcoins and do not learn the other party's secret. The only difference between the CS protocol and the SCS protocol is that if the SCS protocol is not interrupted during the commitment phase, then *both* parties are committed. This means that an honest party can be sure that her opponent either reveals the secret by the time t or transfers $d\,\mathsf{\ss}$ to her. Moreover, it is guaranteed that the party which reveals a secret would get her deposit back. Again, we allow negligible probabilities that the above statements do not hold.

We construct the SCS protocol assuming the Bitcoin modification from Sect. 3. The detailed description of the SCS protocol is presented on Fig. 2. In SCS protocol we assume that both parties already know the hashes h_A and h_B of *both* secrets concatenated with some random strings ρ_A and ρ_B (resp.). More precisely: $h_A := H(s_A || \rho_A)$ and $h_B := H(s_B || \rho_B)$, where $\rho_A \leftarrow \{0,1\}^\alpha$ and $\rho_B \leftarrow \{0,1\}^\alpha$. The reason for this will become clear in Sect. 5. The idea behind the protocol is as follows. First the parties use the existing transactions T^A and T^B to construct the transaction *Commit*. The transaction *Commit* has two outputs—one is used to commit A to s_A and the other one to commit B to s_B. The first output can be claimed by A with revealing her secret or after time t by B. The latter option is technically achieved by signing at the very beginning of the protocol a transaction *Fuse^A*, which redeems *Commit*, can be claimed only by B and has a time-lock t. The second output of *Commit* is analogous. The proof of the following lemma appears in the extended version of this paper.

Lemma 1. *The* SCS *scheme from Fig. 2 is a simultaneous Bitcoin-based commitment scheme assuming the modification from Sect. 3.*

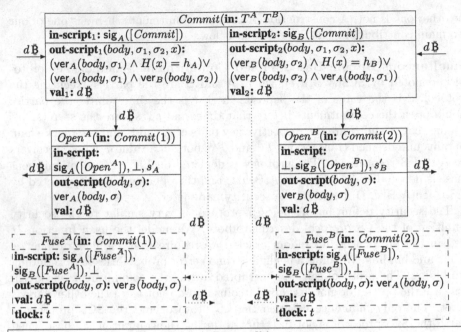

Pre-condition:

1. A holds the key pair A and B holds the key pair B.
2. A knows the secret s_A, B knows the secret s_B, both players know the hashes $h_A = H(s'_A)$ and $h_B = H(s'_B)$, where $s'_A := (s_A || \rho_A)$, $s'_B := (s_B || \rho_B)$, and $\rho_A, \rho_B \leftarrow \{0,1\}^\alpha$ are random strings known only to A and B respectively.
3. There are two unredeemed transactions T^A, T^B of value $d\mathcal{B}$, which can be redeemed with the keys A and B respectively.

The SCS.Commit(A, B, d, t) phase

1. Both players compute the body of the transaction $Commit$ using T^A and T^B as inputs.
2. Both players compute the bodies of the transactions $Fuse^A$ and $Fuse^B$ using appropriate outputs ($Commit(1)$ and $Commit(2)$ respectively) of the $Commit$ transaction. Then, they sign $Fuse^A$ and $Fuse^B$ and exchange the signatures.
3. A signs the transaction $Commit$ and sends the signature to B.
4. B signs the transaction $Commit$ and broadcasts it.
5. Both parties wait until the transaction $Commit$ is included in the block chain.
6. If the transaction $Commit$ does not appear on the block chain until time $t - 2\mathsf{max}_{\mathsf{BB}}$, where $\mathsf{max}_{\mathsf{BB}}$ is a maximal possible delay between broadcasting the transaction and including it in the block chain (what means that B did not perform Step. 4), then A immediately redeems the transaction T^A and quits the protocol. Analogously, if A did not send her signature to B until time $t - 2\mathsf{max}_{\mathsf{BB}}$, then B redeems the transaction T^B and quits the protocol.

The SCS.Open(A, B, d, t) phase

7. A and B broadcast the transactions $Open^A$ and $Open^B$ respectively, what reveals the secrets s_A and s_B.
8. If within time t the transaction $Open^A$ does not appear on the block chain, then B broadcasts the transaction $Fuse^A$ and gets $d\mathcal{B}$. Similarly, if within time t the transaction $Open^B$ does not appear on the block chain, then A broadcasts the transaction $Fuse^B$ and gets $d\mathcal{B}$.

Fig. 2. The SCS protocol. The scripts' arguments, which are omitted are denoted by $\bot$.

5   Two-Party Computation

The concept of secure two-party computations has already been informally described in the introduction. For the lack of space we do not provide full security definitions of these protocols, and only briefly sketch the constructions. The reader may refer to [11,21] for more on this topic. A common paradigm [22] for constructing secure multiparty protocols is to: (1) create a protocol secure only against passive (also called "semi-honest") adversaries, i.e. adversaries, which honestly perform the protocol, and then (2) "compile" such a protocol to be secure against any type of adversarial behavior.

The problem that such a compiler needs to address is that a malicious party can send a different message than she is supposed to send according to the protocol. One can deal with this problem using the zero-knowledge protocols [24]. This is possible since in every protocol a message which should be sent by a party is determined by (a) the public inputs, (b) the party's private inputs, (c) the messages that she received earlier, and (d) the party's internal randomness. The idea is to attach to each message a zero-knowledge proof that this message was computed correctly. Since a message can depend on private inputs and the internal randomness of the sender (which are not known to the receiver), the players commit at the beginning of the protocol to their private inputs and the randomness and later use these commitments in the proof (they actually never open them). Moreover, we need to ensure that the bits used as internal randomness are indeed random, but it can be easily achieved by masking them with the bits chosen by the other party. More details can be found, e.g., in [21].

This compiler works as long as all the parties are interested in completing the protocol. However, the technique described above cannot be used to force a party to send a message if she loses interest in the execution. It is easy to see that in general, there is no "purely cryptographic" way to force a party to execute the protocol until the very end. This may have particularly bad consequences if one of the parties learns the output and, depending on its value either completes the protocol, or halts (preventing the other party from learning the output). This is precisely the problem of the lack of fairness described in the introduction.

In this paper we propose a new way to achieve fairness in two-party computation based on Bitcoin deposits. The idea is that before starting the execution of the protocol both parties make a Bitcoin deposit of an agreed amount $d\,\text{B}$. If the protocol terminates successfully, then both parties get their deposits back. However, if one of the parties interrupts the protocol after she learned the output, the other party takes both deposits—her own and the opponent's one, so she gains $d\,\text{B}$. We would like to stress that making such a deposit is completely safe—the party making it is guaranteed to get it back if she follows the protocol regardless of the other party's behavior.

Our construction is based on the two-party computation protocol by Goldreich and Vainish [23]. We do not provide the details of this protocol here (for its full description the reader may consult, e.g. [11]). Let us just describe its most relevant part. The property which we take advantage of is that at the end of the protocol's execution the parties hold additive shares of the result of the computation, but none of the parties learned anything about the actual output. This means that the parties holds respectively bit strings s_A and s_B, such that the result of the computation is equal to $s_A \oplus s_B$. In the original protocol, the parties reconstruct the result by revealing their shares. More precisely, each party sends its share to the other party and makes a zero-knowledge proof that it is indeed its share of the result. Of course, one of the parties has to reveal her share first (or at least a part of it) and the other party can quit the protocol at this moment, leaving the honest party with no information about the output[9].

In FairComp protocol, which we present in this section the parties reconstruct the result in a different and *fair* way. Fairness of that protocol means that one of the following things happened: either (1) at the end of its execution both parties followed the protocol and they both know the result of the computation, or (2) one of the parties interrupted the protocol at the beginning and none of the parties learned anything about the result, or (3) only a malicious party learned the result, and she paid the other party an agreed amount of bitcoins.

The idea behind FairComp protocol is as follows. Suppose that the parties are called Alice and Bob. At the very beginning Alice and Bob agree on a value of a deposit equal to d Ƀ. Then they execute the two-party protocol [11,23] together with the zero-knowledge proofs in order to make it secure against the active adversary. However, they *do not* reconstruct the result. Then, Alice sends a hash h_A of her share concatenated with some random string to Bob and makes a zero-knowledge proof that she indeed computed h_A in that way. Similarly, Bob sends h_B to Alice and makes an analogous proof. Later, the parties execute SCS protocol to simultaneously commit themselves to respectively h_A and h_B. When the commitment is done, the parties reveal their shares. If any of them does not reveal its share, the honest party can claim the opponent's deposit. The description of the protocol is presented on Fig. 3.

We now have the following lemma whose proof appears in the extended version of this paper.

Lemma 2. *The* FairComp *protocol from Fig. 3 is a fair two party computation protocol assuming the modification from Sect. 3.*

6   Extensions

The result from the previous section can be extended in various ways. It is for example relatively easy to see that the deposits in the SCS and FairComp do not need to be equal for both parties. Another generalization is that (in theory, and very inefficiently) one can use an arbitrary commitment scheme, not necessarily the one based on hashes (the details of this will be provided in the extended version of this paper).

Probably the most interesting extension is to make the payoffs in the FairComp protocol depend on the result of the computation. More precisely, the FairComp

---

[9] Except of that, what she can learn from her inputs and from the function being computed.

Pre-condition:
1. A holds a key pair A and B holds the key pair B.
2. The parties agree on a function they want to jointly compute and on a value of deposits equal $d\,\mbox{B}$ each.

The computation phase

The parties execute the two-party protocol of Goldreich and Vainish [23] additionally secured against an active adversary with zero-knowledge proofs, but they do not reconstruct the secret. At the end of the execution A holds s_A and B holds s_B, such that the result of the computation in equal to $s_A \oplus s_B$.

The commitment phase

1. A computes her secret s'_A as a concatenation of her share s_A and some random string ρ_A of length α, where α is a security parameter.
2. A sends $h_A := H(s'_A)$ to B and makes a zero-knowledge proof to B that this value is indeed equal to $H(s_A||\rho_A)$ for some string ρ_A.
3. Similarly, B computes $s'_B := s_B||\rho_B$ for some random string ρ_B of length α, sends $h_B := H(s'_B)$ to A and makes an analogous proof.
4. The parties execute SCS.Commit(A, B, d, t) protocol for some moment of time t in the future.

The opening phase

5. The parties execute SCS.Open(A, B, d, t) protocol.
6. If A reveals s'_A before time t, then B computes s_A as a prefix of s'_A of an appropriate length and computes the result of the computation $s := s_A \oplus s_B$. Otherwise, B earns $d\,\mbox{B}$ from $Fuse^A$ transaction (See Fig. 2).
7. Similarly, if B reveals s'_B before time t, then A computes s_B as a prefix of s'_B of an appropriate length and computes the result of the computation $s := s_A \oplus s_B$. Otherwise, A earns $d\,\mbox{B}$ from $Fuse^B$ transaction (See Fig. 2).

Fig. 3. The FairComp protocol.

protocol can be easily extended to handle a situation when the result of the computation determines the winner, which will be given some reward (an agreed amount of bitcoins). To achieve this it is enough to add a third output with the value equal to the value of the reward to the *Commit* transaction used in the execution of SCS.Commit in Step. 4 of FairComp protocol. The output script would take as arguments both secrets s'_A, s'_B and a signature. It would check if both provided secrets are correct $(H(s'_A) = h_A \wedge H(s'_B) = h_B)$, compute s_A and s_B as prefixes of respectively s'_A and s'_B, compute the actual result $(s := s_A \oplus s_B)$, check which party is a winner and verify if the signature is the winner's signature on that transaction (this idea is very similar to the ones used in [2,5]).

The idea described above can be further extended to handle a situation, where the reward may be split arbitrarily among the parties depending on the result of the computation, e.g. the result is a fraction between 0 and 1, which determines how big part of the reward will be given to one of the parties (the other party gets the rest of the reward). Suppose that the reward is equal to $1\,\mbox{B}$. The parties have to add to *Commit* transaction, not one additional output, but a number of them—one with value 0.5 Ƀ, one with value 0.25 Ƀ, one with value 0.125 Ƀ and so on[10]. Similarly as earlier, each output script expects both secrets and a signature. It computes the results of the computation, checks, which party should be given the appropriate part of the reward and verifies if the signature is that party's signature.

Acknowledgments. We would like to thank the anonymous reviewers for their valuable comments.

References

1. Abadi, M., Glew, N.: Certified email with a light on-line trusted third party: design and implementation. In: WWW '02
2. Andrychowicz, M., Dziembowski, S., Malinowski, D., Mazurek, Ł.: Secure multi-party computations on Bitcoin. Cryptology ePrint Archive (2013). http://eprint.iacr.org/2013/784
3. Andrychowicz, M., Dziembowski, S., Malinowski, D., Mazurek, L.: How to deal with malleability of Bitcoin transactions. CoRR, abs/1312.3230 (2013)
4. Ateniese, G., Nita-Rotaru, C.: Stateless-recipient certified e-mail system based on verifiable encryption. In: Preneel, B. (ed.) CT-RSA 2002. LNCS, vol. 2271, pp. 182–199. Springer, Heidelberg (2002)
5. Back, A., Bentov, I.: Note on fair coin toss via Bitcoin (2013). http://www.cs.technion.ac.il/~idddo/cointossBitcoin.pdf
6. Ben-Or, M., Goldreich, O., Micali, S., Rivest, R.L.: A fair protocol for signing contracts. IEEE Trans. Inf. Theor. **36**(1), 40–46 (1990)
7. Blum, M.: Coin flipping by telephone. In: CRYPTO 1981 (1981)
8. Boneh, D., Naor, M.: Timed commitments. In: Bellare, M. (ed.) CRYPTO 2000. LNCS, vol. 1880, pp. 236–254. Springer, Heidelberg (2000)
9. Clark, J., Essex, A.: CommitCoin: carbon dating commitments with Bitcoin. In: Keromytis, A.D. (ed.) FC 2012. LNCS, vol. 7397, pp. 390–398. Springer, Heidelberg (2012)
10. Cleve, R.: Limits on the security of coin flips when half the processors are faulty. In: STOC '86
11. Cramer, Ronald: Introduction to secure computation. In: Damgård, Ivan Bjerre (ed.) EEF School 1998. LNCS, vol. 1561, p. 16. Springer, Heidelberg (1999)
12. Damgård, I.B.: Practical and provably secure release of a secret and exchange of signatures. In: Helleseth, T. (ed.) EUROCRYPT 1993. LNCS, vol. 765, pp. 200–217. Springer, Heidelberg (1994)
13. Der Spiegel International. Swiss Bank Data: German Tax Officials Launch Nationwide Raids, April 2013
14. Pfitzmann, B., et al.: Optimal efficiency of optimistic contract signing. In: PODC '98
15. Miers, I., et al.: Zerocoin: anonymous distributed e-cash from Bitcoin. IEEE S&P (2012)

---

[10] The number of outputs created this way is limited and not greater than 30 as a bitcoin is not infinitely divisible. The smallest amount of bitcoins is called "satoshi" and is equal to 10^{-8} Ƀ.

16. Barber, S., Boyen, X., Shi, E., Uzun, E.: Bitter to better—how to make bitcoin a better currency. In: Keromytis, A.D. (ed.) FC 2012. LNCS, vol. 7397, pp. 399–414. Springer, Heidelberg (2012)
17. Gordon, S., et al.: Complete fairness in secure two-party computation. J. ACM **58**(6), 1–37 (2011)
18. Even, S., Yacobi, Y.: Relations among public key signature schemes. Technical report 175, Computer Science Department, Technion, Israel (1980)
19. Garay, J.A., Jakobsson, M.: Timed release of standard digital signatures. In: Blaze, M. (ed.) FC 2002. LNCS, vol. 2357, pp. 168–182. Springer, Heidelberg (2003)
20. Goldreich, O., Micali, S., Wigderson, A.: How to play any mental game. In: STOC 1987 (1987)
21. Goldreich, O.: The Foundations of Cryptography: Basic Applications, vol. 2. Cambridge University Press, Cambridge (2004)
22. Goldreich, O., Micali, S., Wigderson, A: Proofs that yield nothing but their validity and a methodology of cryptographic protocol design. In: FOCS '86
23. Goldreich, O., Vainish, R.: How to solve any protocol problem - an efficiency improvement. In: CRYPTO '87
24. Goldwasser, S., Micali, S., Rackoff, C.: The knowledge complexity of interactive proof systems. SIAM J. Comput. **18**(1), 186–208 (1989)
25. Pinkas, B.: Fair secure two-party computation. In: Biham, E. (ed.) EUROCRYPT 2003. LNCS, vol. 2656, pp. 87–105. Springer, Heidelberg (2003)
26. Bitcoin wiki: Contracts. http://en.bitcoin.it/wiki/Contracts. Accessed 24 Nov 2013
27. Bitcoin wiki: Dominant Assurance Contracts. http://en.bitcoin.it/wiki/Dominant_Assurance_Contracts. Accessed 19 Jan 2014
28. Bitcoin wiki: Transaction malleability. https://en.bitcoin.it/wiki/Transaction_Malleability. Accessed 20 Jan 2014
29. Yao, A.C.-C.: How to generate and exchange secrets. In: FOCS 1986 (1986)
30. Zhou, J., Gollmann, D.: A fair non-repudiation protocol. In: IEEE S&P (1996)
31. Zhou, J., Gollmann, D.: Certified electronic mail. In: Martella, G., Kurth, H., Montolivo, E., Bertino, E. (eds.) ESORICS 1996. LNCS, vol. 1146, pp. 160–171. Springer, Heidelberg (1996)

Increasing Anonymity in Bitcoin

Amitabh Saxena[1], Janardan Misra[1(✉)], and Aritra Dhar[2]

[1] Accenture Technology Labs, Bangalore 560066, India
{amitabh.saxena,janardan.misra}@accenture.com
[2] Indraprastha Institute of Information Technology, New Delhi, India
aritra1204@iiitd.ac.in

Abstract. Bitcoin prevents double-spending using the *blockchain*, a public ledger kept with every client. Every single transaction till date is present in this ledger. Due to this, true anonymity is not present in bitcoin. We present a method to enhance anonymity in bitcoin-type cryptocurrencies. In the blockchain, each block holds a list of transactions linking the sending and receiving addresses. In our modified protocol the transactions (and blocks) do not contain any such links. Using this, we obtain a far higher degree of anonymity. Our method uses a new primitive known as *composite signatures*. Our security is based on the hardness of the Computation Diffie-Hellman assumption in bilinear maps.

Keywords: Bitcoin · Cryptocurrency · Aggregate signatures · Plausible deniability · Anonymity

1 Introduction

Bitcoin (symbol ฿) is virtual currency based on peer-to-peer technology. It is designed to operate without any central authority and enables transaction confirmation using a reward system [1–3]. The first transaction of every block is a reward (currently ฿ 25) to whoever first provides a solution to a hard puzzle as a "proof-of-work". The puzzle is constructed from unconfirmed transactions and the proof-of-work serves as a tamper-proof ledger.

In bitcoin, funds are exchanged between *addresses* which are hashes of public keys The addresses serve as pseudonyms and provide some anonymity. However, bitcoin raises serious privacy concerns because all the information is public and permanently stored. Furthermore, digital signatures used in transactions provide cryptographic proofs of funds transfer.

Our contribution: We propose a method to enhance the anonymity of bitcoin-type currencies using a new primitive known as *composite signatures*. Our method removes any cryptographic proofs of funds transfer and obfuscates the links between inputs and outputs. Multiple transactions are combined into a larger transaction to hide the links of the individual transactions. Our anonymity comes in the form of *plausible deniability*.

© IFCA/Springer-Verlag Berlin Heidelberg 2014
R. Böhme et al. (Eds.): FC 2014 Workshops, LNCS 8438, pp. 122–139, 2014.
DOI: 10.1007/978-3-662-44774-1_9

The rest of the paper is organized as follows. We review related works in Sect. 2. We give an overview of bitcoin in Sect. 3. We describe our method to enhance anonymity using composite signatures in Sect. 4. We give the definition and construction of composite signatures in Sect. 5. A summary of our method is given in Sect. 6. Finally, we describe how to integrate our protocol with existing bitcoin protocol in Sect. 7.

2   Related Work

Aggregate signatures: In aggregate signatures [4] many individual signatures can be combined into and replaced with one short object - the aggregate signature. They were proposed to increase efficiency of verifying multiple signatures.

Composite signatures: The aggregate signatures of [4], however, have another useful property that is not captured (and not needed) in standard definitions such as in [4]. The property is that the aggregation process is *one-way* - given just the aggregate signature, it is very hard to compute the individual signatures. This was used in *verifiably encrypted signatures* [4]. Coron and Naccache proved in [5] that extracting any sub-aggregate signature in a *non-adaptive attack* (where the adversary makes only one sign query) is as hard as solving the CDH problem. Composite signatures capture this property in the stronger *adaptive chosen key and message attack*, where the adversary is allowed to make several sign queries on messages of his choice before outputting a forgery.

There are other extensions of aggregate signatures such as sequential aggregate signatures [6–8], ordered multi-signatures [9,10], history-free sequential aggregate signatures [11] and sequential aggregate signatures with lazy verification [12]. However, none exploit the one-way property of aggregate signatures.

Anonymity in Bitcoin: Elli Androulaki et.al [13] discuss privacy issues in bitcoin such as discovering which public addresses are controlled by the same user. They classify the problem into Activity Unlinkability or Address Unlinkability and User Profile Indistinguishability. and propose several heuristic techniques to reveal user privacy in multi-input transactions. Furthermore, they perform behavioral analysis to link multiple public addresses to same user. Fergal Reid and Martin Harrigan [14] on the other hand considered the topological structure of two networks derived from bitcoin's public transaction history and analyze implications for the anonymity and currency theft. In [15], Dorit Ron and Adi Shamir used the transaction graph of [14] to find that several large transactions were likely used to obfuscate the funds from a larger transaction earlier on.

Current and proposed approaches for increasing anonymity rely on "mixers" that mix bitcoins from various different sources before sending to destinations. Zerocoin [16] is a technique that uses zero-knowledge proofs and commitment schemes to unlink sending and receiving addresses and uses an alternate currency as an intermediate exchange medium. Our technique does not rely on alternate currencies or zero-knowledge proofs. Note that although our method also does not provide true anonymity, the anonymity offered is far higher than what is currently offered in bitcoin. Our method can be used in conjunction with other proposed approaches (such as zerocoin). Compared to zerocoin, it is easier to integrate our method with bitcoin.

The CoinJoin [17] protocol is similar to ours. CoinJoin's goal is to unlink inputs in the same wallet. Several parties agree on the inputs and outputs of a transaction. The total funds in the inputs should cover the total funds of the outputs. Finally, the parties individually sign the transaction for the inputs they control. Once all the inputs are signed, the transaction is broadcast. The difference in our method is that the input/outputs of other parties need not be known a priori. Additionally, our method is non-interactive while CoinJoin requires interaction with other parties. Finally, in CoinJoin, parties cannot later deny knowledge of the outputs and other inputs.

3   Overview of Bitcoin

Although the bitcoin protocol is quite complex, only a few concepts are necessary to understand our idea. These are: *transaction, input, output, reference, block* and *confirmation*. We describe these below. For simplicity, we consider an address as a public key itself rather than its hash.

Transaction. Roughly speaking, a transaction consists of a set of *inputs* (source of funds) and *outputs* (destination of funds).

Example: Suppose Alice is the owner of address A which received x bitcoins in a previous transaction. She wants to send $y \leq x$ bitcoins to Bob's address B. Alice constructs a transaction with A as the input and B as one of the outputs. She also inserts ref, the reference to the previous transaction's output where A received those x bitcoins. The entire amount x must be transferred from A. Alice sends y bitcoins to B, sets a transaction fee t and sends the remaining amount $z = x - y - t$ to her *change address* C, which is the other output. The change address is simply any address owned by Alice (possibly A). The message

$$\text{``}(ref\text{: remove } ฿x \text{ from } A), (\text{put } ฿y \text{ in } B), (\text{put } ฿z \text{ in } C)\text{''}$$

is signed under A.

Notation: We will use the following notation:

- $X \overset{ref}{\rightarrow} x$ is the message "$(ref$: remove $฿x$ from $X)$". This is an input.
- $X \leftarrow x$ is the message "put $฿x$ in X". This is an output.
- $\sigma_X(m)$ is signature on message m under public key X.

Alice's transaction is then $(m, \sigma_A(m))$, where $m = (A \overset{ref}{\rightarrow} x, B \leftarrow y, C \leftarrow z)$.

Transactions: The above scenario had a single input. In reality, a bitcoin transaction can have multiple inputs with no particular link between any source-destination pair. The entire transaction is signed under every input public key. The only requirement is that the sum of the funds at the inputs is greater than or equal to the sum of funds at the outputs. Any difference is considered a transaction fee. More formally, define m to be the message

$$M \stackrel{\text{def}}{=} (A_1 \stackrel{ref_1}{\rightarrow} x_1, A_2 \stackrel{ref_2}{\rightarrow} x_2, \ldots, A_n \stackrel{ref_n}{\rightarrow} x_n, B_1 \leftarrow y_1, B_2 \leftarrow y_2, \ldots, B_l \leftarrow y_l),$$
(1)

where: $(A_1, x_1, ref_1), (A_2, x_2, ref_2), \ldots, (A_n, x_n, ref_n)$ are n tuples each consisting of an address A_i, amount of funds x_i and a reference to a previous transaction where A_i received x_i bitcoins, and $(B_1, y_1), (B_2, y_2), \ldots, (B_l, y_l)$ are l pairs of addresses and amount of funds. A valid transaction tx is a tuple:

$$tx \stackrel{\text{def}}{=} (M, \sigma_{A_1}(M), \sigma_{A_2}(M), \ldots, \sigma_{A_n}(M))$$
(2)

such that each signature $\sigma_{A_i}(M)$ verifies correctly and the following holds:

1. $\sum_{i=1}^{l} y_i \leq \sum_{i=1}^{n} x_i$
2. Each ref_i for $1 \leq i \leq n$ was never used in any prior transaction.

The ordering of the signatures in tx is determined from the ordering of messages inside M (which is fixed due to the signatures).

Referencing outputs: In future, when spending the funds from any of the outputs (say $B_i \leftarrow y_i$) of the above transaction, a reference $ref_{B_i \leftarrow y_i}$ to that output needs to be provided. Let tx be the string of Eq. 2. Then

$$ref_{B_i \leftarrow y_i} \stackrel{\text{def}}{=} (Hash(tx), i)$$

Because ref is constructed from the hash of a previous transaction, it is guaranteed that two different transactions are distinct unless the outputs, input and ref are identical (a forbidden scenario). Due to this, it is also guaranteed (with high probability) that the $refs$ generated by using hashes of two different transactions are also different. In fact, this is how bitcoin prevents double spending (see below). A ref can be used in a transaction at most once. Bitcoin clients maintain a list of unused $refs$ to do this check.

Unspent outputs (and double-spends): An unspent output is essentially an unused reference, one that has never been used in any transaction. The protocol design guarantees that references to two different outputs will be distinct (see above). Each client maintains a set called 'unspent outputs'. Each output of every transaction is added to this set, and removed when is it used as a reference in another transaction. A transaction with a reference not in this list is considered a double spend and is not processed.

Validating Transactions: A new transaction is valid if all the references are unused. If so, the transaction is accepted as *valid* but *unconfirmed*, and is relayed on the network. The clients add each such transaction to a pool of unconfirmed transactions. Unconfirmed transactions can be double-spent.

Confirming Transactions. A miner is a client who confirms new transactions by solving a hard puzzle and providing the solution as a 'proof-of-work' as follows:

1. A bunch of unconfirmed transactions along with one reward transaction (known as the *coinbase transaction*) are combined into a 'block'.
2. Hash of the previous block h_{pr} is added to the block.
3. A nonce is added to the block.
4. Hash(b) of the final block b is computed.

If the output of the hash contains at least a specified number of leading zeros, the puzzle is solved, otherwise the miner tries with different nonces until the puzzle is solved or some other miner broadcasts the solution of a puzzle for a block referencing h_{pr}. A correct solution implies that the corresponding block is 'mined' and all transactions contained in it are confirmed.

Confirmations: The number of confirmations of a transaction are the number of blocks in the blockchain that have been accepted by the network since the block that includes the transaction. The possibility of double-spending a transaction decreases exponentially with the number of confirmations. The default client requires 6 confirmations for normal transactions and 100 confirmations for reward transactions before they can be spent.

Transaction pool management: Each client maintains a pool of unverified (but valid) transactions. An element is removed from this pool when that transaction gets included in a mined block. This ensures that even if a transaction is not included in an immediate block, it is kept in the pool until it gets mined.

Anonymity. Transactions are *not* anonymous; since each input public-key signs the entire transaction, some information is inherently leaked. In particular,

1. Each output is linked to the inputs via the signatures.
2. Each input is also linked to the previous output via the *ref*.
3. The inputs themselves are linked together (they belong to the same wallet).

4   Increasing Anonymity

The links between inputs and outputs result in loss of anonymity. We describe a slight modification to the protocol that removes these links. The modification is so minor that apart from the way signatures and references are computed, the rest of the design remains the same. Yet, the anonymity gained is significant.

The intuition for anonymity is that because inputs and outputs in a transaction are linked cryptographically, a miner and other intermediaries can 'dilute' the information contained in a transaction by inserting more information before processing it further. The final mined block will have the input-output links in each individual transaction highly obfuscated. The only information will be the set of inputs and outputs of an entire block.

Our protocol uses a primitive called *composite signatures* described below.

Composite Signatures. The symbol $\sigma_X(m)$ denotes a signature on message m under public key X. Roughly speaking, composite signatures are an extension of aggregate signatures with the following properties:

1. **Composition:** A number of individual signatures $\sigma_{X_1}(m_1), \sigma_{X_2}(m_2), \ldots, \sigma_{X_n}$ (m_n) can be combined into a composite signature $\sigma_{\{X_1, X_2, \ldots, X_n\}}(\{m_1, m_2, \ldots, m_n\})$, which proves that each m_i was signed under public key X_i. The composite signature is said to be on the set $\{(m_1, X_1), (m_2, X_2), \ldots (m_n, X_n)\}$.
2. **Incremental composition:** More signatures can be added to the composite signature at any time.
3. **One-way:** It is computationally hard to obtain any sub-composite signature given just the composite signature. Informally, given the composite signature on a set $S = \{(m_1, X_1), (m_2, X_2), \ldots (m_n, X_n)\}$ of (message, public-key) pairs, it is hard to compute the composite signature on any subset $S' \subsetneq S$.
4. **No ordering:** The signature does not maintain order. It is impossible to decide if a composite signature was computed 'all at once' or incrementally.

Composite signatures are formally defined in Sect. 5.

A Modified Protocol. Consider the message from the original protocol:

$$M \overset{\text{def}}{=} (A_1 \overset{ref_1}{\rightarrow} x_1, A_2 \overset{ref_2}{\rightarrow} x_2, \ldots, A_n \overset{ref_n}{\rightarrow} x_n, B_1 \leftarrow y_1, B_2 \leftarrow y_2, \ldots, B_l \leftarrow y_l),$$

M is a combination of messages $m_1, m_2, \ldots, m_n, \overline{m}_1, \overline{m}_2, \ldots, \overline{m}_l$, where:

$$m_i \overset{\text{def}}{=} (A_i \overset{ref_i}{\rightarrow} x_i) \ (1 \leq i \leq n) \qquad \text{[Inputs]}$$

$$\overline{m}_i \overset{\text{def}}{=} (B_i \leftarrow y_i) \ (1 \leq i \leq l) \qquad \text{[Outputs]}$$

Transactions: Instead of defining a transaction as in Eq. 2 (repeated below):

$$tx \overset{\text{def}}{=} (M, \sigma_{A_1}(M), \sigma_{A_2}(M), \ldots, \sigma_{A_n}(M)),$$

we define it using composite signatures as follows::

$$tx \overset{\text{def}}{=} (M, \sigma_{\{A_1, A_2, \ldots, A_n, \overline{A}_1, \overline{A}_2, \ldots, \overline{A}_l\}}(\{m_1, m_2, \ldots, m_n, \overline{m}_1, \overline{m}_2, \ldots, \overline{m}_l\})), \quad (3)$$

such that each $\overline{A}_i$ is a randomly generated public key, called a *masking key*, and the pairs $(\overline{A}_i, \overline{m}_i)$ are unique. Define $\Lambda \overset{\text{def}}{=} \{A_1, A_2, \ldots A_n, \overline{A}_1, \overline{A}_2, \ldots \overline{A}_l\}$ and $\Pi \overset{\text{def}}{=} \{m_1, m_2, \ldots m_n, \overline{m}_1, \overline{m}_2, \ldots \overline{m}_l\}$. Equivalently, $tx \overset{\text{def}}{=} (\Pi, \sigma_{(\Lambda)}(\Pi))$.

Observe that in the above transaction, unlike the original bitcoin protocol, each 'regular' public key signs a message containing only its own address. Consequently, the signatures never link the sending addresses to the receiving addresses or other sending addresses. The one-way property of composite signatures preserves the security of the original protocol; it is infeasible to isolate any signatures spending funds from the inputs.

Confirming a transaction: A transaction tx is valid if each of the inputs has an unused reference to a previous output. Confirmation of tx requires a miner to solve a puzzle for a block containing that transaction, constructed as follows:

1. A number of unconfirmed transactions $tx_1, tx_2, \ldots tx_\alpha$ are collected for inclusion in the block, where each tx_i is defined as:

$$tx_i \stackrel{\text{def}}{=} (\Pi_i, \sigma_{\Lambda_i}(\Pi_i)) \qquad (1 \leq i \leq \alpha)$$

Additionally, a coinbase (reward) transaction tx_c with no inputs is created:

$$tx_c \stackrel{\text{def}}{=} (\Pi_c, \sigma_{\Lambda_c}(\Pi_c)),$$

2. It is verified that each (masking-key, output) pair from all the transactions combined together is unique. Not only do we require that the pairs are unique in each transaction but also in all the transactions combined together.
3. A final block b is computed as follows:
   (a) Hash of the previous block h_{pr} is computed.
   (b) A combined composite signature σ_b is computed. That is,

$$\sigma_b \stackrel{\text{def}}{=} \sigma_{(\Lambda_c \cup \Lambda_1 \cup \Lambda_2 \cup \ldots \Lambda_\alpha)}(\Pi_c \cup \Pi_1 \cup \Pi_2 \cup \ldots \Pi_\alpha)$$

   (c) Assume some canonical ordering of all inputs and outputs. Define

$$\Pi_b \stackrel{\text{def}}{=} \Pi_c \cup \Pi_1 \cup \Pi_2 \cup \ldots \Pi_\alpha,$$

   where the elements of Π_b are arranged in the canonical order.
   (d) The final mined block b is computed as:

$$b \stackrel{\text{def}}{=} (h_{pr}, \Pi_b, \sigma_b, \theta_b),$$

   where θ_b is a nonce s.t. $Hash(b)$ has a certain number of leading zeros.

Referencing the outputs: In this modified protocol, we don't reference simply the outputs, but rather the (masking-key, output) pairs. Let $(\overline{A}_j, \overline{m}_j)$ be some (masking-key, output) pair in one of transactions included in the above block. Recall that such a pair is unique in a block (even if the output may be repeated). We compute a reference to the above pair as:

$$ref_{(\overline{A}_j, \overline{m}_j)} \stackrel{\text{def}}{=} (Hash(b), Hash(\overline{A}_j, \overline{m}_j))$$

Since the reference contains the hash of the block, an output can only be spent if its transaction has been included in a mined block. This makes the new transaction incompatible with services that allow spending from unconfirmed transactions (such as satoshidice.com). However, this also makes the protocol more robust to DoS attacks. To summarize, in the modified protocol, **it is not possible to spend from unconfirmed transactions.**

Security: Composite signatures provide security against two distinct types of forgery. The first type, called *ordinary forgery* is the one that all conventional signature schemes are expected to satisfy. This involves forging a signature under an input public-key to steal funds. The second one, called *extraction forgery* occurs when two signatures can be 'separated' given their composition. This will also allow an attacker to steal funds.[1] Since extraction of any sub-composite signature is infeasible, peers can only add further signatures to a transaction. Double spending and replay attacks are prevented in a manner similar to the original protocol. We maintain a list of unused $refs$, and reject the transaction that contains a ref that has been used. The references are unique because:

1. The reference is a hash of the block and the (masking-key, output) pair.
2. Each block is unique because it contains a hash of the previous block.
3. The (masking-key, output) pairs in a block are unique.

We additionally consider the case where the sender uses a weak or compromised masking key. This is similar to a double spending attack. The receiver should not trust the transaction until it is confirmed.

Anonymity: First observe that each input and output is cryptographically linked to only one public key (the regular key or a masking key). Therefore given a transaction as in Eq. 3, it is impossible to prove that the signer knew any outputs. Furthermore, signatures from many transactions can be composed to obfuscate the input-output relationships (we discuss this below). Additionally, once a transaction is confirmed in a block, it is removed from memory and only the confirmed block is stored. The block alone does not leak any information about the input-output links. Consequently, if the individual transactions are not saved, this information is eventually erased with time.

Enhancing Anonymity. We can enhance anonymity via *plausible deniability*.

Joiners: To further enhance anonymity, we propose the notion of *joiners* as follows. The senders will leave a certain amount of funds free for their peers (this is additional to the transaction fee). This transaction is called *partial* and the free funds are the *joining bonus*. This transaction is sent to only one peer. Peers receiving any transaction with free funds can add their addresses as outputs and claim the joining bonus to make the transaction *full* before broadcasting it to the network. The joining bonus is not specifically marked to make it indistinguishable from normal funds. Given a full transaction, it should not be possible to distinguish which outputs consume the joining bonus.

Even with access to the individual transactions, it would still be impossible to prove with certainty that the sender indeed sent those funds to some given output, since it is possible that the outputs were added later on by a joiner. To ensure that transaction fees don't get consumed by joiners, a special output can be used for transaction fees. To ensure that the original partial transaction is never broadcast, a spender should send it to only to one peer. Once the transaction is full, it will be broadcast to the network. Clients attempting to disrupt the network by broadcasting partial transactions will be handled as explained below in the section on transaction pool management. Similarly if a misbehaving peer drops a partial transaction, this can be detected and the transaction resent to a different peer.

---

[1] If an attacker can extract signatures, he can isolate the input and add any output.

Merging services: A merging service accepts various transactions from clients (over a private channel) and once sufficient of them are obtained, it merges them by aggregating the signatures before broadcasting to the network. Clients attempting to disrupt the network by sending the same transactions to multiple merging services will be handled in a similar way as for joiners.

Using the Knapsack problem: Given a 'merged' or 'joined' transaction, it may still be possible to deduce some input-output relationships from the amount of funds going in and out. We use the knapsack problem to further obfuscate this information. The knapsack problem [18–20] can be described as follows. Given a positive rational number X and a set W of positive rational numbers $w_1, w_2, ...w_n$, find a subset S of W (if it exists) such that $Sum(S) \leq X$.

The recipient generates a number of addresses to receive funds into. The sender randomly splits the funds into those addresses and broadcasts the transaction. Other joiners/merging services add further transactions also generated in a similar manner. In the merged transaction, any subset of inputs and outputs with sums close to each other can potentially belong to one sub-transaction. However, if there are overlapping or multiple solutions, then it is impossible to prove this fact with certainty, thereby ensuring plausible deniability.

Revealing the masking keys: To enhance deniability, the masking private keys can be publicized after a few confirmations. In this case, a partial transaction (presented later) cannot act as a cryptographic proof of knowledge of the outputs.

Transaction Pool Management. Referring to the joiner protocol above, suppose a malicious peer transmits a partial transaction $tx = A$ to j joiners, where A is a set of inputs and outputs. This will result in multiple full transactions $AB_1, AB_2, \ldots AB_j$, one for each joiner. Since an output can only be used once, only one of these transactions will be accepted. In such a situation, a peer will reject all new transactions, while a miner could pick one that maximizes fees.

The remaining aspects of the protocol such as rules for pruning and broadcasting shall be the same as the original protocol.

5   Composite Signatures

Our protocol uses a primitive called composite signatures, which we define here.
Message-descriptor: A message-descriptor is a set $\{(m_1, pk_1), (m_2, pk_2), \ldots, (m_n, pk_n)\}$ of (message, public-key) pairs.

Algorithms. A composite signature scheme has four algorithms:

1. **KeyGen**(K) The algorithm takes in a security parameter K and outputs a (public-private) key pair pk, sk.
2. **Sign**(sk, m) The algorithm takes in a private key sk and a message m. It outputs a single-key signature σ. This single-key signature is equivalent to a composite signature on the single pair $\{(m, pk)\}$

3. **Compose**$((\ell_1, \sigma_1), (\ell_2, \sigma_2))$ The algorithm takes in two (message-descriptor, signature) pairs. If both signatures are valid and $\ell_1 \cap \ell_2 = \emptyset$, it outputs a composite signature σ on the message-descriptor $\ell_1 \cup \ell_2$, otherwise it outputs an error symbol $\perp$. Validity is checked by the **Verify** algorithm below.
4. **Verify**(ℓ, σ) The algorithm takes in a message descriptor

$$\ell = \{(m_1, pk_1), (m_2, pk_2), \ldots, (m_n, pk_n)\},$$

and σ, a purported composite signature on ℓ. If the messages in ℓ are not unique, the algorithm outputs Invalid. Otherwise it invokes a deterministic poly-time procedure and outputs either Valid or Invalid.

The composite signatures exhibit an abelian group structure under composition. Given a set of composite signatures, we can compute composite signatures on any union of their message descriptors. Furthermore, these are the only composite signatures we should be able to compute. We capture this below.

Security. Security is defined using the following interaction with a forger A.

1. *Setup:* A chooses n. We generate n (public-private) keypairs $\{(pk_i, sk_i)\}_{i \in [1..n]}$ with security parameter K. We give the set $PK = \{pk_i\}_{i \in [1..n]}$ to A.
2. *Queries:* A makes up to α *sign* queries. Each sign query i consists of ℓ_i, a message-descriptor with public keys from PK. If the pairs in ℓ_i are unique, we respond with an composite signature on ℓ_i, otherwise we return the error symbol $\perp$. Let L be the set of message-descriptors in all sign queries.
3. *Output:* A outputs (ℓ_A, σ_A), a purported (message-descriptor, signature) pair possibly containing public keys not from PK. Let $PK_A = \{pk | (m, pk) \in \ell_A\}$. A wins if the following conditions hold:
   (a) **Verify**$(\ell_A, \sigma_A) = $ Valid.
   (b) The set $PK \cap PK_A$ is non-empty.
   (c) ℓ_A is *not signable* (Definition 1 below).

Notation: Let $\ell'_A = \{(m, pk) | (m, pk) \in \ell_A \wedge pk \in PK\}$. Assign a unique prime number to each element of the set $\{(m, pk) | ((m, pk) \in \ell \wedge \ell \in L) \vee (m, pk) \in \ell'_A\}$. Then each $\ell \in L$ corresponds to a unique integer $integer(\ell)$ obtained by multiplying the primes corresponding to its constituent (m, pk) pairs. Let Z be the set $\{integer(\ell) | \ell \in L\}$. Let $z_A = integer(\ell'_A)$, obtained by multiplying the primes corresponding to ℓ'_A.

Definition 1. *(Signable Set) The set ℓ_A is* **signable** *iff there exists a solution in* **non-negative integers** x_i *to the equation* $z_A = \prod_{z_i \in Z} z_i^{x_i}$.

In a weaker notion, we allow integer solutions. We call this weakly signable.

Example. Suppose $L = \{\ell_1, \ell_2, \ell_3\}$, with $\ell_1 = \{(m_1, pk_1), (m_2, pk_2)\}$, $\ell_2 = \{(m_2, pk_2), (m_3, pk_3)\}$ and $\ell_3 = \{(m_3, pk_3), (m_4, pk_4)\}$. Let $\ell_A = \{(m_1, pk_1), (m_4, pk_4)\}$. Let us assign the primes as: $(m_1, pk_1) \to 2, (m_2, pk_2) \to 3, (m_3, pk_3) \to$

$5, (m_4, pk_4) \rightarrow 7$. We have $Z = \{6, 15, 35\}$ and $z_A = 14$. Then ℓ_A is weakly signable because $14 = 6 \cdot 15^{-1} \cdot 35$. However, ℓ_A is not signable since there are no solutions in non-negative integers to $14 = 6^{x_1} \cdot 15^{x_2} \cdot 35^{x_3}$.

Observe that the signable sets form a monoid under the signature aggregation operation, while the weakly signable sets form a group. The signable sets are exactly those sets that can be generated by aggregating the collected signatures using this operation.

Definition 2. *A composite signature scheme* $\{KeyGen, Sign, Compose, Verify\}$ *is secure if for sufficiently large K, there is no probabilistic poly-time A that wins with non-negligible advantage in K.*

Intuition: In the above definition, aggregation of signatures is represented by multiplication of the primes. The game captures the fact that it is possible to generate new signatures by aggregating smaller signatures (represented by signable numbers - obtained by multiplying elements of Z). Furthermore, it may additionally be possible to generate new signatures by 'reversing the aggregation algorithm' when only one input is unknown (represented by weakly signable numbers - obtained by multiplying *and dividing* elements of Z).

Construction. Our construction is derived from the aggregate signatures of [4] by appending the public key and a random string to the message.
Bilinear pairing: Let G_1 and G_2 be two cyclic multiplicative groups both of prime order q. A bilinear pairing is a map $\hat{e} : G_1 \times G_1 \mapsto G_2$ satisfying:

- *Bilinearity*: $\hat{e}(a^x, b^y) = \hat{e}(a, b)^{xy}$ $\forall a, b \in G_1$ and $x, y \in \mathbb{Z}_q$.
- *Non-degeneracy*: If g is a generator of G_1 then $\hat{e}(g, g)$ is a generator of G_2.
- *Computability*: The map $\hat{e}$ is efficiently computable.

We require a case where the discrete logarithm problem in G_1 is believed to be hard. Such bilinear pairings are known to exist (see [4]). Our security depends on the hardness of the following problem in G_1:
Computation Diffie-Hellman (CDH) problem: Given g^x, g^y for a generator g of G_1 and unknowns $x, y \in \mathbb{Z}_q$, compute g^{xy}.

Algorithms: Select a security parameter κ. Let $\hat{e} : G_1 \times G_1 \mapsto G_2$ be a bilinear map over groups (G_1, G_2) of prime order q, and g be a generator of G_1. Denote by Σ the alphabet $\{0, 1\}$. Let $H : \Sigma^* \times \Sigma^\kappa \times G_1 \mapsto G_1$ be a cryptographic hash function. These parameters are public.

1. **KeyGen:** The private key is $x \xleftarrow{R} \mathbb{Z}_q$ and the public key is $pk = g^x \in G_1$.
2. **Sign:** To sign a message m under the above public key pk, generate $r \xleftarrow{R} \Sigma^\kappa$ and compute the signature $\sigma \in (G_1, \Sigma^\kappa)$ as:

$$\sigma = (H(m, r, pk)^x, r)$$

3. **Compose:** Two (message-descriptor, signature) pairs, $(\ell_1, \sigma_1), (\ell_2, \sigma_2)$ are given. Ensure that $\mathbf{Verify}(\ell_1 \sigma_1) = \mathbf{Verify}(\ell_2, \sigma_2) = \mathtt{valid}$ and $\ell_1 \cap \ell_2 = \emptyset$. Then parse σ_1 and σ_2 as (σ_1', R_1) and (σ_2', R_2) respectively and compute the composite signature σ on $\ell_1 \cup \ell_2$ as $\sigma = (\sigma_1' \sigma_2', R_1 \cup R_2)$.

4. **Verify**(ℓ, σ): Here $\ell = \{(m_1, pk_1), (m_2, pk_2), \ldots, (m_k, pk_k)\}$ is a message-descriptor of length k and σ is a purported composite signature on ℓ. To verify σ, first ensure that all pairs are distinct. Then parse σ as $(\sigma', \{r_1, r_2, \ldots, r_k\}) \in G_1 \times (\Sigma^\kappa)^k$ and check that the following holds:

$$\hat{e}(\sigma', g) \stackrel{?}{=} \prod_{i=1}^{k} \hat{e}(H(m_i, r_i, pk_i), pk_i)$$

Verification works because:

$$LHS = \hat{e}(\prod_{i=1}^{k} \sigma_i', g) = \hat{e}(\prod_{i=1}^{n} H(m_i, r_i, pk_i)^{x_i}, g) = \prod_{i=1}^{n} \hat{e}(H(m_i, r_i, pk_i), g^{x_i}) = RHS$$

Security: Security is based on the hardness of the CDH problem (Theorem 1).

Theorem 1. *Let H be a random oracle and let ϵ be the probability of an attacker breaking the composite signature scheme after making at most α sign queries and at most γ queries to H, such that the forgery contains at most β keys. Then we can solve the CDH problem in G_1 with probability $\geq \frac{\epsilon}{3} \left(1 - \frac{\alpha + \gamma - 1}{2^\kappa}\right)^{\hat{n}\alpha}$.*

The proof of Theorem 1 is given in Appendix A.

6   Composite Signatures and Cryptocurrencies

As discussed earlier, composite signatures can be used to enhance anonymity in cryptocurrencies (such as bitcoin) by unlinking the input and output addresses from where funds move. We summarize the ideas below.

In bitcoin transactions, the sending addresses (i.e., public keys) are linked to the other sending addresses and receiving addresses in a transaction. This link is 'hard' in the sense that it provides a cryptographic proof of funds transfer between those addresses. For example, suppose owner of address pk_1 wants to transfer 1 bitcoin to address pk_2. The transaction will be the message "**Take 1 bitcoin from pk_1; Put 1 bitcoin in pk_2**", signed under the public key pk_1. This transaction cryptographically links the addresses pk_1 and pk_2. The owner of pk_1 cannot later deny sending the funds to pk_2.

Composite signatures enable significantly higher anonymity by removing linkages from sending and receiving addresses. This allows senders to release funds without referring to receiving addresses or other sending addresses. Using composite signatures, the transaction in the above example will consist of two messages (1) the message "**Take 1 bitcoin from pk_1**" signed under pk_1, and (2) the message "**Put 1 bitcoin in pk_2**" signed under a randomly generated public key (which we call the masking key). The two signatures will then be combined into one composite signature and broadcast to the network. Other peers may add more signatures from their transactions before broadcasting further (to increase unlinkability). Since individual signatures in a composite signature cannot be extracted, the composite signature serves as a secure record of the transaction, despite the fact that messages do not contain references to other public keys. Senders can claim *plausible deniability*, since the composite signature cannot serve as proofs of knowledge of the receiving addresses.

We proposed the use of 'joiners', 'merging services' and the knapsack problem [19] to further increase plausible deniability.

Anti-censorship and participation incentive: The proposal also has a desirable anti-censorship property. Because composite spends cannot be de-aggregated, if a miner learns of a 'desirable' spend only after it is aggregated with censored spends, it must take all or none. The prospect of open aggregates also allows relaying nodes to participate in collecting transaction fees.

7   Integrating with Bitcoin

The modified transactions described here use composite signatures instead of ordinary signatures (such as ECDSA). Their construction uses bilinear pairings on elliptic curves. Some examples of such pairings are: Weil pairing [21], the Tate-Lichtenbaum pairing [22] and the Eta Pairing [23].

Efficiency: Public keys are elements of G_1, which are elements of a suitable finite field. Based on [24,25], such elements can be represented in about 30 bytes for 128 bits of security. The signatures constitute one group element and n κ-bit strings (the random rs). The size of signatures increases linearly. Below we consider the possibility of using a weaker scheme where these rs are removed. Signature verification requires several pairing computations, which can be performed fairly efficiently [24,25] (< 10 ms on a Pentium).

Increasing efficiency: Our composite signature construction extends the aggregate signatures of [4] by including a random string r in the signature. The signatures of [4] are constant-size (about 30 bytes) because the r is not included. However, they do not satisfy the security of Definition 2. In practice, however, a weaker security notion is sufficient. In the weaker notion we require the forgery ℓ_A to be not weakly signable (Definition 1). We posit that the construction of [4] is secure in this weaker sense. Furthermore, for our application, an even weaker form of security - the non-adaptive case - should be sufficient. This requires the adversary to output a forgery after making only one sign query. The signatures of [4] satisfy this model [5]. Therefore, we envisage the construction of [4] to be used in our application.

Based on above parameters, transaction size is comparable to that in the existing protocol. In order to verify transactions/blocks created via composite signatures, all relevant masking keys need to be available. These can either be part of the payload or kept in a publicly database (with hashes as payloads). The remaining details of the protocol (such as pruning, etc.) remain the same.

The modified protocol can possibly co-exist with the current protocol. We add the new type of transaction output based on composite signatures. These outputs can be mixed with standard outputs. A composite signature based output will be spent using the new protocol described here. A transaction can even be constructed using a mix of these outputs. We leave this as further work.

8   Conclusion and Future Work

Bitcoin is a popular peer-to-peer cryptocurrency with a weak form of anonymity. We presented an enhancement of the bitcoin protocol to increase anonymity. Our method is based on a new cryptographic primitive known as *composite signatures*. Composite signatures are an extension of Boneh et al.'s aggregate signatures [4] and have the property that multiple signatures can be aggregated into one signatures such that once aggregated, the individual signatures cannot be recovered. We gave the security model of composite signatures and presented a construction with a security proof under the random oracle model and the computational Diffie-Hellman assumption in bilinear maps. We also presented a weaker notion of composite signatures (Definition 1), which may be interesting because the publicly computable signatures exhibit a group structure.

Composite signatures can be used to enhance anonymity in cryptocurrencies such as bitcoin by unlinking the input and output addresses from where funds move. In the current bitcoin protocol the sending addresses are linked to the other sending addresses and receiving addresses in a transaction. This link is 'hard' in the sense that it provides a cryptographic proof of funds transfer between those addresses. We use composite signatures to remove all linkages from the sending and receiving addresses. This enables senders to sign messages releasing funds without mentioning the receiving addresses or other sending addresses, thereby providing plausible deniability. Additionally, several transactions can be combined into one large transaction (possibly via the knapsack problem) in order to further obfuscate the links.

A   Proof of Theorem 1

Proof. Let $g, g^x, g^y \in G_1$ be the given CDH instance we need to solve (our goal is to compute g^{xy}). We show how to solve this using A as a black-box.

Setup: We generate $a_1, a_2, \ldots a_n \xleftarrow{R} \mathbb{Z}_q$ and set the target public keys as $pk_i = g^{x+a_i}$ for $1 \leq i \leq n$. The set $PK = \{pk_i\}_{i \in [1..n]}$ is given to A.

H-list: A can query the random oracle H on points from $\Sigma^* \times \Sigma^\kappa \times G_1$. To respond to such queries, we maintain a list called the H-list, which is initially empty and contains tuples of the type

$$(m, r, pk, h, b, c, d) \in \Sigma^* \times \Sigma^\kappa \times G_1 \times G_1 \times \mathbb{Z}_q \times \mathbb{Z}_2 \times \pm 1,$$

such that $h = g^{cdy+b}$ always holds.

H-Queries: On $H(m_i, r_i, pk_i)$ query, if a tuple $(m_i, r_i, pk_i, h_i, b_i, c_i, d_i)$ exists in the H-list, we respond with $h_i = H(m_i, r_i, pk_i)$, otherwise we add such an entry as follows. Generate $b_i \xleftarrow{R} \mathbb{Z}_q$ uniformly and set $d_i = 1$. If $pk_i \notin PK$, set $c_i = 0$, otherwise set $c_i = 1$. Finally, set $h_i = g^{c_i y + b_i}$ and respond with $h_i = H(m_i, r_i, pk_i)$. In effect, $h_i = g^{b_i}$ if $pk_i \notin PK$, otherwise $h_i = g^{b_i + y}$.

Sign queries: Let $\ell = ((m_1, pk_1), (m_2, pk_2), \ldots (m_k, pk_k))$ be any sign query for $k \leq n$. To respond to this, we generate k random numbers $r_1, r_2, \ldots r_k \xleftarrow{R} \Sigma^\kappa$ and for each $i \in [1..k]$ we check the H-list for entries starting with (m_i, r_i, pk_i). If any such entry exists, we report failure and abort, otherwise we add the entries as follows. We uniformly select k pairs $((c_1, d_1), (c_2, d_2), \ldots (c_k, d_k)) \in (\mathbb{Z}_2 \times \pm 1)^k$ such that $\sum_{i=1}^k c_i d_i = 0$ and $k - \sum_{i=1}^k c_i \in \mathbb{Z}_2$. The latter says that at most one of the c_is can be 0.[2] We then generate $b_1, b_2, \ldots b_k \xleftarrow{R} \mathbb{Z}_q$ and for each $i \in [1..k]$, we set $h_i = g^{c_i d_i y_i + b_i}$. We add $(m_i, r_i, pk_i, h_i, b_i, c_i, d_i)$ to the H-list.

Let $\sigma' = g^{\sum_{i=1}^k (x + a_i)(c_i d_i y + b_i)} = g^{xy \sum_{i=1}^k c_i d_i + \sum_{i=1}^k x b_i + a_i c_i d_i y + a_i b_i}$. We know that $\sum_{i=1}^k c_i d_i = 0$ (by construction). Therefore, $\sigma' = g^{\sum_{i=1}^k x b_i + a_i c_i d_i y + a_i b_i}$, a value that can be computed by us. Also, $\sigma = (\sigma', \{r_1, r_2, \ldots r_k\})$ is a valid signature on ℓ, which is our response to the query.

Output: Finally, A outputs a pair (σ_A, ℓ_A). If σ_A is not a valid forgery on ℓ_A, we report failure. Let PK_A be the set of public keys in this forgery. Some of these keys may not be from PK. Let $PK^\# = PK_A \setminus PK$ and $PK^* = PK \cap PK_A$.

By construction, all c_is in the H-list corresponding to the messages signed under $PK^\#$ are 0. Therefore, the respective b_is are the discrete logarithms (to base g) of the corresponding h_is. Hence, we can compute the sub-composite signature corresponding to the messages of PK^*, denoted by σ_* (we compute this by first computing the sub-composite signature corresponding to the messages of $PK^\#$ and "dividing" σ_A by that).

Let $((a_1^*, b_1^*, c_1^*, d_1^*), \ldots, (a_{k^*}^*, b_{k^*}^*, c_{k^*}^*, d_{k^*}^*))$ be tuples containing a_is and H-list entries corresponding to PK^*. If $\sum_{i=1}^{k^*} c_i^* d_i^* = 0$, we report failure and abort, otherwise σ_* corresponds to a signature we could not have computed ourselves, which can be used to solve the CDH problem as follows. We know that $\sigma_* = (\sigma_*', \{r_1^*, \ldots r_{k^*}^*\})$ such that $\sigma_*' = g^{\sum_{i=1}^{k^*} (x + a_i^*)(c_i^* d_i^* y + b_i^*)} = g^{xy \sum_{i=1}^{k^*} c_i^* d_i^*} \cdot g^{\sum_{i=1}^{k^*} x b_i^* + a_i^* c_i^* d_i^* y + a_i^* b_i^*} = g^{xyz} \cdot w$ for some nonzero w and z that we know. Thus, we can compute $g^{xy} = (\sigma_*' / w)^{1/z}$.

It now remains to bound the probability of success. Define events:

- $\mathcal{E}_1 =$ We do not abort during sign queries.
- $\mathcal{E}_2 = \mathcal{E}_1$ and A outputs a successful forgery.
- $\mathcal{E}_3 = \mathcal{E}_2$ and $\sum_{i=1}^{k^*} c_i^* d_i^* \neq 0$.

Then $\Pr[success] = \Pr[\mathcal{E}_3 | \mathcal{E}_2] \cdot \Pr[\mathcal{E}_2 | \mathcal{E}_1] \cdot \Pr[\mathcal{E}_1]$.

---

[2] These pairs can be generated as follows. First set all c_is to 1. If k is odd, randomly set one of the c_is to 0. Then for those c_is that are 1, randomly set half of the d_is to $+1$ and the rest to -1.

Claim 1. $\Pr[\mathcal{E}_1] \geq \left(1 - \frac{\alpha+\gamma-1}{2^\kappa}\right)^{n\alpha}$

Proof. Consider the number of entries in the H-list corresponding to a given (message, public-key) pair (m, pk). Each H-query can add at most one entry to the H-list for this pair. Since a sign query can contain at most one instance of the pair (m, pk), therefore, each sign query can add at most one entry in the H-list for this pair. Therefore there can be a maximum of $\alpha+\gamma-1$ entries in the H-list corresponding to (m, pk). Now select $r \xleftarrow{R} \Sigma^\kappa$ and consider the event that an entry beginning with (m, r, pk) exists in the H-list. Since there are 2^κ possible ways to select r, we can be assured that $\Pr[\text{no entry in H-list for } (m, r, pk)] \geq 1 - \frac{\alpha+\gamma-1}{2^\kappa}$. Now there can be maximum n pairs in a sign query. Therefore, $\Pr[\text{we do not abort in one sign query}] \geq \left(1 - \frac{\alpha+\gamma-1}{2^\kappa}\right)^n$, and so

$$\Pr[\mathcal{E}_1] = \Pr[\text{we do not abort in } \alpha \text{ sign queries}] \geq \left(1 - \frac{\alpha+\gamma-1}{2^\kappa}\right)^{n\alpha} \qquad \square$$

Claim 2. $\Pr[\mathcal{E}_2|\mathcal{E}_1] = \epsilon$.

Proof. If we do not abort during sign queries, then the view of the adversary is identical to a real simulation, and it follows that $\Pr[\mathcal{E}_2|\mathcal{E}_1] = \epsilon$. $\qquad\square$

Claim 3. $\Pr[\mathcal{E}_3|\mathcal{E}_2] \geq 1/3$

Proof. Split H-list entries into two disjoint sets based on how they are generated:

1. S_1: Sign queries on single (message, public-key) pairs. Here $\Pr[c = 0] = 1$.
2. S_2: H-queries or sign queries on two or more (message, public-key) pairs. It can be checked that $\Pr[c = 0] \leq 1/3$ for such entries.

Let the forgery contain k^* (message, public-key) pairs. Let $\{(m_i^*, r_i^*, pk_i^*)\}_{i \in [1..k^*]}$ be the set of tuples corresponding to the forgery. We ensure that an entry for each tuple exists in the H-list (by simulating H-queries ourselves if necessary).

Lemma 1. *If the forgery is valid (i.e., ℓ_A is not signable), then at least one of the tuples in the forgery must must correspond to an element of S_2.*

Proof. If all tuples $\{(m_i^*, r_i^*, pk_i^*)\}_{i \in [1..k^*]}$ in the forgery correspond to elements from S_1, then A made sign queries on every pair (m_i^*, pk_i^*), possibly more than once. By definition, ℓ_A is signable. Hence the forgery cannot be valid. $\qquad\square$

For any signature σ_ℓ from the sign queries or the forgery, define $f(\sigma_\ell) = \sum_{i=1}^k c_i d_i$, obtained from corresponding entries $(m_i, r_i, pk_i, h_i, b_i, c_i, d_i)$ in the H-list. A's goal is to maximize $\Pr[\neg\mathcal{E}_3|\mathcal{E}_2] = \Pr[f(\sigma_*) = 0]$.

Since we did not abort during the sign queries, each tuple (m_i^*, r_i^*, pk_i^*) was used in at most one sign query. Therefore A's view of any of the c_i^*s for tuples from S_2 is independent of any queries. Extending Lemma 1, we can see that if ℓ_A is not signable, then A's view of $f(\sigma_*)$ is independent of all queries. An upper bound for $\Pr[\neg\mathcal{E}_3|\mathcal{E}_2]$ then gives us the worst case scenario.

Keeping tuples from S_1 in the forgery is not useful for A, since $c_i = 0$ for such values and so $f(\sigma_*)$ is independent of them. Therefore, assume that A's forgery contains only elements from S_2. Now S_2 can be further divided into: (1) S_2' consisting of entries due to H-queries and (2) S_2'' consisting of entries due to sign queries. Since for elements of S_2'', the d_is are uniformly distributed between ± 1, while for those of S_2', the d_is are guaranteed to be $+1$, a symmetric argument shows that including elements from S_2' is not beneficial to A since it only biases $f(\sigma_*)$ towards nonzero. Therefore, assume that A's forgery contains only elements from S_2''. A counting argument shows that if all elements are from S_2'', then $\Pr[f(\sigma_*) = 0] \leq 2/3$, with the maximum occurring when A extracts a 2-tuple signature from a 4-tuple signature. Hence $\Pr[\mathcal{E}_3|\mathcal{E}_2] \geq 1/3$ □

This proves Theorem 1.   □

References

1. Nakamoto, S.: Bitcoin: A Peer-to-Peer Electronic Cash System
2. Martins, S., Yang, Y.: Introduction to bitcoins: a pseudo-anonymous electronic currency system. In: Proceedings of the 2011 Conference of the Center for Advanced Studies on Collaborative Research, CASCON '11, Riverton, NJ, USA, pp. 349–350. IBM Corp. (2011)
3. Bitcoin Developers. Bitcoin client source code (github) (2008)
4. Boneh, D., Gentry, C., Lynn, B., Shacham, H.: Aggregate and verifiably encrypted signatures from bilinear maps. In: Biham, E. (ed.) EUROCRYPT 2003. LNCS, vol. 2656, pp. 416–432. Springer, Heidelberg (2003)
5. Coron, J.-S., Naccache, D.: Boneh et al.'s k-Element aggregate extraction assumption is equivalent to the diffie-hellman assumption. In: Laih, C.-S. (ed.) ASIACRYPT 2003. LNCS, vol. 2894, pp. 392–397. Springer, Heidelberg (2003)
6. Lysyanskaya, A., Micali, S., Reyzin, L., Shacham, H.: Sequential aggregate signatures from trapdoor permutations. In: Cachin, C., Camenisch, J.L. (eds.) EUROCRYPT 2004. LNCS, vol. 3027, pp. 74–90. Springer, Heidelberg (2004)
7. Zhu, H., Bao, F., Li, T., Wu, Y.: Sequential aggregate signatures for wireless routing protocols. In: 2005 IEEE Wireless Communications and Networking Conference, vol. 4, pp. 2436–2439 (2005)
8. Ma, D.: Practical forward secure sequential aggregate signatures. In: Abe, M., Gligor, V.D. (eds.), ASIACCS, pp. 341–352. ACM (2008)
9. Boldyreva, A., Gentry, C., O'Neill, A., Yum, D.H.: Ordered multisignatures and identity-based sequential aggregate signatures, with applications to secure routing. In: CCS '07: Proceedings of the 14th ACM Conference on Computer and Communications Security, pp. 276–285. ACM, New York (2007)
10. Lu, S., Ostrovsky, R., Sahai, A., Shacham, H., Waters, B.: Sequential aggregate signatures and multisignatures without random oracles. In: Vaudenay, S. (ed.) EUROCRYPT 2006. LNCS, vol. 4004, pp. 465–485. Springer, Heidelberg (2006)
11. Fischlin, M., Lehmann, A., Schröder, D.: History-free sequential aggregate signatures. In: Visconti, I., De Prisco, R. (eds.) SCN 2012. LNCS, vol. 7485, pp. 113–130. Springer, Heidelberg (2012)
12. Brogle, K., Goldberg, S., Reyzin, L.: Sequential aggregate signatures with lazy verification from trapdoor permutations. In: Wang, X., Sako, K. (eds.) ASIACRYPT 2012. LNCS, vol. 7658, pp. 644–662. Springer, Heidelberg (2012)

13. Androulaki, E., Karame, G., Roeschlin, M., Scherer, T., Capkun, S.: Evaluating user privacy in bitcoin. Cryptology ePrint Archive, Report 2012/596 (2012)
14. Reid, F., Harrigan, M.: An analysis of anonymity in the bitcoin system. In: Altshuler, Y., Elovici, Y., Cremers, A.B., Aharony, N., Pentland, A. (eds.) Security and Privacy in Social Networks, pp. 197–223. Springer, New York (2013)
15. Ron, D., Shamir, A.: Quantitative analysis of the full bitcoin transaction graph. Cryptology ePrint Archive, Report 2012/584 (2012). http://eprint.iacr.org/
16. Zerocoin: Anonymous distributed e-cash from bitcoin (2012)
17. Maxwell, G.: Coinjoin: Bitcoin privacy for the real world (2013)
18. Pisinger, D.: Where are the hard knapsack problems. Comput. Oper. Res. **32**, 2271–2284 (2005)
19. Chvatal, V.: Hard knapsack problems. Oper. Res. **28**(6), 1402–1411 (1980)
20. Micciancio, D.: Generalized compact knapsacks, cyclic lattices, and efficient one-way functions. Comput. Complex. **16**(4), 365–411 (2007). (Prelim. In: FOCS 2002)
21. Miller, V.S.: The Weil pairing, and its efficient calculation. J. Cryptology **17**(4), 235–261 (2004)
22. Uchida, Y., Uchiyama, S.: The tate-lichtenbaum pairing on a hyperelliptic curve via hyperelliptic nets. In: Abdalla, M., Lange, T. (eds.) Pairing 2012. LNCS, vol. 7708, pp. 218–233. Springer, Heidelberg (2013)
23. Hess, F., Smart, N.P., Vercauteren, F.: The Eta pairing revisited. IEEE Trans. Inf. Theor. **52**(10), 4595–4602 (2006)
24. Shinohara, N., Shimoyama, T., Hayashi, T., Takagi, T.: Key length estimation of pairing-based cryptosystems using η_T pairing. In: Ryan, M.D., Smyth, B., Wang, G. (eds.) ISPEC 2012. LNCS, vol. 7232, pp. 228–244. Springer, Heidelberg (2012)
25. Scott, M.: Scaling security in pairing-based protocols. IACR Cryptology ePrint Archive **2005**, 139 (2005)

Rational Zero: Economic Security for Zerocoin with Everlasting Anonymity

Christina Garman, Matthew Green, Ian Miers[✉], and Aviel D. Rubin

Department of Computer Science, The Johns Hopkins University, Baltimore, USA
{cgarman,mgreen,imiers,rubin}@cs.jhu.edu

Abstract. Zerocoin proposed adding decentralized cryptographically anonymous e-cash to Bitcoin. Given the increasing popularity of Bitcoin and its reliance on a distributed pseudononymous public ledger, this anonymity is important if only to provide the same minimal privacy protections from nosy neighbors offered by conventional banking. Unfortunately, at 25 KB, the non-interactive zero-knowledge proofs for spending a zerocoin are nearly prohibitively large. In this paper, we consider several improvements. First, we strengthen Zerocoin's anonymity guarantees, making them independent of the size of these proofs. Given this freedom, we explore several techniques for drastically reducing proof size while ensuring that forging a single zerocoin is more difficult than the block mining process used to maintain Bitcoin's distributed ledger. Provided a zerocoin is worth less than the reward for a Bitcoin block, forging a coin is not an economically rational action. Hence we preserve Zerocoin's absolute anonymity guarantees while achieving drastic reductions in proof size by limiting ourselves to security against rational attackers.

Keywords: Privacy · e-cash

1 Introduction

Bitcoin is an electronic currency built atop a distributed transaction ledger. While Bitcoin has achieved widespread success, it has significant weaknesses related to transaction privacy [16,21]. Zerocoin [17] attempts to address these issues by extending Bitcoin with a new form of anonymous electronic cash. To add privacy while retaining Bitcoin's decentralized nature, Zerocoin uses a novel construction based on digital commitments and efficient zero-knowledge proofs that a commitment is in a list of commitments. While this construction achieves strong anonymity and prevents double spending, it can incur significant costs. In particular, to achieve cryptographically strong protection against double spending, Zerocoin uses large "spend proofs" that grow rapidly as λ, the resistance of the proofs to forgery, increases. Even for the modest $\lambda = 80$ security level (ensuring forgery effort of 2^{80} operations), Zerocoin spend proofs exceed 25 KB. Since these proofs must be stored in the block chain, the large size of these proofs makes it challenging to deploy Zerocoin in practice.

© IFCA/Springer-Verlag Berlin Heidelberg 2014
R. Böhme et al. (Eds.): FC 2014 Workshops, LNCS 8438, pp. 140–155, 2014.
DOI: 10.1007/978-3-662-44774-1_10

In this work we explore extensions to Zerocoin that may substantially decrease the size of these proofs. Our key observation is a need for revised assumptions. Zerocoin was designed on the assumption that all proofs must by computationally infeasible to forge. We observe that this requirement is, in a certain sense, an anachronism of cryptographic formalism. For example, in the real world we do not require that physical money be impossible to forge, merely that it be impossible to forge while making a profit. Indeed this is already true of Zerocoin: the Bitcoin block chain, upon which Zerocoin's integrity depends, does not itself provide strong cryptographic guarantees against powerful attackers. Instead, the Bitcoin protocol depends on the weaker assumption that an attacker cannot amass more than 50 % of the Bitcoin network's computational power.[1] Thus in some sense, cryptographically unforgeable zerocoins are simply impossible: even if the Zerocoin primitives resist forgery, Bitcoin's block chain can be manipulated to provide the same effect. However, the standard game-based approaches of the type used in the original security analysis of Zerocoin do not provide us any insight into safely reducing the Zerocoin security parameter. Given that this would offer a substantial performance improvements, it is interesting to consider new methods of analysis.

A primary contribution of this paper is a new methodology for examining the computational cost of forging non-interactive zero-knowledge proofs relative to the computational costs of Bitcoin mining. Our main result is as follows: by using the payout from mining a new block as a baseline, we can actually quantify the cost of forging a non-interactive zero-knowledge proof. As a result, we are able to construct game theoretic arguments for Zerocoin's resistance to forgery assuming a rational actor who wishes to profit from forging such a coin.

In and of itself, unfortunately, this new perspective does not allow us to lower the security parameter λ as far as we would like nor, consequently, realize the full reduction in proof size and increase in proof performance. To fully realize these savings, we examine two different techniques for increasing the cost of coin forgery without raising Zerocoin's proof sizes. In our new model, the security parameters are chosen based on economic considerations — such as the value of a zerocoin.

An immediate concern with our new approach is that there exist other factors that cannot be priced as easily as coin forgery. One such factor is the user's *anonymity*. There are no known techniques for pricing the value of a user's long-term transaction privacy, since this price is subjective and may vary from user to user. Moreover, we cannot easily predict the future cost of de-anonymization attacks. Indeed, since Zerocoin transcripts may be retained for long periods of time, the cost of executing an offline attack on a user's anonymity may decrease enormously over time as new computational techniques (e.g., quantum computers) become available. We must be careful in our protocol changes, since even a minor weakening of the zero-knowledge characteristics of Zerocoin's proofs could have significant long-term impact on the anonymity of users. Thus a necessary

---

[1] Some recent results raise questions about this 50 % number [9].

prerequisite of our above analysis is an explicit separation of Zerocoin's security as a real-world currency from its anonymity as a "pure" cryptographic protocol.

Fortunately we are able to address this concern in our work. In fact, through some simple enhancements to the Zerocoin protocol, we are able to provide an even stronger guarantee than what is provided by the original Zerocoin paper. Specifically, our new construction ensures that proofs will provide long-term statistical zero-knowledge even when the hash function they are instantiated with proves to be non-ideal, i.e., it behaves very differently from a random oracle.[2] Not just does this provide stronger anonymity guarantees, it safely allows the use of the block hash as part of the zero-knowledge proof even though the block may have adversarially controlled input. This proves to be a crucial step to increasing the cost of forging a zerocoin.

Our analysis is somewhat unusual in that it applies only to the zero-knowledge property of the proofs; we continue to analyze the soundness of the proofs under the assumption of an ideal hash. The key benefit of our approach is that we are able to retain the efficiency of the original Fiat-Shamir proofs while ensuring that user anonymity is protected over long periods of time. This gives us everlasting anonymity in the common reference string model.

Finally, as an independent contribution, we outline a construction for divisible Zerocoin. The original Zerocoin protocol proposes a new form of electronic cash in which individual coins all have the same value. While the Bitcoin-equivalent value of each zerocoin can be adjusted by protocol convention (and multiple denominations of Zerocoin can be instantiated simultaneously), this property can still be quite restrictive. In this work we show how to modify the Zerocoin protocol to create *divisible* coins, such that every zerocoin can contain an arbitrary individual denomination which may subsequently be "subdivided" into new coins of arbitrary value.

2   Background

2.1   Bitcoin

Bitcoin is a distributed e-cash system that operates without trusted parties or signing authorities. Indeed, the only cryptographic keys necessary for the system to operate are held by individual users and used to authenticate fund transfers.

At a high level, Bitcoin is a set of transaction semantics built on top of a distributed ledger which is known as the block chain. The exact semantics of the transactions are irrelevant here, so for a more detailed discussion of them and the modifications necessary for Zerocoin, we direct the reader to the original Zerocoin paper by Miers et al. [17] or the original Bitcoin paper [19].

---

[2] Specifically, we are concerned with future vulnerabilities in hash functions such as SHA256 that might allow for practical attacks on the zero-knowledge property of Fiat-Shamir proofs. While this concern seems rarified, existing analyses do not allow us to rule out such attacks.

Of extreme importance to our proposed modifications to Zerocoin, however, is the mechanism by which Bitcoin's ledger is maintained. We detail it here.

Consider a version of Bitcoin where there were a fixed number of network nodes. In this case, we could simply have the nodes vote on the correct version of the ledger. Under the assumption that the majority of the nodes are honest, this results in a correct ledger and hence a valid currency system. Effectively, this is the consensus technique used in Byzantine systems. However, Bitcoin is not such a closed network: anyone can download the software, fire up an instance, and join the network. In particular, one individual can fire up numerous instances and mount a Sybil attack, effectively stuffing the ballot box.

Bitcoin's approach to solving this issue is perhaps most intuitively described as the one-CPU-cyle-one-vote approach. Instead of having each node vote, consider a version of Bitcoin that places a computational requirement on voting and updating consensus. Mounting a Sybil attack would be costly. Bitcoin takes this one step further and instead of voting, actually requires a computationally intensive process to propose an update and has updates accepted only if they add on to the maximally difficult set of updates. Under the assumption that the majority of the computational power of the network is held by honest nodes and the requirements that honest nodes only build updates on valid updates, the longest chain of updates will be the correct consensus value of the ledger. Bitcoin calls this process mining, and we describe it below.

In Bitcoin, each node competes to produce an update to the block chain, known as a block, containing new transactions. The block contains a partial hash collision over (1) the previous block hash (hence block chain), (2) the hash of the transactions, and (3) a nonce. This proof of work is $\mathcal{H}_b(data||nonce) < t$ where t is the difficulty target. The target is picked by the network every two weeks in order to cause the rate at which blocks are created to average 10 min given the network's current computational power. As of November 2013, the current difficulty is $609,482,679.89 \approx 2^{29}$. The number of expected hash calculations required to generate a block is given as $difficulty * 2^{32}$. As a result, it takes 2^{61} expected hash calls to generate a single Bitcoin block. Bitcoin uses the double application of SHA256 as its hash function $\mathcal{H}_b$.

Bitcoin, however, goes yet one step further to ensure block chain integrity: a block is not fully trusted until it has a certain number of confirmations (typically six), meaning that there are six blocks on top of it. As a result, the effort required to manipulate a block and completely ensure it stays on the block chain is at least $2^{61} * 6 \approx 2^{63}$ hash calls.

2.2 Zero-Knowledge Proofs

In a zero-knowledge protocol [11] a user (the prover) proves a statement to another party (the verifier) without revealing anything about the statement other than that it is true.

A three-round example of a zero-knowledge protocol is often referred to as a Sigma protocol because Σ represents the flow of the protocol. The three steps can be described in the following manner: (1) commitment, (2) challenge, and

(3) response. A popular and well-known example of this is the technique of Schnorr [22], used to prove knowledge of a discrete logarithm. The protocol works as follows (Fig. 1):

Given a cyclic group G of order q with generator g and $y = g^x$, prove knowledge of x.

Prover		Verifier
Choose $r \in_R \mathbb{Z}_q$		
Calculate $t = g^r$		
	$\xrightarrow{\text{Send } t}$	
		Choose $c \in_R \mathbb{Z}_q$
	$\xleftarrow{\text{Send } c}$	
Calculate $s = xc + r \pmod{q}$		
	$\xrightarrow{\text{Send } s}$	
		Accept if $g^s = ty^c$

Fig. 1. Schnorr protocol for proving knowledge of a discrete logarithm.

While zero-knowledge protocols are normally viewed in the "general cheating verifier" setting, where no matter the strategy of the verifier he learns no additional information, we can also consider the "honest verifier" (or semi-honest verifier) setting. An honest verifier must follow the protocol specifications exactly but maintains the ability to keep a record of the entire interaction [12]. This is of use to us because the Fiat-Shamir heuristic [10] allows us to transform any three-round (Sigma) honest-verifier zero-knowledge protocol into a non-interactive (one-round) zero-knowledge proof of knowledge with the use of a hash function modeled as a random oracle. We demonstrate an example of the application of the Fiat-Shamir heuristic using the Schnorr protocol in Fig. 2 below:

Prover		Verifier
Choose $r \in_R \mathbb{Z}_q$		
Calculate $t = g^r$		
Compute $c = \mathcal{H}(t)$		
Calculate $s = xc + r \pmod{q}$		
	$\xrightarrow{\text{Send } (t,s)}$	
		Compute $c = \mathcal{H}(t)$
		Accept if $g^s = ty^c$

Fig. 2. The Fiat-Shamir heuristic as applied to the Schnorr protocol.

When referring to the aforementioned proofs we will use the notation of Camenisch and Stadler [7]. For instance, $\mathsf{NIZKPoK}\{(x,y) : h = g^x \ \wedge \ c = g^y\}$ denotes a non-interactive zero-knowledge proof of knowledge of the elements x and y that satisfy both $h = g^x$ and $c = g^y$. All values not enclosed in ()'s are assumed to be known to the verifier.

2.3 Zerocoin

The original Zerocoin protocol added anonymous currency to Bitcoin that was backed by bitcoins. A zerocoin was a commitment to a serial number S. Zerocoins were minted when a user submitted a transaction spending a fixed amount of bitcoins (e.g., 1 bitcoin) and outputting a new zerocoin. The bitcoins were placed in an escrow pool and the new zerocoin added to a list of all zerocoins. Zerocoins could be spent to withdraw the same fixed bitcoins from the escrow pool by revealing the serial number of the coin and proving it came from the list of coins. This proof was examined by the distributed network running Bitcoin and, if valid and the serial number unused, the correct amount of bitcoins were transferred. Specifically, the proof was a zero-knowledge proof that (1) some coin had that serial number and (2) that that coin was on the list of minted coins. Because the proof is zero-knowledge, any given coin spend cannot be traced to its withdrawal and hence is anonymous.

The naive version of this proof, instantiated as "either this coin, or this coin, or this coin, or ...", is of size $O(n)$. The principal cryptographic contribution of the original paper was finding a compact representation of the list of coins that still admitted a commitment scheme containing a serial number. Miers et al. accomplished this by using a cryptographic accumulator [3] to represent the list of coins as one group element, a proof due to Camenisch and Lysyanskaya [6] to prove that a committed value is accumulated, and finally a double discrete log proof [8] to prove that the committed value is actually a commitment to a serial number. This results in a proof that is constant size regardless of the number of coins on the list.

Unfortunately, the double discrete log proof is constructed using cut-and-choose methods which effectively repeat a single proof multiple times to decrease the probability of forgery. As a result, the proof is of size $\lambda \cdot 2k$ where k is the size of a single field element and λ is the soundness parameter of the proof. For 1024 bit commitments and an 80 bit security level, this results in a 20 KB double discrete log proof and a total proof size (including the accumulator proof) of 25 KB. Moreover, single threaded runtime for both verification and generation of the proof runs in $O(\lambda \cdot k)$.

Finally, as the proofs for spending a zerocoin need to be publicly verifiable to allow the withdrawal of bitcoins form the escrow pool, they must be non-interactive. To accomplish this, Zerocoin uses the Fiat-Shamir heuristic to transform the above interactive proofs into non-interactive ones. Moreover, the proof is actually used as a signature of knowledge, not just spending a coin, but also signing the Bitcoin address where the withdrawn bitcoins should be deposited.

3   Everlasting Anonymity

The original zero-knowledge proofs in Zerocoin were non-interactive Fiat-Shamir proofs where both the soundness and zero-knowledge property held only in the random oracle model. This is a rather large concern since, at some point in the future, it seems likely SHA256 will be broken in a way that makes it utterly unsuitable for instantiating a random oracle, just as MD5 and MD2 have been broken. Old Zerocoin proofs using that function will still be around, and their anonymity should be preserved if possible. Intuitively, this should not be an issue, however, absent further analysis, one cannot be sure anonymity is maintained.

More significantly, one of our proposed techniques for increasing the cost of forging a zerocoin depends on the prover interacting with the block chain to generate the proof. As the block chain can be adversarially controlled, we need to ensure the proof is still zero-knowledge even in the face of block chain manipulation.

We take the expedient of detailing a simple modification to the proofs that, while still only achieving soundness in the random oracle model, achieves at least statistical zero-knowledge in the common reference string model. In the original (non-interactive) proofs, the challenge (i.e., the second move in a standard three-way "sigma" interactive zero-knowledge proof) was obtained by hashing what would have been the first move in the interactive version. In the random oracle model, a simulator can program a hash function to output arbitrary results. Accordingly, such a simulator could induce a verifier to accept a "proof" even though the simulator knew no witness to the statement being proved. Thus the original proof was zero-knowledge. Obviously when instantiated with an actual hash function, this property no longer strictly holds.

To fix this we propose applying a standard modification for converting from (interactive) honest verifier zero-knowledge proofs to (interactive) non-honest verifier proofs before applying the Fiat-Shamir heuristic: instead of making the first move in the protocol public, first commit to it and then reveal the move only after the challenge is output. Specifically, instead of hashing the first move of the transcript to create a challenge value, we hash a commitment to (the hash of) the first move of the transcript. See Fig. 3 for an example using the Schnorr protocol. As a result, any simulator who can control the common reference string can construct the commitment scheme such that they can equivocate and decommit to a first move that satisfies the generated challenge. This is not a typical approach as Fiat-Shamir proofs rely on the random oracle model themselves. However, by using this approach we get proofs that are at least statistical zero-knowledge in the common reference string model, even if soundness still requires the random oracle model, i.e., from the point of view of a privacy critical system, the proofs fail safe.

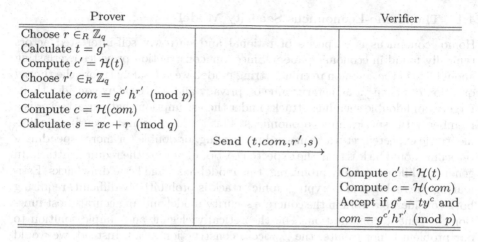

Prover	Verifier
Choose $r \in_R \mathbb{Z}_q$ Calculate $t = g^r$ Compute $c' = \mathcal{H}(t)$ Choose $r' \in_R \mathbb{Z}_q$ Calculate $com = g^{c'} h^{r'} \pmod{p}$ Compute $c = \mathcal{H}(com)$ Calculate $s = xc + r \pmod{q}$	
$\xrightarrow{\quad \text{Send } (t, com, r', s) \quad}$	
	Compute $c' = \mathcal{H}(t)$ Compute $c = \mathcal{H}(com)$ Accept if $g^s = ty^c$ and $com = g^{c'} h^{r'} \pmod{p}$

Fig. 3. Dishonest verifier Schnorr protocol with Fiat-Shamir.

4 Cost Effective Security Against Forgery and Double Spending

Conceptually, payment systems are subject to three types of attacks: theft of funds, forgery of funds, and double (or more) spending of legitimate attacker controlled funds. These are major issues for both theoretical and extent currency and payment systems, and there are a broad range of solutions which vary considerably in terms of both cost and effectiveness. On one end of the spectrum, e-cash schemes typically avoid all three attacks through the use of secure cryptographic primitives which require a staggeringly prohibitive amount of computational power to break. In contrast, on the decidedly low end of the spectrum, debit cards in the US provide little-to-no security against theft/cloning. Instead they leverage fraud detection and minimization procedures to get the costs of such attacks to acceptable levels without imposing too high an overhead on transactions (e.g., verifying multiple forms of ID for every single transaction).

Certainly, the cryptographic approach is superior provided it is achievable with little overhead. Unfortunately for Zerocoin, it is neither completely achievable nor cheap: as mentioned previously, spends for even modest security parameters reach 25 KB and take 0.5 seconds to verify. Moreover, even if Zerocoin was cryptographically secure against such attacks, Bitcoin, upon which it depends, is not. Both double spends and forgery of zerocoins can be accomplished by breaking Bitcoin and without ever touching Zerocoin's underlying cryptographic primitives.

However, the approaches used by centralized credit card companies are antithetical to the decentralized nature of Bitcoin. Moreover, we prefer not to incur the administrative overhead, merchant fees, and chargebacks inherent in the fraud-management approach used by debit cards. Instead we opt for a middle ground: we create cryptographic primitives that are not cost effective to break.

4.1   The Homo-Economicus Security Model

Homo-economicus is a species of rational and narrowly self-interested actors typically found in economic papers. Since our construction provides everlasting anonymity in the common reference string model, we can safely ignore the thorny question of placing a monetary value on privacy and hence safely consider theft, forgery, and double spending attacks under the assumption that our attacker is a member of the species homo-economicus. This leads to a simple security requirement: the expected return from stealing, forging, or double (or more) spending a zerocoin should be less than the expected cost of mounting the required attack. In general, while potentially promising, this model has some large drawbacks. Estimating the real cost of a cryptographic attack is prohibitively difficult, requiring both considerable work in the concrete security model and an accurate cost function for generic computation. The theoretically elegant and simple solution to our problem is not to alter the Zerocoin construction at all. Instead, we would construct a game that, given an attacker who can forge a zerocoin, extracts the computational effort required. One would then assign a monetary value to this work and ensure it is worth more than the resulting forged coin.

We make no such attempt here. Instead, we model our construction only in the expected number of calls an attacker must make to a hash oracle and use the reward for mining a Bitcoin block to establish the market value of computation. While this approach is inherently linked to Bitcoin, it serves our limited purposes well.

Of course, such a model discounts the possibility of someone who is not financially motivated (e.g., a government) wanting to destroy the currency. While this may be a legitimate concern, we note that an attacker who merely wants to disrupt Zerocoin could also easily attack/block the underlying Bitcoin network and likely at far lower cost.

4.2   Zerocoin Attack Surface

We examine how the choice of various security parameters interacts with attacks on Zerocoin and how to minimize these parameters in light of that. Again, due to everlasting anonymity, we neglect attacks on Zerocoin's anonymity properties.

Theft. Actually stealing a user's zerocoin entails spending a coin with the same serial number. Since the Pedersen commitment containing a serial number (i.e., the coin) is information theoretically hiding, an attacker who cannot compromise a user's computer and wallet can only guess blindly. This is a very low probability event and can be made arbitrarily small by increasing the serial number length. If as an absolute minimal bound we assume 512 bit commitments, then we can have 512 bit serial numbers or, in the case of divisible coins, $512 - 64 = 448$ bit serial numbers. A theft probability of 1 in 2^{448} is too small to consider practically and hence we discount theft as a worry.

A second technical consideration for Zerocoin is that proof forgeries can deplete the escrow pool of bitcoins that zerocoins are exchanged for. This would effectively steal someone's coins. A simple solution to this is to operate with no explicit escrow pool, opting instead to destroy bitcoins when minting a zerocoin and create fresh bitcoins when spending one. As a result, forgery of a zerocoin results only in inflation. If forgery is very rare, this is a manageable problem.

Forgery. Factoring the accumulator's RSA modulus allows an attacker to forge the coin membership proof and hence forge an unlimited number of coins. This is perhaps the single biggest target in Zerocoin. As a result, we have little choice but to recommend a large modulus, say 3072 bits.

A second avenue for forging a coin is to forge the zero-knowledge proof in a spend. Each such forgery results in one and only one forged coin (since even a forged proof has a unique serial number). As such, we want to make the cost of conducting n forgeries more than the value of n coins. The bulk of the remaining portion of this section will focus on techniques to accomplish this.

Double Spending. To double spend a coin, one must assign the coin two different serial numbers. This is equivalent to causing the commitment to open to two separate values. Unfortunately, for simple Pedersen commitments, computing a single discrete log value — $\log_g(h)$ or $\log_h(g)$ — allows this to be done an infinite number of times, again giving us a single point of failure. We will discuss a modification to Pedersen commitments that makes this attack more expensive per instance, though does not eliminate entirely the aggregate effect.

4.3 Raising the Cost of Proof Forgeries

Forging a zero-knowledge proof implies guessing the challenge value prior to starting the protocol. For Fiat-Shamir based non-interaction zero-knowledge proofs, where the challenge is provided by the hash of the first move of the protocol, the only way to do this — assuming the hash function is a random oracle — is to repeatedly query the hash function until you get lucky. If the challenge value has length λ then the probability of forging the proof is $P(f) = 2^{-\lambda}$. Normally for zero-knowledge proofs we choose λ such that $P(f)$ is negligible, and hence, even with a concerted offline attack, a forgery is not feasible.

Suppose it takes b expected evaluations of $\mathcal{H}_B$ to mine a Bitcoin block. If v is the value of a coin and p is the payout from mining a block in terms of reward and collected transaction fees, then we need it to take q expected queries of $\mathcal{H}_B$ to forge the proof such that:

$$\frac{p}{b} > \frac{v}{q}$$

I.e., it pays more per hash calculation to try and mine a block than "mine" a proof forgery. Unfortunately, this analysis yields only a small reduction in the security parameter. The payout for mining a block in terms of transactions fees and the reward is roughly 2^4.[3] Mining such a block at current difficulty levels

---

[3] This is discounted to allow for lower payouts from, e.g., a mining cartel's cut.

takes 2^{61} calls to $\mathcal{H}_B$. Assuming a zerocoin is worth one bitcoin, solving the above equation gives us $q = 2^{57}$ and hence $\lambda = 57$.

Proof of Work. Instead of a simple query to $\mathcal{H}_B$, we can make a single instance of the zero-knowledge proof hash function make a tunable number of calls w to $\mathcal{H}_B$ in much the same manner as PBKDF2. Thus it takes $q = 2^{\lambda}w$ expected queries to $\mathcal{H}_B$ to forge a proof.

As a result, we end up with a different boundary condition for forgery unprofitability:

$$\frac{(2^{\lambda}w)p}{b} > v$$

Again assuming the current reward of 25 bitcoins per block plus transaction fees, 2^{61} invocations of $\mathcal{H}_B$ to find a block, and $\lambda = 40$ bit proofs, we end up with approximately $\frac{(2^{40}w)2^4}{2^{61}} > v$. If zerocoins are each worth one bitcoin, this necessitates a value of w of roughly 2^{17} or about 130 thousand hash calls. Since $\mathcal{H}_B$ is the double SHA256 computation used by Bitcoin, we can use the extensive comparisons of Bitcoin mining power across hardware to estimate the cost of this approach. A low end Intel core i3 can compute 1.8 million hashes a second, a now more than a decade old Pentium IV can compute between 0.85 and 1.29 depending on the model, and an AMR Cortex A-9 such as found in the Samsung Galaxy SII can do 1.3 million hashes a second [1]. As such, this approach is surprisingly viable even for very modest hardware.

This approach has one major limitation: it gets worse as mining difficulty increases, and mining difficulty has been increasing very rapidly as application specific integrated circuits (ASIC) mining hardware comes online. Although one could easily (and should) exclude ASICs from forging proofs via trivial changes to the hash function (e.g., changing the padding or using triple SHA256) that invalidate the ASICs but do not affect hash throughput on a general purpose computer, this does not solve the problem. We can do nothing to address the drop in payout per hash that ASICs introduce by upping the number of hashes needed to mine a block but not changing the reward.[4] Thus we would still eventually have to increase w beyond levels feasible on non specialized hardware.

Since the first move in the proof reveals nothing and our proofs allow for dishonest verifiers, this computation can be outsourced. However, paying for that outsourcing represents a catch-22: how do you anonymously pay to spend anonymous currency? While there are potential solutions to this involving small anonymous face-to-face Bitcoin transactions as a bootstrapping mechanism, they are less than ideal.

Rate-Limiting Forgeries. A second option that does not place a computational or financial burden on individuals is to rate limit the proof's hash function. To do this, we split the proof over $n + 1$ blocks. The first block encodes the first

---

[4] Recall that the difficulty of mining a block adjusts to keep blocks spaced at 10 min intervals. Hence greater hashing power necessitates more hashes needed per block.

moves of the protocol. The nth block encodes responses to the challenge value. The λ bit challenge value is generated by taking the first $\frac{\lambda}{n}$ bits from each block of the $1, \ldots, n$ blocks and hashing them to produce a challenge. For an honest prover, this entails no additional work (unlike the proof of work system) as they can satisfy the proof for any challenge and thus must merely wait for the block chain to advance before computing the proof. A dishonest prover, on the other hand, must get a specific challenge. As such, they must either mount many parallel attempts each with a different guess at the challenge value or control the block hashes and hence the challenge. The former can be prevented by merely limiting the number of transactions in a block (Bitcoin already effectively does this by limiting the size of a block).

The likelihood that a challenge value is the one guessed is still $2^{-\lambda}$. However, assuming a maximum of 1000 Zerocoin transactions per block, attempts can only be made every half second. If we assume 40 bit security levels for the proofs, we need an expected 2^{40} hash calls and thus making a single forged zerocoin would take 2^{39} seconds or roughly seventeen thousand years. Even at Bitcoin's current unrealized theoretical maximum transaction throughput of seven transactions a second [14] this would still take over 2400 years. This seems both a prohibitive amount of time for mounting an attack and, as a practical matter, an acceptable rate of coin forgery.

Manipulating the block chain to produce the correct challenge is even more difficult. An attacker must generate far more than n blocks in order to get the correct challenge. They must first generate all n blocks, complete with proof of work for each, and extract the challenge. The overwhelmingly likely case is that the challenge is wrong, and they must repeat the process. If this was done for $n = 2$ blocks and all bits were extracted only from the last block, this would require the attacker to compute 2^{λ} expected blocks to get the right challenge and hence make $2^{\lambda+61}$ calls to $\mathcal{H}_B$ at Bitcoin's current difficulty. The situation, however, is actually worse than that since the last block only contributes $\frac{\lambda}{n}$ bits as input to the hash function the attacker is trying to get to output the guessed challenge value. Thus the attacker cannot merely generate 2^{λ} fresh n^{th} blocks knowing that by the pigeonhole principle one of those will result in the right challenge. Instead, they must actually start with a fresh first block and generate the entire sequence before checking if it works.[5] Not just does this increase the difficulty of mounting such an attack substantially, but because each block depends on the previous one, it adds in a sequential bottleneck that prevents fully parallelizing the attack process. Recall that six blocks is the threshold for normal Bitcoin transactions to be considered confirmed and as such the mere ability to compute six blocks efficiently, let alone $2^{\lambda} \cdot 6$ blocks, constitutes a massive attack on Bitcoin.

---

[5] It is possible to prune some of this work by checking if given, e.g., the first two of n blocks, any assignment of the remaining bits would hash to the correct challenge. We leave to future work the analysis of this strategy along with the best way to skew the sampling of bits from the n blocks to minimize it.

We stress that the above approach is not safe on its own: without the changes described in Sect. 3, adversarial manipulation of the block chain can result in a complete loss of anonymity.

4.4 Raising the Cost of Double Spends

In the original Zerocoin construction of Miers et al., computing a single discrete log of $log_g(h)$ or $log_h(g)$ broke the binding property of Pedersen commitments completely and allowed arbitrary double spends. This is undesirable since a single 1024 bit discrete log instance may be in the range of things solvable by a well-funded organization in six months to a year. We wish to avoid such an attack without using larger moduli.

Instead of using a fixed $g, h \in G$ for our commitment group, we hash the serial number into G to select g, h at random using two different hash functions, $\mathcal{H}, \mathcal{H}'$. When spending a coin, we provide these bases in the proof and then the verifier both checks the proof and that the bases result from the hash of the serial number. As a result, assuming $\mathcal{H}, \mathcal{H}'$ are collision resistant, double spends occur exactly once for any given discrete log computation.

We accomplish this by using the hash of the coin serial number S to select g and h at random. This is enforced at verification time by the verifier simply checking that $g = \mathcal{H}(S)$ and $h = \mathcal{H}'(S)$ for the provided public proof inputs. We briefly outline why this modification preserves both the blinding and binding properties of a Pedersen commitment.

Pedersen commitments are information theoretically blinding because for a fixed commitment c and any given value x, there is randomness r that opens the commitment to that value and all such r values are equally likely, i.e., for a given g^x, there exists an r such that $c = g^x h^r \mod p$. If we replace h with $h' = \mathcal{H}'(x||pad)$, then we merely shift the randomness r by $log_{h'}(h)$ and do not change the distribution on r. Hence this still holds.

Pedersen commitments are computationally binding if the discrete log problem is hard. Given a commitment c that opens to two different values x, x' with randomness r, r', one can compute the discrete log of h with respect to g by substituting in $g^l = h$ and solving $x + lr = x' + lr'$ since $g^x g^{lr} = g^{x'} g^{lr'} = g^{x+lr} = g^{x'+lr'}$. Since g and h are no longer fixed public parameters in our case, we cannot use a single violation of the blinding property to break an instance of the discrete log problem in G. It is probably possible to construct a security proof based on the assumption that the hash function is collision resistant and the discrete log problem is hard. As the rest of our constructions depend on the random oracle model for soundness, we take the expedient of programing the hash function to output the appropriate generators. This is sufficient for our purposes.

Of course, solving l discrete logs in a *fixed* G is not as hard as solving l discrete logs in *distinct* $G_1, \ldots, G_l$. The exact security of this appears not to have been well studied. Some preliminary results indicate that for Pollard's Rho algorithm, the difficulty of computing $l < \epsilon \sqrt[3]{N}$ discrete logs is approximately $\sqrt{2NL}$ where N is the order of the group and $0 < \epsilon < 1$ [2]. The far faster class of index calculus methods are still sub-exponential when run on a fixed group. Specifically, they run in $L_p(\frac{1}{2}, \frac{1}{2})$ instead of $L_p(1, \frac{1}{2})$ with a sub-exponential space requirement $L_p(\frac{1}{2}, \frac{1}{2})$ [18]. What this means in practice is an interesting question. We note that both SSH and the Internet Key Exchange protocol used in IPv6 use groups for Diffie-Hellman that are fixed for far longer timespans than we are contemplating.

5 Divisible Cash

The original Zerocoin construction did not make particularly efficient use of the fact that coins are an information theoretically blinding and computationally binding commitment that can contain arbitrary data. These commitments were merely used as a container for a serial number. Yet there are a whole number of techniques for proving far more interesting statements about commitments. These techniques allow us to construct divisible coins. We are aware of an unpublished result that makes this observation in the context of a different Zerocoin construction entirely. Our purpose in this document is not to introduce divisibility but to point out how it can be achieved using the existing cryptographic construction.

Intuition. Instead of a coin being a commitment to a serial number, we propose committing to a serial number S and a balance B. The coin owner can divide the balance B_0 in an existing coin c_0 into two new coins c_1 and c_2 with balances B_1 and B_2 respectively. She does so by creating two new coins, proving that $B_0 = B_1 + B_2$, and revealing the serial number S_0 of the divided coin c_0. Note that because we do not reveal the balance of any coin in this construction and by the original Zerocoin construction the spends for the resulting c_1 and c_2 are unlinkable to their minting, we lose nothing by explicitly identifying the original coin c_0. As such, we do not need to provide the expensive proof used for a spend, we can just identify the coin outright. This results in a highly efficient proof.

The technical question left to answer is how do we encode both the balance and the serial number in the coin? There are two possible constructions:

– We use multi-message commitments where one message is the serial number and one is the balance.
– We encode both the balance and serial number in one value in the commitment.

While conceptually elegant, multi-message commitments are problematic. In the case of Pedersen commitments [20], a commitment to a vector m of messages n is $(\prod_{i=1}^{n} g_i^{m_i})h^r$. Since the coin is then $g_1^{m_1} g_2^{m_2} h^r$, the double discrete log proof used for a coin spend must prove knowledge of three exponents instead of two. This adds approximately 10 KB to the proof. With the encoding case, we can encode the balance as the l low order bits of the original serial number and use the high $2^{l-\epsilon}$ as the actual serial number. We merely open the coin using the existing spend proof, reveal the encoded value, and then anyone can extract out the serial number and balance.

Dividing a coin c_0 is not as straightforward. We must prove that $B_0 = B_1 + B_2$ and reveal the existing coin's serial number S_0 without revealing anything about the serial numbers for the new coins. We do this as follows:

$$\pi = \mathsf{NIZKPoK}\{(S_1, S_2, r_0, r_1, r_2, B_0, B_1, B_2):$$
$$(B_0 = B_1 + B_2) \wedge_{i=0}^{2} (c_i = g^{B_i + 2^{l+\epsilon}S_i} h^{r_i} \wedge 0 \le B_i < 2^l \wedge 0 \le S_i < 2^l)\}$$

This proof can be accomplished with a variety of standard techniques for efficiently proving range restrictions [4,5,13,15]. The granularity of the ranges these techniques admit vary and will define both the size l of the serial number and balance and space ϵ between the two values.

6   Conclusion

We demonstrate several useful extensions to Zerocoin. First, by removing the random oracle assumption for the zero-knowledge property of the proofs, we get everlasting security in the common reference string model. Second, and most importantly, we provide a means to model the cost of forging a coin and hence allow for cryptographic parameters to be picked to make such forgery uneconomic. As a result, we argue that one can safely reduce the soundness of the proofs from 80 bits to 40, reducing proof size from 25 KB to 10 KB and nearly halving proof generation and verification time on a single threaded implementation (or increasing throughput on a multithreaded one). The techniques used to accomplish this are specific both to Bitcoin and certain instantiations of hash functions for Fiat-Shamir proofs. We are hopeful future work will provide a general model for game-theoretic security for e-cash.

References

1. Mining hardware comparison. https://en.bitcoin.it/wiki/Mining_hardware_comparison. Accessed 23 Nov 2013
2. Kuhn, F., Struik, R.: Random walks revisited: extensions of pollard's rho algorithm for computing multiple discrete logarithms. In: Vaudenay, S., Youssef, A.M. (eds.) SAC 2001. LNCS, vol. 2259, pp. 212–229. Springer, Heidelberg (2001)
3. Benaloh, J.C., de Mare, M.: One-way accumulators: a decentralized alternative to digital signatures. In: Helleseth, T. (ed.) EUROCRYPT 1993. LNCS, vol. 765, pp. 274–285. Springer, Heidelberg (1994)
4. Boudot, F.: Efficient proofs that a committed number lies in an interval. In: Preneel, B. (ed.) EUROCRYPT 2000. LNCS, vol. 1807, pp. 431–444. Springer, Heidelberg (2000)
5. Camenisch, J.L., Chaabouni, R., Shelat, A.: Efficient protocols for set membership and range proofs. In: Pieprzyk, J. (ed.) ASIACRYPT 2008. LNCS, vol. 5350, pp. 234–252. Springer, Heidelberg (2008)
6. Camenisch, J.L., Lysyanskaya, A.: An efficient system for non-transferable anonymous credentials with optional anonymity revocation. In: Pfitzmann, B. (ed.) EUROCRYPT 2001. LNCS, vol. 2045, p. 93. Springer, Heidelberg (2001)

7. Camenisch, J.L., Stadler, M.A.: Efficient group signature schemes for large groups. In: Kaliski Jr., B.S. (ed.) CRYPTO 1997. LNCS, vol. 1294, pp. 410–424. Springer, Heidelberg (1997)
8. Camenisch, J.L.: Group signature schemes and payment systems based on the discrete logarithm problem. Ph.D. thesis, ETH Zürich (1998)
9. Eyal, I., Sirer, E.G.: Majority is not enough: bitcoin mining is vulnerable (2013)
10. Fiat, A., Shamir, A.: How to prove yourself: practical solutions to identification and signature problems. In: Odlyzko, A.M. (ed.) CRYPTO 1986. LNCS, vol. 263, pp. 186–194. Springer, Heidelberg (1987)
11. Goldreich, O., Micali, S., Wigderson, A.: Proofs that yield nothing but their validity and a methodology of cryptographic protocol design. In: FOCS (1986)
12. Goldreich, O.: A short tutorial of zero-knowledge (2010)
13. Groth, J.: Non-interactive zero-knowledge arguments for voting. In: Ioannidis, J., Keromytis, A.D., Yung, M. (eds.) ACNS 2005. LNCS, vol. 3531, pp. 467–482. Springer, Heidelberg (2005)
14. Lee, T.B.: Bitcoin needs to scale by a factor of 1000 to compete with Visa. Here's how to do it, November 2013. http://www.washingtonpost.com
15. Lipmaa, H.: On diophantine complexity and statistical zero-knowledge arguments. In: Laih, C.-S. (ed.) ASIACRYPT 2003. LNCS, vol. 2894, pp. 398–415. Springer, Heidelberg (2003)
16. Meiklejohn, S., Pomarole, M., Jordan, G., Levchenko, K., McCoy, D., Voelker, G.M., Savage, S.: A fistful of bitcoins: characterizing payments among men with no names. In: Internet Measurement Conference (2013)
17. Miers, I., Garman, C., Green, M., Rubin, A.D.: Zerocoin: anonymous distributed e-cash from bitcoin. In: IEEE Symposium on Security and Privacy (2013)
18. Mihalcik, J.: An analysis of algorithms for solving discrete logarithms in fixed groups. Master's thesis, Navel Post Graduate School (March 2010)
19. Nakamoto, S.: Bitcoin: A peer-to-peer electronic cash system, 2009 (2012). http://www.bitcoin.org/bitcoin.pdf
20. Pedersen, T.P.: Non-interactive and information-theoretic secure verifiable secret sharing. In: Feigenbaum, J. (ed.) CRYPTO 1991. LNCS, vol. 576, pp. 129–140. Springer, Heidelberg (1992)
21. Reid, F., Harrigan, M.: An analysis of anonymity in the Bitcoin system. In: Security and Privacy in Social Networks (SOCIALCOM) (2011)
22. Schnorr, C.P.: Efficient signature generation for smart cards. J. Cryptol. 4(3), 239–252 (1991)

Bitcoin Poster Abstracts

On Offline Payments with Bitcoin
(Poster Abstract)

Alexandra Dmitrienko[1]([✉]), David Noack[2],
Ahmad-Reza Sadeghi[2], and Moti Yung[3]

[1] Fraunhofer SIT/CASED, Darmstadt, Germany
alexandra.dmitrienko@sit.fraunhofer.de
[2] TU Darmstadt/CASED, Darmstadt, Germany
{ahmad.sadeghi,david.noack}@trust.cased.de
[3] Google, New York, USA
moti@cs.columbia.edu

Bitcoin [2] is a decentralized digital currency which relies neither on banks nor on any other central authority for issuing of coins or transaction verification. Currently, Bitcoin experiences enormous success driven by large interest from users, politics, but also by speculation. Particularly, despite being conjured to be a giant bubble, the value of a bitcoin[1] increased from USD $5 in May 2012 to temporarily over USD $1,200 in December, and fluctuating between USD 500$ and USD 800$ since then. According to coinmap.org, as of February 2014 there are at least over 3000 shops, hotels, bars or even medical practices worldwide that accept local Bitcoin payments. This is an increase of 2000 locations over the last 3 month and not including online-shops or online-services[2].

The two most important challenges of digital cash, explicit and undeniable ownership of coins and double-spending prevention, are addressed in Bitcoin by means of asymmetric cryptography and a distributed time-stamping service based on proof-of-work (PoW). Users of the Bitcoin network own addresses in form of asymmetric key pairs. To spend bitcoins, a user issues a transaction that, amongst others, includes a signature of the sender, the amount and the address (public key) of the receiver. All transactions are committed to the Bitcoin network and recorded in a public transaction history known as the blockchain. Building the blockchain requires solving cryptographic puzzles which is computationally hard to perform, but easy to verify. Special Bitcoin clients, called miners, are working on integration of new transactions into the blockchain, and get awarded with bitcoins as soon as they discover a new valid block. Regular Bitcoin clients can track the transaction history to ensure that the bitcoin they are going to receive has never been spent before.

An important characteristic of the Bitcoin system is that clients require *online access* to the blockchain for a certain amount of *time* to be able to verify any transaction. However, these requirements render Bitcoin *not* suitable for offline payment scenarios, where neither the sender nor the receiver have

---

[1] As usual we use capitalized Bitcoin to denote the system and lowercase bitcoin to refer to monetary currency.
[2] https://en.bitcoin.it/wiki/Trade

© IFCA/Springer-Verlag Berlin Heidelberg 2014
R. Böhme et al. (Eds.): FC 2014 Workshops, LNCS 8438, pp. 150–160, 2014.
DOI: 10.1007/978-3-662-44774-1_11

connection to the Bitcoin network. Furthermore, immediate payments with Bitcoin, where transactions have to be accepted or rejected immediately, are insecure [1] even in online settings.

In this work we aim to overcome these shortcomings and extend the existing Bitcoin system. Particularly, we propose a solution which allows for *offline* and *immediate* secure payments with Bitcoin. We rely on a trusted wallet, a trusted resource-constrained platform component which cannot be tampered with and controls usage of private keys of corresponding Bitcoin addresses. It prevents the user from spending a single coin twice, rendering double-spending attacks impossible by design. However, using trusted wallet is not sufficient to enable secure offline payments. This is because any input to the trusted wallet can be manipulated and due to resource constrains of typical wallet environments, which makes transaction verification challenging. For instance, these constraints render full blockchain validation within the wallet environment infeasible, as downloading and verification the whole blockchain takes days even on resource-rich platforms such as PCs[3].

To address these challenges, we design a lightweight transaction verification mechanism. Our solution exploits the fact that valid transactions and their confirmations expose a unique signature consisting of the computational effort and time required to generate them that only the Bitcoin network can achieve, but unlikely the adversary. We provide a thorough security and risk analysis of our solution and suggest concrete security parameters for a reasonable trade-off between adversary model and efficiency. Moreover, we eliminate small remaining risks of attacks by introducing an additional security parameter which limits transaction amounts to keep them smaller than costs of potential attacks. We then perform rigorous analysis of associated attack costs and show that a reasonable transaction limit lies in a range of thousands of dollars (per transaction), which is sufficient to satisfy most payment scenarios. Further, if larger transactions are required, they can be split into several smaller transactions, transparently to the user.

We prototyped our solution for mobile Android clients and utilized a microSD security card as a wallet environment. Our performance analysis demonstrates the feasibility of our approach in practice. Furthermore, our extension is compatible to the original Bitcoin system which makes our solution suitable for immediate deployment.

References

1. Karame, G.O. Androulaki, E., Capkun, S.: Double-spending fast payments in bitcoin. In: Proceedings of the 2012 ACM Conference on Computer and Communications Security (2012)
2. Nakamoto, S.: Bitcoin: a peer-to-peer electronic cash system. Technical report (2008). www.bitcoin.org/bitcoin.pdf

---

[3] http://bitcoin.stackexchange.com/questions/9816/how-long-does-it-take-to-download-the-blockchain-its-been-over-a-day-and-still

One Weird Trick to Stop Selfish Miners: Fresh Bitcoins, A Solution for the Honest Miner (Poster Abstract)

Ethan Heilman[(✉)]

Boston University, Boston, USA
heilman@bu.edu

1 Abstract

In "Majority is not Enough: Bitcoin Mining is Vulnerable", Eyal and Sirer study a Bitcoin mining strategy called selfish mining [1]. Under selfish mining, miners strategically withhold blocks to cheat Bitcoin's mining incentive system. This represents a 'tragedy of the commons' in which selfish behavior is incentivized over honest behavior, eventually causing most miners to adopt the selfish strategy, despite it being harmful to Bitcoin [2] as a whole.

The success of selfish mining depends on two parameters: α, the mining power of the selfish cartel and γ, the ratio of honest mining power that, during a block race, mines on a block released by the selfish cartel. We can view the minimum value of α, such that selfish mining is successful, as the security threshold for a particular γ.

Using Eq. 1, Eyal and Sirer show, if $\gamma = 0$, then selfish mining is profitable at $\alpha \geq 0.33$ or 33 %, whereas if $\gamma = 0.99$, then selfish mining is profitable at $\alpha \geq 0.009$. Eyal and Sirer propose a defense against selfish mining which fixes $\gamma = 0.5$. This raises the threshold for a selfish cartel to be profitable to at least 25 % or $\alpha \geq 0.25$.

$$\frac{1-\gamma}{3-2\gamma} < \alpha < \frac{1}{2} \tag{1}$$

We introduce a new defense, called FP (Freshness Preferred), improving on the previous best result of Eyal and Sirer. FP changes the Bitcoin protocol by adding unforgeable timestamps to blocks and preferring blocks with more recent blocks to blocks with older timestamps. We use Random Beacons [3] to prevent miners from faking timestamps from the future. Thus, as selfish mining is based on the strategic withholding of blocks, our strategy decreases the profitability of selfish mining because withheld blocks will lose block races against newly minted or "fresh" blocks.

Under FP we show that γ can be found as a function of t, $\gamma = 1 - e^{-\frac{(1-\alpha)}{600} \times t}$, where t is the refresh rate of the random beacon. We plug our equation for γ into Eq. 1 to find Eq. 2, the equation for the threshold of mining power to successfully selfishly mine within FP.

© IFCA/Springer-Verlag Berlin Heidelberg 2014
R. Böhme et al. (Eds.): FC 2014 Workshops, LNCS 8438, pp. 161–162, 2014.
DOI: 10.1007/978-3-662-44774-1_12

$$\text{threshold of } \alpha \text{ needed} = \frac{1 - (1 - e^{-\frac{(1-\alpha)}{600} \times t})}{3 - 2 \times (1 - e^{-\frac{(1-\alpha)}{600} \times t})} \tag{2}$$

Using the NIST random beacon [5], which generates random 512-bit strings every 60 s, as our model, we set $t = 60$ s and find that under all $\alpha \leq 0.32$, selfish mining is less profitable than honest mining, raising the mining power to selfishly mine to 32 % [4].

Next, we consider the mining power to selfishly mine within FP, assuming a cartel that can forge timestamps. Using the heuristic of "overestimate the attacker and underestimate the defender", we assume the cartel has no propagation delay, that it learns about honest blocks instantly, and that the honest miner has a lengthy propagation delay of 100 s and a block race window of 120 s. Under these assumptions, we find that the threshold for selfish mining with forgeries is 30 %.

FP with forgeable timestamps, while resistant to selfish mining, enables a new attack we call slothful mining. A slothful miner chooses timestamps slightly greater than the current time. The slothful miner can then withhold and mine on any block they discover, until the timestamp matches the current time, without hurting their chances of winning a block race. Slothful mining is not possible if the timestamps are unforgeable and therefore slothful mining motivates the use of unforgeable timestamps in FP.

We propose a incentive-compatible deployment scheme for FP. If the default miners significantly outnumber the FP miners, FP miners are at a disadvantage because if there is a block race between default miners and FP miners, the FP miners will likely lose. To solve the incentive problem, FP miners initially use the default block preference behavior, but they still add timestamps. When more than half of the most recent blocks in the blockchain for 30 days include unforgeable timestamps, then FP miners begin preferring the most recent blocks, as this behavior has become incentive-compatible. See our full report for details [4].

Acknowledgments. We thank Sharon Goldberg for comments and suggestions on drafts of this paper.

References

1. Eyal, I., Sirer, E.G.: Majority is not enough: bitcoin mining is vulnerable. arXiv:1311.0243 (2013). http://arxiv.org/abs/1311.0243
2. Nakamoto, S.: Bitcoin: a peer-to-peer electronic cash system. The Cryptography Mailing List (2008). http://Bitcoin.org/Bitcoin.pdf
3. Rabin, M.: Transaction protection by beacons. J. Comput. Syst. Sci. **27**(2), 256–267 (1983). (Elsevier, Amsterdam)
4. Heilman, E.: One Weird Trick to Stop Selfish Miners: Fresh Bitcoins. A Solution for the Honest Miner. Cryptology ePrint Archive, Report 2014/007 (2013). https://eprint.iacr.org/2014/007.pdf
5. Iorga, M.: NIST, NIST Randomness Beacon (2013). http://www.nist.gov/itl/csd/ct/nist_beacon.cfm

From Bitcoin to the Brixton Pound: History and Prospects for Alternative Currencies (Poster Abstract)

Garrick Hileman[✉]

London School of Economics, London, UK
g.hileman@lse.ac.uk

The rise of Bitcoin has led to renewed interest in alternative currencies. While alternative currencies have regularly featured on the economic landscape over the last half-millennia we have a limited understanding of several salient questions, such as which factors explain their rise and decline. An alternative currency is considered here to be any medium of exchange other than legal tender. A new taxonomy is introduced below to more precisely define the many different types of alternative currencies and to address the disparate lexicon found in the literature. Alternative currencies can be broadly classified as either *tangible* (Table 1) or *digital* (Table 2).

Table 1. Classification framework - tangible alternative currencies

	Historical	Contemporary
Intrinsic utility	Metals, cigarettes in post-WWII Berlin	African SIM airtime minutes
Token	17th–19th c. British tokens, 1930s Great Depression-era scrip	Chiemgau, Brixton pound, BerkShares

Tangibles possessing *intrinsic utility* were likely some of the earliest currencies. Often referred to as 'commodity money', these currencies derive their value from relative scarcity and non-monetary utility. Unlike other monetary instruments, the value in such currencies is not an abstraction, nor dependent upon governance. They are also not geographically bound, making them well suited for earlier nomadic peoples. *Token* currencies have comparatively less intrinsic value, which is instead derived from social agreements such as honoring them for exchange or limiting supply. Also referred to as 'local' or 'community' currencies, token currencies are often issued by commercial enterprises and other organizations for use within a limited range.

Table 2. Classification framework - digital alternative currencies

	Closed	Open
Centralized	Linden Dollar, World of Warcraft Gold	Flooz, Beenz
Decentralized	N/A	Bitcoin, Litecoin

© IFCA/Springer-Verlag Berlin Heidelberg 2014
R. Böhme et al. (Eds.): FC 2014 Workshops, LNCS 8438, pp. 163–165, 2014.
DOI: 10.1007/978-3-662-44774-1_13

Table 3. Socio-economic forces driving demand for alternative currencies

Localism	Protect independent retailers, promote community commerce
Technology	Open source software, mobile devices, cryptography advances
Political economy	Economic distress, 'Too Big to Fail', inflation, privacy
Environmentalism[a]	Impact of globalization, 'peak oil', industrial food
Inefficiencies	Expensive credit card and wire transfer fees, long waiting
Financial Repression	Bypass capital controls, avoid liquidation of savings
Speculation	Currency appreciation due to wider acceptance

[a] Historical precedent is found for all forces identified in this Table except environmentalism.

Digital alternative currencies can be distinguished by the degree they must be transacted in a *closed* system versus in the *open* marketplace. Second Life's Linden dollar is largely transacted inside a bounded environment. Governance structure, which in the Linden dollar's case is *centralized*, is a second distinguishing characteristic. Open digital currencies such as Bitcoin can be transacted outside any clearly demarcated environment. Bitcoin's governance can also be characterized as relatively *decentralized* due to its open source software and other features.

A survey of historical and contemporary alternative currencies shows they arise for similar reasons, such as recessions or to promote local commerce (Table 3).

Compared to national currencies, alternative currencies tend to cease circulating following their introduction within a relatively short time for three broad reasons: *technological innovation*, *regulation*, and *insufficient demand*.

Technological innovation can be any advancement that impacts the use of an alternative currency. The ultimate decline of thousands of British merchant tokens circulating throughout the 17th–19th centuries [1] was hastened by two innovations: the adoption of the 'standard formula', whereby the market rather than authorities determine the mix of denominations, and new low-cost minting technology [2].

Governments have periodically sought to eliminate the use of alternative currencies through regulation. The King of England succeeded in temporarily banning the use of British tokens [3]. A more decisive regulatory action occurred with the Austrian Freigeld, which was introduced in 1932 only to be outlawed by authorities in 1933.

Insufficient demand for an alternative currency can occur for many reasons, including limited acceptance, improved economic conditions, low institutional support, low social motivation, fraud, and other factors. Many of the aforementioned played a role in the demise of the hundreds of short-lived U.S. scrip currencies introduced during the 1930s Great Depression [4].

References

1. Whiting, J.R.S.: Trade Tokens a Social and Economic History. David & Charles, Newton Abbot (1971)
2. Sargent, Thomas J., Velde, François R.: The Big Problem of Small Change, Princeton Economic History of the Western World. Princeton University Press, New Jersey (2002)

3. Searle, W.G.: The Coins, Tokens and Medals of the Town. County and University of Cambridge. Cambridge Antiquarian Society, Cambridge (1871)
4. Harper, J.W.C.: Scrip and other forms of local money. Department of Economics, University of Chicago (1948)

Part II Applied Homomorphic Cryptography and Encrypted Computing

High-Speed Fully Homomorphic Encryption
Over the Integers

Xiaolin Cao, Ciara Moore[✉], Máire O'Neill, Neil Hanley,
and Elizabeth O'Sullivan

Centre for Secure Information Technologies, Queen's University Belfast,
Belfast, Northern Ireland, UK
cmoore50@qub.ac.uk

Abstract. A fully homomorphic encryption (FHE) scheme is envisioned as a key cryptographic tool in building a secure and reliable cloud computing environment, as it allows arbitrary evaluation of a ciphertext without revealing the plaintext. However, existing FHE implementations remain impractical due to very high time and resource costs. To the authors' knowledge, this paper presents the first hardware implementation of a full encryption primitive for FHE over the integers using FPGA technology. A large-integer multiplier architecture utilising Integer-FFT multiplication is proposed, and a large-integer Barrett modular reduction module is designed incorporating the proposed multiplier. The encryption primitive used in the integer-based FHE scheme is designed employing the proposed multiplier and modular reduction modules. The designs are verified using the Xilinx Virtex-7 FPGA platform. Experimental results show that a speed improvement factor of up to 44 is achievable for the hardware implementation of the FHE encryption scheme when compared to its corresponding software implementation. Moreover, performance analysis shows further speed improvements of the integer-based FHE encryption primitives may still be possible, for example through further optimisations or by targeting an ASIC platform.

1 Introduction

Fully homomorphic encryption (FHE) is a significant breakthrough in cryptographic research in recent years [1]. A FHE scheme can be used to arbitrarily perform computations on a ciphertext without compromising the content of the corresponding plaintext. Thus, a practical FHE scheme will open the door to numerous new security technologies and privacy related applications, such as privacy-preserving search and cloud-based computing.

A working example of FHE was introduced by Gentry in 2009 [2]. Since then, several FHE schemes and corresponding software implementations based on various computationally hard problems have been proposed [1–11]. The first software implementation of the lattice-based FHE scheme was reported by Gentry and Halevi (GH) with a public key size ranging from 17 Megabytes (MB) to 2.3 Gigabytes, and a ciphertext homomorphic evaluation time of 6 s to 30 min [6].

© IFCA/Springer-Verlag Berlin Heidelberg 2014
R. Böhme et al. (Eds.): FC 2014 Workshops, LNCS 8438, pp. 169–180, 2014.
DOI: 10.1007/978-3-662-44774-1_14

The FHE scheme over the integers was introduced in 2010 by van Dijk *et al.* [3], then Coron *et al.* [8] extended this scheme by reducing the public key size, resulting in a bitwise encryption time ranging from 0.05 s to 3 min. Coron *et al.* [9] further reduced the public key size to no more than 10.1 MB with a longer encryption time, ranging from 0.05 s to 7 min. A recent FHE software implementation was on an NVIDIA C2050 GPU [12]; using the Integer-FFT algorithm [13] for multiplication, the Montgomery algorithm to perform modular reduction within the Integer-FFT execution and Barrett modular reduction [14] to implement the GH FHE scheme [6]. This implementation resulted in a speed improvement of almost 7 compared to the original results [6]. However, it is clear that there is still a long way to go before a practical FHE scheme can be deployed in real-life applications.

To date, there have been few hardware implementations of FHE schemes. Cousins *et al.* [15,16] proposed a hardware implementation on an FPGA platform using the Matlab HDL Coder tool; however they do not report any implementation or simulation results. More recently, an ASIC implementation of a multiplier for the GH FHE scheme is proposed by Doröz *et al.* [17]; this implementation shows comparable performance to the original software implementation. An FPGA implementation of a multiplier for the GH FHE scheme was proposed by Wang and Huang [18] and is stated to be about twice as fast as the previously mentioned GPU implementation [12]. Further to this, an ASIC design of the full GH FHE scheme, without key generation, is proposed in [19]. Timings show this ASIC implementation is considerably faster than the original implementation in software [6] and also the encryption and recrypt steps are faster than for the GPU platform implementation [12].

The objective of this paper is to accelerate the encryption primitives in integer-based FHE using FPGA technology. This particular FHE algorithm is chosen because of the comparatively simpler theory, smaller key size and comparable performance to the GH scheme. Moreover, the introduction of a batched FHE scheme over the integers promises further efficiency improvements [20]. Multiplication is a key element in these FHE schemes and features in the encryption, decryption and evaluation steps. Large-integer FFT multiplication has also been used in the previously mentioned hardware and GPU implementations of other FHE schemes. In this paper we focus initially on the hardware architecture of a large integer multiplier using the FFT algorithm and how this can speed up the encryption step of an integer-based FHE scheme. Future work will investigate the impact of the hardware multiplier on the other steps within the FHE scheme.

Specifically, we present the first hardware implementation of an encryption primitive required for FHE over the integers. Our contributions are as follows: (i) the proposal of a novel large-integer hardware multiplier architecture using the Integer-FFT multiplication algorithm; (ii) a large-integer architecture of Barrett modular reduction using the proposed multiplier as a sub-module is presented along with an analysis of the suitability of four different moduli; (iii) the first hardware architecture for the encryption primitive of FHE over the integers is designed utilising the proposed multiplier and modular reduction; (iv) our implementations are verified for a Xilinx Virtex-7 FPGA, and the results show our design achieves a significant performance improvement of a factor of 44.72 over equivalent software implementations. An extended version of this work is available on the ePrint Archive [21], where the encryption primitives of two integer-based schemes [8,9] are implemented; there was little difference between the synthesis implementation results of these primitives and thus this paper only presents results for the implementation of the integer-based scheme [8] with the fastest running time.

The rest of the paper is organised as follows. In Sect. 2, the background information is introduced. In Sect. 3 the proposed hardware architectures of the FHE encryption primitive is described. Implementation and performance results are given in Sect. 4. Finally, Sect. 5 concludes the paper.

2   Related Work

2.1   Encryption Primitive in FHE Over the Integers

First proposed by van Dijk *et al.* [3], the integer-based FHE scheme was later extended upon by Coron *et al.* [8,9] by reducing the public key size. The encryption primitive of the scheme [8], denoted by CMNT here, is implemented in this paper. The encryption step is as follows:

$$C = (M + 2R + 2 \sum_{1 \leq i,j \leq \theta} B_{i,j} \times A_{i,0} \times A_{j,1}) \bmod A_0 \tag{1}$$

where C denotes the ciphertext; $M \in \{0,1\}$ is a 1-bit plaintext; R is a random signed integer in the range $(-2^\rho, 2^\rho)$ and $A_0 \in [0, 2^\varphi)$ is a part of the public key. $\{B_{i,j}\}$ where $1 \leq i,j \leq \theta$ is a random integer sequence, and each $B_{i,j}$ is a δ-bit integer. $\{A_{i,0}\}$ and $\{A_{i,1}\}$ where $1 \leq i \leq \theta$ are two public key sequences, and each entry is a φ-bit integer. The parameter bit-lengths of four test groups [8], used in the performance comparison in Sect. 4, are listed in Table 1. For further information on the parameter selection and the parameter security levels, see [8,9].

Table 1. Four parameter groups for CMNT FHE scheme

Group	δ	$\rho = 4\delta$	$\varphi \times 10^{-6}$	θ
Toy	42	168	0.16	12
Small	52	208	0.86	23
Medium	62	248	4.20	44
Large	72	288	19.0	88

To implement (1), the first challenge is the very large multiplication. The multiplication algorithm typically used for very large bit-length operands is the Integer-FFT [13,22,23]. It computes large bit-length multiplication by dividing it into smaller bit-length multiplication and then accumulating. For example, the widely used open-source GMP library uses the Schönhage-Strassen Integer-FFT algorithm [13] for multiplication when the operand bit-length is greater than 2^{15} bits [24]. There exist many Integer-FFT variants which aim to improve the speed of small bit-length multiplication, as it is the bottleneck of the Integer-FFT algorithm. However, the use of the embedded multipliers on a Xilinx Virtex-7 FPGA can address this issue, as they are specifically optimised for high-speed performance of up to 750 MHz [25]. Thus, the basic Integer-FFT algorithm [23] combined with these embedded multipliers is used in our work.

The large modular reduction is also a considerable challenge. Generally, the modular reduction algorithms used in traditional long bit-length cryptographic implementations are Montgomery [26] and Barrett reduction [14]. However, due to heavy pre-computation and post-processing costs, Montgomery reduction is only suitable in scenarios where successive modular operations with the same operands are required, such as exponentiation for example. In contrast, Barrett reduction only requires a one-time pre-computation, and therefore is used in our implementation.

The objective of this work is to accelerate the speed of the encryption step outlined in (1) rather than deal with storage bottlenecks. Therefore, it is assumed that there is sufficient off-chip memory available for the designed FPGA accelerator to store intermediate variables and final results. This is a reasonable assumption as the accelerator can be viewed as a powerful coprocessor device, sharing memory with a main workstation over a high speed PCI bus. However, it is acknowledged that with off-chip memory I/O can become a bottleneck and the latency of the bus becomes an issue. Investigations into such issues will be the subject of future work.

2.2 The Integer-FFT Multiplication Algorithm

Integer-FFT multiplication treats each multiplication operand as a sequence of smaller, computationally efficient numbers instead of a single large integer. The input parameters for Integer-FFT multiplication are:

- p, an m-bit number, the modulus in Integer-FFT modular reduction
- q_i, the prime factors of p
- k, the FFT point number
- ω, the twiddle factor of the FFT
- b, the base unit bit-length when transforming the input operand into a b-bit digit sequence

To ensure the Integer-FFT algorithm works correctly, the FFT point number k must divide $q_i - 1$ for every prime factor q_i of p (if p is a prime, q_i equals p). The twiddle factor ω is a primitive k^{th} root of unity, that is $\omega^k \equiv 1 \, (\mathrm{mod} \, \mathrm{p})$ and $\omega^{k/q_i} - 1 \not\equiv 0 \, (\mathrm{mod} \, \mathrm{p})$ for any prime divisor q_i of p [13], and all operations used in the FFT should be modular with respect to the modulus p. The requirement for a suitable base unit bit-length is $k(2^b - 1)^2/2 < p$ [23].

Table 2. The four integer-FFT moduli

Group	p	m	k	ω	b
Special Modulus [27]	$2^{32} + 1$	33	64	2	8
Special Modulus [27]	$2^{64} + 1$	65	128	2	24
Solinas Modulus [23, 28]	$2^{64} - 2^{32} + 1$	64	128	7	28
General Modulus [23]	$2^{32} - 2^{20} + 1$	32	64	17	12

As the selection of a reasonable modulus, p, heavily influences the modular multiplication performance, four different moduli, as defined in Table 2, are implemented and compared in this work. Further details on the moduli are given in Sect. 3.3. The Integer-FFT algorithm [13, 23] is outlined in Algorithm 1.

Algorithm 1. Integer-FFT Multiplication [23]

Input: x, y, b, z
Output: $c = x \times y$

1 Compute the FFT of the digits of x and y, with respect to the base b, where each digit is treated as a FFT sample;
2 Multiply the FFT results component by component: $z_i = FFT(x_i) \times FFT(y_i)$;
3 Compute the inverse FFT (IFFT): $c_i = IFFT(z_i)$;
4 Resolve the carry chain: when $c_i \geq b$, set $c_{i+1} = c_i \,\mathbf{div}\, b$ and set $c_i = c_i \,\mathbf{mod}\, b$;
5 **return** c

2.3 The Barrett Modular Reduction

Two Barrett modular reduction hardware architectures have been designed for this work. The first is for small integer reduction used in the Integer-FFT algorithm, and the second is for the proposed large integer Barrett reduction design. Both adopt the Barrett reduction algorithm introduced in [29], outlined in Algorithm 2.

The essence of Barrett reduction is that the intermediate parameter $\hat{\sigma}$ given in Algorithm 2 is used to estimate x/p, where $\lfloor . \rfloor$ is the floor operation. Then $x - \hat{\sigma}p$ is used to approximate $x \pmod{p}$. The advantage of this algorithm is that it has been proven that if $\beta < -2$ and $\alpha > m$, at most one subtraction is required in the final reduction [29].

3 The Proposed FHE Encryption Architecture

3.1 Multiplier Architecture Overview

The multiplier architecture consists of a shared RAM, a finite state machine (FSM) controller and an Integer-FFT unit. The shared RAMs are assumed to be off-chip and are used to store the input operands, the intermediate results

Algorithm 2. Barrett Reduction Algorithm

Input: x ($2m$-bit), p (m-bit) and a pre-computed constant $p_1 = \lfloor 2^{m+\alpha}/p \rfloor$
Output: $y = x \,(\mathrm{mod}\, p)$

1 $\hat{\sigma} = \left\lfloor \dfrac{\lfloor x/2^{m+\beta} \rfloor \times \lfloor 2^{m+\alpha}/p \rfloor}{2^{\alpha-\beta}} \right\rfloor$
2 $p_2 = \hat{\sigma} \times p$;
3 $y_1 = x - p_2$ and $y_2 = y_1 - p$;
4 If $y_2 < 0$, $y = y_1$, otherwise $y = y_2$;
5 **return** y

and final results. The FSM controller is responsible for distributing the signals to schedule the algorithm. The proposed FSM scheduling mechanism can be viewed as a combination of school-book [24] and Integer-FFT [13] multiplication. The core element of the design is an Integer-FFT module that executes a block multiplication to calculate partial products, while the FSM controller schedules an iterative school-book multiplication to accumulate the block products. The proposed architecture, depicted in Fig. 1, is fully pipelined and the RAM read, RAM write and Integer-FFT operations are executed in parallel.

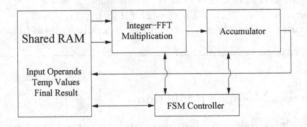

Fig. 1. Overview of the proposed hardware multiplier

3.2 The FFT/IFFT Module and Butterfly Unit

Various FFT algorithms and architectures can be used to implement the FFT algorithm for different optimisation goals [22,23]. In this work, a radix-2 fully parallel architecture is adopted for FFT and IFFT in order to obtain the highest throughput. There are $\log_2 k$ butterfly stages for a k-point FFT, and each butterfly stage is composed of $k/2$ parallel butterfly units.

The IFFT needs to multiply $k^{-1}(\mathrm{mod}\, p)$, which is not required in the FFT. If an identical architecture is used to implement both the IFFT and FFT, a point-wise module multiplication stage is additionally required for the IFFT and the cycle latency is increased. This problem can be solved by pre-computing $\hat{\omega}^{-1} = (k\omega)^{-1}(\mathrm{mod}\, p)$ to incorporate $k^{-1}(\mathrm{mod}\, p)$ into the IFFT twiddle factors, then $\hat{\omega}^{-1}$ is used in the final IFFT butterfly stage, while the previous stages use ω^{-1}. In order to meet the butterfly requirement of both FFT and IFFT, a unified butterfly unit is proposed in Fig. 2. The multiplication at the bottom left-hand side in Fig. 2, $x_{down} \times \omega_{down}$, is the same for all FFT/IFFT butterfly stages, as is the operation of X_{up}/X_{down} on the right-hand side of Fig. 2. However, the operation of $x_{up} \times \omega_{up}$ on the upper left-hand side of Fig. 2 is only required in the final stage of the IFFT.

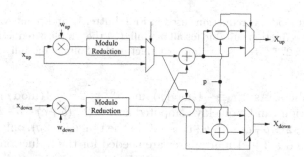

Fig. 2. The proposed FFT/IFFT butterfly unit

In the design presented here, if the special modulus $p = 2^{m-1} + 1$ is used, each m-bit multiplier in a butterfly is implemented using a bit-shift operation, as the kth primitive root of unit, ω, equals 2, as stated in Table 2. Otherwise, each butterfly multiplier is designed using a multi-stage pipelined multiplier and implemented using FPGA embedded multipliers using Xilinx Core Generator [25] tools. This prevents the multipliers becoming the bottleneck in our design.

3.3 The Modular Reduction Module

The small integer modular reduction is very simple, only requiring an addition/subtraction operation; it is illustrated in the right half of Fig. 2. Therefore, this subsection introduces the modular reduction unit used after the butterfly and point-wise multiplication. Three modular reduction methods are designed and tested in our work: Barrett reduction with any modulus (in this case $2^{32} - 2^{20} + 1$); the simplest reduction method with the modulus in the special form $2^{m-1} + 1$; and modular reduction using the suitable Solinas modulus, $2^{64} - 2^{32} + 1$ [28].

The Barrett reduction architecture is shown in Fig. 3(a) and it requires two multipliers and two subtractions. Following Algorithm 2, in our design we set $\beta = -4$ and $\alpha = m + 4$; thus the pre-computed constant is $p_1 = 2^{2m+4}/p$. The second design with special form modulus [13] is shown in Fig. 3(b) and the reduction $y = x(\bmod p)$ is easily obtained using the logic in Fig. 3(b) as follows: let $y_1 = x[m - 2: 0] + x[2m - 1: 2m - 2] - x[2m - 3: m - 1]$ and $y_2 = y_1 + p$; if $y_1 < 0$, $y = y_2$; else $y = y_1$ [30]. As no multiplication is required, this circuit consumes less hardware resources than traditional Barrett reduction and offers faster performance.

In Fig. 3(c) the Solinas modulus $p = 2^{64} - 2^{32} + 1$ is used and the 128-bit multiplication can be expressed as $x = 2^{96}a + 2^{64}b + 2^{32}c + d$, where a, b, c and d

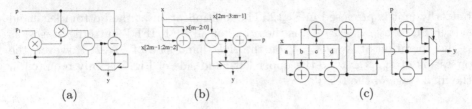

Fig. 3. Proposed modular reductions used in FFT butterfly and point-wise multiplication: (a) Barrett reduction suitable for all moduli; (b) the simplest reduction for special form moduli, $p = 2^{m-1} + 1$; (c) a simpler reduction for Solinas moduli

are 32-bit numbers. As $2^{96} \equiv -1 (\mathrm{mod}\, p)$ and $2^{64} \equiv 2^{32} - 1 (\mathrm{mod}\, p)$, the Solinas modular reduction can be quickly computed as $x \equiv 2^{32}(b+c) - a - b + d (\mathrm{mod}\, p)$. Since the result, $2^{32}(b+c) - a - b + d$, is within the range $(p, 2p)$, only an addition, a subtraction and a $3 \rightarrow 1$ multiplexer are needed for the reduction. This is still much simpler than Barrett reduction as no multiplication is required. However, given the modulus and twiddle factor restrictions described in Sect. 2, not every Solinas modulus is suitable [23].

The FHE encryption architecture is tightly coupled with the large Barrett modular reduction using the FSM controller since only one instance of the proposed multiplier is implemented; the FSM controller occupies a very small percentage of area compared to the multiplier. The encryption primitive in (1) is implemented by firstly executing the pipelined multiplier and accumulation modules in parallel and secondly performing the large Barrett reduction.

4   Implementation, Performance and Comparison

The proposed architectures are designed and implemented using Xilinx FPGA technology. The synthesis tool used is Xilinx ISE Design Suite 14.1 and Modelsim 6.5a is used as the functional and post-synthesis timing simulation tool. The optimisation objective of the synthesis tool is set to speed. The target device is the Virtex-7 XC7VX980T-2FFG1926. The test vectors are generated as random numbers using C++ according to the parameters given in Table 1.

The proposed multiplier architecture is implemented as a fully pipelined and parallel circuit. At the outer interface, three RAM read buses and one RAM write bus are implemented, so large multiplication operands can be read into the multiplier and final block product accumulation can be executed simultaneously. At the inner layer, the Integer-FFT multiplier is also pipelined. The basic computation bit-length in the Integer-FFT is determined by modulus bit-length rather than base unit bit-length, so increasing base unit bit-length will not reduce speed performance. However, base unit bit-length is related to the multiplication result, so the larger the base unit bit-length, the lower the latency.

In our implementations the ratio of multiplication operand block bit-length $kb/2$ and data bus bit-width d, $kb/2d$, is equal to 8. The data bus bit-width is then equal to 32, 192, 224 and 48 for the moduli respectively. The clock cycle count therefore equals 8 for each $\frac{kb}{2}$-bit input operand, and for each output block product except the first block product. The pipeline stage number in each FFT butterfly stage is designed to also equal 8.

We have implemented the FHE encryption primitive with the moduli listed in Table 2 and the synthesis results are shown in Table 3. It should be noted that, in general, post place and route of the design will give slightly worse results. For each design, the FFT point number k is fixed and is unrelated to multiplication operand bit-length.

Table 3. Synthesis results of FHE encryption primitive

Integer-FFT modulus	Frequency (MHz)	# DSPs	# Slice registers	# Slice LUTs
Special: CMNT $2^{32} + 1$	292.410	256	191176	237031
Special: CMNT $2^{64} + 1$	179.346	2048	956974	1215166
Solinas: CMNT $2^{64} - 2^{32} + 1$	166.450	18496	1123001	954955
General: CMNT $2^{32} - 2^{20} + 1$	254.054	6292	213788	171450

For the small integer multiplications used in the FFT butterfly and point-wise multiplication, Xilinx Core Generator is employed to generate a 4-stage pipelined multiplier using Virtex-7 FPGA embedded multipliers. From Table 3 the special modulus design with modulus $2^{32} + 1$ requires the least hardware resources, as no multiplication is needed in the FFT butterfly unit. Also, this design which uses the modulus with the smallest bit-length has the highest frequency, as the multipliers needed for point-wise multiplication in the Integer-FFT algorithm contain the critical path and are implemented as 4-stage pipelined multipliers. However this does not mean that the special modulus design will offer the best performance, as the other moduli allow larger base unit bit-length, which implies that in one clock cycle the Solinas modulus multiplier can produce the longest product. We also find that only the implementation with the smallest modulus, $2^{32} + 1$, is within the hardware resource budget of the targeted XC7VX980T FPGA device. Moreover the implementation with the second special modulus, $2^{64} + 1$, can fit on the largest available XC7V2000T FPGA device. Thus an ASIC platform would be required for the implementations with the other two moduli; however this would mean the design would no longer be able to take advantage of the embedded multipliers available on Xilinx Virtex-7 FPGAs and therefore alternative design approaches might be more suitable.

The running time of the proposed hardware implementation of the encryption primitive using the parameter groups from Table 1 is compared with the corresponding previously reported software results in Table 4. The running time is obtained by averaging the latency of the simulated test vectors and multiplying by the clock frequency. It can be seen that the special modulus multiplier has a higher frequency but still requires more execution time than the Solinas modulus multiplier. This is because in the multiplication circuit, the throughput is mainly determined by the product of data bus bit-width, base unit bit-length and circuit frequency, rather than just the frequency. Comparing moduli, it is also clear to see that although the special moduli can use a simple twiddle factor of 2, its base unit bit-length is much smaller than for the other modulus types when almost the same bit-length modulus is employed. Therefore the Solinas modulus is the best choice of moduli, enabling a comparatively simpler modular reduction and a larger base unit bit-length.

Table 4. Average running time of proposed FHE encryption design

Integer FFT Modulus	Toy	Small	Medium	Large
CMNT $2^{32} + 1$	0.003 s	0.050 s	0.872 s	15.735 s
CMNT $2^{64} + 1$	0.000854 s	0.0139 s	0.239 s	4.284 s
CMNT $2^{64} - 2^{32} + 1$	0.000815 s	0.0130 s	0.221 s	3.958 s
CMNT $2^{32} - 2^{20} + 1$	0.003 s	0.057s	1.003 s	18.110 s
CMNT on Intel Core2 Duo E8500 [8]	0.05 s	0.79 s	10 s	2 min 57 s

Table 4 also shows that a hardware design of the encryption step in integer-based FHE with a Solinas modulus is 61.35 and 44.72 times faster than the corresponding software implementation of CMNT for the toy and large parameter groups respectively. Moreover, for the implementations with special moduli $2^{32} + 1$ and $2^{64} + 1$, which both fit on to FPGA devices, speed up factors of 11.25 and 41.32 are achieved for the large parameter group respectively. It must be noted that we only give experimental results using small FFT parameters (i.e., $k \leq 128$ and $m \leq 65$). As the product of data bus bit-width and frequency determines multiplier performance, we believe that there is much potential for speed improvement of the integer-based FHE encryption primitives if larger FFT parameters are used. Ongoing work focuses on the use of a Solinas prime modulus for a lower cost design that can achieve a comparable speed to this implementation.

5   Conclusion

In this paper, the first hardware implementations of the encryption primitive employed in the integer-based FHE scheme by Coron *et al.* [8] are presented. For this purpose, an Integer-FFT based hardware multiplier module and a Barrett modular reduction module are proposed. These hardware architectures are designed and verified on a Xilinx Virtex-7 device. When the encryption primitive is implemented with a particular Integer-FFT modulus, such as the special modulus $2^{32} + 1$, the synthesis results show that a speed improvement factor of up to 11.25 is possible compared to the corresponding software implementation for the large scale test data used in FHE over the integers; moreover this design fits on a Virtex-7 FPGA device. This speed improvement factor could be increased to at least 44 if another Integer-FFT modulus such as the Solinas modulus is used; however an ASIC device would also need to be targeted, which would provide further inherent improvements in speed. The modulus size is limited in terms of practical or implementable FPGA design due to the excessive hardware cost. As our implementations only use at most 128-point FFT and small base unit bit-lengths of at most 28 for the proposed hardware multiplier, there is still potential to further improve the encryption speed in FHE over the integers by increasing the FFT point and targeting an ASIC platform.

References

1. Gentry, C.: A fully homomorphic encryption scheme. Ph.D. thesis, Stanford University (2009). http://crypto.stanford.edu/craig
2. Gentry, C.: Fully homomorphic encryption using ideal lattices. In: Proceedings the 41st Annual ACM Symposium on Theory of Computing, pp. 169–178 (2009)
3. van Dijk, M., Gentry, C., Halevi, S., Vaikuntanathan, V.: Fully Homomorphic Encryption over the Integers. In: Gilbert, H. (ed.) EUROCRYPT 2010. LNCS, vol. 6110, pp. 24–43. Springer, Heidelberg (2010)
4. Smart, N.P., Vercauteren, F.: Fully homomorphic encryption with relatively small key and ciphertext sizes. In: Nguyen, P.Q., Pointcheval, D. (eds.) PKC 2010. LNCS, vol. 6056, pp. 420–443. Springer, Heidelberg (2010)
5. Brakerski, Z., Vaikuntanathan, V.: Fully homomorphic encryption from ring-LWE and security for key dependent messages. In: Rogaway, P. (ed.) CRYPTO 2011. LNCS, vol. 6841, pp. 505–524. Springer, Heidelberg (2011)
6. Gentry, C., Halevi, S.: Implementing gentry's fully-homomorphic encryption scheme. In: Paterson, K.G. (ed.) EUROCRYPT 2011. LNCS, vol. 6632, pp. 129–148. Springer, Heidelberg (2011)
7. Brakerski, Z., Gentry, C, Vaikuntanathan, V.: Fully homomorphic encryption without bootstrapping. Cryptology ePrint Archive, Report 2011/277 (2011)
8. Coron, J.-S., Mandal, A., Naccache, D., Tibouchi, M.: Fully homomorphic encryption over the integers with shorter public keys. In: Rogaway, P. (ed.) CRYPTO 2011. LNCS, vol. 6841, pp. 487–504. Springer, Heidelberg (2011)
9. Coron, J.-S., Naccache, D., Tibouchi, M.: Public key compression and modulus switching for fully homomorphic encryption over the integers. In: Pointcheval, D., Johansson, T. (eds.) EUROCRYPT 2012. LNCS, vol. 7237, pp. 446–464. Springer, Heidelberg (2012)
10. Lauter, K., Naehrig, M., Vaikuntanathan, V.: Can homomorphic encryption be practical? Cryptology ePrint Archive, Report 2011/405 (2011)
11. Gentry, C., Halevi, S., Smart, N.P.: Homomorphic evaluation of the AES circuit. Cryptology ePrint Archive, Report 2012/099 (2012)
12. Wang, W., Hu, Y., Chen, L. Huang, X., Sunar, B.: Accelerating fully homomorphic encryption using GPU. In: High Performance Extreme Computing Conference 2012, pp. 1–5, IEEE (2012)
13. Schönhage, A., Strassen, V.: Schnelle multiplikation grosser Zahlen. Computing (Springer) 7(3), 281–292 (1971)
14. Barrett, P.: Implementing the rivest shamir and adleman public key encryption algorithm on a standard digital Signal Processor. In: Odlyzko, A.M. (ed.) CRYPTO 1986. LNCS, vol. 263, pp. 311–323. Springer, Heidelberg (1987)

15. Cousins, D.B., Rohloff, K., Peikert, C., Schantz, R.: SIPHER: scalable implementation of primitives for homomorphic encryption - FPGA implementation using Simulink. In: IEEE High Performance Extreme Computing Conference (2011)
16. Cousins, D.B., Rohloff, K., Peikert, C., Schantz, R.: SIPHER: An update on SIPHER (Scalable Implementation of Primitives for Homomorphic EncRyption) - FPGA implementation using Simulink. In: IEEE Conference on High Performance Extreme Computing, pp. 1–5 (2012)
17. Doröz, Y., Öztürk, E., Sunar, B.: Evaluating the Hardware Performance of a Million-Bit Multiplier. In:Digital System Design, pp. 955–962 (2013)
18. Wang, W., Huang, X.: FPGA implementation of a large-number multiplier for fully homomorphic encryption. In: International Symposium on Circuits and Systems, pp. 2589–2592 (2013)
19. Doröz, Y., Öztürk, E., Sunar, B.: Accelerating Fully Homomorphic Encryption in Hardware. Under review. http://ecewp.ece.wpi.edu/wordpress/vernam/files/2013/09/Accelerating-Fully-Homomorphic-Encryption-in-Hardware.pdf
20. Cheon, J.H., Coron, J.-S., Kim, J., Lee, M.S., Lepoint, T., Tibouchi, M., Yun, A.: Batch fully homomorphic encryption over the integers. In: Johansson, T., Nguyen, P.Q. (eds.) EUROCRYPT 2013. LNCS, vol. 7881, pp. 315–335. Springer, Heidelberg (2013)
21. Cao, X., Moore, C., O'Neill, M., O'Sullivan, E., Hanley, N.: Accelerating fully homomorphic encryption over the integers with super-size hardware multiplier and modular reduction. Cryptology ePrint Archive, Report 2013/616 (2013)
22. Craven, S., Patterson, C., Athanas, P.: Super-sized multiplies: how do FPGAs fare in extended digit multipliers?. In: 7th International Conference on Military and Aerospace Programmable Logic Devices (2004)
23. Emmart, N., Weems, C.: High precision integer multiplication with a GPU using Strassen's algorithm with multiple FFT sizes. Parallel Process. Lett. **21**(3), 359–375 (2011)
24. GMP, The GNU Multiple Precision Arithmetic Library [Online]. Multiplication Algorithms. http://gmplib.org/manual/Multiplication-Algorithms.html
25. Xilinx Product Specification: LogiCORE IP Multiplier v11.2. http://www.xilinx.com/support/documentation/ip-documentation/mult-gen-ds255.pdf
26. Montgomery, P.: Modular multiplication without trial division. Math. Comput. **44**(170), 519–521 (1985)
27. Kalach, K., David, J.P.: Hardware implementation of large number multiplication by FFT with modular arithmetic. In: 3rd International IEEE-NEWCAS Conference, pp. 267–270 (2005)
28. Solinas, J.A.: Generalized Mersenne Numbers. Issue 39 of Research report, University of Waterloo. Faculty of Mathematics (1999)
29. Dhem, J.F.: Design of an efficient public-key cryptographic library for RISC-based smart cards. Ph.D thesis, Université catholique de Louvain (1998). http://users.belgacom.net/dhem/these/
30. Zimmermann, R.: Efficient VLSI implementation of modulo $(2^n \pm 1)$ addition and multiplication. In: IEEE Symposium on Computer Arithmetic, pp. 158–167 (1999)

Practical and Privacy-Preserving Policy Compliance for Outsourced Data

Giovanni Di Crescenzo[1]([⊠]), Joan Feigenbaum[2], Debayan Gupta[2],
Euthimios Panagos[1], Jason Perry[3], and Rebecca N. Wright[3]

[1] Applied Communication Sciences, Middlesex County, NJ, USA
{gdicrescenzo,epanagos}@appcomsci.com
[2] Yale University, New Haven, CT, USA
{joan.feigenbaum,debayan.gupta}@yale.edu
[3] Rutgers University, Middlesex County, NJ, USA
{jasperry,rebecca.wright}@cs.rutgers.edu

Abstract. We consider a scenario for data outsourcing that supports performing database queries in the following three-party model: a client interested in making database queries, a data owner providing its database for client access, and a server (e.g., a cloud server) holding the (encrypted) outsourced data and helping both other parties. In this scenario, a natural problem is that of designing efficient and privacy-preserving protocols for checking compliance of a client's queries to the data owner's query compliance policy. We propose a cryptographic model for the study of such protocols, defined so that they can compose with an underlying database retrieval protocol (with no query compliance policy) in the same participant model. Our main result is a set of new protocols that satisfy a combination of natural correctness, privacy, and efficiency requirements. Technical contributions of independent interest include the use of equality-preserving encryption to produce highly practical symmetric-cryptography protocols (i.e., *two orders of magnitude faster* than "Yao-like" protocols), and the use of a query rewriting technique that maintains privacy of the compliance result.

1 Introduction

The recent information technology trend of outsourcing "big data" in the "cloud" is being embraced in banking, finance, government and other areas. Banks and financial institutions need to process huge data volumes on a daily basis; in government, large databases are needed in many contexts (e.g., no-fly lists, metadata of communication records, etc.). Cloud storage and computing provide tremendous efficiency and utility for users (as exemplified by the "database-as-a-service" application paradigm), but they also create privacy risks. To mitigate these risks, database-management systems can use *privacy-preserving* data-retrieval protocols that allow users to submit queries and receive results in a way that users learn nothing about the contents of a database except the results of their queries, data owners do not learn which queries are submitted. Of critical importance

© IFCA/Springer-Verlag Berlin Heidelberg 2014
R. Böhme et al. (Eds.): FC 2014 Workshops, LNCS 8438, pp. 181–194, 2014.
DOI: 10.1007/978-3-662-44774-1_15

for the success of database management systems is the notion of *access control*, which requires carefully crafted *data-access policies*. Compliance of these policies can be enforced by the database-management system but might need to be confidential, as the policies themselves may reveal sensitive facts about the data and its owner. In this paper, we formalize, design, and analyze practical and privacy-preserving policy compliance protocols for outsourced data.

Our Problem: Our goal is to augment natural encrypted database retrieval solutions with a query authorization property based on compliance to a policy, while preserving the privacy and efficiency properties of the basic database retrieval solution. For consistency with the database-as-a-service model, and to achieve practical solutions, we consider a 3-party model, shown in Fig. 1, including a client C (interested in private data retrieval), a data owner D (offering data for retrieval conditioned on compliance to a query-specific policy), and a server S (e.g., a cloud server) helping both parties to achieve their goals. In this paper, we focus on the policy-compliance building block. Our solutions can be combined in a modular fashion with database retrieval (DR) protocols in this 3-party model, provided that they satisfy some natural structure and properties (described later). Such protocols already exist in the literature (e.g., [5,11,18]).

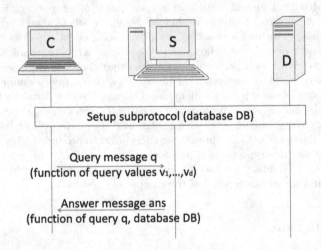

Fig. 1. Structure of a database-retrieval protocol

Our Contributions. We investigate the modeling and design of database policy compliance (DPC) protocols that combine with known DR protocols, as shown in Fig. 2, and that satisfy the following novel set of requirements:

1. *Preservation of Query Correctness*: A client that could retrieve all of the records that satisfy its query using a DR protocol can still do so if the query is compliant;

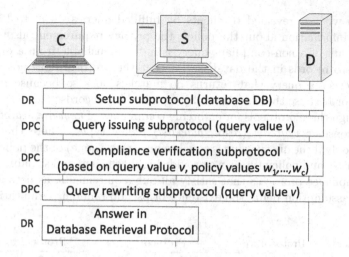

Fig. 2. Composition of a DR protocol with a DPC protocol

2. *Compliance Completeness*: All queries that satisfy (resp., do not satisfy) the policy are found to be compliant with probability 1 (resp., with negligible[1] probability);

3. *Compliance Soundness*: For any efficient (and even malicious) adversary impersonating the client, the data owner can correctly compute (except with negligible probability) the policy compliance of whichever query message is received and answered by the server according to the DR protocol;

4. *Privacy*: Privacy of database values, policy values and query values is preserved, in that no efficient semi-honest adversary corrupting one among the parties C, S, D learns more information at the end of the protocol than whatever is efficiently computable from the following: the system parameters (which are intended to be known by all parties), the compliance bit b (if the corrupted party is D, who is intended to learn b), the query message Q' (if the corrupted party is S, who is intended to learn Q'), where Q' has the same distribution as the query message Q in the DR protocol when the query is compliant, or otherwise represents a query that does not match any records in DB (to reduce leakage of the policy-compliance result to S or C);

5. *Efficiency*: The protocol should have low time, communication and round complexity. One of the most significant design criteria we target to reduce computational overhead of query compliance checking is to minimize or eliminate costly public-key cryptographic operations and to achieve protocols faster than a direct application of secure function evaluation techniques.

Implicit in the above privacy requirement is the fact that the protocol does not reveal new information about the data owner's policy to client and server,

---

[1] A function is *negligible* if for any positive polynomial p and all sufficiently large natural numbers $\sigma \in \mathcal{N}$, it is smaller than $1/p(\sigma)$.

other than what is revealed to clients by fulfilled queries. Still, to hide some additional information about the policy, the privacy requirement also demands that the result of a non-compliant query is indistinguishable from a query that matches zero records in the database, so that the protocol does not reveal to clients whether a query that returns no matches does so because it is non-compliant or because there are actually no matching records[2].

We design three protocols for enforcing compliance of *keyword search* queries. We only consider *whitelist* (resp., *blacklist*) policy types, where the query is compliant only if the query value is equal to one (resp., none) of the policy values. For such query and policy types, we provide highly efficient and scalable database policy compliance protocols that satisfy all our requirements, as detailed below (the PRP assumption being the existence of pseudo-random permutations).

Requirement	Protocol π_1	Protocol π_2	Protocol π_3
Correctness preservation	If DR protocol satisfies Added Property 1	If DR protocol satisfies Added Property 2	If DR protocol satisfies Added Property 1
Compliance completeness	Under no complexity assumption	Under no complexity assumption	Under no complexity assumption
Compliance soundness	(not satisfied)	Under no complexity assumption	Under no complexity assumption
Privacy	Under PRP assumption (some leakage to S)	Under PRP assumption (some leakage to S)	Under PRP assumption And based on SFE
Time	Linear in policy size	Linear in policy size	Linear in policy size
Communication	Linear in policy size	Linear in policy size	Linear in policy size
Rounds	$O(1)$ in policy size	$O(1)$ in policy size	$O(1)$ in policy size

An additional important property is that all our 3 DPC protocols only require $O(1)$ cryptographic operations per query and policy value, and are about two orders of magnitude faster than 2-party arbitrary function evaluation protocols [19], which require at least $\Omega(\ell)$ cryptographic operations per query and policy value, where ℓ denotes the length of these values (even in recent optimized solutions). Just like achieved previously for DR protocols in the 3-party model, our DPC protocols not only minimize or eliminate costly public-key cryptography operations, but they provide concrete time efficiency, which we document through performance numbers from our implementations (in Sect. 4). Our solutions rest on two main technical contributions: (1) using equality-preserving symmetric encryption with multiple keys shared among different subsets of

---

[2] Of course, sometimes a client is able to distinguish these cases due to auxiliary information.

parties (building on [3]) for efficient 3-party computation on encrypted data, and (2) performing policy-based query rewriting to make the results of non-compliant queries indistinguishable from queries matching no records. Formal definitions and proofs are omitted due to space restrictions.

Related Work. To the best of our knowledge, there is no previous work on privacy-preserving, efficient, *query* policy compliance checking for database queries. That is, although there has been previous work on 3-party protocols in which the data set being searched is encrypted, the query is kept private, and queries are only allowed if they satisfy certain structural conditions, we are unaware of previous work in which the restriction on allowable queries (i.e., the policy) depends on the query and/or is kept private from the clients. Existing work in this area focuses on policy conditions that mainly depend on the database attributes (see, e.g., [5,8,11,18]) or on the identity of the clients (see, e.g., [4,10,13,16], or consider different kinds of access control in such systems (see, e.g., [12,14]).

Our work is also somewhat related (in a complementary way) to a number of areas in theoretical and applied cryptography, including private information retrieval [6], searchable symmetric encryption [17], searchable public-key encryption [2] and oblivious RAMs [9]. Previous cryptographic work in a 3-party model (also referred as commodity-based, server-assisted, server-aided model) seems to have originated in [1], with respect to oblivious transfer protocols, and [7], with respect to private information retrieval.

2   Models, Definitions and Properties

We discuss models and DR protocol properties used in the rest of the paper, and further clarify the privacy and security properties that our DPC protocols must satisfy.

Data, Query and Policy Models. We model a *database table* (briefly, database) as a matrix DB with n rows and m columns, where each row is associated with a data *record*, each column is associated with a data *attribute*, and each database entry $DB(i, j)$ is the value of the j-th attribute of the i-th record. The database *schema* consists of n, m, and the *domains* of each of the m attributes (*i.e.*, the j-th domain is the set of values that the j-th attribute of a record can take), and is assumed to be known by all parties that participate in the protocol. We assume that domains are large in that a randomly chosen domain element is, with very high probability, not in DB. (If DB does not satisfy these conditions, then simple padding of domain strings can be used to make it so.)

A *query* q contains a database attribute and a *query value* v from the corresponding attribute domain. We consider keyword-match queries of the following form (using SQL notation): "SELECT * FROM *main* WHERE attribute_name = v".

A data owner's *query compliance policy* (briefly, *policy*) contains, for each attribute $j \in \{1, \ldots, m\}$, a set $W_j = \{w_{j,1}, \ldots, w_{j,c_j}\}$ of *policy values* drawn from the j-th domain. All of the clients that access DB through this data owner are subject to the same policy. On input a query value v, an attribute name (or, equivalently, an attribute index j), and a set of attribute values W_j, the policy returns 1 (resp., 0) to denote query compliance (resp., non-compliance). We mainly consider the *whitelist* and *blacklist* policies:

1. *Whitelist*: If query q refers to the j-th attribute, then p returns 1 iff $v \in W_j$;
2. *Blacklist*: If query q refers to the j-th attribute, then p returns 1 iff $v \notin W_j$.

Intuitively, a blacklist policy captures the notion of a set of forbidden query values, while a whitelist policy restricts queries to a specified set of allowed values. We assume that the lengths c_j of whitelists and blacklists and the lengths of the policy values $w_{j,k}$ are system parameters known to all parties (although our protocols will keep the latter values hidden from C).

DR Protocol Properties. We consider DR protocols, as depicted in Fig. 1, with the following structure:

1. C, D and S run a preliminary setup subprotocol
   (this enables S to later answer C's query on the database owned by D)
2. Given a query q, C constructs a *query message* Q and sends it to S
3. S computes an *answer message* *ans* and sends it to C
4. Based on Q and *ans*, C can compute database records that satisfy q, if any.

The *unique-query* property requires that, for any database DB and any properly formatted query message Q, there is at most one pair (attribute_name, v) for which C could have generated query message Q. When such a pair exists, we refer to v as the "query value associated with Q."

The *query-correctness* property requires that, for any database DB, any input pair (attribute_name, v), and any Q with associated query value v, at the end of the DR protocol, C can compute all records in DB that satisfy query attribute_name $= v$.

We also impose some additional structural properties on DR protocols:

1. *Added DR Property 1:* At the end of step 1, S stores $F(k_{c,d}; DB(i,j))$, for each database entry $DB(i,j)$, where F is a pseudo-random permutation and $k_{c,d}$ denotes a key shared between C and D;
2. *Added DR Property 2:* At the end of step 1, for each database entry $DB(i,j)$, S stores the triple encryption $F(k_{c,d}; F(k_{c,s}; F(k_{c,d}; DB(i,j))))$, where F is a pseudo-random permutation and $k_{c,d}$ (resp., $k_{c,s}$) denotes a key shared between C and D (resp., C and S).

Note the following simple DR protocol satisfying Property 1: query values and data values are encrypted via a pseudo-random permutation, a query message contains the encrypted query value, and the answer message contains the records with encrypted data values equal to the encrypted query value. Other examples can be found in the literature (see, e.g., [11, 18]). It should also be noted that any protocol satisfying Property 1 can be turned into one that satisfies Property 2, and that our techniques will work with a number of variations of these example properties.

DPC Protocol Properties. Our DPC protocols compose with DR protocols as follows (see Fig. 2): after the DR setup subprotocol, instead of a single query message Q sent from C to S, we now have three subprotocols (a query subprotocol, a compliance-verification subprotocol, and a query rewriting subprotocol) after which a query message is sent to S, and then the answer step of the DR protocol can be executed.

The requirements we demand from any DPC protocol were already informally described and motivated in Sect. 1. Here, we only further clarify its input/output behavior and privacy requirement. The inputs to a DPC protocol are a security parameter 1^σ (known to all parties), an attribute name and query value v (private inputs to C), and a database DB (schema known to all parties, but contents private to D). The outputs of a DPC protocol are a query message Q' (communicated privately to S) and a bit b (communicated privately to D) indicating whether the query complies with the policy ($b = 1$) or not ($b = 0$). We consider privacy in multiple runs of the DPC protocol against a semi-honest probabilistic polynomial-time adversary Adv (with history as auxiliary input) corrupting up to one party, by a natural adaptation of the real/ideal security framework, as typically used in the cryptography literature. Briefly speaking, a (real-world) execution of multiple runs of the DPC protocol are executed, does not leak to Adv more than the ideal-world leakage, defined as follows. On input of a query value v given by C, a database DB, policy values $w_1, \ldots, w_c$, and policy p input by D, each ideal execution of a single DPC protocol returns:

1. the output b of policy p on input query value v and policy values $w_1, \ldots, w_c$ to D
2. a random query message Q' to S, where Q' has no matching records if $b = 0$ or has associated query value v if $b = 1$.

In our first two protocols, we admit some additional leakage to S, and consider the variant of the above definition, where such leakage is also admitted in the ideal world.

Our design also targets a number of additional security properties, which can be obtained using network security protocols such as TLS: *confidentiality* of the communication between all participants, message *sender authentication*, message *receiver authentication*, and *communication integrity* protection.

3   DPC Protocols

In this section we present our three DPC protocols (whose properties are detailed in Sect. 1). Our first protocol π_1 falls short of satisfying all requirements formulated in Sects. 1 and 2 in two ways: (a) it does not satisfy compliance soundness (i.e., a malicious C could send inconsistent encryptions for compliance verification and query rewriting; thus, the compliance verification test would pass on a query value different than the one used for query rewriting); (b) privacy against D is only satisfied if the protocol is allowed to leak any repeated occurrences of the same query value. Our second protocol π_2 extends π_1 so to eliminate (a), and

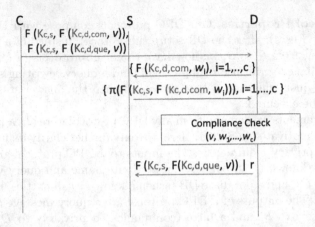

Fig. 3. The basic keyword match policy compliance protocol π_1

protocol π_3 eliminates both (a) and (b). In the following protocol descriptions, keys are named with two subscripts indicating by which parties they are shared. For example, a private key shared by C and S would be named $k_{c,s}$. There may optionally be a third subscript *com* or *que*, to indicate whether the key is used for policy compliance checking or query rewriting. Thus, $k_{c,d,com}$ means a key shared by C and D and used for compliance checking. We assume a standard secure 2-party key agreement protocol is executed in an initialization phase to produce these keys.

Protocol π_1. Our most basic protocol π_1 allows efficient enforcement of policy compliance for keyword search queries with whitelist policies (blacklist policies can be supported with minor modifications).

A pictorial description of the protocol can be found in Fig. 3. In the first step, C sends to D two double encryptions of its query value v, once using key $k_{c,d,que}$ as the inner layer, and a second time using key $k_{c,d,com}$. Then, D and S interact to analogously compute ciphertexts for the policy values, as follows: first, D encrypts each of the policy values $w_1, \ldots, w_c$ using key $k_{c,d,com}$ and sends the resulting ciphertexts to S; then, S further encrypts each of these ciphertexts using key $k_{c,s}$, and returns the resulting ciphertexts, *reordered using a random permutation* π, to D. At this point, D computes the whitelist policy output by simply checking whether one or zero of the policy value ciphertexts is equal to the ciphertext received by C. After the policy compliance calculation, if the query is compliant, D simply forwards the received encryption $k_{c,d,que}$ to S, who can remove the outer layer of encryption and fulfill the query. Otherwise, D performs *query rewriting*, sending S a random value indistinguishable from a double-encrypted query.

As described in the introduction, the two main technical ideas embedded in this protocol are: (1) using "equality-preserving encryption" to allow D to calculate the policy output without revealing the policy values to S or C and without learning why the policy was or was not satisfied (i.e., which policy value(s) w_i may have textually matched value(s) in the query); (2) using "query rewriting" to allow D to rewrite the query q obtained by C into a query q' which guarantees that the same database records match q and q' if q is compliant, or no records match q' otherwise, without S or C obtaining any additional information on which is the case.

Protocol π_2: Soundness Against Malicious Clients. One problem with protocol π_1 is that a malicious C can violate the soundness property by sending two different queries for compliance verification and query rewriting. Protocol π_2 prevents this attack with minimal modifications from π_1. As a preliminary observation, we see that since C only sends one query message, the only opportunity for C to provide malicious input is before the compliance verification subprotocol. This naturally leads us to examine ways in which we could modify protocol π_1 to require only one input from C. Note that we cannot use the same encryption for both compliance checking and query rewriting, since that would allow S to identify encrypted query values that match policy items it has seen during the setup phase.

We can resolve this by storage of a triple encryption $F(k_{c,d}, F(k_{c,s}, F(k_{c,d}, v)))$ of each database value, as in Added DR Property 2, instead of a single encryption $F(k_{c,d}, v)$, as in π_1. The structure of the protocol is similar as for π_1. At query time, C encrypts the query value with *both* of its keys and sends the resulting doubly-encrypted value $F(k_{c,s}, F(k_{c,d}, v))$ to D. Then D encrypts each of the policy values w_i using key $k_{c,d}$ and sends them to S, which then re-encrypts each of these using key $k_{c,s}$, randomly permutes the order of keywords, and returns the re-encrypted values to D.

As before, D checks the encrypted query for equality with the double-encrypted policy values. If the query is non-compliant, D sends to S a random query indistinguishable from a triple-encrypted real query; otherwise, D re-encrypts $F(k_{c,s}, F(k_{c,d}, v))$ using $k_{c,d}$, and sends the triple-encrypted value $F(k_{c,d}, F(k_{c,s}, F(k_{c,d}, v)))$ to S for its answer generation in the DR protocol. Note that the outermost layer of encryption prevents S from identifying whether the query matches policy items it had previously encrypted from D—thus eliminating the need for separate *com* and *que* encryptions.

The resulting DPC protocol π_2 inherits the same properties as π_1, plus compliance soundness under a different assumption on the method used to encrypt the database values in the DR protocol (namely, Added Property 2). The triply-encrypted database of Added DR Property 2 can be generated during the setup phase as follows. First, D encrypts all items in the database with $k_{c,d}$ and sends them to S, which re-encrypts them using $k_{c,s}$ and returns them to D. Then D adds a third layer of encryption, again using $k_{c,d}$, and sends the triply-encrypted database to S. This interaction between D and S may be expensive, as it involves every item in the database being encrypted and sent over the network three times; this may render this method undesirable to practitioners, especially when dealing with large databases. We address this issue as well in π_3.

Protocol π_3: Privacy Across Multiple Queries. Protocols π_1, π_2 come with some leakage to D across multiple query executions: D learns, by checking for

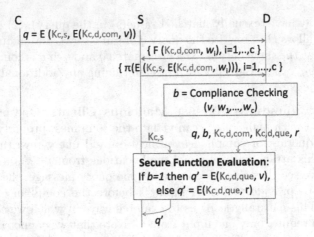

Fig. 4. Protocol π_3: Keyword search policy compliance with (multi-query) security against D

repetitions in the first message sent by C to D, whether the query value in the current execution is equal to a previously executed query. Although not a major form of leakage, it remains of interest to see if we can prevent it at some affordable efficiency cost.

We now describe a protocol π_3 that keeps all properties in π_1, the compliance soundness property achieved in π_2 and satisfies privacy against D without the mentioned leakage. (It also avoids the database setup inefficiency mentioned at the end of the description of π_2.) Protocol π_3 uses an additional cryptographic tool: 2-party Secure Function Evaluation (SFE) protocols [19]. Recall that in such protocols, two parties P_1 and P_2, with private inputs x_1 and x_2, respectively, can jointly compute a functionality $f(x_1, x_2) = (f_1, f_2)$, such that P_1 receives $f_1(x_1, x_2)$, and P_2 receives $f_2(x_1, x_2)$, and it is required that nothing is learned by either party other than the output.

Instead of using a triple encryption as in π_2, protocol π_3 uses a different shared key $k'_{c,d}$ for query rewriting. After the policy check, which remains unchanged, D and S perform a two-party SFE protocol, returning to S a newly-encrypted form of the query.

First, C sends $F(k_{c,s}, F(k_{c,d}, v))$ to D, at which point the same policy compliance check as in π_2 takes place. After the compliance check, D and S engage in a two-party SFE protocol, where D inputs $F(k_{c,s}, F(k_{c,d}, v)), k_{c,d}, k'_{c,d}$, a random query r, and the (one-bit) result of the compliance check. S inputs $k_{c,s}$. Together, the two parties securely compute the following output, which is received only by S: if the query was non-compliant, random value r is output; if the query was compliant, the doubly-encrypted value $F(k_{c,s}, F(k_{c,d}, v))$ is decrypted twice to produce v, which is then encrypted using key $k'_{c,d}$, and the result, $F(k'_{c,d}, v)$ is released to S. S then proceeds to compute the answer based on the DR protocol.

The resulting DPC protocol π_3, illustrated in Fig. 4, inherits the same properties as π_1 and π_2, plus multi-query privacy against D. However, π_3 is not strictly better than π_1, π_2 since two-party SFE protocols come with added running time, even when considering recent implementation advances (see, e.g., [15] and follow-up work). Accordingly, we only used two-party SFE executions on very short ℓ-bit inputs (as opposed to a generic SFE solution which would require inputs as large as the policy itself).

4 Performance Results

In this section we report initial performance results related to implementations of our basic DPC protocols. We focus on results for π_1 as π_2 and π_3 exhibit similar behaviour. Specifically, π_2 is only slower than π_1 by a small constant multiplicative factor and π_3 is only slower than π_2 by a small constant additive factor.

Setup. The Data Owner and Server processes were running on a Dell PowerEdge R710 server with two Intel Xeon 2.66 Ghz processors and 48 GB of memory, running 64-bit Ubuntu 12.04.1. The R710 server was connected to a Dell Power-Vault MD1200 disk array containing 12 2TB 7.2 K RPM SAS drives arranged in a RAID6 configuration. The Client was running on a Dell PowerEdge R810 server with two Intel Xeon 2.40 GHz processors and 64 GB of memory, running 64-bit Red Hat Enterprise Linux Server release 6.3 and connected to the R710 server via switched Gigabit Ethernet.

The database was populated by generating random values about fictitious people using demographic information from the US Census Bureau. A single table with 23 columns was used (e.g., last name *lname*, state *state*, and zip code *zip*), including several columns containing large text fields and one column containing binary data (*fingerprint*). We considered the following policies:

Policy	Compliant queries must include:
F	All queries are rejected as non compliant
T	All queries are accepted as compliant
B1	A conjunction of at least 3 keyword queries on *state*, *lname*, and *zip*
B2	A conjunction of at least 3 keyword queries on *state*, *lname*, and any one of the remaining columns, excluding *fingerprint*
W1	A keyword query on *lname* with query value in a 1-entry whitelist
W2	A keyword query on *lname* with query value in a 100-entry whitelist
W3	A keyword query on *lname* with query value in a 1000-entry whitelist
W4	A keyword query on *lname* with query value in a 10000-entry whitelist
W5	A keyword query on *lname* with query value in a 20000-entry whitelist

Compliance policy $B2$ was expressed as a disjunction of 23 sub-policies of $B1$
type, each of them requiring keyword query conjunctions on *state*, *lname*, and an
additional (and different) database column. We considered the following queries:

Query	Template
$Q1$	SELECT * FROM main WHERE lname=value
$Q2$	SELECT * FROM main WHERE state=value AND lname=value AND zip=value

Results. Each query template was executed several times using different values.
We note that policies F, T, $B1$ and $B2$ only refer to the query structure or
database attributes and do not depend on query values, contrarily to queries
$W1, \ldots, W5$, which depend on values in the query and in the (variable-length)
whitelist.

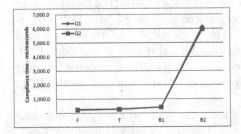

Fig. 5. Query compliance checking
overhead for policies F, T, $B1$, and $B2$.

Fig. 6. Query compliance checking
overhead for policies $W1$, $W2$, $W3$,
$W4$, and $W5$.

Figure 5 shows results when checking compliance for policies F, T, $B1$, and
$B2$ for $Q1$ and $Q2$ queries. Such checking was based on the query structure
only and, thus, there is no impact from cryptographic operations on the mea-
sured running time. Three main observations can be derived from this figure:
(1) running time for $B1$ is almost the same as for the trivial policies T and F;
(2) running time for $B1$ and $B2$ is almost the same for the two policy types $Q1$
and $Q2$, with differences smaller than 3 %; and (3) running time for $B1$ and $B2$
is essentially linear with policy size.

Figure 6 shows computation results when running protocol π_1 for query
classes $Q1$ and $Q2$ and policies $W1, \ldots, W5$. These policies depend on query
values and, hence, trigger execution of π_1, with its cryptographic operations.
Two main observations can be derived from this figure. First, running time is
almost the same again for the two policy types $Q1$ and $Q2$, with differences of
less than 7 % for shorter policies and less than 2 % as policies get longer. Second,
the time required by π_1 grows linearly with the size of the whitelist. Specifically,

as the size of the whitelist grows, so does the time it takes to doubly encrypt its values, send/receive them between D and S, and checking by using sequential scan whether an attribute value referenced in C's query belongs to the doubly encrypted and permuted whitelist values. (Here, a speedup from the use of binary search does not seem to impact the running time substantially, due to the double encryption and network communication required).

When comparing the two figures, we observe that the impact of running π_1 when checking compliance is essentially minimal for policies with short-size whitelists (i.e., a factor of about 10, calculated by comparing the running time for $F, T, B1$ with the running time of policies $W1, W2, W3$).

Acknowledgement. Supported by the Intelligence Advanced Research Projects Activity (IARPA) via Department of Interior National Business Center (DoI/NBC) contract number D13PC00003. The second, third, fifth and sixth authors also acknowledge DARPA contract FA8750-13-2-0058 for some of the time spent on revising this paper. The U.S. Government is authorized to reproduce and distribute reprints for Governmental purposes notwithstanding any copyright annotation hereon. Disclaimer: The views and conclusions contained herein are those of the authors and should not be interpreted as necessarily representing the official policies or endorsements, either expressed or implied, of IARPA, DARPA, DoI/NBC, or the U.S. Government.

References

1. Beaver, D.: Commodity-based cryptography (extended abstract), pp. 446–455. In: STOC (1997)
2. Boneh, D., Di Crescenzo, G., Ostrovsky, R., Persiano, G.: Public key encryption with keyword search. In: Cachin, C., Camenisch, J.L. (eds.) EUROCRYPT 2004. LNCS, vol. 3027, pp. 506–522. Springer, Heidelberg (2004)
3. Brickell, E., Di Crescenzo, G., Frankel, Y.: Sharing block ciphers. In: Clark, A., Boyd, C., Dawson, E.P. (eds.) ACISP 2000. LNCS, vol. 1841, pp. 457–470. Springer, Heidelberg (2000)
4. Camenisch, J., Kohlweiss, M., Rial, A., Sheedy, C.: Blind and anonymous identity-based encryption and authorised private searches on public key encrypted data. In: Jarecki, S., Tsudik, G. (eds.) PKC 2009. LNCS, vol. 5443, pp. 196–214. Springer, Heidelberg (2009)
5. Ceselli, A., Damiani, E., De Capitani di Vimercati, S., Paraboschi, S.: Modeling and assessing inference exposure in encrypted databases. ACM TISSEC **8**, 119–152 (2005)
6. Chor, B., Kushilevitz, E., Goldreich, O., Sudan, M.: Private information retrieval. J. ACM **45**(6), 965–981 (1998)
7. Di Crescenzo, G., Ishai, Y., Ostrovsky, R.: Universal service-providers for database private information retrieval, pp. 91–100. In: PODC (1998)
8. Evdokimov, S., Günther, O.: Encryption techniques for secure database outsourcing. In: Biskup, J., López, J. (eds.) ESORICS 2007. LNCS, vol. 4734, pp. 327–342. Springer, Heidelberg (2007)
9. Goldreich, O., Ostrovsky, R.: Software protection and simulation on oblivious RAMs. J. ACM **43**(3), 431–473 (1996)

10. Goyal, V., Pandey, O., Sahai, A., Waters, B.: Attribute-based encryption for fine-grained access control of encrypted data. In: ACM CCS Conference, pp. 89–98 (2006)
11. Hacigümüs, H., Iyer, B.R., Li, C., Mehrotra, S.: Executing SQL over encrypted data in the database-service-provider model, pp. 216–227. In: SIGMOD Conference (2002)
12. Hamlen, K.W., Kagal, L., Kantarcioglu, M.: Policy enforcement framework for cloud data management. IEEE Data Eng. Bull. **35**(4), 39–45 (2012)
13. Jarecki, S., Lincoln, P.: Negotiated privacy. In: Okada, M., Babu, C.S., Scedrov, A., Tokuda, H. (eds.) ISSS 2002. LNCS, vol. 2609, pp. 96–111. Springer, Heidelberg (2003)
14. Li, M., Yu, S., Cao, N., Lou, W.: Authorized private keyword search over encrypted data in cloud computing, pp. 383–392. In: ICDCS (2011)
15. Malkhi, D., Nisan, N., Pinkas, B., Sella, Y.: Fairplay - secure two-party computation system, pp. 287–302. In: USENIX Security Symposium (2004)
16. Miklau, G., Suciu, D.: Controlling access to published data using cryptography, pp. 898–909. In: VLDB (2003)
17. Song, D., Wagner, D., Perrig, A.: Practical techniques for searches on encrypted data, pp. 44–55. In: IEEE Symposium on Security and Privacy (2000)
18. Yang, Z., Zhong, S., Wright, R.N.: Privacy-preserving queries on encrypted data. In: Gollmann, D., Meier, J., Sabelfeld, A. (eds.) ESORICS 2006. LNCS, vol. 4189, pp. 479–495. Springer, Heidelberg (2006)
19. Yao, A.C.C.: How to generate and exchange secrets (extended abstract), pp. 162–167. In: FOCS (1986)

Bandwidth Efficient PIR from NTRU

Yarkın Doröz[1]([✉]), Berk Sunar[1], and Ghaith Hammouri[2]

[1] Worcester Polytechnic Institute, Worcester, USA
ydoroz@wpi.edu
[2] Crags Inc, Boylston, USA

Abstract. We present a private information retrieval (PIR) scheme based on somewhat homomorphic encryption (SWHE). In particular, we customize an NTRU-based SWHE scheme in order to evaluate a specific class of fixed depth circuits relevant for PIR implementation, thus achieving a more practical implementation. In practice, a SWHE that can evaluate a depth 5 circuit is sufficient to construct a PIR capable of retrieving data from a database containing 4 billion rows. We leverage this property in order to produce a more practical PIR scheme. Compared to previous results, our implementation achieves a significantly lower bandwidth cost (more than 1000 times smaller). The computational cost of our implementation is higher than previous proposals for databases containing a small number of bits in each row. However, this cost is amortized as database rows become wider.

Keywords: Private information retrieval · Homomorphic encryption · NTRU

1 Introduction

The problem of Private Information Retrieval (PIR) is one of the simplest yet most useful concepts in cryptography. Simply put, a PIR scheme allows Alice to store a database D at a remote server (Bob) with the promise that Alice can retrieve $D(i)$ without revealing i or $D(i)$ to Bob. The notion of an information theoretic PIR scheme was first introduced in [22] where the limits on Bob's knowledge of i were based on information theoretic arguments. In such a setting, it can easily be shown that in a PIR scheme with a single server (single copy of the database D) the only way to hide access to D in the information theoretic setting is for Bob to send the entire database D back to Alice. Many solutions were proposed in order to produce a secure information theoretic PIR scheme when Alice can communicate with several servers storing a copy of D [22–24]. While these constructions are interesting from a theoretical point of view they are difficult to achieve in a practical setting. For the remainder of this text we focus only on single database PIRs.

As such Chor and Gilboa [25,26] introduced the concept of computational PIRs (cPIR). In cPIR, Alice is content to have the difficulty of Bob retrieving i (or information about i) based on computational difficulty. That is Alice would

© IFCA/Springer-Verlag Berlin Heidelberg 2014
R. Böhme et al. (Eds.): FC 2014 Workshops, LNCS 8438, pp. 195–207, 2014.
DOI: 10.1007/978-3-662-44774-1_16

like Bob to face a computationally *difficult* problem in order to extract any significant information about i or $D(i)$. Since the introduction of cPIR many schemes have been proposed. In [27] Kushilevitz and Ostrovsky presented the first single server PIR scheme based on the computational difficulty of deciding the quadratic residuosity of a number modulo a product of two large primes.

Other cPIR constructions include [28] which is based on the computational difficulty of deciding whether a small prime p divides $\phi(m)$ for any composite integer m of unknown factorization where $\phi()$ denotes Euler's totient function. In [29] another cPIR scheme was presented that generalizes the scheme in [28] while using a slight variation on the security assumption. Most notably, the construction in [29] achieves a communication complexity of $O(k + d)$ where k is the security parameter satisfying $k > \log(N)$, N is the database size, and d is the bit-length of the retrieved data. In [7] Lipmaa presented a different yet quite interesting cPIR scheme that leverages a (length-flexible) additively homomorphic public-key encryption scheme and provides better communication complexity performance. Later in [3], an efficient PIR scheme is produced using a partially homomorphic encryption algorithm. This was later followed by a lattice based cPIR construction by Aguilar-Melchor and Gaborit [30].

In 2007 the computational practicality of PIRs was raised by Sion and Carbunar [20] who concluded that no existing construction is as efficient as the trivial PIR scheme. The authors observe that any computational PIR scheme that requires one or more modular multiplications per database bit cannot be as efficient as the trivial PIR scheme. Later, Olumofin and Goldberg [21] revisited the performance analysis and found that the lattice-based PIR scheme by Aguilar-Melchor and Gaborit [30] to be an order of magnitude more efficient than the trivial PIR in situations that reflect average consumer internet bandwidth.

In all these constructions the challenge has been to find an efficient scheme based on a difficult computational problem. The aforementioned schemes utilize a variety of approaches and a diverse set of tools to construct cPIR schemes. However, it has always been clear that given a fully or somewhat homomorphic encryption (SWHE or FHE) scheme achieving a cPIR construction would be conceptually as simple as carrying out normal information retrieval. Although fully homomorphic encryption schemes have been introduced in 2009 [1] efficiency has been the biggest hindrance preventing any practical implementation. As such, FHE schemes have yet to be shown to be useful in progressing a practical realization of a private information retrieval. However, a number of new FHE schemes [4–6,10,11] and optimizations such as modulus and key switching [8], batching and SIMD optimizations [9] have been introduced in just the last few years which improved the efficiency of FHE implementation roughly by two orders of magnitude per year.

Our Contribution. Motivated by these advances, in this work we take a first step towards using a SWHE scheme along with optimizations developed for leveled SWHE implementation to construct an efficient cPIR. We construct a rather simple implementation of a PIR scheme from a batched leveled SWHE implementation based on the NTRU encryption scheme. Our scheme has excellent bandwidth performance compare to previous implementations (more than 1000 times smaller). The computational cost of our implementation is higher than previous proposals for databases containing a small number of bits in each row. However, this cost is amortized as the database rows become wider.

2   Homomorphic Encryption Based PIR Schemes

In this section we briefly survey 3 representative cPIR schemes constructed out of homomorphic encryption schemes most relevant to our proposal. We note that this survey is only intended to provide a basis for later comparison.

2.1   Kushilevitz-Ostrovsky PIR

At the essence of the K-O scheme [2] is the use of a secure homomorphic operations and the idea of conceptually storing the database as a matrix. To elaborate, we can think of Bob as having a database D of size 2^h with each location containing a single bit (this can easily be extended for longer strings). Bob then stores D in a matrix M of size $2^{h/2} \times 2^{h/2}$. For any location i in the database D, this process can be done by using the first $h/2$ bits of i to represent the number of the row in M and the last $h/2$ bits of i to represent the number of the column in M where i will be placed. Now for Alice to recover the entry $D(i)$, she will take the first $h/2$ bits of i encode them into a one hot encoding A and carry out the same process for the lower $h/2$ bits of i to produce B. Finally, Alice uses a partially homomorphic encryption scheme E to encrypt each bit in A and B. Thus Alice sends to Bob $(E(A_0) \ldots E(A_{h/2-1}), E(B_0) \ldots E(B_{h/2-1}))$. With this information Bob can now carryout some homomorphic operations between the encrypted bits sent by Alice and the data stored within the matrix M in order to produce an encrypted output which encodes the bit $D(i)$ and can then be sent to Alice for decryption. The matrix is of size $2^{h/2} \times 2^{h/2} = N$ and therefore the communication complexity becomes $\mathcal{O}(\sqrt{N})$.

2.2   Boneh-Goh-Nissim (BGN) Scheme

The BGN cryptosystem is a partially homomorphic encryption scheme [3] capable of evaluating 2-DNF expressions in encrypted form. For example, given two encryptions of messages, we can obtain an encryption of the sum of the messages without decryption or compromising privacy. Indeed, the cryptosystem remains semantically secure. Being (in part) based on the Paillier cryptosystem, BGN inherits its additive homomorphic properties. Moreover, with the clever introduction of pairings, BGN is capable of homomorphically evaluating *one level of multiplication* operations.

The BGN algorithm constructs a homomorphic encryption scheme using finite groups or composite order that support bilinear maps. The construction outlined in [3] uses groups over elliptic curve where homomorphic additions translate into elliptic curve point addition and homomorphic multiplication translates into a pairing operation. Leveraging the single multiplication afforded by pairing operation Boneh, Goh and Nissim also manage to reduce the communication complexity in the basic step of the Kushilevitz-Ostrovsky PIR protocol from $\mathcal{O}(\sqrt{N})$ to $\mathcal{O}(\sqrt[3]{N})$. In contrast, the computational efficiency of BGN (for the server side PIR computation) scheme lies the pairing operation. Guillevic [18] developed optimized implementations to support BGN which reveals that parings over composite order elliptic curves are far less efficient than parings over prime order curves and also require significantly larger parameter sizes to reach the same security level.

2.3   Aguilar-Melchor-Gaborit's Lattice Based PIR

Most of the single server cPIR schemes rely on costly algebraic operations with large operands such as modular multiplications [2,32,33], or pairing operations on elliptic curves [3] to realize the homomorphic evaluations. In contrast, the PIR scheme by Aguilar-Melchor and Gaborit [30,31] makes use of a new lattice based construction replacing costly modular operations, with much cheaper vector addition operations in lattices. The security is based on the differential hidden lattice problem, which they relate like in many lattice based construction to NP-complete problems in coding theory. Via this connection the scheme is also related to the NTRU scheme [13].

Very briefly, the PIR schemes works as follows. The scheme utilizes a secret random $[N, 2N]$ matrix M of rank N over a field $\mathbb{Z}_p$ which is used to generate a set of *different matrices* obtained by multiplication by invertible random matrices. These matrices are disturbed by the user by the introduction of noise in half of the matrix columns to obtain softly disturbed matrices (SDMs) and hardly disturbed matrices (HDMs). To retrieve an element from the database the client sends a set of SDMs and one HDM to the PIR server. The PIR server inserts each of its elements in the corresponding matrix with a multiplicative operation OP and sums all the rows of the resulting matrices collapsing the PIR server reply to a single noisy vector over $\mathbb{Z}_p$.

While they proposed full fledged protocol and implementation [30,31], their analysis was limited to server-side computations on a small database consisting of twelve 3 MB files. Later Olumofin and Goldberg [21] performed extensive experiments with a broad set databases sizes under realistic network bandwidth settings determining that the lattice based Aguilar-Melchor and Gaborit PIR scheme is one order of magnitude more efficient than a simple PIR.

3   From SWHE to PIR

Consider a database D with $|D| = 2^\ell$ rows. Clearly ℓ index bits are sufficient to address all rows. Assume the data bit contained in row i is denoted by D_i. We may retrieve an element of D with given index $x \in \{0,1\}^\ell$ which holds D_x by computing:

$$f(x) = \sum_{y \in [2^\ell]} (x = y)D_y \pmod 2, \tag{1}$$

where the bitwise comparison $(x = y)$ may be computed as $\prod_{i \in [\ell]}(x_i + y_i + 1)$. Here $[\ell] = \{0, 1, \ldots, \ell - 1\}$ for $\ell > 0$ and $[\ell] = \{\}$ otherwise. The function of the inner loop is to check if each bit of the given x matches the corresponding bit of the y value currently processed. The boolean result is multiplied with the current data value D_y and added to the sum. All of the summed terms except the one where there was a match becomes zero and therefore does not affect the result. Therefore, $f(x) = D_x$.

This arithmetic retrieval formulation allows us to build PIRs and sPIRs. In this case the index value x is in encrypted form. Therefore, the database curator does not know which row is read from the database. We wish the curator to still be able to retrieve and serve the requested row. The data in the row itself can also be in encrypted form in which case the protocol is referred to as a symmetric PIR or sPIR in short. In this setting, if the index x is encrypted using a homomorphic encryption scheme E we may evaluate $f(x)$ homomorphically. From the formulation of $f(x)$ we need E to be able to compute a large number of homomorphic additions (XORs) $O(2^\ell)$ and a small number of multiplications (ANDs) ℓ and $\ell + 1$ if the rows are encrypted[1].

4   Picking the SWHE Scheme

To build a PIR for a database of size 2^ℓ as described in Sect. 3 we need an efficient SWHE instantiation that can evaluate a circuit of depth $\lceil \log_2(\ell) \rceil$. In practice a depth 5 or 6 circuit will suffice since that will give us an ability to construct a PIR for a database of size 2^{32} and 2^{64}, respectively.

For this we make use of the modified NTRU scheme [13] introduced by Stehlé and Steinfeld [12] with a number of optimizations introduced to this construction by Lopez-Alt, Tromer and Vaikuntanathan [11] to turn Stehlé and Steinfeld's scheme into a full fledged fully homomorphic encryption scheme. Here we only need to support a few levels and therefore the full Lopez-Alt, Tromer and Vaikuntanathan scheme is not needed. Stehlé and Steinfeld [12] formalized the security setting and reduced the security of their NTRU variant to the ring learning with error (RLWE) problem. More specifically, they show that if the secret polynomials are selected from the discrete Gaussian distribution with rejection then the public key is indistinguishable from a uniform sample. Unfortunately, the reduction does not carry over to the fully homomorphic setting since relaxation of parameters e.g. a larger modulus is needed to accommodate the noise growth during homomorphic evaluation as noted in [11]. We next summarize our instantiation of the scheme in [12] in a way that supports restricted homomorphic evaluations but does not require all the machinery of [11].

We require the ability to sample from a probability distribution χ on B-bounded polynomials in $R_q := \mathbb{Z}_q[x]/(x^n+1)$ where a polynomial is "B-bounded" if all of its coefficients lie in $[-B, B]$. For example, we can sample each coefficient from a discrete Gaussian with mean 0 and discard samples outside the

---

[1] Note that we restricted the database entries D_i to be bits but a w-bit entry can also easily be handled by considering w parallel and independent function evaluations.

desired range. Each AND gate evaluation incurs significant noise growth and therefore we use the modulus reduction technique introduced by Brakerski, Gentry and Vaikuntanathan [10]. We assume we are computing a leveled circuit with gates alternating between XOR and AND and modulus reduction taking place after each AND level. We use a decreasing sequence of odd prime moduli $q_0 > q_1 > \cdots > q_d$ where d is the depth of the PIR circuit. In this way, the key (public and evaluation keys) can become quite large and it remains a practical challenge to manage the size of this data and handle it efficiently. For this implementation we specialize the prime moduli q_i by requiring $q_i | q_{i+1}$ as was proposed in [16]. This allows us to eliminate the need for key switching and to reduce the public key size significantly. Also in this implementation we do not use relinearizations as proposed in [11] since we are in a single user setting and we have a shallow well structured circuit (a perfect binary tree) to evaluate. This will significantly improve the efficiency of implementation since relinearization is an expensive operation [16]. The primitives are as follows:

- KeyGen: We choose a decreasing sequence of primes $q_0 > q_1 > \cdots > q_d$ and a polynomial $\Phi_m(x)$, the m-th cyclotomic polynomial of degree $n = \varphi(m)$. For each i, we sample $u^{(i)}$ and $g^{(i)}$ from distribution χ, set $f^{(i)} = 2u^{(i)} + 1$ and $h^{(i)} = 2g^{(i)} \left(f^{(i)}\right)^{-1}$ in ring $R_{q_i} = \mathbb{Z}_{q_i}[x]/\langle \phi(x) \rangle$. (If $f^{(i)}$ is not invertible in this ring, re-sample.)
- Encrypt: To encrypt a bit $b \in \{0, 1\}$ with a public key $(h^{(0)}, q_0)$, random samples s and e are chosen from χ and compute the ciphertext as $c^{(0)} = h^{(0)}s + 2e + b$, a polynomial in R_{q_0}.
- Decrypt: To decrypt the ciphertext c with the corresponding private key $f^{(i)} = f^{2^i} \in R_{q_i}$, multiply the ciphertext and the private key in R_{q_i} then retrieve the message via modulo two reduction: $m = c^{(i)}f^{(i)} \pmod{2}$.
- XOR: For two ciphertexts $c_1^{(0)} = \mathsf{Encrypt}(b_1)$ and $c_2^{(0)} = \mathsf{Encrypt}(b_2)$ then their homomorphic XOR is evaluated by simply adding the ciphertexts $\mathsf{Encrypt}(b_1 + b_2) = c_1^{(0)} + c_2^{(0)}$.
- AND: Polynomial multiplication is realized in two steps. We first compute $\tilde{c}^{(i-1)}(x) = c_1^{(i-1)} \cdot c_2^{(i-1)} \pmod{\phi(x)}$ and then perform a modulus reduction operation as $\tilde{c}^{(i)}(x) = \left\lfloor \frac{q_1}{q_0} \tilde{c}^{(i-1)}(x) \right\rceil_2$ where the subscript 2 on the rounding operator indicates that we round up or down in order to make all coefficients equal modulo 2.

4.1   Concrete Setting

To instantiate the Stehlé Steinfeld variant of NTRU for depth d we need to pick a large enough q_0 value to reduce the modulus d times. For instance, for a selection of $B = 2$ and if we cut by 24 bits in each iteration we need at least 200 bits. For such a q parameter we can then select n based on the Hermite factor. The Hermite factor was introduced by Gama and Nguyen [14] to estimate the hardness of the shortest vector problem (SVP) in an n-dimensional lattice L and is defined as

$$\gamma^{2n} = \frac{||b||}{\text{vol}(L)^{\frac{1}{2n}}}$$

where $||b||$ is the length of the shortest vector or the length of the vector for which we are searching. The authors also estimate that, for larger dimensional lattices, a factor $\delta^n \leq 1.01^n$ would be the feasibility limit for current lattice reduction algorithms. In [15], Lindner and Peikert gave further experimental results regarding the relation between the Hermite factor and the recovery time as $t(\gamma) := \log(T(\gamma)) = 1.8/\log(\gamma) - 110$. For instance, for $\gamma^n = 1.0066^n$, we need about 2^{80} seconds on an AMD Opteron running at 2.5 Ghz [15]. Since we are using a construction based on NTRU we need to determine the desired Hermite factor for the NTRU lattice. Coppersmith and Shamir in [19] show that an attacker would gain useful information with a lattice vector as close as norm $q/4$ to the original secret key vector. Therefore we take $||b|| = q/4$ and $\text{vol}(L) = q^n$ and compute the Hermite factor for the NTRU lattice as $\gamma = (\sqrt{q}/4)^{1/(2n)}$.

To select parameters we also need to consider the noise growth. Since we no longer use relinearization, the powers of the secret key will grow exponentially through the levels of evaluation. To cope with the growth we use the modulus reduction as described in Sect. 4. Following the noise analysis of [16] (Sect. 5) we can express the correctness condition as $||c^{2^i} f^{2^d}||_\infty < q_d/2||$ assuming we are evaluating a depth d circuit. Also note that instantiation we fix χ to choose from $\{-1, 0, 1\}$ with probabilities $\{0.25, 0.5, 0.25\}$, respectively. With modulus reduction rate of $\kappa \approx q_{i+1}/q_i$ the following equation holds $c^{2^d} f^{2^d} = (\dots((c^2\kappa + p_1)^2\kappa + p_2)^2 \dots \kappa + p_{2^i})f^{2^d}$. In Table 1 we computed the Hermite factor and supported depth for various sizes of q_0 and n for our scheme.

Table 1. Hermite factor and supported circuit depth (γ, d) for various q and n.

n	$\log_2(q)$				
	512	640	768	1024	1280
2^{13}	$(1.01083, 5)$	$(1.0135, 5)$	$(1.0162, 6)$	$(1.0218, 6)$	$(1.0273, 7)$
2^{14}	$(1.00538, 5)$	$(1.0067, 5)$	$(1.0081, 6)$	$(1.0108, 6)$	$(1.0135, 6)$
2^{15}	$(1.00269, 5)$	$(1.0033, 5)$	$(1.0040, 6)$	$(1.0054, 6)$	$(1.0067, 6)$

5   The NTRU Based PIR Protocol

In our encryption scheme we are able to batch additional information to the ciphertext polynomials. This allows us to perform retrieval using two different query mechanisms:

Bundled Query one query is used to to retrieve data stored at different rows of the database (different indicies are queried).

Single Query the query retrieves data from a single row (a single index) but processes more indices at a time during the PIR server computation.

Next we explain an FHE optimization technique named *batching* and show how it gives us the two query methods.

Batching. Batching was introduced by Smart and Vercauteren [8,9]. It allows us to evaluate a circuit on multiple independent data inputs simultaneously by embedding them into the same ciphertext. The independent data inputs are encoded to form special binary polynomials that are used as message polynomials. Addition and multiplication of these the message polynomials has the effect of evaluating XOR and AND operations on the packed message bits. The encoding is achieved using the Chinese Remainder Theorem. First we set $R_{q_0} = \mathbb{Z}_{q_0}/\langle \Phi_m(x) \rangle$, where $\Phi_m(x)$ is defined as the mth cyclotomic polynomial. The cyclotomic polynomial $\Phi_m(x)$ is factored into equal degree irreducible polynomials over $\mathbb{F}_2$ $\Phi_m(x) = \prod_{i \in [\varepsilon]} F_i(x)$. where $\lambda = \deg(F_i)$ is the smallest integer that satisfies $m|(2^\lambda - 1)$. A message polynomial $m(x)$ in the residue space is represented as $m_i = m(x) \pmod{F_i(x)}$. Therefore; given a message bit vector $\mathbf{m} = \{m_0, m_1, m_2, m_3 \ldots, m_\varepsilon\}$ we may compute the corresponding message polynomial using inverse CRT $m(x) = \mathsf{CRT}^{-1}(\mathbf{m})$. Using these special formed messages, we can perform bit level AND and XOR operations: $m_i \cdot m_i' = m(x) \cdot m'(x) \pmod{F_i(x)}$ and $m_i \oplus m_i' = m(x) + m'(x) \pmod{F_i(x)}$.

Bundled Query. The batching technique allows us to embed multiple indices into a query ciphertext and thereby facilitate retrieval of multiple database entries. First recall our PIR function $\sum_{y \in [2^\ell]} [\prod_{i \in [\ell]} (x_i + y_i + 1)] D_y$, which we will now evaluate on encrypted x and y values. Using the batching technique we may evaluate ε retrievals with indices $\beta[1], \ldots, \beta[\varepsilon]$ simultaneously. First we form their bit representation as:

$$\beta[1] = (\beta_{\ell-1}[1] \; \beta_{\ell-2}[1] \; \cdots \; \beta_0[1])$$
$$\beta[2] = (\beta_{\ell-1}[2] \; \beta_{\ell-2}[2] \; \cdots \; \beta_0[2])$$
$$\vdots \qquad \vdots \qquad \vdots \qquad \vdots$$
$$\beta[\varepsilon] = (\beta_{\ell-1}[\varepsilon] \; \beta_{\ell-2}[\varepsilon] \; \cdots \; \beta_0[\varepsilon])$$

Using the columns of the bit matrix on the RHS, we can compute the batched polynomial versions of the index bits $\tilde{\beta}_i(x)$ as:

$$\tilde{\beta}_i(x) = \mathsf{CRT}^{-1}(\beta_i[1], \beta_i[2], \ldots, \beta_i[\varepsilon])$$

Later, these polynomials are encrypted as: $\xi_i(x) = h(x)s_i(x) + 2e_i(x) + \tilde{\beta}_i(x)$ for $i \in [\ell]$. The query $Q = [\xi_i(x), \ldots, \xi_{\ell-1}(x)]$ is then send to the PIR server. In order to perform parallel comparisons vector row index bit $\{y_i, y_i, \ldots, y_i\}$ should also converted into a polynomial representation using inverse-CRT. Since we are dealing with bits $y_i = \{0, 1\}$, the inverse-CRT will result in $\{0, 1\}$ polynomials, and thus $y_i(x) = y_i$. This is true for data D_y as well. Then, we can rewrite the PIR equation as: $r(x) = \sum_{y \in [2^\ell]} \left(\prod_{i \in [\ell]} (\xi_i(x) + y_i(x) + 1) \right) D_y(x)$. Given that $y_i(x)$ has small coefficient, i.e. 1 or 0, the additions are done over the least coefficient term in the polynomial. Furthermore, having $D_y(x) = \{0, 1\}$ we may skip the product evaluations unless $D_y(x) = 1$. Once $r(x)$ is homomorphically evaluated simultaneously over the ℓ ciphertexts, the response (a single cipher-text) $R = r([\xi_0(x), \ldots, \xi_{\ell-1}(x)])$ is sent back to the PIR client. The ciphertext response is first decrypted and the individual data entries are recovered using modular reductions: $D_i = \mathsf{dec}(r(x)) \pmod{F_i(x)}$.

Single Query. In the single query mode we will also perform batching as in the Bundled Query mode. However, here we will place the same index into all index slots. The resulting polynomials are encrypted as before giving us a query $Q = [\xi_i(x), \ldots, \xi_{\ell-1}(x)]$. Though this is similar to the Bundled Query, the PIR server side computation is handled quite differently. For parallel comparisons we batch the row bits of y_i and D_y as well:

$$y_i(x) = \mathrm{CRT}^{-1}\{y_i[1], \ldots, y_i[\varepsilon]\}, D_y(x) = \mathrm{CRT}^{-1}\{D_y[1], \ldots, D_y[\varepsilon]\}.$$

These conversions are done on-the fly and are not precomputed. Working in modulo 2 arithmetic makes the evaluations sufficiently fast and easy such that it only adds a small overhead. Although precomputation is an option, storing converted message polynomials would take extra space. The comparison equation will stay the same with the Bundled Query, but $y_i(x)$ and $D_y(x)$ will now binary polynomials. Therefore, we require polynomial addition inside the product and a polynomial multiplication with $D_y(x)$. Since in each iteration we are comparing ε indecies simultaneously we can process the database ε times faster. This speedup comes at a price where each iteration need to carryout a multiplication by the polynomial representation of the batched D_y.

The response ciphertext is first decrypted and then reduced to recover the evaluation bits as before: $z_i = \mathsf{dec}(r([\xi_0(x), \ldots, \xi_{\ell-1}(x)])) mod F_i(x)$. In a Single Query each z_i refers to a subsection of the summation therefore to compute the overall result we perform a final bit summation $D_y = \sum_{i \in \varepsilon} z_i mod 2$.

6   Performance

We implemented the proposed PIR protocol with both the Single and Bundled Querying modes in C++ where we relied on Shoup's NTL library version 6.0 [17] for the lattice operations. Table 2 shows minimal parameters to support various evaluation depths. Each depth can support upto 2^{2^d} entries, e.g. $d = 5$ can support 4 Billion entries. The parameter ε denotes the number of message slots that we can bundle. The query and response sizes are given in Table 2 *without* normalization by ε. In the Bundled Query mode sizes may be normalized with ε to determine the bandwidth per query. In Table 3, we present the time performance for query processing. The reported times are normalized per row of the database and per query. The time is split into two components: the time

Table 2. Polynomial parameters and query/response sizes necessary to support various database sizes N.

max N	$(\log q, n)$	ε	Query size (MB)	Response size (KB)
4 Billion	(512, 16384)	1024	32	784
65536	(250, 8190)	630	3.9	154
256	(160, 4096)	256	0.625	44

required to compare the encrypted index to the index of the currently processed row, and the time required to add the data in the current row to the summation. While the computation cost in comparison is quite high we should note that we are paying primarily for the index comparison. In the Bundled Query case, once the index comparison is completed we may simply reuse the comparison result and only compute an addition operation for each additional bit in the same database entry. In this sense, our results are similar to the other lattice based PIR construction by Melchor and Gaborit [30]. The index comparison may be considered as a one time overhead to be paid for each row that would be amortized as database rows get wider. Still due to the large vector sizes data aggregation will be rather slow. For instance; in a Bundled Query with $d = 4$ and 1 GBytes of data in a row, the processing time will be about 8 times slower than a Kushilevitz and Ostrovsky implementation as given in [21].

Table 3. Index comparison and data aggregation times per entry in the database for (d, ε) choices of $(5, 1024), (4, 630)$ and $(3, 256)$ on Intel Pentium @ 3.5 Ghz.

Depth (d)	Bundled query (msec)			Single query (msec)		
	5	4	3	5	4	3
Index comparison	4.45	0.71	0.31	4.56	2.03	1.29
Data aggregation	0.22	0.09	0.04	37	7.45	3.40

What we loose in computational efficiency, we make up for in terms of bandwidth. In Table 4, we give Complexity and Query size comparisons. As before, N is the size of the database and α is the ciphertext size that differs in each scheme[2]. In the Bundled Query case, for instance, the query is formed by $\ell = 2^d = 32$ ciphertexts each made of Mbytes. By normalizing with ε index retrievals in a single query, per retrieval we are paying about 32 KB. The query size of our scheme is smaller by a factor of 1024, 1200, and 3072 when compared to BGN, Melchor-Gaborit and Kushilevitz-Ostrovsky, respectively.

Finally, we would like to point out that for all practical purposes the size α of the ciphertexts in the query and response can be considered *almost* independent of the database size. Therefore, the size of the ciphertext, i.e. α is very mildly

---

[2] For [30], we used the given size of 37.5 MB for 20,000 entries since it does not provide a complexity. The size will grow significantly when N goes to 2^{32}.

Table 4. Comparison of query sizes for databases upto 2^{32}, 2^{16} and 2^8 entries. Bandwidth complexity is given in the number of ciphertexts; α denotes the ciphertext size.

	BW	α			Query size		
	Compl.	$d=5$	$d=4$	$d=3$	$d=5$	$d=4$	$d=3$
Boneh-Goh-Nissim	$\alpha\sqrt{N}$	6144	6144	6144	96 MB	384 KB	24 KB
Kushilevitz-Ostrovsky	$\alpha\sqrt{N}$	2048	2048	2048	32 MB	128 KB	8 KB
Ours (single)	$\alpha \log N$	8388608	2047500	655360	**32 MB**	**249 KB**	**80 KB**
Ours (bundled)	$\alpha \log N$	8192	3250	2560	**32 KB**	**406 B**	**320 B**

effected when the database size is increased. Indeed, as seen in Table 4 when the table size is grown from 256 entrees to 2^{16} entries, the ciphertext size grows only about by 1.26 times in the bundled case.

Acknowledgments. Funding for this research was in part provided by the US National Science Foundation CNS Awards #1117590 and #1319130.

References

1. Gentry, C.: Fully homomorphic encryption using ideal lattices. In: Symposium on the Theory of Computing (STOC), pp. 169–178 (2009)
2. Kushilevitz, E., Ostrovsky, R.: Replication is not needed: single database, computationally-private information retrieval. In: FOCS '97 (1997)
3. Boneh, D., Goh, E.-J., Nissim, K.: Evaluating 2-DNF formulas on ciphertexts. In: Kilian, J. (ed.) TCC 2005. LNCS, vol. 3378, pp. 325–341. Springer, Heidelberg (2005)
4. Gentry, C., Halevi, S., Smart, N.P.: Homomorphic evaluation of the AES circuit. In: Safavi-Naini, R., Canetti, R. (eds.) CRYPTO 2012. LNCS, vol. 7417, pp. 850–867. Springer, Heidelberg (2012)
5. Gentry, C., Halevi, S.: Implementing Gentry's fully-homomorphic encryption scheme. In: Paterson, K.G. (ed.) EUROCRYPT 2011. LNCS, vol. 6632, pp. 129–148. Springer, Heidelberg (2011)
6. Bos, J.W., Lauter, K., Loftus, J., Naehrig, M.: Improved security for a ring-based fully homomorphic encryption scheme. In: Stam, M. (ed.) IMACC 2013. LNCS, vol. 8308, pp. 45–64. Springer, Heidelberg (2013)
7. Lipmaa, H.: An oblivious transfer protocol with log-squared communication. In: Zhou, J., López, J., Deng, R.H., Bao, F. (eds.) ISC 2005. LNCS, vol. 3650, pp. 314–328. Springer, Heidelberg (2005)
8. Gentry, C., Halevi, S., Smart, N.: Fully homomorphic encryption with polylog overhead. Manuscript (2011)
9. Smart, N.P., Vercauteren, F.: Fully homomorphic SIMD operations. Manuscript (2011) http://eprint.iacr.org/2011/133
10. Brakerski, Z., Gentry, C., Vaikuntanathan, V.: Fully homomorphic encryption without bootstrapping. In: ITCS, pp. 309–325 (2012)
11. Lopez-Alt, A., Tromer, E., Vaikuntanathan, V.: On-the-fly multiparty computation on the cloud via multikey fully homomorphic encryption. In: Proceedings of the 44th Symposium on Theory of Computing, pp. 1219–1234. ACM (2012)

12. Stehlé, D., Steinfeld, R.: Making NTRU as secure as worst-case problems over ideal lattices. In: Paterson, K.G. (ed.) EUROCRYPT 2011. LNCS, vol. 6632, pp. 27–47. Springer, Heidelberg (2011)

13. Hoffstein, J., Pipher, J., Silverman, J.H.: NTRU: a ring-based public key cryptosystem. In: Buhler, J.P. (ed.) ANTS 1998. LNCS, vol. 1423, pp. 267–288. Springer, Heidelberg (1998)

14. Gama, N., Nguyen, P.Q.: Predicting lattice reduction. In: Smart, N.P. (ed.) EUROCRYPT 2008. LNCS, vol. 4965, pp. 31–51. Springer, Heidelberg (2008)

15. Lindner, R., Peikert, C.: Better key sizes (and attacks) for LWE-based encryption. In: Kiayias, A. (ed.) CT-RSA 2011. LNCS, vol. 6558, pp. 319–339. Springer, Heidelberg (2011)

16. Doröz, Y., Hu, Y., Sunar, B.: Homomorphic AES evaluation using NTRU, IACR ePrint Archive. Technical report 2014/039, January 2014. http://eprint.iacr.org/2014/039.pdf

17. NTL: A library for doing number theory. http://www.shoup.net/ntl

18. Guillevic, A.: Comparing the pairing efficiency over composite-order and prime-order elliptic curves. In: Jacobson, M., Locasto, M., Mohassel, P., Safavi-Naini, R. (eds.) ACNS 2013. LNCS, vol. 7954, pp. 357–372. Springer, Heidelberg (2013)

19. Coppersmith, D., Shamir, A.: Lattice attacks on NTRU. In: Fumy, W. (ed.) EUROCRYPT 1997. LNCS, vol. 1233, pp. 52–61. Springer, Heidelberg (1997)

20. Sion, R., Carbunar, B.: On the computational practicality of private information retrieval. In: NDSS'07 (2007)

21. Olumofin, F., Goldberg, I.: Revisiting the computational practicality of private information retrieval. In: Danezis, G. (ed.) FC 2011. LNCS, vol. 7035, pp. 158–172. Springer, Heidelberg (2012)

22. Chor, B., Goldreich, O., Kushilevitz, E., Sudan, M.: Private information retrieval. In: FOCS 95: Proceedings of the 36th Annual Symposium on the Foundations of Computer Science, October 1995, pp. 41–50 (1995)

23. Ambainis, A.: Upper bound on the communication complexity of private information retrieval. In: Degano, P., Gorrieri, R., Marchetti-Spaccamela, A. (eds.) ICALP 1997. LNCS, vol. 1256, pp. 401–407. Springer, Heidelberg (1997)

24. Ishai, Y., Kushilevitz, E.: Improved upper bounds on information-theoretic private information retrieval. In: Proceedings of the 31th ACM Symposium on TC (1999)

25. Chor, B., Gilboa, N.: Computationally private information retrieval. In: Proceedings of the 29th STOC, pp. 304–313 (1997)

26. Ostrovsky, R., Shoup, V.: Private information storage. In: Proceedings of the 29th STOC, pp. 294–303 (1997)

27. Kushilevitz, E., Ostrovsky, R.: Replication is not needed: single database, computationally-private information retrieval. In: FOCS 97, p. 364 (1997)

28. Cachin, C., Micali, S., Stadler, M.A.: Computationally private information retrieval with polylogarithmic communication. In: Stern, J. (ed.) EUROCRYPT 1999. LNCS, vol. 1592, pp. 402–414. Springer, Heidelberg (1999)

29. Gentry, C., Ramzan, Z.: Single-database private information retrieval with constant communication rate. In: Caires, L., Italiano, G.F., Monteiro, L., Palamidessi, C., Yung, M. (eds.) ICALP 2005. LNCS, vol. 3580, pp. 803–815. Springer, Heidelberg (2005)

30. Aguilar-Melchor, C., Gaborit, P.: A lattice-based computationally-efficient private information retrieval protocol. In: WEWORC 2007, July 2007

31. Aguilar Melchor, C., Crespin, B., Gaborit, P., Jolivet, V., Rousseau, P.: High-speed PIR computation on GPU. In: SECURWARE'08, pp. 263–272 (2008)
32. Goldwasser, S., Micali, S.: Probabilistic encryption. J. Comput. Syst. Sci. **28**(2), 270–299 (1984)
33. Paillier, Pascal: Public-key cryptosystems based on composite degree residuosity classes. In: Stern, Jacques (ed.) EUROCRYPT 1999. LNCS, vol. 1592, pp. 223–238. Springer, Heidelberg (1999)

Toward Practical Homomorphic Evaluation of Block Ciphers Using Prince

Yarkın Doröz[✉], Aria Shahverdi, Thomas Eisenbarth,
and Berk Sunar

Worcester Polytechnic Institute, Worcester, MA, USA
{ydoroz,ashahverdi,teisenbarth,sunar}@wpi.edu

Abstract. We present the homomorphic evaluation of the Prince block cipher. Our leveled implementation is based on a generalization of NTRU. We are motivated by the drastic bandwidth savings that may be achieved by scheme conversion. To unlock this advantage we turn to *lightweight* ciphers such as Prince. These ciphers were designed from scratch to yield fast and compact implementations on resource-constrained embedded platforms. We show that some of these ciphers have the potential to enable near practical homomorphic evaluation of block ciphers. Indeed, our analysis shows that Prince can be implemented using only a 24 level deep circuit. Using an NTRU based implementation we achieve an evaluation time of 3.3 s per Prince block – one and two orders of magnitude improvement over homomorphic AES implementations achieved using NTRU, and BGV-style homomorphic encryption libraries, respectively.

Keywords: Homomorphic encryption · NTRU · Prince · Lightweight block ciphers

1 Introduction

An encryption scheme is *fully homomorphic* (FHE scheme) if it permits the efficient evaluation of any boolean circuit or arithmetic function on ciphertexts [1]. Gentry proposed the first FHE scheme [2,3] based on lattices that supports addition and multiplication circuits for arbitrary depth. Since addition and multiplication on any non-trivial ring give us a universal set of logic gates, this scheme – if made efficient – allows one to employ *any* untrusted computing resources without risk of revealing sensitive data. In [4], van Dijk, et al., proposed a FHE scheme based on integers. In 2010, Gentry and Halevi [5] presented a variant of Gentry's FHE; this publication introduced a number of optimizations as well as the first actual FHE implementation. For other optimizations see also [6–8]. Although these earlier schemes have achieved full homomorphism, there is a serious bottleneck that prevents deployment.

To address this problem, some newer FHE schemes were proposed in recent years. In [9], Brakerski, Gentry and Vaikuntanathan proposed a new FHE scheme (BGV) based on LWE problems. Instead of re-encryption, this new scheme

© IFCA/Springer-Verlag Berlin Heidelberg 2014
R. Böhme et al. (Eds.): FC 2014 Workshops, LNCS 8438, pp. 208–220, 2014.
DOI: 10.1007/978-3-662-44774-1_17

uses other lightweight methods to refresh ciphertexts. These methods cannot thoroughly refresh ciphertexts (as re-encryption does), but they limit noise growth so that the scheme can evaluate much deeper circuits. The re-encryption process is then reserved as an optimization only for extremely complicated circuits instead of a necessity for the majority of practical circuits. Gentry, Halevi and Smart [8] proposed a customized LWE-based FHE scheme tailored to achieve efficient evaluation of the AES cipher without bootstrapping. Their implementation is highly customized to evaluate AES efficiently and makes use of batching [7], key and modulus switching techniques [9]. Their byte-sliced and SIMD implementations take about 5 min and 40 min, respectively, to evaluate an AES block.

In [10], Alt-López, Tromer and Vaikuntanathan adopted this idea to Stehlé and Steinfeld's generalized NTRU scheme [11] and developed an FHE scheme (ATV) that supports inputs from multiple public keys. Bos et al. [12] presented a leveled FHE scheme and its implementation derived from ATV. The ATV scheme is modified by adopting a tensor product technique introduced by Brakerski [14] such that the security depends only on standard lattice assumptions (and no longer on the decisional small polynomial ratio assumption). Furthermore, modulus switching is no longer needed due to the reduced noise growth. Lastly, the authors advocate use of the Chinese Remainder Theorem on the message space to improve the flexibility of the scheme. In [15] Doröz, Hu and Sunar propose another implementation based on the ATV scheme [10]. Similar to earlier proposals the implementation is batched, bit-sliced and features modulus switching techniques. The authors also introduce a specialization of the modulus to reduce the public key size and thereby memory required during evaluation. The scheme is generic, i.e. *not* customized to efficiently evaluate any specific class of circuits such as AES. When used to evaluate an AES block the implementation performs one order of magnitude faster than the implementation of [8].

More recent FHE schemes displayed significant improvements over earlier constructions in both time complexity and in ciphertext size. Nevertheless, both latency and message expansion rates remain roughly two orders of magnitude higher than those of traditional public-key schemes. This rapid emergence of a diverse set of homomorphic encryption schemes has brought with it the need to transform one ciphertext into another. Bootstrapping [2], relinearization [16], and modulus reduction [9,16] are tools of this form, allowing someone other than the holder of the original private key to transform one encryption into one or more encryptions using the same scheme and (typically) a different key and/or different parameters. One important type of ciphertext transformation was introduced by Brakerski and Vaikuntanathan. In [16, Sect. 1.1], the technique of *relinearization* is introduced as a way to re-encrypt quadratic polynomials as linear polynomials under a new key, thereby making their security argument independent of lattice assumptions and dependent only on a standard LWE hardness assumption.

Lauter, Naehrig and Vaikuntanathan [17] discuss tools for making somewhat homomorphic encryption schemes more practical including *scheme conversion*. First, they present two natural options for encryption of integers and demonstrate the versatility afforded by efficient transforms between bitwise representation and integer representation with a larger modulus. The authors of [17] also use this conversion idea to facilitate efficient communication with a cloud server. If cloud computations are to be performed with a FHE scheme, data can be uploaded to the server under a more compact scheme such as AES provided it has a relatively simple decryption circuit. If computations on ciphertexts are to be carried out, the decryption circuit of the target scheme is evaluated homomorphically to re-encrypt this data under the FHE. The result of these computations is a collection of very large ciphertexts and, at present, no method is known to transform these back to AES encryptions. But Lauter et al. observe that the dimension reduction technique of Brakerski and Vaikuntanathan [16] is useful here to reduce the ciphertext size (i.e., the overall FHE is the same, but the parameters are smaller, prohibiting further computation) before transmitting the results back to the client. In [17], efficient implementation is left as an important open problem.

Motivated by this need, we propose the use of *lightweight block ciphers* to facilitate efficient conversion. As a research area lightweight block ciphers [18] emerged from the proliferation of severely constrained embedded and mobile computing applications such as RFIDs, sensor network nodes etc. Such applications demand cryptographic primitives that can be computed with very little power in compact chips. Driven by this strong need, a new class of lightweight block ciphers were designed from scratch with security *and* implementation efficiency in mind. Here we exploit the synergy between block ciphers designed for constrained environments and the efficiency bottleneck of homomorphic encryption schemes to achieve efficient homomorphic evaluation of a block cipher.

Our Contribution. In this work,

- we present a survey of lightweight block ciphers. We show that some lightweight block ciphers are more suitable than others. In contrast some lightweight ciphers have worse homomorphic evaluation performance than traditional block ciphers, e.g. AES since our metric (circuit depth) is related to but different than the metrics used in the construction of lightweight ciphers.
- we present a leveled homomorphic implementation of the Prince cipher. Our implementation makes use of the NTRU based library developed by Doröz, Hu and Sunar [15]. Specifically, we optimize the Prince cipher for shallow circuit implementation, and based on the depth characteristics, chose optimal but secure parameters for the library to evaluate Prince efficiently. With the chosen parameters, the batched implementation evaluates 1024 blocks in 57 min, with 3.3 s per block amortization.
- more broadly, we motivate the study of lightweight block cipher design for homomorphic evaluation bringing a new metric, i.e. *circuit depth*, to the attention of block cipher designers.

2   Background

2.1   The ATV-FHE Scheme

NTRU based FHE schemes present a viable alternative to the currently dominant BGV style constructions. We follow the methodology proposed in [15] by Doröz et al. which builds on the NTRU based homomorphic encryption scheme (ATV) by Alt-López, Tromer and Vaikuntanathan [10]. The ATV scheme uses a variant of NTRU proposed by Stehlé and Steinfeld [11] to develop a leveled multi-key FHE that features a new operation named relinearization. The authors note that although the transformation to a fully homomorphic system deteriorates the efficiency, their construction is a leading candidate for a practical FHE scheme.

We next briefly outline the *single key version* of the ATV scheme. All operations are performed in $R_q = \mathbb{Z}_q[x]/\langle x^n + 1 \rangle$ where n represents the lattice dimension and q is the prime modulus. A polynomial is B-bounded if all of its coefficients lie in $[-B, B]$. In the primitives we often sample "small" polynomials $f \in R$ such that f is B-bounded. The error distribution χ is the truncated discrete Gaussian distribution $\mathbb{D}_{\mathbb{Z}^n, r}$ for standard deviation $r > 0$. A sample from this distribution is a $r\sqrt{n}$-bounded polynomial $e \in \mathbb{R}$. For a detailed treatment of the discrete Gaussian distribution see [19]. With these definitions we are now ready to outline the primitives of the public key encryption scheme:

KeyGen. We choose a decreasing sequence of primes $q_0 > q_1 > \cdots > q_d$ and a polynomial $\phi(x) = x^n + 1$. For each i, we sample $u^{(i)}$ and $g^{(i)}$ from distribution χ, set $f^{(i)} = 2u^{(i)} + 1$ and $h^{(i)} = 2g^{(i)} \left(f^{(i)} \right)^{-1}$ in ring $R_{q_i} = \mathbb{Z}_{q_i}[x]/\langle \phi(x) \rangle$ (If $f^{(i)}$ is not invertible, re-sample). We then sample, for $i = 0, \ldots, d$ and for $\tau = 0, \ldots, \lfloor \log q_i \rfloor$, $s_\tau^{(i)}$ and $e_\tau^{(i)}$ from χ and publish evaluation key $\left\{ \zeta_\tau^{(i)}(x) \right\}_\tau^i$ where $\zeta_\tau^{(i)}(x) = h^{(i)} s_\tau^{(i)} + 2e_\tau^{(i)} + 2^\tau \left(f^{(i-1)} \right)^2$ in $R_{q_{i-1}}$.

Encrypt. To encrypt a bit $b \in \{0, 1\}$ with a public key $(h^{(0)}, q_0)$, Encrypt first generates random samples s and e from χ and sets $c^{(0)} = h^{(0)} s + 2e + b$, a polynomial in R_{q_0}.

Decrypt. To decrypt the ciphertext c with the corresponding private key $f^{(i)}$, Decrypt multiplies the ciphertext and the private key in R_{q_i} then compute the message by modulo two: $m = c^{(i)} f^{(i)} \pmod 2$.

Eval. We assume we are computing a leveled circuit with gates alternating between XOR and AND. Arithmetic operations are performed directly on ciphertexts as follows: Suppose $c_1^{(0)} = \mathsf{Encrypt}(b_1)$ and $c_2^{(0)} = \mathsf{Encrypt}(b_2)$. Then XOR is effected by simply adding ciphertexts: $\mathsf{Encrypt}(b_1 + b_2) = c_1^{(0)} + c_2^{(0)}$. Polynomial multiplication incurs a much greater growth in the noise, so each multiplication step is followed by a modulus switching. First, we compute $\tilde{c}^{(0)}(x) = c_1^{(0)} \cdot c_2^{(0)} \pmod{\phi(x)}$ and then perform Relinearization, as described below, to obtain $\tilde{c}^{(1)}(x)$ followed by modulus switching $\mathsf{Encrypt}(b_1 \cdot b_2) = \lfloor \frac{q_1}{q_0} \tilde{c}^{(1)}(x) \rceil_2$ where the subscript 2 on the rounding operator indicates that we round up or down in order to make all coefficients equal modulo 2. The same process holds for evaluating with ith level ciphertexts, e.g. computing $\tilde{c}^{(i)}(x)$ from $c_1^{(i-1)}$ and $c_2^{(i-1)}$.

In addition to the primitives [10] defines another operation named **Relinearization** that computes $\tilde{c}^{(i)}(x)$ from $\tilde{c}^{(i-1)}(x)$ extending $\tilde{c}^{(i-1)}(x)$ as a linear combination of 1-bounded polynomials $\tilde{c}^{(i-1)}(x) = \sum_\tau 2^\tau \tilde{c}_\tau^{(i-1)}(x)$ where $\tilde{c}_\tau^{(i-1)}(x)$ takes its coefficients from $\{0,1\}$. Also define $\tilde{c}^{(i)}(x) = \sum_\tau \zeta_\tau^{(i)}(x)\tilde{c}_\tau^{(i-1)}(x)$ in R_{q_i}.

Note that by augmenting the public key with the evaluation keys $\zeta_\tau^{(i)}(x)$, i.e. encrypted shifted versions of f^2, it becomes possible to homomorphically evaluate the product of c with the encrypted f^2 using a shallow circuit of only additions. The authors propose the use of relinearization (with modulus switching) after both addition and multiplication operations and define evaluation key parameters accordingly. To relinearize after additions, we need shifted versions of the secret key f encrypted with respect to the new modulus, whereas for after multiplications, we need the same but of f^2 instead.

2.2   The DHS FHE Library

Doröz, Hu and Sunar (DHS) [15] proposed a customized leveled implementation of the ATV FHE scheme. The code is written in C++ and relies on the library functions provided by NTL software package linked with GMP. The implementation introduces a number of optimizations, including a modulus specialization technique to reduce the public key size. The main features of the DHS implementation are as follows:

– The arithmetic is performed over $R_q = \mathbb{Z}_q[x]/\langle\Psi_m(x)\rangle$ where the modulus q takes the special form $q = p^k$ and $p > 2$ is a prime, and $\Psi_m(x)$ denotes the mth cyclotomic polynomial and $n = \varphi(m) = \deg(\Psi)$. Noise vectors are chosen from the discrete Gaussian noise distribution χ [19].
– Circuit evaluation is divided into levels by the multiplication (AND) operations. Modulus switching is implemented at the end of each level. Since the moduli are special: $q = p^k$, after every multiplication first relinearization is performed which is then followed by modulus switching. Due to the special structure, the public key in one level can also be promoted to the next level via modular reduction. For instance, to evaluate a depth d circuit, the scheme uses the public key in the first level defined over $q_0 = p^d$ which is then promoted to the following levels that use $q_1 = p^{d-1}, q_2 = p^{d-2}, \ldots, q_{d-1} = p$ by on-the-fly modular reduction with the new modulus, significantly reducing the memory requirement.
– The authors analyze the noise growth during circuit evaluation and determined that to keep the noise stable over the levels of the evaluation one needs to cut after each relinearization by

$$\log(p) \approx \log\left(\epsilon[an(6B^2 + 2B)\log(aq_0) + n^{3/2}(2B+1)^2B^2]\right)$$

bits where ϵ is small constant chosen to minimize the error probability, $B = 2$ from the χ distribution, and a represents the maximum number of ciphertexts summed before multiplication in each level. Also note that in instantiation we fix χ to choose from $\{-1, 0, 1\}$ with probabilities $\{0.25, 0.5, 0.25\}$, respectively.

- The implementation is bit-sliced and uses the batching technique proposed by Smart and Vercauteren [6,7] (see also [8]). For this the modulus polynomial $\Psi_m(x)$ is factorized over $\mathbb{F}_2$ into equal degree polynomials $F_i(x)$ which define the message slots in which message bits are embedded using the Chinese Remainder Theorem. Therefore, the number of message slots is found as $\ell = \varphi(m)/t$ where $\deg(F_i(x)) = t$ may be determined by finding the smallest integer d such that $m|(2^t - 1)$.

The ATV library contains 5 main operations; KEYGEN, ENCRYPTION, DECRYPTION, MODULUS SWITCH and RELINEARIZATION. The most critical operation for circuit evaluation is RELINEARIZATION. The other operations have negligible effect on the run time.

The authors also implement the 128-bit AES circuit to compare the performance of their scheme to the earlier AES implementation by Gentry, Halevi and Smart [8]. The implementation manages to evaluate the 10 round AES circuit in 31 h with 2048 message slots with a 55 sec per AES block evaluation time making it 48 times faster than the generic SIMD implementation, 6 times faster than the AES customized byte-sliced implementation by Gentry, Halevi and Smart.

2.3 A Lightweight Block Cipher: Prince

Several lightweight block ciphers have been proposed with the goal of permitting a compact hardware implementation or good performance at small memory footprint in software. Examples include ciphers like Present, KATAN, TEA, HIGHT, etc. An overview of implementation properties can be found in [20]. Among these, Prince is a lightweight block cipher that has been optimized for low latency and a small hardware footprint [21]. It features a 64-bit block size, 128-bit key size. Prince implements a substitution-permutation network which iterates for 12 rounds. The round function is AES-like and operates on a 4 by 4 array of nibbles, with 4-bit S–boxes, shift rows and mix columns operations. The round key remains constant, but is augmented with a 64-bit round constant to ensure variation between rounds. An interesting feature of Prince is the inflective property: encryption and decryption only differ in the round key, i.e. decryption can use the same implementation as encryption, only the round key needs to be modified. Figure 1 shows the structure of the Prince cipher. To implement Prince, the following operations have to be realized:

Key Schedule. The 128-bit key is split into two parts k_0 and k_1. k_0 is used to generate another key $k_0' = (k_0 >>> 1) \oplus (k_0 >> 63)$. The keys k_0 and k_0' are used as pre- and post-whitening keys, i.e. are XOR-added to the state before and after all round functions are performed. The round key k_1 is the same for all rounds and is also XOR-added during the key addition phase.

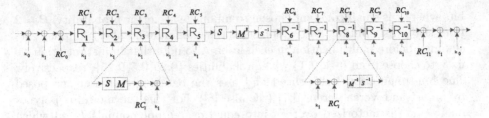

Fig. 1. The Prince cipher

Round Constant Addition. Prince defines different round constants RC_i for each round. A noteworthy property of the round constants is that $RC_i \oplus RC_{11-i} = \alpha$ for $0 \leq i \leq 11$, with $\alpha = \texttt{c0ac29b7c97c50dd}$. The round constant addition is a binary addition, just as the round key addition. Both operations can be merged.

S–box. The S–box layer uses a mapping of 4-bit to 4-bit, as defined in the following table. The S–box is the only operation of Prince that is not linear in the bits, and hence needs costly AND operations (or binary multiplication) for its implementation. While other S–boxes are possible for Prince, we chose to use the original S–box, since the maximum depth of multiplication is already optimal for the standard S–box. More details on how we implemented the S–box is given in Sect. 3.2.

Linear Layer. The linear layer consists of two parts: a shift rows which is similar to the shift rows used in AES and simply changes the order of the nibbles. Hence, it is a free operation in a bit-oriented implementation. The mix columns equivalent XOR-adds three input bits to compute one output bit in such a way that the operation is invertible. Again, this operation is linear and easily implementable.

i	0	1	2	3	4	5	6	7	8	9	A	B	C	D	E	F
$S[i]$	B	F	3	2	A	C	9	1	6	7	8	0	E	5	D	4

All operations also need an implementation of their inverse, as the last six rounds use the inverse operations.

3   NTRU Based Homomorphic Evaluation

In this section we describe our implementation in detail. Specifically, we first present a study of the depth characteristics of popular lightweight block ciphers among which we identify the Prince cipher as the most promising for homomorphic evaluation. Later we present in detail a shallow circuit implementation of Prince. In what follows, we select optimal parameters for the Doröz et al. [15] leveled ATV FHE implementation to support evaluation of the Prince circuit.

3.1   Picking a Lightweight Block Cipher

We are looking for any cipher that provides efficient encryption while permitting a *shallow* circuit implementation, i.e. the number of consecutive multiplication levels should be minimized. Therefore we turn our attention to lightweight block ciphers [22]. There are two main factors that increase the number of consecutive multiplications: The size and complexity of the S–boxes, as higher non-linearity usually results in higher-degree terms, i.e. an increased number of consecutive binary multiplications. PRESENT [18], for example, has very simple S–boxes, resulting in a shallow circuit for each individual S–box. Another important factor is the number of rounds, where PRESENT is less optimal due to the rather high number of rounds. Prince, a recently proposed block cipher [21], has roughly the same complexity for the S–boxes, but has only 12 rounds which make it a much more efficient choice for our purposes. The more complex linear layer is not a problem, since it does not introduce new binary multiplications. We present an overview of the complexity of different lightweight ciphers in Table 1.

Table 1. Comparison of the complexity of common lightweight block ciphers in number of rounds, algebraic degree of the S–box function, algebraic degree of a round excluding the S–box, per round and total number of multiplicative levels.

Cipher	# Rounds	ALGEBRAIC DEGREE		TOTAL DEPTH	
		S–box	Rem. Round	Per Round	Full Cipher
AES-128 [23]	10	8	0	3	30
Present [18]	31	4	0	2	62
Prince [21]	12	4	0	2	24
HIGHT [24]	32	N/A	8	3	96
SEA$_{96,8}$ [25]	93	3	8	4	372
KATAN-64 [26]	254	N/A	1	1	254
Simon-64/96 (64/128) [27]	42 (44)	N/A	1	1	42 (44)

Note that the cipher *depth* is almost fully determined by the consecutive levels of binary AND-statements. The two software-oriented ciphers, namely SEA and HIGHT, feature Feistel-structure and a high number of rounds. The number of rounds, together with the Feistel structure, results in a high depth circuit, making them a bad choice for our purposes. Furthermore, additions mod 2^n add significant depth due to high nonlinearity for the most significant output bits. While there are [12, 13] FHE implementations capable of evaluating integer operations they do not support mixing of integer and bit-oriented operations as required by most block ciphers. Hence, the hardware-oriented ciphers such as Present and Prince seem more appropriate. Certain possible cipher-specific optimizations are likely missed in the table. Katan, for example, allows the evaluation of a few rounds in parallel, since independent bits are processed in consecutive rounds. We did not explore this further due to the big starting disadvantage in the number of rounds. It can be seen that AES already offers quite a low depth, due to the low number of rounds. In practice, the depth 30 implementation of AES is not attainable since the number of multiplications grows significantly. Instead at best a depth 40 implementation is used in practice [15]. Either way, the Prince cipher offers a significant improvement over AES.

3.2 Prince as a Shallow Circuit

As described in Sect. 2.3, Prince can be implemented in a way that every operation is done on a single bit. Consecutive AND operations are costly in the ATV FHE scheme so it is a necessity to prevent them as much as possible. The only part of Prince that is nonlinear is the S–box layer. To determine an optimal representation of the S–box, we use Mathematica to obtain the Algebraic Normal Form (ANF), which represents all equations only in terms of XOR or AND statements. The following table gives the resulting ANF representation of the Prince S–box $S(A, B, C, D) = (S_0, S_1, S_2, S_3)$. According to the table the S–box requires 28 AND-operations. Further optimization, making use of efficient reuse of intermediate terms, enables a significant reduction of two-input AND operations. The values for AB, AC, AD, BC, BD, CD can simply be stored and used whenever it is necessary instead of recalculating them every time. There exist four more terms in the formula that can be saved and used again; these values are ABD, ABC, ACD, BCD. To be more efficient, for calculating the first two terms and the next two terms we will use the saved value AB and CD, respectively. The resulting depth of the multiplication is 2 i.e. one for calculating terms such as AB and one for calculating terms such as ABD. Hence the total number of ANDs for S–box would be 10—much less than by straight implementation of the ANF. The same procedure is applied to optimize the implementation of the inverse S–box.

$$
\begin{array}{l|l}
S_0 & A \oplus C \oplus AB \oplus BC \oplus ABD \oplus ACD \oplus BCD \oplus 1 \\
S_1 & A \oplus D \oplus AC \oplus AD \oplus CD \oplus ABC \oplus ACD \\
S_2 & AC \oplus BC \oplus BD \oplus ABC \oplus BCD \oplus 1 \\
S_3 & A \oplus B \oplus AB \oplus AD \oplus BC \oplus CD \oplus BCD \oplus 1
\end{array}
$$

3.3 Parameter Selection for the ATV FHE

We follow the parameter selection process of [15] for our ATV Prince implementation. In Table 2 we summarize the chosen parameters for Prince and AES. Clearly, the 24 levels of Prince give us an advantage over the 40 level AES in selecting smaller parameters: The polynomial degree of Prince is half the size of AES with $n = 16384$. The per level cutting rate is $\log(p) = 20$ bits, better than

Table 2. Parameters for the AES [15] and our Prince implementations.

	n	$\log(q_0)$	δ	LEVELS	$\log(p)$	MESSAGE SLOTS
AES [15]	32768	1271	1.0067	40	31	2048
Prince	16384	500	1.0052	24	20	1024

expected than the noise analysis in [15] predicts. The reason is simple; the Prince S–box has AND operations with three gates, e.g. $A \cdot B \cdot C$, and therefore in the second level two polynomials with different noise levels are multiplied, whereas [15] assumes the product inputs bear the same level of noise. With $\log(p) = 20$, the modulus may be chosen as $\log(q_0) = 500$ which is less than half as long as the AES modulus, i.e. 1271-bits used in [15]. With $n = 16384$ and $\log(q_0)$, our Hermite factor is $\delta = 1.0052$. This gives us a 130-bit security level, which actually exceeds the security claims of Prince. The only disadvantage of our Prince evaluation is that we have fewer message slots, exactly half of those of the AES evaluation.

4   Implementation Results

We ran our implementation on a single thread on Intel Core i7 3770 K running 3.5 Ghz with 32 GBytes of memory. The most expensive Prince operation is the evaluation of the S–box circuit, since it is the only operation that contains multiplications and therefore requires Relinearization. The S–box is evaluated using 6 Relinearizations, resulting in 1,152 Relinearizations for the entire evaluation. The execution completes in 57 min compared to 31 h [15] and 36 h [8] for AES. This shows about ×30 speedup. A block of Prince encryption takes 3.3 s compared to 55 s for AES blocks. Another significant advantage of Prince is that at 1 Gbytes the public key is much smaller. Therefore we can run our implementations on standard machines (Table 3).

Table 3. Performance comparison of Prince against AES implementations.

	TOTAL TIME	#BLOCKS	PER BLOCK seconds	PK Size GBytes
AES [15]	31 h	2048	55	13.1
AES-Byte Sliced [8]	65 h	720	300	n/a
AES-SIMD Sliced [8]	36 h	54	2400	n/a
Prince (Ours)	**57 min**	1024	**3.3**	1.0

5   Conclusion

We presented a customized implementation of the lightweight block cipher Prince using a leveled fully homomorphic encryption scheme based on NTRU. For this we surveyed lightweight block ciphers and analyzed them with respect to a new metric: circuit depth. Our analysis determined that the Prince block cipher is the most suitable for homomorphic evaluation as it can be implemented using only a depth 24 circuit. Using the recently proposed ATV library [15] we developed an optimized shallow circuit implementation of Prince, which yielded an amortized 3.3 s per block evaluation running time, one to two orders of magnitude faster than previous homomorphic AES evaluation proposals [8,15].

With this work, we presented a near practical block cipher implementation that could be used for scheme conversion [17]. We also aim to further motivate research in the field of lightweight cryptography under the new *shallow circuit* or *circuit depth* metric.

Acknowledgments. Funding for this research was in part provided by the US National Science Foundation CNS Awards #1117590, #1319130, and #1261399.

References

1. Rivest, R.L., Adleman, L., Dertouzos, M.L.: On data banks and privacy homomorphisms. In: Foundations of Secure Computation (1978)
2. Gentry, C.: Fully homomorphic encryption using ideal lattices. In: Symposium on the Theory of Computing (STOC), pp. 169–178 (2009)
3. Gentry, C.: A Fully Homomorphic Encryption Scheme. Ph.D. thesis, Department of Computer Science, Stanford University (2009)
4. van Dijk, M., Gentry, C., Halevi, S., Vaikuntanathan, V.: Fully homomorphic encryption over the integers. In: Gilbert, H. (ed.) EUROCRYPT 2010. LNCS, vol. 6110, pp. 24–43. Springer, Heidelberg (2010)
5. Gentry, C., Halevi, S.: Implementing gentry's fully-homomorphic encryption scheme. In: Paterson, K.G. (ed.) EUROCRYPT 2011. LNCS, vol. 6632, pp. 129–148. Springer, Heidelberg (2011)
6. Gentry, C., Halevi, S., Smart, N.P.: Fully homomorphic encryption with polylog overhead. Manuscript (2011)
7. Smart, N.P., Vercauteren, F.: Fully homomorphic SIMD operations (2011). http://eprint.iacr.org/2011/133
8. Gentry, C., Halevi, S., Smart, N.P.: Homomorphic evaluation of the AES circuit. In: Safavi-Naini, R., Canetti, R. (eds.) CRYPTO 2012. LNCS, vol. 7417, pp. 850–867. Springer, Heidelberg (2012)
9. Brakerski, Z., Gentry, C., Vaikuntanathan, V.: Fully homomorphic encryption without bootstrapping. In: Innovations in Theoretical Computer Science, ITCS, pp. 309–325 (2012)
10. Alt-López, A., Tromer E., Vaikuntanathan, V.: On-the-fly multiparty computation on the cloud via multikey fully homomorphic encryption. In: Proceedings of the 44th STOC, pp. 1219–1234. ACM (2012)

11. Stehlé, D., Steinfeld, R.: Making NTRU as secure as worst-case problems over. In: Paterson, K.G. (ed.) EUROCRYPT 2011. LNCS, vol. 6632, pp. 27–47. Springer, Heidelberg (2011)

12. Bos, J.W., Lauter, K., Loftus, J., Naehrig, M.: Improved security for a ring-based fully homomorphic encryption scheme. In: Stam, M. (ed.) IMACC 2013. LNCS, vol. 8308, pp. 45–64. Springer, Heidelberg (2013)

13. Coron, J.-S., Naccache, D., Tibouchi, M.: Public key compression and modulus switching for fully homomorphic encryption over the integers. In: Pointcheval, D., Johansson, T. (eds.) EUROCRYPT 2012. LNCS, vol. 7237, pp. 446–464. Springer, Heidelberg (2012)

14. Brakerski, Z.: Fully homomorphic encryption without modulus switching from classical GapSVP. In: Safavi-Naini, R., Canetti, R. (eds.) CRYPTO 2012. LNCS, vol. 7417, pp. 868–886. Springer, Heidelberg (2012)

15. Doröz, Y., Hu, Y., Sunar, B.: Homomorphic AES Evaluation using NTRU, IACR ePrint Archive. Technical report 2014/039 January 2014. http://eprint.iacr.org/2014/039.pdf

16. Brakerski, Z., Vaikuntanathan, V.: Efficient fully homomorphic encryption from (standard) LWE. In: 2011 IEEE 52nd Annual Symposium on Foundations of Computer Science (FOCS), IEEE (2011)

17. Lauter, K., Naehrig, M., Vaikuntanathan, V.: Can homomorphic encryption be practical?. In: Proceedings of the 3rd ACM CCSW (Cloud Computing Security Workshop), ACM (2011)

18. Bogdanov, A.A., Knudsen, L.R., Leander, G., Paar, C., Poschmann, A., Robshaw, M., Seurin, Y., Vikkelsoe, C.: PRESENT: an ultra-lightweight block cipher. In: Paillier, P., Verbauwhede, I. (eds.) CHES 2007. LNCS, vol. 4727, pp. 450–466. Springer, Heidelberg (2007)

19. Micciancio, D., Regev, O.: Worst-case to average-case reductions based on gaussian measures. SIAM J. Comput. 37(1), 267–302 (2007)

20. Eisenbarth, T., Gong, Z., Güneysu, T., Heyse, S., Indesteege, S., Kerckhof, S., Koeune, F., Nad, T., Plos, T., Regazzoni, F., Standaert, F.-X., van Oldeneel tot Oldenzeel, L.: Compact implementation and performance evaluation of block ciphers in ATtiny devices. In: Mitrokotsa, A., Vaudenay, S. (eds.) AFRICACRYPT 2012. LNCS, vol. 7374, pp. 172–187. Springer, Heidelberg (2012)

21. Borghoff, J., Canteaut, A., Güneysu, T., Kavun, E.B., Knezevic, M., Knudsen, L.R., Leander, G., Nikov, V., Paar, C., Rechberger, C., Rombouts, P., Thomsen, S.S., Yalçın, T.: PRINCE – A low-latency block cipher for pervasive computing applications. In: Wang, X., Sako, K. (eds.) ASIACRYPT 2012. LNCS, vol. 7658, pp. 208–225. Springer, Heidelberg (2012)

22. Eisenbarth, T., Paar, C., Poschmann, A., Kumar, S., Uhsadel, L.: A Survey of lightweight-cryptography implementations. IEEE Des. Test Comput. 24(6), 522–533 (2007)

23. Daemen, J., Rijmen, V.: The design of Rijndael: AES-the advanced encryption standard. Information Security and Cryptography, vol. XVII, pp. 1–238. Springer, Heidelberg (2002)

24. Hong, D., Sung, J., Hong, S.H., Lim, J.-I., Lee, S.-J., Koo, B.-S., Lee, C.-H., Chang, D., Lee, J., Jeong, K., Kim, H., Kim, J.-S., Chee, S.: HIGHT: a new block cipher suitable for low-resource device. In: Goubin, L., Matsui, M. (eds.) CHES 2006. LNCS, vol. 4249, pp. 46–59. Springer, Heidelberg (2006)

25. Standaert, F.-X., Piret, G., Gershenfeld, N., Quisquater, J.-J.: SEA: a scalable encryption algorithm for small embedded applications. In: Domingo-Ferrer, J., Posegga, J., Schreckling, D. (eds.) CARDIS 2006. LNCS, vol. 3928, pp. 222–236. Springer, Heidelberg (2006)
26. De Cannière, C., Dunkelman, O., Knežević, M.: KATAN and KTANTAN — a family of small and efficient hardware-oriented block ciphers. In: Clavier, C., Gaj, K. (eds.) CHES 2009. LNCS, vol. 5747, pp. 272–288. Springer, Heidelberg (2009)
27. Canniere, C.D., Dunkelman, O., Knezevic, M.: The SIMON and SPECK Families of Lightweight Block Ciphers. Cryptology ePrint Archive, Report 2013/404 (2013). http://eprint.iacr.org/

A Scalable Implementation of Fully Homomorphic Encryption Built on NTRU

Kurt Rohloff[⊠] and David Bruce Cousins

Raytheon BBN Technologies, 10 Moulton St., Cambridge, MA, USA
{krohloff,dcousins}@bbn.com

Abstract. In this paper we report on our work to design, implement and evaluate a Fully Homomorphic Encryption (FHE) scheme. Our FHE scheme is an NTRU-like cryptosystem, with additional support for efficient key switching and modulus reduction operations to reduce the frequency of bootstrapping operations. Ciphertexts in our scheme are represented as matrices of 64-bit integers. The basis of our design is a layered software services stack to provide high-level FHE operations supported by lower-level lattice-based primitive implementations running on a computing substrate. We implement and evaluate our FHE scheme to run on a commodity CPU-based computing environment. We implemented our FHE scheme to run in a compiled C environment and use parallelism to take advantage of multi-core processors. We provide experimental results which show that our FHE implementation provides at least an order of magnitude improvement in runtime as compared to recent publicly known evaluation results of other FHE software implementations.

1 Introduction

Recent breakthroughs in Homomorphic Encryption have shown that it is theoretically possible to securely run arbitrary computations over encrypted data without decrypting the data [10,11]. There has been recent work on designing and implementing variations of Somewhat Homomorphic Encryption (SHE) and Fully Homomorphic Encryption (FHE) schemes [2,6,9,12,13,15,18,23,24, 28]. These implementations have become increasingly practical with published results on both the runtime of isolated EvalAdd and EvalMult operations for some implementation [12,23,24] and evaluations of composite functions like AES [9,15,28].

Current approaches to design FHE schemes rely on bootstrapping to arbitrarily increase the size of computation supported by an underlying SHE scheme.

Sponsored by the Defense Advanced Research Projects Agency (DARPA) and the Air Force Research Laboratory (AFRL) under Contract No. FA8750-11-C-0098. The views expressed are those of the authors and do not necessarily reflect the official policy or position of the Department of Defense or the U.S. Government. Distribution Statement "A". (Approved for Public Release, Distribution Unlimited.)

© IFCA/Springer-Verlag Berlin Heidelberg 2014
R. Böhme et al. (Eds.): FC 2014 Workshops, LNCS 8438, pp. 221–234, 2014.
DOI: 10.1007/978-3-662-44774-1_18

Many current implementations of SHE and FHE schemes rely on the manipulation of very large integers so that the schemes are both secure and capable of supporting the evaluation of sufficiently large circuits. Prior SHE and FHE implementation designs [12,15,23,24], for the most part, rely on single-threaded execution on commodity CPU-type hardware, partially due to the difficulty of or lack of native support for multi-threaded execution with underlying software libraries [20,25]. This, in addition to the inherent computational cost of secure computing using known SHE and FHE schemes, prevented the practical use of SHE and FHE.

In this paper we report on our work to design, implement and evaluate a scalable Fully Homomorphic Encryption (FHE) scheme which addresses the limitations for secure arbitrary computation. Our implementation uses a variation of a not previously implemented bootstrapping scheme [1] simplified for power-of-2 rings. We also use a "double-CRT" representation of ciphertexts which was also discussed in [15]. With this double-CRT representation, we can select parameters so that ciphertexts are secure when represented as matrices of 64-bit integers, but still support the secure execution of programs on commodity computing device without expending unnecessary computational overhead manipulating large multi-hundred-bit or even multi-thousand-bit integers.

We implement in software specialized lattice primitives such as Ring Addition, Ring Multiplication and the Chinese Remainder Transform (CRT). We use our primitive implementations to construct the FHE operations of Key Generation (KeyGen), Encryption (Enc), Decryption (Dec), Evaluation Addition (EvalAdd), Evaluation Multiplication (EvalMult) and Bootstrapping (Boot). We use supporting Modulus Reduction (ModReduce), Ring Reduction (RingReduce) and Key Switching (KeySwitch) operations to augment the EvalMult operation and support larger depth computations without bootstrapping or decreasing the security of our scheme.

We implemented this scheme to run in a compiled C environment and use parallelism to take advantage of multi-core processors. Taken together, our implementation of these concepts points the way to a practical implementation of FHE with a more efficient (and less frequent) use of the bootstrapping operation. We evaluate the performance of our software library as a set of compiled executables in a commodity CPU-based multi-core Linux environment. The evaluated performance of our library compares favorably with evaluations of the reported experimental CPU-based evaluation results of other recent SHE and FHE schemes implemented in software such as in [12,23,24].

This paper is organized as follows. In Sect. 2 we discuss how we represent ciphertexts in our implementation. In Sect. 3 we define our NTRU-based FHE scheme. In Sect. 4 we discuss parameter selection for our NTRU-based scheme to provide practical secure computing on commodity computing hardware. In Sect. 5 we discuss our experimental results from our FHE scheme implemented in Matlab. We conclude the paper with a discussion of our insights and next steps in Sect. 6. Data tables experimental runtime results can be seen in Appendix A.

2 Double-CRT Ciphertext Representation

Previous SHE/FHE designs and implementations use two primary parameters to tune the security provided and the supported depth of homomorphic computation (without resorting to bootstrapping): the ring dimension n and the ciphertext modulus q. With these parameters, fresh ciphertexts are typically represented as n-element integer arrays, where each array element consists of at least $\log_2(q)$ bits. In previous implementations the ring dimension n typically ranged from 512 (2^9) to 16384 (2^{14}) and beyond, while several hundred to several thousand bits was typically required to represent q. In the previous implementations that use this "large-q" approach, the practicality challenge derives from the difficulty of supporting both a large ring dimension n (which provides comparatively better security) and a large q (which increases the depth of computation supported).

The requirement of a very large q is potentially problematic, because the number of clock cycles to support mod-q operations using naive "big integer" arithmetic grows at least linearly (and often quadratically) with the number of bits used to represent q for even the simplest operations, e.g., modular addition and multiplication. We use a variation of the double-CRT approach discussed in [15] to circumvent this problem using the standard technique of a "residue number system" (based on the Chinese remainder theorem over the integers) to represent ciphertexts as t length-n integer vectors of mod-q_i values instead of a single integer vector mod q where $q = q_1 * \cdots * q_t$ for pairwise coprime moduli q_i. For our ciphertext representation we use t length-n integer vectors of mod-q_i values represented as a $n \times t$ integer matrix. With our double-CRT approach, the number of moduli (t) grows to support the secure execution of larger programs, but more bits are not required to represent the moduli $q_1, \cdots, q_t$. Our implementation supports the secure execution of depth $t - 1$ programs with t moduli.

The double-CRT representation is an extension of the Chinese Remainder Transform (CRT) [19] representation used in prior SHE and FHE implementations. Chinese remainder transforms are used to convert ciphertexts from the natural "power basis" representation to the double-CRT representation. This conversion can mathematically be represented as a multiplication by square $n \times n$ matrices, but admits a fast, highly parallel evaluation procedure that is closely related to the Cooley-Tukey Fast Fourier Transform (and others.)

As we discuss more in Sect. 4 below, each of the moduli $q_1, \cdots, q_t$ can be represented as 64-bit integers and still support the secure execution of non-trivial programs. These 64-bit representations greatly improve the practicality of our approach to SHE and FHE. By using 64-bit modular operations to manipulate ciphertexts, keys, etc., we support faster low-level execution of the SHE operations on commodity 64-bit (or even 32-bit) processors.

An advantage of our double-CRT NTRU approach is that the FHE operations can be highly parallelized. Similar to the standard CRT representation, by using a double-CRT representation, the EvalAdd, EvalMult operations and key sub-operations in Bootstrapping, Modulus Reduction, Ring Switching and Key

Switching can become t naively parallelized operations. This greatly simplifies the secure execution of programs using our FHE implementation as compared to other, non-CRT representations of ciphertexts.

3 Cryptosystem

In this section we describe the somewhat homomorphic cryptosystem we use that is very similar to the NTRU system [16], though it was not until recently that its homomorphic properties were noticed independently by López-Alt et al. [18] and Gentry et al. [14].

For ease of implementation and design simplicity, we limit our description to power-of-2 cyclotomic rings. For ring dimension n which is a power of 2, define the ring $R = \mathbb{Z}[x]/(x^n + 1)$ (i.e., integer polynomials modulo $x^n + 1$). For a positive integer q, define the quotient ring $R_q = R/qR$ (i.e., integer polynomials modulo $x^n + 1$, with coefficients from $\mathbb{Z}_q = \mathbb{Z}/q\mathbb{Z}$).

3.1 Basic NTRU-Type System

In this subsection we provide a mathematical description of a somewhat homomorphic NTRU-based scheme. The message space is R_p for some integer $p \geq 2$, and most arithmetic operations are performed modulo some $q \gg p$ that is relatively prime with p. Fast addition and multiplication in R_q can be performed by using the mod-q Chinese Remainder Transform (CRT) representation of elements. The basic operations of the scheme are as follows:

- Gen: choose a short $f \in R$ such that $f = 1 \mod p$ and f is invertible modulo q, and a short $g \in R$. Output $pk = h = g \cdot f^{-1} \mod q$ and $sk = f$.

  Note that f is invertible modulo q if and only if each of its mod-q CRT coefficients is nonzero. The CRT coefficients of f^{-1} (modulo q) are just the mod-q inverses of those of f.

  Concretely, the short elements f and g can be chosen from discrete Gaussians. E.g., we can let $f = p \cdot f' + 1$ for some Gaussian-distributed f'. Note that such an f will have expectation (center) 1. Using a zero-centered f can have some advantages, and may be chosen using a more sophisticated sampling algorithm.

- Enc($pk = h, \mu \in R_p$): choose a short $r \in R$ and a short $m \in R$ such that $m = \mu \mod p$. Output $c = p \cdot r \cdot h + m \mod q$.

  Concretely, m can naively be chosen as $m = p \cdot m' + \mu$ for a Gaussian-distributed m', but again, such an m is not zero-centered. It is typically better to choose m as a zero-centered random variable congruent to μ modulo p.

- Dec($sk = f, c \in R_q$): compute $\bar{b} = f \cdot c \mod q$, and lift it to the integer polynomial $b \in R$ with coefficients in $[-q/2, q/2)$. Output $\mu = b \mod p$.

The homomorphic operations are defined as follows:

- EvalAdd(c_0, c_1): output $c = c_0 + c_1 \mod q$.
- EvalMult(c_0, c_1): output $c = c_0 \cdot c_1 \mod q$.

With the use of EvalMult, the decryption procedure needs to be modified. Define the "degree" of ciphertexts as follows: a freshly generated ciphertext has degree 1, and the degree of $c =$ EvalMult(c_0, c_1) is the sum of the degrees of c_0 and c_1. Then decryption of a ciphertext c of degree at most d is the same as above, except that we instead compute $\bar{b} = f^d \cdot c \mod q$.

3.2 Key Switching

Key switching converts a ciphertext of degree at most d, encrypted under a secret key f_1, into a degree-1 ciphertext c_2 encrypted under a secret key f_2 (which may or may not be the same as f_1). This requires publishing a "hint"

$$a_{1\to2} = m \cdot f_1^d \cdot f_2^{-1} \mod q,$$

for a short $m \in R$ congruent to 1 modulo p. (Concretely, we can choose $m = p \cdot e + 1$ for a Gaussian-distributed e, though a zero-centered m is better.)

- KeySwitch$(c_1, a_{1\to2})$: output $c_2 = a_{1\to2} \cdot c_1 \mod q$.

Note that $a_{1\to2}$, c_1, c_2 can all be stored and operated upon in CRT form, so key switching is very efficient: the hint is just one ring element, and the procedure involves just one coordinate-wise multiplication of the CRT vectors. This compares quite favorably to key-switching procedures for other cryptosystems, which typically require decomposing a ciphertext into several short ring elements and performing several ring multiplications.

3.3 Ring Reduction

Ring reduction maps a ciphertext from ring n to smaller ring $n' = n/2^a$, where typically $a = 1$. Although we describe a ring reduction operation for power-of-2 rings, more general ring switching approaches exist and can be obtained from simple generalizations of the approach we describe here.

The basic ring switching operation is a Decompose algorithm, which maps a dimension n ring to dimension n' elements. Decompose(c) works as follows:

- Let $c = (c_0, ..., c_{n-1})$ be in the power basis and let $w = n/n'$.
- We output ciphertexts c_i' for each $i = 0, ..., w-1$ where $c_i' = (c_i, c_{w+i}, c_{2w+i}, ..., c_{(m'-1)w+i})$. I.e., c_i' just consists of those entries of c whose indices are i mod w.

Before applying Decompose we first key-switch the ciphertext to one which can be decrypted by a "sparse" secret key sk, whose only nonzero entries in the power basis are at indices equal to 0 mod w. We perform the ring-switching on a ciphertext c, by performing key-switching on c to get cp (encrypted under sk), then call Decompose(cp) to get the $/c_i'/$. The ciphertext c should only have plaintext data only in its indices 0 mod w. Otherwise, this data is lost during the ring reduction operation.

3.4   Modulus Reduction

Modulus reduction, initially proposed in [3], converts a ciphertext from modulus q to a smaller modulus (q/q'), where q' divides q (and so is also relatively prime with p), while also reducing the underlying noise by about a q' factor.

The basic description is as follows: given a ciphertext $c \in R_q$, we add to it a small integer multiple of p that is congruent to $-c \mod q'$. This ensures that the underlying noise remains small, the plaintext remains unchanged, and the resulting ciphertext is divisible by q'. Then we can divide both the ciphertext and modulus by q', which reduces the underlying noise term by a q' factor as well.

Note that the final step (of dividing by q') implicitly multiplies the underlying message by $(q')^{-1} \mod p$. We can either keep track of these extra factors as part of the ciphertext and correct for them as the final step of decryption, or we can just ensure that $q' = 1 \mod p$, so that division by q' does not affect the underlying message.

The following formal procedure uses the fixed (ciphertext-independent) value $v = (q')^{-1} \mod p$, which can be computed in advance and stored.

- ModReduce(c, q, q')

  1. compute a short $d \in R$ such that $d = c \mod q'$.
  2. compute a short $\Delta \in R$ such that $\Delta = (vq' - 1) \cdot d \mod (pq')$. E.g., all of Δ's integer coefficients can be in the range $[-pq'/2, pq'/2)$.
  3. let $d' = c + \Delta \mod q$. By construction, d' is divisible by q'.
  4. output $(d'/q') \in R_{(q/q')}$.

Following [15], the above is most efficient to implement when $q = q_1 \cdots q_t$ is the product of several small, pairwise relatively prime moduli; when q' is one of those moduli (say, $q' = q_t$ without loss of generality); and when c is represented in "double-CRT" form, i.e., each of c's mod-q CRT coefficients is itself represented in (integer) CRT form as a vector of mod-q_i values, one for each i. Then the above steps can be computed as follows:

1. Computing d is done by inverting the mod-q_t CRT on the vector of mod-q_t components of c (leaving the other mod-q_i components unused), and interpreting the resulting coefficients as integers in $[-q_t/2, q_t/2)$.
2. Computing Δ is done by multiplying the coefficients of d by the fixed scalar $(vq_t - 1)$ modulo pq_t.
3. Adding Δ to c is done by computing the double-CRT representation of Δ (i.e., applying each mod-q_i CRT to Δ), and adding it entry-wise to c's double-CRT representation.

   Note that the mod-q_t CRTs of Δ and c are just the negations of each other (by construction), so their sum is the all-zeros vector. Therefore, there is no need to explicitly compute the mod-q_t CRT of Δ.
4. Computing d'/q_t is done by dropping the mod-q_t components in the double-CRT representation of d' (which are all zero anyway), and multiplying every mod-q_i component by the fixed scalar $q_t^{-1} \mod q_i$. (These scalars can be computed in advance and stored.)

3.5   Composed EvalMult

We use the Key Switching, Ring Reduction and Modulus Reduction operations as supporting functions with EvalMult to improve noise management and enable more computation between calls to the Bootstrapping operation. Taken together, we form a composite operation, which we call ComposedEvalMult, from the sequential execution of an EvalMult, Key Switching and Modulus Reduction operation.

Ring Reduction is called during some ComposedEvalMult operations, depending on the level of security provided by a ciphertext resulting from the result of the Ring Reduction operation. As Modulus Reduction operations are performed the security provided by a ciphertexts increases (as described in Sect. 4.) Ring Reduction correspondingly reduces the level of security provided by a ciphertext. We implemented our FHE library such that a minimum level of security δ' is provided at all times, and this level of δ' is a parameter selectable by the library user. If a call to a Ring Reduction operation will result in a level of security $\delta \leq \delta'$, then the RingReduction is performed in the ComposedEvalMult operation.

Our conception is that due to the ModReduction and RingReduction component of ComposedEvalMult, it is feasible to coordinate the choice of the original ciphertext width t and the scheduling of ComposedEvalMult operations so that the final ciphertext resulting from secure circuit evaluation and which needs to be decrypted is only one column wide with respect to a single modulus q_1 and provides a level of security at least as great as the original ciphertexts resulting from the encryption operation. More explicitly, if we need to support a depth $t-1$ computation, the initial encryptions should only be t columns wide to ensure that the final ciphertext is 1 column wide. Whereas the runtime of Encryption, EvalAdd, ComposedEvalMul depend on the ring dimension and depth of computation supported, the Decryption operation would hence depend only on the final ring dimension after all ring switching has been completed. If we need to decrypt a ciphertext that has multiple columns we our double-CRT representation, we could perform multiple ModReduction operations to reduce this $t > 1$ ciphertext until we are left with a single mod-q_1 column.

3.6   Bootstrapping

The basis of our bootstrapping approach comes from a new approach to homomorphic rounding. This approach to bootstrapping is described in detail in [1]. We provide a high-level overview of this operation here, simplified for our restriction to power-of-2 rings. This operation has the following steps:

1. *Round the ciphertext*: For each entry v for residue i, we output $round(v * q/q_i)$, where the inner expression is rational, and "round" means taking the nearest integer. Generally $q = 2^\ell$ is chosen experimentally, but as small as possible.
2. *Convert the plaintext modulus*: This is no-op under our simplifying assumptions.

3. *Lift the ciphertext and plaintext moduli*: This is also a no-op under our simplifying assumptions.
4. *Scale the ciphertext*: We scale up the ciphertext by a Q/q' factor (rounding to nearest integers in the power basis), and embed into dimension N (new ring dimension) as well. The plaintext modulus is still q'.
5. *Compute the homomorphic trace*: The following steps are performed iteratively $\log_2(N)$ times:
   (a) "Lift" the ciphertext modulus to $2Q$, which has the effect of making the plaintext modulus $2q$.
   (b) Apply the automorphism from [1], with appropriate key switching to put the result into the same key as the original ciphertext in the iteration.
   (c) Sum the original and resulting ciphertexts.
   (d) Divide the ciphertexts by 2.
6. *Perform a homomorphic rounding*: This operation is described in Appendix B of [1].

4   Parameter Selection

The selection of n and $q_1, \ldots, q_t$ depends heavily on the plaintext modulus p, the depth of computation that needs to be supported, and the desired security level. We capture the primary concerns influencing the selection of a ring dimension n and the moduli $q_1, \ldots, q_t$ at a high level as follows:

- The necessary ring arithmetic should be easily supported on the computation substrate – i.e., that mod-q_i operations (for $i \in \{1, \ldots, t\}$) require few clock cycles.
- The moduli $q_1, \ldots, q_t$ are sufficiently large to enable sufficient noise shrinkage via modulus reduction.
- The ring dimension n and noise parameters are sufficiently large so the scheme provides adequate security.
- The ring dimension n is not so large that it becomes overly time-consuming and memory-intensive to manipulate the ciphertexts.
- The plaintext modulus p and any noise added to the ciphertext during encryption is sufficiently small that we can evaluate reasonably sized circuits with correct decryption.

Table 1. Dependence of bit lengths of moduli q_i, as a function of ring dimension for $p = 2$.

Ring dimension n	512	1024	2048	4096	8192	16384
Bit length $\log_2(q_i)$	44	45	47	48	50	51

We choose to add discrete Gaussian noise to the fresh ciphertexts where $r = 6$ represents the selected probability distribution parameter. We have found theoretically that the smallest modulus q_1 needs to satisfy the expression

$$q_1 > 4pr\sqrt{nw} \tag{1}$$

in order to ensure successful decryption, where the parameter $w \approx 6$ represents an "assurance" measure for correct decryption (essentially, the probability of decryption failure is bounded by the probability that a normally distributed variable is more than $w\sqrt{2\pi}$ standard deviations from its mean), and $p \cdot r$ is the Gaussian parameter of the noise used in fresh ciphertexts. (Hence r is the Gaussian parameter of the underlying NTRU-like problem.)

After selecting q_1, we select the remaining $q_i \in \{q_2, \ldots, q_t\}$ such that

$$q_i > 4p^2 r^5 n^{1.5} w^5, \tag{2}$$

which ensures that modulus reduction by a factor of q_i sufficiently reduces the noise after a ComposedEvalMult operation. For implementation simplicity, we set q_1 to be the smallest feasible solution to $q_1 > 4p^2 r^5 n^{1.5} w^5$. Consequently all q_i are represented by $\log_2(q_t)$ bits, leading to simpler implementations.

Table 1 shows how many bits are required to represent $q_1, \ldots, q_t$ for varying ring dimensions for $p = 2$. Note that all $q_1, \ldots, q_t$ can be represented in less than 64 bits.

Following [5,17,22,26], we use the standard "root Hermite factor" δ as the primary measure of concrete security for a set of parameters. The most recent experimental evidence [5] suggests that $\delta = 1.007$ would require roughly 2^{40} core-years on recent Intel Xeon processors to break. Using the estimates from [17,22], we found that in order to achieve a security level δ for a depth of computation $d = t - 1$ using the t moduli $q_1, \ldots, q_t$, we need to ensure that

$$n \geq \lg(q_1 \cdots q_t)/(4 \lg(\delta)). \tag{3}$$

Table 2 shows how δ varies as a function of the ring dimension and depth of computation supported. Based on our analysis, if we impose the requirement that $\delta \leq 1.007$, then we would need to use ring dimension $n = 16324$ to support depth $d = 13$ computations.

Table 2. Security level δ, as a function of depth of computation supported and ring dimension for $p = 2$.

Dim. \ Depth	1	3	5	7	9	11	13	15	17	19
512	1.015	1.045	1.077	1.109	1.143	1.178	1.213	1.250	1.288	1.327
1024	1.007	1.023	1.038	1.054	1.070	1.087	1.104	1.121	1.138	1.155
2048	1.004	1.012	1.020	1.028	1.036	1.044	1.053	1.061	1.069	1.078
4096	1.002	1.006	1.010	1.014	1.018	1.022	1.026	1.030	1.035	1.039
8192	1.0011	1.003	1.005	1.007	1.009	1.011	1.013	1.016	1.018	1.020
16384	1.0005	1.0016	1.003	1.003	1.005	1.006	1.007	1.008	1.009	1.010

5   Evaluation Experiments

We implemented our scheme in the Mathworks Matlab environment and used the Matlab coder toolkit [21] to generate an ANSI C representation of our implementation. We subsequently hand-modified our auto-generated ANSI C to incorporate the pthreads library [4] to leverage parallelism. We compiled this ANSI

C using gcc to run as an executable in a Linux environment. We believe that additional performance improvements could be obtained by implementing our FHE scheme natively in C.

We chose to implement our scheme in Matlab because it provides an interpreted computation environment for rapid prototyping with native support for vector and matrix manipulation which simplifies implementation development. We found the Matlab syntax to be a natural fit for writing software to support the primitive lattice operations needed for our double-CRT NTRU-based SHE design.

We wrote our Matlab implementation of our double-CRT NTRU SHE scheme using the Matlab fixed-point toolbox. The Matlab fixed-point toolbox also provides a path toward generated HDL implementations of our design that can be deployed for practical use on highly parallel computing hardware such as FPGAs. Part of our vision for the use of our SHE design is to develop an FPGA implementation of FHE [7,8].

We ran our compiled implementation on a 64core server with 2.1 GHz Intel Xeon processors and 1TB of RAM in a CentOS environment. Although we had access to many resources, we used at most 10 GB of memory and 20 cores during the evaluation of our software implementation.

We collected data on the runtime of the Encryption, EvalAdd, ComposedEvalMult, Decryption and Bootstrapping operations over selections of depth of computation supported and ring dimension. We ran 100 iterations of this collection procedure for each combination of t and ring dimension. We used different randomly selected key sets, plaintexts and encryption noise on every iteration to mitigate minor variations in performance that may arise due to these experimental random variables on every iteration. Tables of the raw mean runtime results can be seen in Tables 3, 4, 5, 6 and 7 in Appendix A.

We collected data on the runtime of the Encryption, EvalAdd and ComposedEvalMult operations for settings of $t \in \{2, 4, 6, ..., 20\}$ and for ring dimensions $n \in \{512, 1024, 2048, 4096, 8192, 16384\}$. We collected data on the runtime of the Decryption operation of final ciphertexts, for computations with fresh (input) ciphertexts with ring dimensions $n \in \{512, 1024, 2048, 4096, 8192, 16384\}$ and depth of computation $t - 1$ for $t \in \{2, 4, 6, ..., 20\}$. Note that due to ring switching, decryption runtime is dependent only on the dimension of the final ciphertext, which is a function of the initial ciphertext and depth of computation. We collected data on the runtime of the Bootstrapping operation for settings of the "maximum" ring dimensions $n \in \{512, 1024, 2048, 4096, 8192, 16384\}$ ciphertexts are expressed in where the resulting ciphertext supports a depth one computation before another bootstrapping operations is required. As discussed in [1], the depth of computation required for bootstrapping is logarithmic in the ring dimension. We are currently exploring practical trade-offs associated with the impacts on the scheduling of bootstrapping to enable more computation between bootstrapping calls.

Our experimental results shows that run times grow linearly with ring dimension n and the ciphertext width t where $t-1$ is the depth of computation supported before bootstrapping or decryption could still be performed and have a high probability of recovering a correctly decrypted ciphertext. This makes intuitive sense because as we double either the ring dimension or the ciphertext width, we roughly double the amount of computation that needs to be performed with every Encryption, EvalAdd and ComposedEvalMult operation. Similar results hold for Decryption (Table 6) which shows a linear dependence of runtime on ring dimension, but under the assumption that decryption occurs after $t-1$ ModReduction operations, including ModReduction operations bundled in ComposedEvalMult operations. Our initial results show that Bootstrapping runtime is similarly linear with respect to the maximum ring dimension. As compared to the results reported in [12, 23, 24], our FHE software implementation provides order-of-magnitude improvements in the runtime of the FHE operations.

6 Discussion and Looking Forward

Our FHE implementation is part of our long-term vision to support a general, practical and secure computing capability through a layered services architecture. Part of our vision is to provide software interfaces in our design for our highly optimized implementations of the basic FHE operations (KeyGen, Encrypt, EvalAdd, EvalMult, Decrypt) for users to construct general applications that require secure computation on encrypted data with automated calls to supporting operations such as Ring Switching, Key Switching, Modulus Reduction and Bootstrapping. Inherent to this architecture vision is our FHE implementation of lattice-based computational primitives which form a lower layer of our envisioned architecture. We use these primitives such as ring addition, ring multiplication, modulus operations and the Chinese Remainder Transforms to run on commodity computing devices such as CPUs and FPGAs. We designed this modular approach to the implementation of the SHE operations and the underlying core primitives which allows us to (1) augment these operations with additional operations such as a bootstrapping operation (which enables FHE), or (2) replace the implementations of a subset of the operations or primitives as implementation advances are made.

A further aspect of our layered architecture vision is our ability to mix-and-match a computing substrate at lower levels of our architecture. Although not an immediate focus of the results reported here, the double-CRT representation, coupled with the 64-bit integer representation, simplifies parallelization of our FHE scheme for easier porting to other, high-performance and low-cost parallel computing environments such as FPGAs [7, 8] and possibly even GPUs [27]. If ported to a dedicated FPGA co-processor, the runtime of our underlying SHE/FHE implementation can be greatly improved upon as compared to the runtime of the corresponding interpreted CPU-only implementation which we discuss herein.

Taken together, we see our design and experimentation with our NTRU-based FHE scheme as a stepping-stone to a practical implementation of FHE through our layered architecture vision. Our primary path forward is to increasingly leverage the inherent parallelism of our design at multiple levels of our implementation. At a low level we are working to port our lattice-based primitives to operate on commodity FPGAs. This higher level parallelism offers the possibility of more practical SHE and FHE on both multi-core CPUs or multiple parallel FPGAs operating as "FHE co-processors".

Acknowledgement. The authors wish to acknowledge the helpful feedback and guidance of Prof. Chris Peikert in preparing the material discussed in this paper.

A   Experimental Results

Table 3. Encryption Runtime (ms) vs. Depth of computation supported and ring dimension for $p = 2$.

Dim. \ Depth	1	3	5	7	9	11	13	15	17	19
512	2.32	2.83	2.86	3.27	3.39	3.25	4.38	4.64	5.35	5.66
1024	3.87	5.33	5.17	5.98	5.68	5.63	6.94	8.40	9.04	9.20
2048	6.26	6.48	7.01	7.47	7.94	8.78	12.70	13.03	13.05	14.52
4096	12.08	12.27	13.04	14.87	17.38	17.65	20.73	17.46	21.57	22.13
8192	24.53	25.18	26.13	29.07	30.81	32.15	34.43	32.46	36.16	37.90
16384	52.30	55.02	58.05	59.71	60.29	61.98	63.44	64.99	69.96	72.89

Table 4. EvalAdd Runtime (ms) vs. Depth of computation supported and ring dimension for $p = 2$.

Dim. \ Depth	1	3	5	7	9	11	13	15	17	19
512	0.21	0.32	0.42	0.54	0.64	0.73	1.26	2.11	2.90	3.12
1024	0.30	1.04	0.47	0.57	0.72	0.74	1.40	2.72	2.85	2.93
2048	0.37	0.45	0.55	0.67	0.80	1.00	1.97	3.00	3.04	3.24
4096	0.56	0.65	0.74	0.91	1.92	2.07	2.25	2.43	3.73	3.54
8192	0.89	1.01	1.20	1.36	2.46	2.70	3.69	3.23	5.05	5.44
16384	1.58	1.82	2.12	2.39	3.99	4.19	4.27	4.77	7.16	7.29

Table 5. ComposedEvalMult Runtime (ms) vs. Depth of computation and Ring Dim. for $p = 2$.

Dim. \ Depth	1	3	5	7	9	11	13	15	17	19
512	16.03	22.73	23.32	22.65	22.87	22.96	24.35	25.24	25.37	25.78
1024	29.15	37.85	39.05	39.11	38.79	39.24	39.49	39.59	39.52	39.68
2048	49.17	66.31	66.77	67.41	67.15	68.38	68.22	69.27	69.45	71.09
4096	99.56	140.42	140.71	141.42	141.26	142.75	143.52	145.51	144.61	148.31
8192	196.83	279.37	280.42	284.40	283.98	285.69	289.59	286.55	292.69	295.69
16384	463.92	623.19	622.74	628.87	630.43	633.37	639.52	642.80	651.20	659.88

Table 6. Decryption Runtime (ms) vs. Depth of computation supported and Initial Ring Dim. for $p = 2$.

Dim. \ Depth	1	3	5	7	9	11	13	15	17	19
512	0.40	0.26	0.13	0.14	0.10	0.10	0.06	0.06	0.06	0.06
1024	0.87	0.38	0.18	0.11	0.11	0.11	0.11	0.11	0.05	0.05
2048	1.92	0.84	0.38	0.38	0.22	0.22	0.22	0.22	0.12	0.12
4096	3.36	1.70	0.84	0.86	0.37	0.39	0.38	0.22	0.22	0.21
8192	7.22	3.43	1.67	1.72	0.85	0.87	0.86	0.87	0.39	0.40
16384	15.36	7.18	3.37	3.37	1.67	1.67	1.67	1.73	0.87	0.85

Table 7. Bootstrapping Runtime (s) vs. Ring dimension for $p = 2$.

Ring Dimension	512	1024	2048	4096	8192	16384
Runtime (s)	5.8	13	26	60	125	275

References

1. Alperin-Sheriff, J., Peikert, C.: Practical bootstrapping in quasilinear time. In: Canetti, R., Garay, J.A. (eds.) CRYPTO 2013, Part I. LNCS, vol. 8042, pp. 1–20. Springer, Heidelberg (2013)
2. Bos, J.W., Lauter, K., Loftus, J., Naehrig, M.: Improved security for a ring-based fully homomorphic encryption scheme. In: Stam, M. (ed.) IMACC 2013. LNCS, vol. 8308, pp. 45–64. Springer, Heidelberg (2013)
3. Brakerski, Z., Vaikuntanathan, V.: Efficient fully homomorphic encryption from (standard) LWE. In: FOCS, pp. 97–106 (2011)
4. Butenhof, D.: Programming with POSIX (R) Threads. Addison-Wesley Professional, Reading (1997)
5. Chen, Y., Nguyen, P.Q.: BKZ 2.0: better lattice security estimates. In: Lee, D.H., Wang, X. (eds.) ASIACRYPT 2011. LNCS, vol. 7073, pp. 1–20. Springer, Heidelberg (2011)
6. Cheon, J.H., Coron, J.-S., Kim, J., Lee, M.S., Lepoint, T., Tibouchi, M., Yun, A.: Batch fully homomorphic encryption over the integers. In: Johansson, T., Nguyen, P.Q. (eds.) EUROCRYPT 2013. LNCS, vol. 7881, pp. 315–335. Springer, Heidelberg (2013)
7. Cousins, D.B., Rohloff, K., Peikert, C., Schantz, R.: SIPHER: scalable implementation of primitives for homomorphic encryption - FPGA implementation using Simulink. In: Fifteenth Annual Workshop on High Performance Embedded Computing (HPEC), HPEC '11 (2011)
8. Cousins, D.B., Rohloff, K., Peikert, C., Schantz, R.: An update on scalable implementation of primitives for homomorphic encryption - FPGA implementation using simulink. In: Sixteenth Annual Workshop on High Performance Embedded Computing (HPEC), HPEC '12 (2012)
9. Doroz, Y., Hu, Y., Sunar, B.: Homomorphic AES evaluation using NTRU. Cryptology ePrint Archive, Report 2014/039 (2014). http://eprint.iacr.org/
10. Gentry, C.: A fully homomorphic encryption scheme. Ph.D. thesis, Stanford University, Stanford, CA, USA, 2009. AAI3382729

11. Gentry, C.: Fully homomorphic encryption using ideal lattices. In: Proceedings of the 41st Annual ACM Symposium on Theory of Computing, STOC '09, pp. 169–178. ACM, New York (2009)
12. Gentry, C., Halevi, S.: Implementing gentry's fully-homomorphic encryption scheme. In: Paterson, K.G. (ed.) EUROCRYPT 2011. LNCS, vol. 6632, pp. 129–148. Springer, Heidelberg (2011)
13. Gentry, C., Halevi, S.: HElib (2014). https://github.com/shaih/HElib
14. Gentry, C., Halevi, S., Lyubashevsky, V., Peikert, C., Silverman, J., Smart, N.: Personal communication (2011)
15. Gentry, C., Halevi, S., Smart, N.P.: Homomorphic evaluation of the AES circuit. In: Safavi-Naini, R., Canetti, R. (eds.) CRYPTO 2012. LNCS, vol. 7417, pp. 850–867. Springer, Heidelberg (2012)
16. Hoffstein, J., Pipher, J., Silverman, J.H.: NTRU: a ring-based public key cryptosystem. In: Buhler, J.P. (ed.) ANTS 1998. LNCS, vol. 1423, pp. 267–288. Springer, Heidelberg (1998)
17. Lindner, R., Peikert, C.: Better key sizes (and attacks) for LWE-based encryption. In: Kiayias, A. (ed.) CT-RSA 2011. LNCS, vol. 6558, pp. 319–339. Springer, Heidelberg (2011)
18. López-Alt, A., Tromer, E., Vaikuntanathan, V.: On-the-fly multiparty computation on the cloud via multikey fully homomorphic encryption. In: STOC, pp. 1219–1234 (2012)
19. Lyubashevsky, Vadim, Peikert, Chris, Regev, Oded: On ideal lattices and learning with errors over rings. In: Gilbert, Henri (ed.) EUROCRYPT 2010. LNCS, vol. 6110, pp. 1–23. Springer, Heidelberg (2010)
20. MAGMA. V2.18-11 (2012). http://magma.maths.usyd.edu.au/magma/
21. MATLAB. R2012b. The MathWorks Inc., Natick, Massachusetts (2012)
22. Micciancio, D., Regev, O.: Lattice-based cryptography. In: Bernstein, D.J., Buchmann, J., Dahmen, E. (eds.) Post-Quantum Cryptography, pp. 147–191. Springer, Heidelberg (2009)
23. Naehrig, M., Lauter, K., Vaikuntanathan, V.: Can homomorphic encryption be practical? In: Proceedings of the 3rd ACM Workshop on Cloud Computing Security Workshop, CCSW '11, pp. 113–124. ACM, New York (2011)
24. Perl, H., Brenner, M., Smith, M.: Poster: an implementation of the fully homomorphic Smart-Vercauteren cryptosystem. In Proceedings of the 18th ACM Conference on Computer and Communications Security, CCS '11, pp. 837–840. ACM, New York (2011)
25. Shoup, V.: NTL: a Library for doing number theory. Courant Institute, New York University, New York, NY (2012). http://shoup.net/ntl/
26. van de Pol, J.: Quantifying the security of lattice-based cryptosystems in practice. In: Mathematical and Statistical Aspects of Cryptography (2012)
27. Wang, W., Hu, Y., Chen, L., Huang, X., Sunar, B.: Accelerating fully homomorphic encryption on GPUs. In: Proceedings of the IEEE High Performance Extreme Computing Conference (2012)
28. Wu, D., Haven, J.: Using homomorphic encryption for large scale statistical analysis (2012)

Restructuring the NSA Metadata Program

Seny Kamara[✉]

Microsoft Research, Seattle, USA
senyk@microsoft.com

Abstract. During the Summer of 2013, it was revealed through the documents leaked by Edward Snowden that the NSA was collecting the metadata of every US-to-foreign, foreign-to-US and US-to-US call from the largest US telephone providers. This led to public outcry and to President Obama calling for the restructuring of this program. The options initially considered included keeping the data at the providers, entrusting the data to a private entity, entrusting the data to a non-NSA government agency or ending the program all-together.

In this work, we show how cryptography can be used to design a privacy-preserving alternative to the NSA metadata program. We present a protocol based on structured encryption, in particular on graph encryption, and secure function evaluation that provides the following guarantees: (1) providers learn no information about NSA queries; (2) NSA queries can only be executed if validated by a given certification process; (3) the NSA learns nothing about the data beyond what can be inferred from the query results. In addition, these properties are achieved whether the data is stored at the providers, the NSA or on a third-party cloud.

1 Introduction

On June 5th, 2013, Glenn Greenwald published the first document from the Edward Snowden leaks in the Guardian [10]. This was a top secret court order compelling Verizon to hand the metadata of its calls to the National Security Agency (NSA) on a daily basis. This metadata was to include (among other things) the to and from numbers, the time and the duration of every foreign-to-US, US-to-foreign and US-to-US call. The revelation that the NSA was collecting information concerning *every* US citizen was astonishing to many and led to public outcry.

The Snowden revelations have motivated many important questions in a variety of disciplines including in Ethics, Law, Public Policy and Diplomacy. This work explores and formulates new problems in cryptography motivated by these disclosures. In particular, we consider the following question:

> *Can we design a practical privacy-preserving alternative to the NSA telephony metadata program?*

Answering this question will first require us to understand how the program works—as much as is possible from only public sources—and to formulate an

© IFCA/Springer-Verlag Berlin Heidelberg 2014
R. Böhme et al. (Eds.): FC 2014 Workshops, LNCS 8438, pp. 235–247, 2014.
DOI: 10.1007/978-3-662-44774-1_19

appropriate notion of privacy for this setting. While we do propose a concrete cryptographic protocol for this problem, we stress that our proposal should be viewed as a first step and that *our main interest is in formulating and motivating further research in this direction.* It is also worth mentioning that by *practical*, we roughly mean: built out of efficient cryptographic primitives like symmetric-key encryption and hash functions and not from primitives that are currently mostly of theoretical interest like fully-homomorphic [8] or functional encryption [1].

To properly model the problem, we provide in Sect. 1.1 an overview of how the program works. Our understanding is based on various public sources including [4,5] but we note that this may not reflect exactly how the program works in practice and that there are likely many important aspects of it that have not been disclosed. To provide context for our work, we provide in the full version [13] a high-level survey of the legal questions surrounding the NSA metadata program. This is not needed to understand the protocols we present.

1.1 How the NSA Metadata Program Works

We provide an overview of how the metadata program works. Our understanding of the program relies mostly on the findings of President Obama's Review Group on Intelligence and Communications Technologies [4]. Each day, the telephone providers hand the metadata of every US-to-foreign, foreign-to-US and US-to-US call to the NSA. This metadata consists of the origin and destination numbers, the time and duration of the call, the international mobile subscriber identity (IMSI) number, the trunk identifier and telephone calling card numbers [4]. This data is stored by the NSA and each record has to be deleted after 5 years. The data can only be queried by a subset of 22 NSA analysts (two of which are supervisors) that have received special training. Furthermore, the dataset can only be queried by phone number and each query has to go through an internal NSA certification process. In particular, each query to the database has to be found to be relevant to a particular investigation by at least two analysts. If this is the case, the query has to be approved by at least one of the two supervisors and found to be associated with one of a set of FISA-court-approved Terrorist organizations. If the query passes this certification process, the analyst is allowed to query the database and receives the metadata associated with every number that called or was called from the query number and every number that was either called from or called any one of the latter numbers. Viewing the database as an undirected graph with phone numbers as vertices and edges between any two numbers for which there was a call, the analyst receives the metadata associated with any number that is at most 2 hops away from the query number.[1]

---

[1] Originally, the program allowed for 3-hop queries but this was reduced to 2 hops by the Obama Administration as of January 17th.

1.2   Our Approach

While the current NSA metadata program has an internal process for query certification and is claimed to include technological procedures to minimize the exposure of private information,[2] the program does not provide any *cryptographic* privacy guarantees. This simply follows from the fact that the telecommunications companies provide the metadata in plaintext to the NSA. At a high-level, our goal in designing a new system will therefore consist of having the providers hand *encrypted* metadata to the NSA in such a way that analysts can then issue (cryptographically-enforced) certified queries on the encrypted data.

To achieve this we design a cryptographic protocol we refer to as MetaCrypt which relies in part on two important building blocks. The first is graph encryption (a special case of structured encryption) [3] which encrypts graphs in such a way that they can be privately queried. The second is secure function evaluation (SFE) which enables a set of parties to evaluate a function without revealing information about their inputs to each other [9,17]. We review both building blocks in Sect. 5. Our protocol makes a non-trivial use of these primitives and there are several technical difficulties to overcome in order to arrive at a final solution.

To analyze the security of our proposal, we isolate four properties we believe are crucial to any satisfactory solution:

1. isolation: the database should be protected from outsiders;
2. query privacy: the analyst queries should remain hidden from the providers and the server;
3. data privacy: the analyst should not learn any information about the database beyond what it can infer from the 2-hop queries it makes;
4. query certification: the analyst should only be able to make queries that satisfy the certification process described above (i.e., two analysts agree about the relevance of the query, at least one supervisor approves it and the associated organization is on a FISA-approved list of organizations).

In the full version of this work [13], we formalize these security properties in the ideal/real-world paradigm which is typically used to analyze the security of multi-party computation protocols. This paradigm has several advantages including modularity and simplicity.

Applications beyond the metadata program. Though the focus of this work is on the metadata program, the cryptographic techniques and protocols introduced have applications beyond this specific application. In particular, our main protocol can be used in any setting where a client wishes to privately query a set of privacy-sensitive graph datasets generated by various providers.

---

[2] Unfortunately, we could not find any details of how these mechanisms worked in public sources.

2   Related Work

As far as we know, the first discussion of privacy-preserving alternatives to the NSA programs appeared in a blog post of the author from July, 2013 [12]. There, a protocol is described that would enable an intelligence agency to privately query encrypted data generated by a provider in such a way that the query is certified by a third-party judge. The protocol makes use of MACs, secure two-party computation [17] and a keyword OT protocol of Freedman, Ishai, Pinkas and Reingold [7]. In [11], Jarecki, Jutla, Krawczyk, Rosu and Steiner describe a protocol similar in functionality to the one proposed in [12] but that, in addition, supports boolean keyword searches over the encrypted data. Concurrently with this work, Kroll, Felten and Boneh describe in [15] a set of protocols that allow an investigator to privately retrieve the encrypted records of providers in such a way that investigator queries are certified by a judge. The protocols of [15] provide accountability but, unlike the solutions proposed in [11,12], do not support any form of search functionality over encrypted records (i.e., investigators can only access a record by an identifier).

We note that none of the protocols above are directly applicable to the problem considered in this work. This is simply because, as discussed in Sect. 1.1, the NSA metadata system is designed to support 2-hop neighbor queries on the *call graph* (i.e., the graph that underlies the providers' datasets) and such a functionality is not directly supported by these works. Presumably, 2-hop neighbor queries could be instantiated on top of these protocols by having the client perform an interactive breadth-first search, but this would require $O(d)$ rounds, where d is the degree of the vertex queried.

In this work, we provide a solution with a completely non-interactive query phase. More precisely, it only uses interaction to certify queries, not to execute the 2-hop queries over the encrypted datasets. We achieve this in part by making use of a 1-hop graph encryption scheme which, roughly speaking, allows one to encrypt a graph in such a way that it can be privately queried. Graph encryption was introduced by Chase and Kamara in [3], where constructions supporting various types of queries were proposed (adjacency queries, 1-hop neighbor queries and focused sub-graph queries). Graph encryption is a special case of structured encryption which encrypts arbitrarily-structured data in such a way that it can be privately queried [3]. To certify queries, we make use of secure multi-party computation as introduced by Yao for the two-party case [17] and by Goldreich, Micali and Wigderson for the n-party case [9].

In the 90's, a team at NSA led by Binney, Loomis and Wiebe designed a system called ThinThread for large-scale data analysis. The system was designed to provide some form of privacy protection for US citizens. Unfortunately, it was never deployed on a large scale and the only official document that discusses it is so heavily redacted that no information about its design can be gleaned [16].

3 Preliminaries and Notation

Graphs and graph databases. A graph $G = (V, E)$ consists of a set of vertices V and a set of edges $E \subseteq V \times V$. For any vertex $v \in V$, we denote its d-hop neighbors by $\Gamma_d^G(v)$ and its neighbors at a distance of at most d hops by $\Gamma_{\leq d}^G(v)$. Given two graphs $G = (V, E)$ and $G' = (V', E')$ such that $E' \subseteq (V \cup V') \times (V \cup V')$, we refer to the graph $G'' = (V \cup V', E \cup E')$ as the sum of G and G' and to G' as an update to G. We sometime write $G'' = G + G'$.

We view the metadata generated by a telecommunications provider as a directed graph, $G = (V, E)$, where the vertices $v \in V$ correspond to telephone numbers and where there is a directed edge from v_1 to v_2 if there is a call from the number associated with v_1 to the number associated with v_2. We associate to each *undirected* edge $e = \{v_1, v_2\}$ in E: (1) a unique identifier $\mathsf{id}(e)$ that is independent of the numbers/vertices in e; and (2) a document $D_{\mathsf{id}(e)}$ that stores information about calls between v_1 and v_2 such as time, originating number, destination number and duration. We refer to a graph $G = (V, E)$ and its auxiliary documents $\mathbf{D} = \{D_{\mathsf{id}(e)}\}_{e \in E}$ as a graph database $\mathsf{GDB} = (G, \mathbf{D})$. We denote the documents associated with edges 2 hops away from v as follows:

$$\mathsf{GDB}(v) = \left\{ D_{\mathsf{id}(v,w)} \in \mathbf{D} : w \in \Gamma_1^G(v) \right\} \bigcup \left\{ D_{\mathsf{id}(w,z)} \in \mathbf{D} : z \in \Gamma_1^G(w) \right\}_{w \in \Gamma_1^G(v)}.$$

Parties and adversarial structures. The participants in our protocol include t providers $(\mathsf{Prv}_1, \ldots, \mathsf{Prv}_t)$ that generate the metadata; a server Srv that stores the (encrypted) metadata; two analysts An_1 and An_2 which query the metadata; two supervisors Sup_1 and Sup_2 that validate queries; and a FISA judge J that provides a watch list WL of organizations. The analysts and supervisors are assumed to belong to a single *agency*. In our security analysis, we will consider the cases where the server is managed by the providers and where the server is managed by the agency. We assume private and authenticated channels between all parties.

4 The MetaDB Functionality

As mentioned in Sect. 1, we use the ideal/real-world paradigm to analyze the security of our protocol. Here, we give an overview of the ideal functionality that captures the security properties we want (a detailed security definition is provided in the full version). The functionality, which we refer to as the MetaDB functionality, supports the operations of the NSA metadata program as described in Sect. 1.1, but with privacy guarantees for the analyst queries and the graph databases, and with a cryptographically-enforced query certification process.

The functionality is executed between t providers $(\mathsf{Prv}_1, \ldots, \mathsf{Prv}_t)$, a server Srv, two analysts An_1 and An_2, two supervisors Sup_1 and Sup_2 and a judge J. It is parameterized by three leakage functions $\mathcal{L}_S$, $\mathcal{L}_N$ and $\mathcal{L}_U$ and is a $(t+6)$-party reactive functionality. Throughout, we will assume that the first analyst An_1 is primarily interested in making the query and that the purpose of the second analyst An_2 is to provide support for the query (i.e., to satisfy the constraint that at least two analysts must determine that the query is relevant to the investigation). This is without loss of generality since the roles can be inversed.

In the first phase, each provider Prv_i sends its graph database $GDB_i = (V_i, E_i, \mathbf{D}_i)$ to the trusted party while the judge J sends a watch-list WL. At the end of this phase, the functionality sends leakage $(\mathcal{L}_S(GDB_1), \ldots, \mathcal{L}_S(GDB_t))$ to the server Srv. In the next phases the parties either update the data or query it. To query the data, the parties do the following. The two analysts send their query vertices v and v' to the functionality and the two supervisors Sup_1 and Sup_2 send tuples (v_1, b_1, org_1) and (v_2, b_2, org_2), respectively. Here, v_1 and v_2 are the vertices under consideration, b_1 and b_2 are bits indicating whether the respective vertices are authorized, and org_1 and org_2 are the organizations associated with the vertex. If $v = v'$ and if at least one of the supervisors' inputs has the form $(v, 1, org)$, the functionality checks that $org \in WL$. If this is the case, it returns the documents $\bigcup_{i=1}^{t} GDB_i(v)$ to analyst An_1. It also sends leakage $(\mathcal{L}_N(GDB_1, v), \ldots, \mathcal{L}_N(GDB_t, v))$ to the server Srv. To update a graph database, each provider Prv_i sends a tuple $up_i = (V_i^+, E_i^+, \mathbf{D}_i^+)$, where V_i^+ is either a set of new vertices or $\bot$, E_i^+ is a set of new edges in $(V_i \times V_i^+) \cup (V_i \times V_i^+)$ and $\mathbf{D}_i^+ = \{D_{id(e^+)}\}_{e^+ \in E_i^+}$ is a set of new documents. The functionality then sends leakage $(\mathcal{L}_U(GDB_1, up_1), \ldots, \mathcal{L}_U(GDB_t, up_t))$ to the server.

Other certification processes. We briefly note that while the MetaDB functionality captures a very specific certification process—essentially the one described in [4]—any new or different process could be easily formalized by changing or extending the functionality described above. Since our concrete protocol relies in part on (general-purpose) secure function evaluation for query certification, it could also be extended to capture a new/different certification process.

5   Cryptographic Building Blocks

We review the building blocks used in the MetaCrypt protocol. These include SFE [9,17] and graph encryption [3]. An SFE protocol allows n parties to evaluate a function f on their private inputs $\mathbf{x} = (x_1, \ldots, x_n)$ in such a way they cannot learn any information about each other's inputs beyond what can be inferred from the result. A graph encryption scheme encrypts a graph $G = (V, E)$ in such that way that the graph structure (i.e., the edges E) is hidden and that it can be queried without disclosing the query. We describe each of these in more detail.

Secure function evaluation. An SFE protocol securely computes any polytime computable function $f : X_1 \times \cdots \times X_n \to Y_1 \times \cdots \times Y_n$. The protocol is executed between n parties $(P_1, \ldots, P_n)$, where the ith party holds input x_i and receives output $y_i = f_i(x_1, \ldots, x_n)$. An MPC protocol is a protocol that securely computes any polynomial-time reactive functionality $\mathcal{F} = (f_1, \ldots, f_\ell)$.

5.1   Graph Encryption

Graph encryption was introduced in [3] as a special case of structured encryption. A graph encryption scheme takes a graph $G = (V, E)$ and produces an encrypted graph EGR that hides the structure of the graph.[3] The encrypted graph can then be queried using tokens that can only be generated with knowledge of a secret key. In [3], several constructions are proposed that support various kinds of queries, including adjacency queries (i.e., given two vertices, do they share an edge?) and 1-hop neighbor queries (i.e., given a vertex v, return all the vertices that share an edge with v). In this work, we require a scheme that supports 1-hop neighbor queries but that, in addition, is *associative*, *dynamic* and is *edge-centric*. We augment the syntax and security definitions of [3] to capture such a scheme.

Definition 1 (Dynamic graph encryption with 1-hop neighbor queries).
A dynamic and associative graph encryption scheme that supports 1-hop neighbor queries Graph = (Setup, Token, Nghbr, Token$^+$, Add) *consists of five polynomial-time algorithms that work as follows:*

- $(K, \text{EGR}) \leftarrow \text{Setup}(1^k, G, \text{sp})$: *is a probabilistic algorithm that takes as input a security parameter k, a graph $G = (V, E)$ and semi-private information* $\text{sp} = (e, s_e)_{e \in E}$. *It outputs a secret key K and an encrypted graph* EGR.
- $\text{tk} := \text{Token}(K, v)$: *is a deterministic algorithm that takes as input a secret key K and a vertex $v \in V$ and outputs a token* tk.
- $\{(\text{id}, s_{\text{id}})\}_{\text{id} \in I} := \text{Nghbr}(\text{EGR}, \text{tk})$: *is a deterministic algorithm that takes as input an encrypted graph* EGR *and a token* tk *and returns a set of id/string pairs* $\{(\text{id}, s_{\text{id}})\}_{\text{id} \in I}$, *where* $I \subseteq \{\text{id}(e)\}_{e \in E}$.
- $\text{atk} := \text{Token}^+(K, G^+, \text{sp}^+)$: *is a deterministic algorithm that takes as input a secret key K, a graph update G^+ and semi-private information* sp^+ *and returns an add token* atk.
- $\text{EGR}' := \text{Add}(\text{EGR}, \text{atk})$: *is a deterministic algorithm that takes as input an encrypted graph* EGR *and a token* atk *and outputs an encrypted graph* EGR$'$.

A note on deletion. Recall that the metadata program requires the NSA to remove from its database all information associated with calls older than 5 years. Note, however, that the formulation of graph encryption given in Definition 1 does not support deletions. The reason is essentially that since the deletion of the (encrypted) documents cannot be enforced (e.g., the server holding the documents can always make copies) there is no security-related reason for the encrypted graphs to support deletion. The value of supporting deletion would mostly be efficiency (e.g., to avoid returning old documents) but that can be handled using non-cryptographic mechanisms (e.g., not returning any encrypted document that was received past a certain date).

Security. Intuitively, a graph encryption scheme is secure if, given an encrypted graph EGR and a token tk, the adversary cannot learn anything about the underlying graph and query. This exact intuition is difficult to achieve (efficiently) so

---

[3] Typically, the number of vertices is revealed but this can be hidden using padding.

the security guarantee is usually weakened to allow for some form of leakage. The leakage is formalized by parameterizing the security definition with a set of leakage functions $\mathcal{L}_S$, $\mathcal{L}_N$ and $\mathcal{L}_U$ which precisely capture the leakage of the scheme's Setup, Nghbr and update algorithms, respectively. We recall in Definition 2 below the notion of adaptive semantic security for graph encryption which is a special case of the definition from [3] which itself generalizes the definition from [6].

Definition 2 (Adaptive semantic security [3,6]). *Let* Graph = (Setup, Token, Nghbr, Token$^+$, Add) *be a dynamic and associative graph encryption scheme supporting 1-hop neighbor queries and consider the following probabilistic experiments where $\mathcal{A}$ is an adversary, $\mathcal{S}$ is a simulator and $\mathcal{L}_S$, $\mathcal{L}_N$ and $\mathcal{L}_U$ are (stateful) leakage algorithms:*

Real$_{\mathsf{Graph},\mathcal{A}}(k)$*: the adversary $\mathcal{A}$ generates a graph $G = (V, E)$ and semi-private information* sp *from which the challenger creates an encrypted graph* EGR, *where $(K, \mathsf{EGR}) \leftarrow \mathsf{Setup}(1^k, G, \mathsf{sp})$. Given* EGR, *the adversary $\mathcal{A}$ makes a polynomial number of adaptive queries and updates. For each neighbor query v, $\mathcal{A}$ receives a token* tk := Token$_K(v)$ *from the challenger and for each graph update G^+ and semi-private information* sp$^+$ *it receives an add token* atk := Token$^+(K, G^+, \mathsf{sp}^+)$. *Finally, $\mathcal{A}$ returns a bit b that is output by the experiment.*

Ideal$_{\mathsf{Graph},\mathcal{A},\mathcal{S}}(k)$*: the adversary $\mathcal{A}$ outputs a graph $G = (V, E)$ and semi-private information* sp $= (e, s_e)_{e \in E}$. *Given leakage $\mathcal{L}_S(G, \mathsf{sp})$, the simulator $\mathcal{S}$ returns an encrypted graph* EGR. *The adversary then makes a polynomial number of adaptive queries and updates. For each query v the simulator is given $\mathcal{L}_N(G, v)$ and $\{s_{(v,w)}\}_{w \in \Gamma_1^G(v)}$ and returns a token* tk *to $\mathcal{A}$. For each graph update G^+ and new semi-private information* sp$^+$, *the simulator receives $\mathcal{L}_U(G, G^+, \mathsf{sp}^+)$ and returns an add token* atk *to $\mathcal{A}$. Finally, $\mathcal{A}$ returns a bit b that is output by the experiment.*

We say that Graph *is adaptively $(\mathcal{L}_S, \mathcal{L}_N, \mathcal{L}_U)$-secure if for all PPT adversaries $\mathcal{A}$, there exists a PPT simulator $\mathcal{S}$ such that*

$$|\Pr[\mathbf{Real}_{\mathsf{Graph},\mathcal{A}}(k) = 1] - \Pr[\mathbf{Ideal}_{\mathsf{Graph},\mathcal{A},\mathcal{S}}(k) = 1]| \leq \mathsf{negl}(k).$$

Instantiating 1-hop graph encryption. In [3], Chase and Kamara show how to construct a static, non-interactive, associative 1-hop graph encryption scheme from any static, non-interactive, associative, and *chainable* searchable symmetric encryption (SSE) scheme. Roughly speaking, chainability means that the scheme's $\mathcal{L}_S$ leakage does not reveal any information about the semi-private information. For a discussion and formalization see the full version of [3]. Non-interactive means search requires only a single message from the client.

The high-level idea of the CK transformation is as follows: document identifiers are set to the vertex labels and a vertex label v' is added to a document with identifier v if the graph has either a (directed) edge (v, v') or (v', v). A 1-hop undirected neighbor query for vertex v then consists of searching for keyword v.

It is not hard to see that this transformation can be extended to the dynamic case as well if the underlying SSE scheme supports both add operations (i.e., adding documents) and edits (i.e., adding words to an existing document).

Unfortunately, we cannot use the Chase-Kamara transformation here. The reason is that a direct application of it yields a "vertex-centric" 1-hop graph encryption scheme in the sense that the semi-private strings are associated to *vertices* and that the Nghbr algorithm returns *vertex* identifiers. This is in contrast to the kind of scheme we need and that is described above which is "edge-centric" in the sense that the semi-private strings are associated with *edges* and that the Nghbr algorithm returns *edge* identifiers. Nevertheless, in the full version of this work [13], we show how to construct such an edge-centric 1-hop graph encryption scheme based on the dynamic SSE schemes of Kamara, Papamanthou and Roeder [14] and of Cash et al. [2] (in particular, based on the scheme Π_{bas}^{+}).

6   The MetaCrypt Protocol

In this Section, we describe our main protocol, MetaCrypt, which securely computes the MetaDB functionality. The protocol is described in detail in the full version of this work [13] and, at a high level, works as follows. It makes use of an SFE protocol Π, a graph encryption scheme Graph = (Setup, Token, Nghbr, Token^{+}, Add) that supports 1-hop neighbor queries, a public-key encryption scheme PKE = (Gen, Enc, Dec), a pseudo-random function F and a random oracle (RO) H. The RO can be removed at the cost of increased storage complexity. We assume private and authenticated channels between all parties which can be instantiated using standard cryptographic primitives. The protocol supports three operations: setup, queries and updates, which are described next.

Setup. During setup, the agency generates a public/private key pair (pk, sk). The secret key is sent to all its analysts (we discuss in the full version how to augment the protocol to support individual analyst keys) and the public key is sent to the providers (Prv$_1$, ..., Prv$_t$). The t providers encrypt their graph databases GDB$_1$, ..., GDB$_t$ and send the result to the server. This encryption step, however, does not consist of simply applying the underlying graph encryption scheme as there are three main difficulties to overcome. The first is that in our setting—unlike in the standard structured/searchable encryption setting— the intended recipient of the data (the analyst) is not the owner of the data (the provider). The second difficulty is that the graph encryption schemes we have only support 1-hop neighbor queries, whereas we need to handle 2 hops. A third, and more subtle, issue has to do with how the documents are encrypted. In fact, unlike the standard client/server setting where structured/searchable encryption is typically applied, in our setting we cannot use any CPA-secure symmetric encryption scheme to encrypt the documents. The difficulty is that in the adversarial structures we consider, the adversary not only corrupts the server but the analyst as well which means the adversary will have access to the *decrypted* documents that are relevant to the queries. To satisfy our adaptive and simulation-based definition where the ideal adversary learns the contents of the documents only *after* having committed to simulated ciphertexts, the underlying encryption scheme has to be non-committing.

We handle the first issue using hybrid encryption and the third using the "standard" PRF-based symmetric-key encryption scheme—though we replace the PRF with a RO for efficiency reasons. Recall that each graph database GDB consists of a graph $G = (V, E)$ and a set of documents $\mathbf{D}$. Each provider encrypts its documents by computing, for all $e \in E$, $c_{\mathsf{id}(e)} := \langle D_{\mathsf{id}(e)} \oplus H(K_{\mathsf{id}(e)}, r_{\mathsf{id}(e)}), r_{\mathsf{id}(e)} \rangle$, where $K_{\mathsf{id}(e)} := F_{K^h}(\mathsf{id}(e))$, $K^h \xleftarrow{\$} \{0,1\}^k$ and $r_{\mathsf{id}(e)} \xleftarrow{\$} \{0,1\}^k$. Each key $K_{\mathsf{id}(e)}$ is then encrypted under the agency public key pk. We refer to these public-key-encrypted keys as *key encapsulations* and denote them $\mathsf{ke}_{\mathsf{id}(e)}$. The encapsulations are stored as semi-private information in encrypted graphs constructed from G. This is done so that the result of a query includes both the identifiers and the encapsulations of the relevant encrypted documents. After receiving the encrypted documents and encapsulations from the server, the analyst uses the agency secret key sk to recover the symmetric keys with which it decrypts the documents.

To handle 2-hop neighbor queries based on a scheme that only supports 1-hop queries, we use the chaining approach first used in [3] to construct web graph encryption schemes for focused subgraph queries. The high-level idea is to encrypt the graph $G = (V, E)$ twice and to store tokens for the second encryption as semi-private information in the first encryption. More specifically, we generate a second-level encrypted graph by computing $(K^{(2)}, \mathsf{EGR}^{(2)}) \leftarrow \mathsf{Setup}(1^k, G, \mathsf{sp}^{(2)})$, where $\mathsf{sp}^{(2)}$ is the semi-private information $(e, \mathsf{ke}_{\mathsf{id}(e)})_{e \in E}$. We then generate tokens for all vertices $v \in V$ by computing $\mathsf{tk}_v^{(2)} \leftarrow \mathsf{Token}_{K^{(2)}}(v)$ and create a first-level encrypted graph by computing $(K^{(1)}, \mathsf{EGR}^{(1)}) \leftarrow \mathsf{Setup}(1^k, G, \mathsf{sp}^{(1)})$, where $\mathsf{sp}^{(1)}$ is the semi-private information $(e, \langle \mathsf{tk}_{e_2}^{(2)}, \mathsf{ke}_{\mathsf{id}(e)} \rangle)_{e \in E}$, where e_2 is the terminating vertex of e. Finally, the provider sets its key to $K = (K^h, K^{(1)}, K^{(2)})$ and sends an encrypted graph database $\mathsf{EGDB} = (\mathsf{EGR}^{(1)}, \mathsf{EGR}^{(2)}, \{c_{\mathsf{id}(e)}\}_{e \in E})$ to the server.

Updates. To update an encrypted graph database with a new graph $G^+ = (V^+, E^+)$ and new documents $\mathbf{D}^+$, a provider does the following. It first encrypts the documents as in the Setup phase: it generates a key $K_{\mathsf{id}(e^+)} := F_{K^h}(\mathsf{id}(e^+))$ for each new edge $e^+ \in E^+$; creates a key encapsulation $\mathsf{ke}_{\mathsf{id}(e^+)} \leftarrow \mathsf{PKE.Enc}_{\mathsf{pk}}(K_{\mathsf{id}(e^+)})$; and encrypts the document by computing $c_{\mathsf{id}(e^+)} := \langle D_{\mathsf{id}(e^+)} \oplus H(K_{\mathsf{id}(e^+)}, r_{\mathsf{id}(e^+)}), r_{\mathsf{id}(e^+)} \rangle$, where $r_{\mathsf{id}(e^+)} \xleftarrow{\$} \{0,1\}^k$. It then stores the key encapsulations as semi-private information in an update to the second-level encrypted graph. More precisely, it generates an add token $\mathsf{atk}^{(2)} := \mathsf{Token}_{K^{(2)}}^+(G^+, \mathsf{sp}^{(2)})$, where $\mathsf{sp}^{(2)} = (e^+, \mathsf{ke}_{\mathsf{id}(e^+)})_{e^+ \in E^+}$. It then generates second-level query tokens for every vertex in G^+ by computing, for all $v^+ \in V^+$, $\mathsf{tk}_{v^+}^{(2)} := \mathsf{Token}_{K^{(2)}}(v^+)$. These second-level query tokens are then stored as semi-private information in an update to the first-level encrypted graph. Specifically, the provider computes $\mathsf{atk}^{(1)} := \mathsf{Token}_{K^{(1)}}^+(G^+, \mathsf{sp}^{(1)})$, where $\mathsf{sp}^{(1)} = (e^+, \langle \mathsf{tk}_{e_2^+}^{(2)}, \mathsf{ke}_{\mathsf{id}(e^+)} \rangle)_{e^+ \in E^+}$. The provider then sends an update

$(\mathsf{atk}^{(1)}, \mathsf{atk}^{(2)}, \{c_{\mathsf{id}(e+)}\}_{e+\in E+})$ to the server who uses the add tokens to update the encrypted graphs and stores the new ciphertexts. If a new document encryption $c_{\mathsf{id}(e+)}$ is for an edge for which there already exists ciphertexts (perhaps the new document contains metdata on new calls conducted between the vertices), then the server just concatenates the new ciphertext to the olds ones.

Queries. During the query phase, the parties interact in such a way that the analyst An_1 receives a token for his vertex if the latter is certified with respect to the policy outlined in Sect. 1. This phase mainly consists of the execution of an SFE protocol Π between the providers $(\mathsf{Prv}_1, \ldots, \mathsf{Prv}_t)$ who input the keys $(K_1^{(1)}, \ldots, K_t^{(1)})$, the analysts An_1 and An_2 who input their query vertices v and v', the supervisors Sup_1 and Sup_2 who input tuples $(v_1, b_1, \mathsf{org}_1)$ and $(v_2, b_2, \mathsf{org}_2)$ and the judge J who inputs the watch list WL.

The function f that is evaluated is defined as follows. First, it checks whether the query vertices v and v' of the analysts are equal. If so, it verifies that at least one supervisor authorizes the query by verifying that either $b_1 = 1$ or $b_2 = 1$. In the following suppose, without loss of generality, that $b_1 = 1$, i.e., the first supervisor Sup_1 approved the query. The function checks that the vertex v_1 approved by Sup_1 is indeed the same as the vertex input by the analysts. This is to avoid a potential attack where an analyst, say An_1, asks a supervisor, say Sup_1, to approve a query vertex v_1 but inputs a vertex $v \neq v_1$ into the SFE protocol. If this is the case, the function checks that the organization org_1 submitted by Sup_1 is on the watch list submitted by the judge. If this is the case, the function uses the keys $(K_1^{(1)}, \ldots, K_t^{(1)})$ to generate query tokens $(\mathsf{tk}_1^{(1)}, \ldots, \mathsf{tk}_t^{(1)})$ for vertex v. The function returns these tokens to the analyst.

The analyst then sends the tokens to the server who uses them to query the providers' encrypted graph databases $(\mathsf{EGDB}_1, \ldots, \mathsf{EGDB}_t)$. More precisely, for each encrypted database $\mathsf{EGDB}_i = (\mathsf{EGR}_i^{(1)}, \mathsf{EGR}_i^{(2)}, \{c_{\mathsf{id}(e)}\}_{e\in E})$ the server does the following. It queries the first-level encrypted graph by computing $\mathsf{Nghbr}(\mathsf{EGR}_i^{(1)}, \mathsf{tk}_i^{(1)})$. This results in either $\bot$ or a set of tuples $\left(\mathsf{id}(v, w), \langle \mathsf{tk}_w^{(2)}, \mathsf{ke}_{\mathsf{id}(v,w)}\rangle\right)_{w\in\Gamma_1^G(v)}$, consisting of an edge identifier $\mathsf{id}(v, w)$, a second-level token $\mathsf{tk}_w^{(2)}$ and a key encapsulation $\mathsf{ke}_{\mathsf{id}(v,w)}$. For each $w \in \Gamma_1^G(v)$, the server uses the second-level token to query the second-level encrypted graph $\mathsf{EGR}_i^{(2)}$, which results in tuples $\left(\mathsf{id}(w, z), \mathsf{ke}_{\mathsf{id}(w,z)}\right)_{z\in\Gamma_1^G(w)}$, consisting of an edge identifier $\mathsf{id}(w, z)$ and a key encapsulation $\mathsf{ke}_{\mathsf{id}(w,z)}$. The server then returns the encryptions and key encapsulations of all the edges recovered.

Security of the MetaCrypt protocol. To analyze the security of our protocol, we show in the full version that it securely computes the MetaDB functionality. Our analysis, however, is slightly different and less general than what is typically found in the literature. In particular, we are not interested in threshold adversarial structures since, in our setting, each party plays a very distinct role and since, in practice, we are concerned with very specific threats. Specifically, the two main adversarial structures that concern us are: (1) when the adversary corrupts the server Srv, the analysts An_1 and An_2, the supervisors Sup_1 and

Sup_2 and the judge J; and (2) when the adversary corrupts the server Srv and the providers Prv_1 through Prv_t. The first structure captures the setting where the agency-affiliated parties (plus the judge) are corrupted and collude. Showing that our protocol is secure under this structure essentially lets us analyze the security afforded to providers—and by extension to the users whose metadata is included in the datasets—when the Government acts dishonestly. The second structure captures the setting where the providers are corrupted and colluding. Showing that our protocol is secure under this structure lets us reason about the security afforded to the agency when the providers act dishonestly. Notice that in both cases, we include the server in the adversarial structure. This effectively guarantees that the security of the protocol still holds no matter who manages the server. In the full version, we show the security of our protocol in the presence of a semi-honest adversary against these adversarial structures and discuss how to achieve malicious security.

References

1. Boneh, D., Sahai, A., Waters, B.: Functional encryption: definitions and challenges. In: Ishai, Y. (ed.) TCC 2011. LNCS, vol. 6597, pp. 253–273. Springer, Heidelberg (2011)
2. Cash, D., Jaeger, J., Jarecki, S., Jutla, C., Krawczyk, H., Rosu, M., Steiner, M.: Dynamic searchable encryption in very-large databases: data structures and implementation. In: Network and Distributed System Security Symposium, NDSS '14 (2014)
3. Chase, M., Kamara, S.: Structured encryption and controlled disclosure. In: Abe, M. (ed.) ASIACRYPT 2010. LNCS, vol. 6477, pp. 577–594. Springer, Heidelberg (2010)
4. Clarke, R., Morell, M., Stone, G., Sunstein, C., Swire, P.: Liberty and security in a changing world (2013). http://www.whitehouse.gov/sites/default/files/docs/2013-12-12_rg_final_report.pdf
5. United States Foreign Intelligence Surveillance Court. Primary order, April 2013. http://www.dni.gov/files/documents/PrimaryOrder_Collection_215.pdf
6. Curtmola, R., Garay, J., Kamara, S., Ostrovsky, R.: Searchable symmetric encryption: improved definitions and efficient constructions. In: ACM Conference on Computer and Communications Security (CCS '06), pp. 79–88. ACM (2006)
7. Freedman, M.J., Ishai, Y., Pinkas, B., Reingold, O.: Keyword search and oblivious pseudorandom functions. In: Kilian, J. (ed.) TCC 2005. LNCS, vol. 3378, pp. 303–324. Springer, Heidelberg (2005)
8. Gentry, C.: Fully homomorphic encryption using ideal lattices. In: ACM Symposium on Theory of Computing (STOC '09), pp, 169–178. ACM Press (2009)
9. Goldreich, O., Micali, S., Wigderson, A.: How to play ANY mental game. In: ACM Symposium on the Theory of Computation (STOC '87), pp. 218–229 (1987)
10. Greenwald, G.: NSA collecting phone records of millions of verizon customers daily, July 2013. http://www.theguardian.com/world/2013/jun/06/nsa-phone-records-verizon-court-order
11. Jarecki, S., Jutla, C., Krawczyk, H., Rosu, M., Steiner, M.: Outsourced symmetric private information retrieval. In: ACM Conference on Computer and Communications Security (CCS '13), pp. 875–888 (2013)

12. Kamara, S.: Are compliance and privacy always at odds? July 2013. http://outsourcedbits.org/2013/07/23/are-compliance-and-privacy-always-at-odds/
13. Kamara, S.: Restructuring the NSA metadata program. In: Böhme, R., Brenner, M., Moore, T., Smith, M. (eds.) FC 2014 Workshops. LNCS, vol. 8438, pp. 235–248. Springer, Heidelberg (2014). http://research.microsoft.com/en-us/projects/metacrypt/
14. Kamara, S., Papamanthou, C., Roeder, T.: Dynamic searchable symmetric encryption. In: ACM Conference on Computer and Communications Security (CCS '12). ACM Press (2012)
15. Kroll, J., Felten, E., Boneh, D.: Secure protocols for accountable warrant execution, April 2014. http://www.cs.princeton.edu/~felten/warrant-paper.pdf
16. Office of the Inspector General of the Department of Defense. Requirements for the trailblazer and thinthread systems (2004). https://www.fas.org/irp/agency/dod/ig-thinthread.pdf
17. Yao, A.: Theory and application of trapdoor functions. In: IEEE Symposium on Foundations of Computer Science (FOCS '82), pp. 80–91. IEEE Computer Society (1982)

Author Index